T0183870

Lecture Notes in Computer Science 9606

Commenced Publication in 1973
Founding and Former Series Editors:
Gerhard Goos, Juris Hartmanis, and Jan van Leeuwen

Editorial Board

More information about this series at http://www.springer.com/series/7410

Tsuyoshi Takagi (Ed.)

Post-Quantum Cryptography

7th International Workshop, PQCrypto 2016
Fukuoka, Japan, February 24–26, 2016
Proceedings

 Springer

Editor
Tsuyoshi Takagi
Kyushu University
Fukuoka
Japan

ISSN 0302-9743   ISSN 1611-3349   (electronic)
Lecture Notes in Computer Science
ISBN 978-3-319-29359-2   ISBN 978-3-319-29360-8   (eBook)
DOI 10.1007/978-3-319-29360-8

Library of Congress Control Number: 2015960429

LNCS Sublibrary: SL4 – Security and Cryptology

Printed on acid-free paper

This Springer imprint is published by SpringerNature
The registered company is Springer International Publishing AG Switzerland

Preface

PQCrypto 2016, the 7th International Workshop on Post-Quantum Cryptography, was held in Fukuoka, Japan, during February 24–26, 2016. It was organized in cooperation with the International Association for Cryptologic Research.

The aim of PQCrypto is to serve as a forum for researchers to present results and exchange ideas on the topic of cryptography in the era of large-scale quantum computers. The workshop was preceded by a winter school during February 22–23, 2016.

PQCrypto 2016 has received 42 submissions from 21 countries all over the world. The Program Committee selected 16 papers for publication in the workshop proceedings. The accepted papers deal with multivariate polynomial cryptography, code-based cryptography, lattice-based cryptography, quantum algorithms, post-quantum protocols, and implementations. The program featured four excellent invited talks given by Daniel Bernstein (University of Illinois at Chicago), Ernie Brickell (Intel), Steven Galbraith (University of Auckland), and Masahide Sasaki (Quantum ICT Laboratory, NICT), as well as a hot topic session. The Program Committee selected the work "An Efficient Attack on a Code-Based Signature Scheme" by Aurélie Phesso and Jean-Pierre Tillich for the Best Paper Award of PQCrypto 2016. During the workshop, the National Institute of Standards and Technology (NIST) announced a preliminary plan for the submission and evaluation of quantum-resistant algorithms for potential standardization.

Many people contributed to the success of PQCrypto 2016. I am very grateful to all of the Program Committee members as well as the external reviewers for their fruitful comments and discussions on their areas of expertise. I am greatly indebted to the general chair, Kouichi Sakurai, for his efforts and overall guidance. I would also like to thank the general co-chairs, Takanori Yasuda and Kirill Morozov, and the local Organizing Committee, Hiroaki Anada, Shinichi Matsumoto, Duong Hoang Dung, Taku Jiromaru, and Emi Watanabe, for their continuous support.

Finally, I would like to express our gratitude to our partners and sponsors: JST CREST, ISIT, ID Quantique, Fukuoka Convention & Vistors Bureau, The Telecommunications Advancement Foundation, and Inoue Foundation for Science. ISIT's contribution to the organization of this workshop is supported by "Strategic Information and Communications R&D Promotion Programme (SCOPE), no. 0159-0016," Ministry of Internal Affairs and Communications, Japan.

February 2016   Tsuyoshi Takagi

Organization

General Chair

Kouichi Sakurai   Kyushu University and ISIT, Japan

General Co-chairs

Takanori Yasuda   ISIT, Japan
Kirill Morozov   Kyushu University, Japan

Program Chair

Tsuyoshi Takagi   Kyushu University, Japan

Program Committee

Joppe Bos   NXP Semiconductors, Belgium
Johannes Buchmann   TU Darmstadt, Germany
Chen-Mou Cheng   National Taiwan University, Taiwan
Pierre-Louis Cayrel   Jean Monnet University, France
Claude Crépeau   McGill University, Canada
Jintai Ding   University of Cincinnati, USA
Philippe Gaborit   University of Limoges, France
Danilo Gligoroski   Norwegian University of Science and Technology, Norway
Tim Güneysu   Ruhr University of Bochum, Germany
Sean Hallgren   Pennsylvania State University, USA
Yasufumi Hashimoto   University of the Ryukyus, Japan
David Jao   University of Waterloo, Canada
Tanja Lange   TU Eindhoven, The Netherlands
Yi-Kai Liu   NIST, USA
Michele Mosca   University of Waterloo and Perimeter Institute, Canada
Martin Rötteler   Microsoft Research, USA
Nicolas Sendrier   Inria, France
Daniel Smith-Tone   University of Louisville and NIST, USA
Damien Stehlé   ENS Lyon, France
Rainer Steinwandt   Florida Atlantic University, USA
Jean-Pierre Tillich   Inria, France
Keita Xagawa   NTT, Japan
Bo-Yin Yang   Academia Sinica, Taiwan
Zhengfeng Zhang   Chinese Academy of Sciences, China

Local Organizing Committee

Hiroaki Anada   ISIT, Japan
Shinichi Matsumoto   ISIT, Japan
Duong Hoang Dung   Kyushu University, Japan
Taku Jiromaru   Conference Service, Japan
Emi Watanabe   Kyushu University, Japan

External Reviewers

John Baene   Po-Chun Kuo   Fang Song
Shi Bai   Wen-Ding Li   Tobias Schneider
Yun-An Chang   Artur Mariano   Rodolfo Canto Torres
Long Chen   Rafael Misoczki   Saraswathy
Craig Costello   Mohamed Saied   Ramanathapuram
Alain Couvreur   Mohamed   Vancheeswaran
Leo Ducas   Michael Naehrig   Christopher Wolf
Kirsten Eisentraeger   Khoa Nguyen   Jiang Zhang
Vlad Gheorghiu   Edoardo Persichetti
Gerhard Hoffman   Simona Samardjiska

Steering Committee

Daniel J. Bernstein   University of Illinois at Chicago, USA and TU Eindhoven,
                         The Netherlands
Johannes Buchmann   TU Darmstadt, Germany
Claude Crépeau   McGill University, Canada
Jintai Ding   University of Cincinnati, USA
Philippe Gaborit   University of Limoges, France
Tanja Lange   TU Eindhoven, The Netherlands
Daniele Micciancio   University of California at San Diego, USA
Michele Mosca   University of Waterloo, Canada
Nicolas Sendrier   Inria, France
Shigeo Tsujii   Chuo University, Japan
Bo-Yin Yang   Academia Sinica, Taiwan

Partners and Sponsors

CREST, Japan Science and Technology Agency
Institute of Systems, Information Technologies and Nanotechnologies (ISIT)
ID Quantique
Fukuoka Convention and Vistors Bureau
The Telecommunications Advancement Foundation
Inoue Foundation for Science

Contents

IND-CCA Secure Hybrid Encryption
from QC-MDPC Niederreiter

Ingo von Maurich[1]([✉]), Lukas Heberle[1], and Tim Güneysu[2,3]

[1] Horst Görtz Institute for IT-Security, Ruhr University Bochum, Bochum, Germany
{ingo.vonmaurich,lukas.heberle}@rub.de
[2] University of Bremen, Bremen, Germany
tim.gueneysu@uni-bremen.de
[3] DFKI, Bremen, Germany

Abstract. QC-MDPC McEliece attracted significant attention as promising alternative public-key encryption scheme believed to be resistant against quantum computing attacks. Compared to binary Goppa codes, it achieves practical key sizes and was shown to perform well on constrained platforms such as embedded microcontrollers and FPGAs.

However, so far none of the published QC-MDPC McEliece/ Niederreiter implementations provide indistinguishability under chosen plaintext or chosen ciphertext attacks. Common ways for the McEliece and Niederreiter encryption schemes to achieve IND-CPA/IND-CCA security are surrounding constructions that convert them into secured schemes. In this work we take a slightly different approach presenting (1) an efficient implementation of QC-MDPC Niederreiter for ARM Cortex-M4 microcontrollers and (2) the first implementation of Persichetti's IND-CCA hybrid encryption scheme from PQCrypto'13 instantiated with QC-MDPC Niederreiter for key encapsulation and AES-CBC/AES-CMAC for data encapsulation. Both implementations achieve practical performance for embedded microcontrollers, at 80-bit security hybrid encryption takes 16.5 ms, decryption 111 ms and key-generation 386.4 ms.

Keywords: Post-quantum cryptography · Code-based public key encryption · Hybrid encryption · Software · Microcontroller

1 Introduction

Shor's quantum algorithm [21] efficiently solves the underlying problem of RSA (factoring) and can be adapted to break ECC and DH (discrete logarithms). Although quantum computers can handle only few qubits so far, the proof-of-concept of Shor's algorithm was verified several times with 143 being the largest number which was factored into its prime factors, yet [23]. In this context the NSA Central Security Service recently announced preliminary plans to transition its Suite B family of cryptographic algorithms to quantum-resistant algorithms in the "not too distant future"[1].

---

[1] See NSA announcement published at https://www.nsa.gov/ia/programs/suiteb_ cryptography/.

© Springer International Publishing Switzerland 2016
T. Takagi (Ed.): PQCrypto 2016, LNCS 9606, pp. 1–17, 2016.
DOI: 10.1007/978-3-319-29360-8_1

The code-based public-key encryption schemes by McEliece [15] and Nieder-reiter [17] are among the most promising alternatives to RSA and ECC. Their security is based on variants of hard problems in coding theory. McEliece encryption instantiated with *quasi-cyclic moderate density parity-check* (QC-MDPC) codes [7] was introduced in [16], followed by QC-MDPC Niederreiter encryption in [3]. Compared to the original proposal of using McEliece and Niederreiter with binary Goppa codes, QC-MDPC codes allow much smaller keys and were shown to achieve good performance on a variety of platforms [9,12–14] combined with improved decoding and implementation techniques.

However, none of the previous implementations took into account that the plain McEliece and Niederreiter cryptosystems do not provide *indistinguishability under adaptive chosen-ciphertext attacks* (IND-CCA), using QC-MDPC codes does not change this fact. McEliece/Niederreiter can be integrated into existing frameworks which provide IND-CPA or IND-CCA security (e.g., [11,18]). Another approach is to plug Niederreiter into an IND-CCA secure hybrid encryption scheme as recently proposed by Persichetti [20]. It is the first hybrid encryption scheme with assumptions from coding theory and it was proven to provide IND-CCA security and *indistinguishability of keys under adaptive chosen-ciphertext attacks* (IK-CCA) in the random oracle model in [20]. Being a hybrid encryption scheme, it furthermore allows efficient encryption of large plaintexts without requiring to share a symmetric secret key beforehand. Still it is not clear how efficient such a system is in practice, especially when implemented for constrained processors of embedded devices.

Contribution. In this work we provide the first implementation of QC-MDPC Niederreiter for ARM Cortex-M4 microcontrollers for which we also deploy Persichetti's recent hybrid encryption scheme. We base Persichetti's hybrid encryption scheme on QC-MDPC Niederreiter and extend it to handle arbitrary plaintext lengths.

Outline. We summarize the background on QC-MDPC Niederreiter in Sect. 2. Hybrid encryption with Niederreiter based on [20] is presented in Sect. 3. Our implementation of QC-MDPC Niederreiter for ARM Cortex-M4 microcontrollers is detailed in Sect. 4 followed by our implementation of Persichetti's hybrid encryption scheme in Sect. 5. Results and comparisons are given in Sect. 6. We conclude in Sect. 7.

2   QC-MDPC Codes in a Nutshell

In the following we introduce (QC-)MDPC codes, show how the code-based public-key cryptosystem Niederreiter is instantiated with these codes, and explain efficient decoding of (QC-)MDPC codes.

2.1   (QC-)MDPC Codes

A binary linear $[n, k]$ error-correcting code C of length n is a subspace of $\mathbb{F}_2^n$ of dimension k and co-dimension $r = n - k$. Code C is defined by *generator* matrix $G \in \mathbb{F}_2^{k \times n}$ such that $C = \{mG \in \mathbb{F}_2^n \mid m \in \mathbb{F}_2^k\}$. Alternatively, the code is defined by *parity-check matrix* $H \in \mathbb{F}_2^{r \times n}$ such that $C = \{c \in \mathbb{F}_2^n \mid Hc^T = 0^r\}$. The syndrome of any vector $x \in \mathbb{F}_2^n$ is $s = Hx^T \in \mathbb{F}_2^r$. By definition, $s = 0$ for all codewords of C.

A code C is called *quasi-cyclic* (QC) if there exists an integer n_0 such that cyclic shifts of codewords $c \in C$ by n_0 positions yield codewords $c' \in C$ of the same code. If $n = n_0 \cdot p$ for some integer p, the generator and parity-check matrices are composed of $p \times p$ circulant blocks. Hence, storing one row of each circulant block fully describes the matrices.

A (n, r, w)-MDPC code is a binary linear $[n, k]$ error-correcting code whose parity-check matrix has constant row weight w. A (n, r, w)-QC-MDPC code is a (n, r, w)-MDPC code which is quasi-cyclic with $n = n_0 r$.

2.2 The QC-MDPC Niederreiter Cryptosystem

Using QC-MDPC codes in code-based cryptography was proposed in [16] for the McEliece cryptosystem, a corresponding description of QC-MDPC Niederreiter was published in [3]. We introduce the Niederreiter cryptosystem's key-generation, encryption and decryption based on t-error correcting (n, r, w)-QC-MDPC codes.

QC-MDPC Niederreiter Key-Generation. Key-generation requires to generate a (n, r, w)-QC-MDPC code $\mathcal{C}$ with $n = n_0 r$. The private key is a composed parity-check matrix of the form $H = [H_0 \mid \ldots \mid H_{n_0-1}]$ which exposes a decoding trapdoor. The public key is a systematic parity-check matrix $H' = [H_{n_0-1}^{-1} \cdot H] = [H_{n_0-1}^{-1} \cdot H_0 \mid \ldots \mid H_{n_0-1}^{-1} \cdot H_{n_0-2} \mid I]$ which hides the trapdoor but allows to compute syndromes of the public code.

In order to generate a (n, r, w)-QC-MDPC code with $n = n_0 r$, select the first rows $h_0, \ldots, h_{n_0-1}$ of the n_0 parity-check matrix blocks $H_0, \ldots, H_{n_0-1}$ with Hamming weight $\sum_{i=0}^{n_0-1} \mathrm{wt}(h_i) = w$ at random and check that H_{n_0-1} is invertible (which is only possible if the row weight d_v is odd). The parity-check matrix blocks $H_0, \ldots, H_{n_0-1}$ are generated by $r - 1$ quasi-cyclic shifts of the first rows $h_0, \ldots, h_{n_0-1}$. Their concatenation yields the private parity-check matrix H. The public systematic parity-check matrix H' is computed by multiplication of $H_{n_0-1}^{-1}$ with all blocks H_i. Since the public and private parity-check matrices H' and H are quasi-cyclic, it suffices to store their first rows instead of the full matrices. The identity part I of the public key is usually not stored.

QC-MDPC Niederreiter Encryption. Given a public key H' and a message $m \in \mathbb{Z}/\binom{n}{t}\mathbb{Z}$, encode m into an error vector $e \in \mathbb{F}_2^n$ with $wt(e) = t$. The ciphertext is the public syndrome $s' = He^\intercal \in \mathbb{F}_2^r$.

QC-MDPC Niederreiter Decryption. Given a public syndrome $s' \in \mathbb{F}_2^r$, recover its error vector using a t-error correcting (QC-)MDPC decoder Ψ_H with private key H. If $e = \Psi_H(s')$ succeeds, return e and transform it back to message m. On failure of $\Psi_H(s')$ return $\perp$.

Parameters. The following parameters are proposed in [16] among others for QC-MDPC McEliece to achieve a 80-bit security level: $n_0 = 2, n = 9602, r = 4801, w = 90, t = 84$. For a 128-bit security level the parameters are $n_0 = 2, n = 19714, r = 9857, w = 142, t = 134$. The same parameters achieve the same security levels for QC-MDPC Niederreiter [3].

By $d_v = w/n_0$ we denote the Hamming weight of each row of the n_0 private parity-check matrix blocks[2]. With these parameters the private parity-check matrix H consists of $n_0 = 2$ circulant blocks, each with constant row weight d_v. The public parity-check matrix H' consists of $n_0 - 1 = 1$ circulant block concatenated with the identity matrix. The public key has a size of r bit and the private key has a size of n bit which can be compressed since it is sparse ($w \ll n$). Plaintexts are encoded into vectors of length n and Hamming weight t, ciphertexts have length r. For a detailed discussion of the security of QC-MDPC McEliece and QC-MDPC Niederreiter we refer to [3, 16].

2.3   Decoding (QC-)MDPC Codes

Compared to encryption, decryption is a more involved operation in both time and memory. Several decoders were proposed for decoding (QC-)MDPC codes [2,7,9,10,16]. Bit-flipping decoders as introduced by Gallager in [7] were, with some modifications, found to be most suitable for constrained devices [9,13,14]. We transfer the decoder and several optimizations to the QC-MDPC Niederreiter setting and introduce the decoder in its basic form in Algorithm 1 in the Appendix.

The decoder receives a private parity-check matrix H and a public syndrome s' as input and computes the private syndrome $s = H_{n_0-1}s'^\mathsf{T}$. Decoding then runs in several iterations which in general works as follows: the inner loop iterates over all rows of a block of the private-parity check matrix and counts the number of unsatisfied parity-checks $\#_\mathrm{upc}$ by counting the number of shared set bits of each row $H_i[j]$ and the private syndrome s. If $\#_\mathrm{upc}$ exceeds a certain threshold[3], the decoder likely has found an error position and inverts the corresponding bit in a zero-initialized error candidate $e_\mathrm{cand} \in \mathbb{F}_2^n$, thus the name *bit-flipping* decoder. In addition, we include the optimization of directly updating the syndrome s by addition of $H_i[j]$ in case of a bit-flip as proposed in [9]. It was shown in [9,14] that this modification improves the decoding behavior to take less decoding iterations and to reduce the chance of decoding failures. Furthermore, decoding is accelerated because recomputing the syndrome after every decoding iteration is avoided.

---

[2] 80-bit: $d_v = 45$, 128-bit: $d_v = 71$. Note that $n_0 = 2$ and w is even for the parameters used in this paper.

[3] The bit-flipping thresholds used in Algorithm 1 are precomputed from the code parameters as proposed in [7].

The inner loop is repeated for every block H_i of H until all blocks have been processed. Afterwards the public syndrome of the error candidate is computed and compared to the initial public syndrome s'. On a match, the correct error vector was found and is returned. Otherwise the decoder continues with the next iteration. After a fixed maximum of iterations, decoding is restarted with incremented thresholds as proposed in [14] for QC-MDPC McEliece. The failure symbol $\bot$ is returned if even after δ_{max} threshold adaptations the correct error vector is not found.

3 Hybrid Encryption with Niederreiter

Hybrid encryption schemes were introduced in [5]. They are divided into two independent components: (1) a key encapsulation mechanism (KEM) and (2) a data encapsulation mechanism (DEM). The KEM is a public-key encryption scheme that encrypts a randomly generated symmetric session key under the public key of the intended receiver. The DEM then encrypts the plaintext under the randomly generated session key using a symmetric encryption scheme.

Hybrid encryption is usually beneficial in practice because symmetric encryption is orders of magnitude more efficient than pure asymmetric encryption, especially for large plaintexts. On the other hand sole usage of symmetric schemes is not practical due to the symmetric key distribution problem. Hybrid encryption takes the best of two worlds, efficient symmetric data encryption combined with asymmetric key distribution.

3.1 Constructing Hybrid Encryption from Niederreiter

We introduce the Niederreiter hybrid encryption scheme as proposed in [20]. The authors focus on the realization of an IND-CCA secure KEM and assume an IND-CCA symmetric encryption scheme as DEM.

The Niederreiter KEM. Let $\mathcal{F}$ be the family of t-error correcting $[n, k]$-linear codes over $\mathbb{F}_q$ and let n, k, q, t be fixed system parameters. The Niederreiter KEM $\pi_{\text{NR\_KEM}} = (\text{Gen}_{\text{NR\_KEM}}, \text{Enc}_{\text{NR\_KEM}}, \text{Dec}_{\text{NR\_KEM}})$ follows the definition of a generic Niederreiter scheme.

- **Gen$_{\text{NR\_KEM}}$.** Pick a random code $\mathcal{C} \in \mathcal{F}$ with parity-check matrix $H' = (M \mid I_{n-k})$. Output H' (or M) as public-key and the private code description Δ as private key.
- **Enc$_{\text{NR\_KEM}}$.** Given a public-key H', generate a random error $e \in_R \mathbb{F}_q^n$ of weight $\text{wt}(e) = t$ and compute its public syndrome $s' = H'e^T$. The symmetric key k of length l_k is generated from e by a key-derivation function (KDF) as $k = (k_1 \mid\mid k_2) = \text{KDF}(e, l_k)$. The output is (k, s').
- **Dec$_{\text{NR\_KEM}}$.** Decode ciphertext s' to $e = \Psi_\Delta(s')$ using the private code description Δ and decoding algorithm Ψ. Derive symmetric key $k = \text{KDF}(e, l_k)$ if decoding succeeds. Otherwise, k is set to a pseudorandom string of length l_k, [20] suggests to set $k = \text{KDF}(s', l_k)$.

The Standard DEM. Let $\text{Enc}_{k_1}^{\text{SE}}(\cdot)$ and $\text{Dec}_{k_1}^{\text{SE}}(\cdot)$ denote en-/decryption operations of a symmetric encryption scheme under key k_1 and let $\text{Ev}_{k_2}(\cdot)$ denote the evaluation of a keyed message authentication code (MAC) under key k_2 that returns a fixed length message authentication tag τ. The standard DEM $\pi_{\text{DEM}} = (\text{Enc}_{\text{DEM}}, \text{Dec}_{\text{DEM}})$ is the combination of a symmetric encryption scheme with a message authentication code[4].

- **Enc$_{\text{DEM}}$.** Given a plaintext m and key $k = (k_1 \,\|\, k_2)$, encrypt m to $T = \text{Enc}_{k_1}^{\text{SE}}(m)$ and compute the message authentication tag $\tau = \text{Ev}_{k_2}(T)$ of ciphertext T under k_2. The output is $c^* = (T \,\|\, \tau)$.
- **Dec$_{\text{DEM}}$.** Given a ciphertext c^* and key k, split c^* into T, τ and k into k_1, k_2. Then verify the correctness of the MAC by evaluating $\text{Ev}_{k_2}(T) \overset{?}{=} \tau$. If the MAC is correct, plaintext $m = \text{Dec}_{k_1}^{\text{SE}}(T)$ is decrypted and returned. In case of a MAC mismatch, $\perp$ is returned.

The Niederreiter Hybrid Encryption Scheme. The Niederreiter hybrid encryption scheme $\pi_{\text{HY}} = (\text{Gen}_{\text{HY}}, \text{Enc}_{\text{HY}}, \text{Dec}_{\text{HY}})$ is a combination of the Niederreiter KEM $\pi_{\text{NR\_KEM}}$ with the DEM π_{DEM}.

- **Gen$_{\text{HY}}$** invokes $\text{Gen}_{\text{NR\_KEM}}()$ and returns the generated key-pair.
- **Enc$_{\text{HY}}$** is given plaintext m and public key H' and first invokes $\text{Enc}_{\text{NR\_KEM}}(H')$. The returned symmetric keys k_1 and k_2 are used to encrypt the message to $T = \text{Enc}_{k_1}^{\text{SE}}(m)$ and to compute the authentication tag $\tau = \text{Ev}_{k_2}(T)$. The overall ciphertext is $(s' \,\|\, T \,\|\, \tau)$.
- **Dec$_{\text{HY}}$** receives ciphertext $(s' \,\|\, T \,\|\, \tau)$ and invokes $\text{Dec}_{\text{NR\_KEM}}(s')$ to decrypt the symmetric key $k = (k_1 \,\|\, k_2)$. Then it verifies the correctness of the MAC by evaluating $\text{Ev}_{k_2}(T) \overset{?}{=} \tau$. If the MAC is correct, plaintext $m = \text{Dec}_{k_1}^{\text{SE}}(T)$ is decrypted and returned. In case of a MAC mismatch, $\perp$ is returned.

3.2   QC-MDPC Niederreiter Hybrid Encryption

Our instantiation of the Niederreiter hybrid encryption scheme of [20] realizes the KEM using QC-MDPC Niederreiter as defined in Sect. 2.2. We construct the DEM based on AES so that it is capable of handling arbitrary plaintext lengths compared to the impractical one-time pad DEM used in [20]. We target 80-bit and 128-bit security levels in this work. Hence, our DEM uses AES-128 in CBC-mode for message en-/decryption and AES-128 in CMAC-mode for MAC computation following the *encrypt-then-MAC* paradigm. Furthermore, we employ SHA-256 for key derivation of $(k_1 \,\|\, k_2)$ from s'.

For an overall 256-bit security level, appropriate parameters for QC-MDPC Niederreiter should be used (cf. [16]) combined with AES-256-CBC, AES-256-CMAC, and SHA-512.

---

[4] In [20], the DEM is simply assumed to be a fixed length one-time pad of the size of m combined with a standardized MAC. Hence, $\text{Enc}_{k_1}^{\text{SE}}(m) = m \oplus k_1$ and $\text{Dec}_{k_1}^{\text{SE}}(T) = T \oplus k_1$ with m, T, k_1 having the same fixed length.

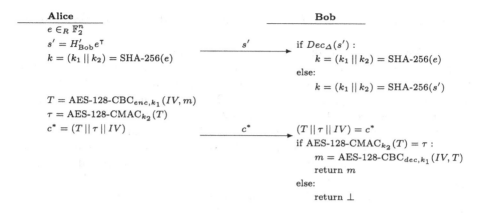

Fig. 1. Alice encrypts plaintext m for Bob using QC-MDPC Niederreiter hybrid encryption with public key H'_{Bob}. Note that we split the transfer of s' and c^* into two steps for illustrative purposes.

Hybrid Key-Generation is simply using QC-MDPC Niederreiter key-generation (cf. Sect. 2.2).

Hybrid Encryption generates a random error vector $e \in_R \mathbb{F}_2^n$ with Hamming weight t, encrypts e using QC-MDPC Niederreiter encryption to s' and derives two 128-bit symmetric sessions keys $k = (k_1 \,\|\, k_2) = \text{SHA-256}(e)$. Message m is encrypted under k_1 by AES-128 in CBC-mode to T starting from a random initialization vector IV. A MAC tag τ is computed over T under k_2 using AES-128 CMAC. The ciphertext is $(s' \,\|\, T \,\|\, \tau \,\|\, IV)$.

Hybrid Decryption extracts the symmetric session keys k_1, k_2 from the QC-MDPC Niederreiter cryptogram, verifies the provided AES-128 CMAC under k_2 and finally decrypts the symmetric ciphertext using k_1 with AES-128 in CBC-mode. The scheme is illustrated in Fig. 1.

Security. Proof for the IND-CCA security of the hybrid scheme is given in [20] assuming IND-CCA secure symmetric encryption. Furthermore, it was shown in [5] that it is possible to construct IND-CCA symmetric encryption from IND-CPA symmetric encryption (AES-CBC with random IVs [1]) by combining it with a standard MAC (AES-CMAC).

4 QC-MDPC Niederreiter on ARM Cortex-M4

The implementation of QC-MDPC Niederreiter presented in the following targets ARM Cortex-M4 microcontrollers as they are a common modern representative of embedded computing platforms. Our implementation covers key-generation, encryption, and decryption. Details on the implementations of the hybrid encryption scheme based on QC-MDPC Niederreiter are presented in Sect. 5.

To allow fair comparison with previous work we focus on the same microcontroller that was used to implement QC-MDPC McEliece in [13]. The STM32F417VG microcontroller [22] features an ARM Cortex-M4 CPU with a maximum clock frequency of 168 MHz, 1 MB of flash memory and 192 kB of SRAM. The microcontroller is based on a 32-bit architecture and features built-in co-processors for hardware acceleration of AES, Triple DES, MD5, SHA-1 as well as true random number generation (TRNG). Our implementations are written in *Ansi-C* with additional use of Thumb-2 assembly for critical functions. The primary optimization goal is performance, the secondary goal is memory consumption, e.g., we make limited use of unrolling only where it has high performance impacts.

4.1   Polynomial Representation

Our implementations use three different ways for polynomial representation. Each representation has advantages which we exploit in different parts of our implementation.

- *poly_t:* is the naïve way to store a polynomial. It simply stores each bit of the polynomial after each other, its size depends on the polynomial's length and is independent of the polynomial's weight.
- *sparse_t:* stores the positions of set bits of the polynomial. This representation needs less memory than *poly_t* if few bits are set in a polynomial. Furthermore, the *sparse_t* representation allows fast iteration of set bits in the polynomial without having to test all positions.
- *sparse_double_t:* stores the polynomial similarly to the *sparse_t* representation but allocates twice the size of the actually required memory. The yet unused memory is prepended. In addition, it holds a pointer indicating the start of the polynomial. This representation is beneficial when rotating sparse polynomials compared to rotation in *sparse_t* representation. Its benefits will be explained in more detail when we talk about efficient decoding in Sect. 4.4.

4.2   QC-MDPC Niederreiter Key-Generation

Generating a random first row candidate h_{n_0-1} for block H_{n_0-1} of length r and Hamming weight d_v is done using the microcontroller's TRNG as source of entropy. Its outputs are used as indexes at which we set bits in the polynomial. Since r is prime and hence not a power of two, we use rejection sampling to ensure a uniform distribution of the sampled indexes. The TRNG provides 32 random bits per call but only $\lceil \log_2(r) \rceil$ random bits (13 bit at 80-bit security level, 14 bit at 128-bit security level) are needed to determine an index in the range of $0 \leq i \leq r - 1$. Hence we derive two random indexes per TRNG call.

As already stated in Sect. 2.2, we have to ensure that H_{n_0-1} is invertible. We therefor apply the *extended Euclidean algorithm* to newly generated first row candidates until an invertible h_{n_0-1} is found.

We generate the remaining first rows h_i, similar to h_{n_0-1} but skip the inverse checking as only H_{n_0-1} has to be invertible. After private key generation, we compute the corresponding public key which is the systematic parity-check matrix $H' = H_{n_0-1}^{-1} \cdot H = [H_{n_0-1}^{-1} \cdot H_0 | \ldots | I]$, so all we need to do is to compute $H_1^{-1} \cdot H_0$ and append the identity matrix since $n_0 = 2$ in our selected parameter sets. As the private key has few set bits ($d_v \ll r$) we store it in sparse representation. The public key is stored in polynomial representation due to its high density. Since the code is quasi-cyclic, we only need to store the first rows of both matrices. The different representations ease and accelerate later usage.

4.3 QC-MDPC Niederreiter Encryption

Given a public key H' and an error vector[5] $e \in \mathbb{F}_2^n$ of weight $\text{wt}(e) = t$, we compute the public syndrome $s' = H'e^{\mathsf{T}}$. Computing s' is done by iterating over set bits in the error vector and accumulating the corresponding rows of H'. Since the error vector is stored in sparse representation, the index of each bit in the error vector specifies the number of cyclic shifts of the first row of public key H'. To avoid repeated shifting, we reuse the previous shifted row and shift it only by the difference to the next bit index. Multiplication of e^{T} by the identity part of H' is skipped. As the public syndrome has high density, we store it in *poly_t* representation.

4.4 QC-MDPC Niederreiter Decryption

For decryption we implement two decoder variants, referred to as Dec_A and Dec_B. They differ in their implementation, the decoding behavior of both remains as explained in Sect. 2.3. We start with Dec_A and subsequently look at the improvements made in Dec_B to accelerate decryption. Furthermore, we discuss general implementation optimizations.

Dec_A starts by computing the private syndrome $s = H_{n_0-1}s'^{\mathsf{T}}$ from the public syndrome s' and the private key H. This is basically the same operation as encryption, however we use the *sparse_t* representation for the private key.

Recovery of the error vector e starts from a zero-initialized error candidate e_{cand} of length n. For each row of the private parity-check matrix blocks we observe in how many positions they differ from the private syndrome s, i.e., counting unsatisfied parity-checks. We implement this step by computing the binary *AND* of the current row of the private parity-check matrix block with s followed by a Hamming weight computation of the result. If the Hamming weight exceeds the decoding threshold $b_{\text{iteration}}$, we invert the corresponding bit in e_{cand}. The position is determined by the current row i and block j with $pos = j * r + i$. Additionally, we *XOR* the current row onto the private syndrome

---

[5] We do not implement constant weight encoding since it is not needed in the hybrid encryption scheme. Encrypting a message $m \in \mathbb{Z}/\binom{n}{t}\mathbb{Z}$ requires to encode it into an error-vector $e \in \mathbb{F}_2^n$ of weight $\text{wt}(e) = t$ and to reverse the encoding after decryption.

for a direct update every time a bit is flipped in e_cand. Updating the syndrome while decoding was shown to drastically increase decoding performance in [9,14] for QC-MDPC McEliece, the results similarly apply to QC-MDPC Niederreiter.

We iterate over the private key row by row from the first block to the last by taking the first row of each block and performing successive cyclic shifts. The *sparse_t* representation allows efficient shifting as we only have to increment d_v indexes to effectively shift the polynomial. However, we have to check for overflows of incremented indexes which translate to carry transfers in the regular *poly_t* representation. An overflow results in additional effort, as we have to transfer every value in memory so that the position of the highest bit is always stored in the highest counter.

After iterating over all rows of the private key, we compute the public syndrome of the current error candidate, i.e., we encrypt e_cand to $s'_\text{cand} = H' e_\text{cand}^\mathsf{T}$, and compare s'_cand to the initial public syndrome s'. On a match, the error vector was found and decryption finishes by returning e. On a mismatch, we continue with the next decoding iteration. After a fixed number of iterations[6], we abort and restart decoding with the original private syndrome and increased decoding thresholds similar to the optimized decoder for QC-MDPC McEliece presented in [14].

Dec_B. The decoding approach of Dec_A has two downsides. First, the public key has to be known during decryption which diverges from standard crypto APIs. Second, costly encryptions have to be performed after each decoding iteration to check whether the current error candidate is the correct error vector. Our decoder Dec_B solves these drawbacks as described in the following.

The first optimization is to transform the private key from *sparse_t* to *sparse_double_t* polynomial representation. This structure allows us to efficiently handle overflows during row rotation. A cyclic shift without carry is equivalent to the *sparse_t* representation in which we increment every bit index of the polynomial. If case of a carry, we pop the last value of the array (with value r), move all array elements by one position, and insert a new value in the beginning (with value 0). We illustrate this operation in Fig. 2.

Using *sparse_double_t*, we avoid direct manipulation of the array in case of a carry which is the costly part of the *sparse_t* representation. Instead, we decrement the pointer by one and insert a zero at the first element. The last element is ignored since the polynomial has known fixed weight d_v and thereby known

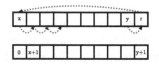

Fig. 2. Carry handling during cyclic rotation in *sparse_t* representation.

---

[6] We found the number of iterations experimentally and set it to five, in line with iteration counts reported in [13,14].

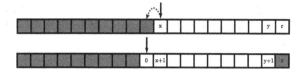

Fig. 3. Carry handling during cyclic rotation in *sparse_double_t* representation. The pointer position is indicated by the black arrow.

length. While the previous approach needs r operations, this approach breaks it down to two operations, independent of the polynomial's length. We illustrate the carry handling in *sparse_double_t* representation in Fig. 3.

Our second optimization checks if the Hamming weight of the error candidate matches the expected Hamming weight $\mathrm{wt}(e) = t$ instead of encrypting e_{cand} after every decoding iteration. If the Hamming weights do not match, we continue with the next decoding iteration immediately. Since Hamming weight computation of a vector is a much cheaper operation than vector matrix multiplication, decryption performance improves.

Our third optimization eliminates the need to encrypt the error candidate to determine whether the correct error vector was found. Instead we test the private syndrome for zero at the end of each decoding iteration. Since the private syndrome is updated every time a bit-flip occurs, it becomes zero once the correct error vector was recovered.

Other general optimizations include writing hot code of the decryption routine in Thumb-2 assembly giving us full control of the executed instructions and allowing us to pay close attention to the instruction execution order to avoid pipeline stalls by interleaving instructions which decreases the number of wasted clock cycles. Furthermore, we store two 16-bit indexes in one 32-bit field of the *sparse_double_t* type[7]. As we indicate the start by a pointer, we do not need to actually shift the values in memory in case of an overflow. A shift by 16 bit would be expensive on a 32-bit architecture. Furthermore, this allows us to increment two values with one `ADD` instruction and we process twice the data with each load and store instruction. To benefit from the burst mode of the load and store instructions (`LDMIA` and `STMIA`), i.e., loading and storing multiple words from/to SRAM, we have to ensure that the memory pointers are 32-bit word aligned. This however is not the case every second overflow since we decrement the *sparse_double_t* pointer in 16-bit steps. To deal with this issue a flag variable is used and, if set, we temporarily decrease the pointer for alignment.

5 QC-MDPC Niederreiter Hybrid Encryption on ARM Cortex-M4

In this section we detail our implementation of the IND-CCA secure QC-MDPC Niederreiter hybrid encryption scheme for ARM Cortex-M4 microcontrollers as

---

[7] 16 bit are sufficient to store the position for both 80-bit and 128-bit security.

introduced in Sect. 3.2. We describe hybrid key-generation, hybrid encryption, as well as hybrid decryption based on our implementation of QC-MDPC Niederreiter (cf. Sect. 4).

5.1 Hybrid Key-Generation

The hybrid encryption scheme requires an asymmetric key-pair for the KEM, and two symmetric keys for the DEM. One symmetric key is used to ensure confidentiality through encryption, the other key is used to ensure message authentication. However, only the asymmetric key pair is permanent, the symmetric keys are randomly generated during encryption. Thus, the implementation of the hybrid key-generation is equal to QC-MDPC Niederreiter key-generation (cf. Sect. 4.2).

5.2 Hybrid Encryption

On input of a plaintext $m \in \mathbb{F}_2^*$ and a QC-MDPC Niederreiter public key H', we generate a random error vector $e \in_R \mathbb{F}_2^n$ with $\mathrm{wt}(e) = t$ using the microcontroller's TRNG and encrypt e under H' using QC-MDPC Niederreiter encryption (cf. Sect. 4.3). Additionally, a hash is derived from e and is split into two 128-bit keys $k = (k_1 \,\|\, k_2) = \text{SHA-256}(e)$.

After generation of k_1 and k_2 the key encapsulation is finished and we continue with data encapsulation. We generate a random 16-byte IV using the microcontroller's TRNG and encrypt message m under k_1 to $T = \text{AES-128-CBC}_{enc,k_1}(IV, m)$. Ciphertext T is then fed into AES-128-CMAC, generating a 16-byte tag τ under key k_2. Finally, we concatenate the outputs to $x = (s' \,\|\, T \,\|\, \tau \,\|\, IV)$.

To accelerate AES operations we make use of the AES crypto co-processor featured by the STM32F417 microcontroller for encryption and MAC generation. Unfortunately, the crypto co-processor only offers SHA-1 acceleration which we refrain from to not lower the overall security level. Thus we created a software implementation of SHA-256 for hashing.

5.3 Hybrid Decryption

Hybrid decryption receives ciphertext $x = (s' \,\|\, T \,\|\, \tau \,\|\, IV)$ and decrypts the public syndrome s' using QC-MDPC Niederreiter decryption with the KEM private key to recover the error vector e (cf. Sect. 4.4). After successful decryption of e, we derive sessions keys k_1 and k_2 by hashing the error vector with SHA-256. We compute the AES-128-CMAC tag τ^* of the symmetric ciphertext T under k_2. If $\tau^* \neq \tau$ we abort decryption, otherwise we AES-128-CBC decrypt T under k_1 to recover plaintext m.

Again we make use of the microcontroller's AES crypto co-processor to accelerate decryption and MAC computation. For SHA-256 we use the same software implementation as during encryption.

6 Implementation Results

In the following we present our implementation results of QC-MDPC Niederreiter and of the hybrid encryption scheme from [20] instantiated with QC-MDPC Niederreiter. Both implementations target ARM Cortex-M4 embedded microcontrollers. We list code size as well as execution time, evaluate the impact of our optimizations and compare the results with previous work. Our code was built with GCC for embedded ARM (arm-eabi v.4.9.3) at optimization level -O2.

6.1 QC-MDPC Niederreiter Results

In order to measure the performance of QC-MDPC Niederreiter key-generation, encryption and decryption, we use randomly chosen instances throughout the measurements. We generate 500 random key-pairs and measure for each key-pair 500 en-/decryptions of randomly chosen plaintexts of n-bit length and Hamming weight t, resulting in 250,000 executions over which we average the execution time. Furthermore, we measure cyclic shifting in $poly\_t$ compared to the sparse polynomial representations to verify our optimizations in more detail. The execution times are listed for 80-bit security, results for 128-bit security are given in parenthesis.

QC-MDPC Niederreiter key-generation takes 376.1 ms (1495.8 ms), encryption 15.6 ms (81.7 ms) and decryption 109.6 ms (477.7 ms) with decoder Dec_B on average. With decoder Dec_A, decryption takes 697.9 ms (3830.2 ms) on average. Both decoders require 2.35 (3.25) decoding iterations on average until decoding succeeds. As embedded microcontrollers usually generate few key pairs in their lifespan, key-generation performance is usually of less practical relevance.

Generating the full private parity-check matrix from its first row in the straightforward $poly\_t$ representation takes 83.4 ms (345.8 ms). Our $sparse\_t$ representation accelerates this to 11.6 ms (34.0 ms), even faster rotations with 7.9 ms (21.2 ms) for the same task are achieved with the $sparse\_double\_t$ representation. By storing private keys in sparse representation with two 16-bit counters in one 32-bit word we reduce the required memory per private key by 85 % (88.5 %) from 9602 bit (19714 bit) to 1440 bit (2272 bit) compared to simply storing the polynomials in their full length.

The code size of 80-bit QC-MDPC Niederreiter including key-generation, encryption and decryption with Dec_A requires 14 KiB flash memory (1.3 %) and additional 4 KiB SRAM (2.0 %). For the 128-bit parameter set we need 19 KiB flash memory (1.9 %) and 4 KiB SRAM (2.0 %). The same implementation with decoder Dec_B requires 16 KiB flash (1.6 %) and 3 KiB SRAM (1.5 %). For 128-bit security we measured 20 KiB flash memory (2.0 %) and 3 KiB SRAM (1.5 %) with Dec_B. In Table 1 the code size of each function is listed separately. Note that the sum of the separate code sizes is greater than the combined implementation since we reuse code.

6.2 QC-MDPC Niederreiter Hybrid Encryption Results

The overall execution time of hybrid encryption schemes is dominated by the asymmetric component for key en-/decapsulation. Hence, we focus on QC-MDPC decoder Dec_B for key decapsulation as it operates much faster compared to Dec_A. We generate 500 random key pairs and en-/decrypt 500 randomly chosen plaintexts with a length of 32 byte for each key pair with the hybrid encryption scheme. We measure short plaintexts to get worst-case performance in terms of cycles/byte, longer plaintexts only marginally affect performance since they are only processed by the symmetric components. We list our results for 80-bit security, results for 128-bit security are given in parenthesis.

Key-generation of the hybrid encryption scheme requires 386.4 ms (1511.8 ms), hybrid encryption takes 16.5 ms (83.2 ms), and hybrid decryption 111.0 ms (477.5 ms) on average. Compared to pure QC-MDPC Niederreiter, the symmetric operations (en-/decryption, MACing, hashing) only add very little to the overall execution time ($< 5\%$) although the hybrid encryption scheme seems more complex at first. The AES computations are hardware accelerated which results in further speedup but even if a Cortex-M4 microcontroller without an AES co-processor would be used we would only see a slight increase in the overall execution time. The required code size of the complete hybrid encryption scheme (QC-MDPC Niederreiter, AES-128-CBC, AES-128-CMAC, SHA-256) is 25 KiB flash (2.4 %) and 4 KiB SRAM (2.0 %) at 80-bit security and 30 KiB flash (2.8 %) and 4 KiB SRAM (2.0 %) at 128-bit security.

6.3 Comparison with Previous Work

Implementation results reported in other work are listed in Table 1 in the Appendix. A direct comparison of QC-MDPC McEliece [13] with our hybrid QC-MDPC Niederreiter implemented on similar ARM Cortex-M4 microcontrollers shows that hybrid QC-MDPC Niederreiter is around 2.5 times faster at the same security level. In addition it provides IND-CCA security and the possibility to efficiently handle large plaintexts. However, one has to keep in mind that the QC-MDPC McEliece implementation of [13] features constant runtime which adds to its execution time.

Compared to QC-MDPC McEliece implemented on an ATxmega256 [9], our encryption runs 50 times faster and decryption runs 25 times faster, in addition we provide IND-CCA security through hybrid encryption. Comparing implementations on ATxmega256 with implementations on STM32F417 is by no means a fair comparison, however both microcontrollers come at a similar price which makes the comparisons relevant for practical applications.

We refrain from comparing our work to the cyclo-symmetric (CS) MDPC Niederreiter implementation on a PIC24FJ32GA002 microcontroller as presented in [3] because it was shown in [19] that the proposed CS-MDPC parameters do not reach the proclaimed security levels and need adaptation. McEliece implementations based on binary Goppa codes targeting the ATxmega256 microcontroller were presented in [6,8]. Again, our implementations outperform both by factors of 5–28. In addition, binary Goppa code public keys are much larger (64 kByte vs. 4801 bit) up to the point of being impractical for embedded devices with constraint memory. The CCA2-secure McEliece implementation based on Srivastava codes presented in [4] also targets the ATxmega256 and is just 4–8 times slower than our hybrid QC-MDPC Niederreiter which seems to make it a good competitor if it would be implemented on the same microcontroller as our work.

7 Conclusion

In this work we presented first implementations of QC-MDPC Niederreiter and of Persichetti's IND-CCA secure hybrid encryption scheme for embedded microcontrollers. We extended the hybrid encryption scheme to handle arbitrary plaintext lengths by choosing well-known symmetric components for data encapsulation and we achieve reasonable performance by combination of new implementation optimizations with transferred known techniques from QC-MDPC McEliece. Furthermore, our implementations operate with practical key sizes which for a long time was one of the major drawbacks of code-based cryptography.

Acknowledgments. This project has received funding from the European Unions Horizon 2020 research and innovation programme under grant agreement No 645622 (PQCRYPTO). The authors would like to thank Rafael Misoczki for helpful feedback and comments when starting this project.

Appendix

Algorithm 1: Syndrome decoder for QC-MDPC codes which returns error vector e or failure $\perp$.

```
1  Input H, s', iterations_max, δ_max, threshold ;
2  Output e ;
3  Compute the private syndrome s ← H_{n_0-1} s'^T;
4  δ ← 0;
5  e_cand ← 0^n;
6  while δ < δ_max do
7      iterations ← 0;
8      while iterations < iterations_max do
9          for i in n_0 do
10             for j in r do
11                 hw ← HammingWeight(H_i[j] & s);
12                 if hw ≥ (threshold[iterations] + δ) then
13                     e_cand[i · r + j] ← e_cand[i · r + j] ⊕ 1;
14                     s ← H_i[j] ⊕ s;
15                 end
16             end
17         end
18         s'_cand ← H' e_cand^T;
19         if s' = s'_cand then
20             return e_cand;
21         end
22         iterations++;
23     end
24     δ++;
25     s ← H_{n_0-1} s'^T;
26 end
27 return ⊥;
```

Table 1. Performance and code size of our implementations of QC-MDPC Niederreiter using Dec_B compared to other implementations of similar public-key encryption schemes on embedded microcontrollers. We abbreviate Niederreiter (NR) and McEliece (McE). As code is reused in the combined implementation its size is smaller than the sum of the three separate implementations.

Scheme	Platform	SRAM [byte]	Flash [byte]	Cycles/op	Time/op [ms]
QC-MDPC NR 80-bit [enc]	STM32F417	2,048	3,064	2,623,432	16
QC-MDPC NR 80-bit [dec]	STM32F417	2,048	8,621	18,416,012	110
QC-MDPC NR 80-bit [keygen]	STM32F417	3,136	8,784	63,185,108	376
QC-MDPC NR 80-bit [combined]	STM32F417	3,136	16,124	-	-
QC-MDPC NR 128-bit [enc]	STM32F417	2,048	4,272	13,725,688	82
QC-MDPC NR 128-bit [dec]	STM32F417	2,048	8,962	80,260,696	478
QC-MDPC NR 128-bit [keygen]	STM32F417	3,136	12,096	251,288,544	1496
QC-MDPC NR 128-bit [combined]	STM32F417	3,136	20,416	-	-
QC-MDPC McE 80-bit [enc] [13]	STM32F407	2,700[a]	5,700[a]	7,018,493	42
QC-MDPC McE 80-bit [dec] [13]	STM32F407	2,700[a]	5,700[a]	42,129,589	251
QC-MDPC McE 80-bit [keygen] [13]	STM32F407	2,700[a]	5,700[a]	148,576,008	884
QC-MDPC McE 80-bit [enc] [9]	ATxmega256	606	5,500	26,767,463	836
QC-MDPC McE 80-bit [dec] [9]	ATxmega256	198	2,200	86,874,388	2,710
Goppa McE [enc] [6]	ATxmega256	512	438,000	14,406,080	450
Goppa McE [dec] [6]	ATxmega256	12,000	130,400	19,751,094	617
Goppa McE [enc] [8]	ATxmega256	3,500	11,000	6,358,400	199
Goppa McE [dec] [8]	ATxmega256	8,600	156,000	33,536,000	1,100
Srivastava McE [enc] [4]	ATxmega256	-	-	4,171,734	130
Srivastava McE [dec] [4]	ATxmega256	-	-	14,497,587	453

[a]Flash and SRAM memory requirements are reported for a combined implementation of key generation, encryption, and decryption

References

1. Bellare, M., Desai, A., Jokipii, E., Rogaway, P.: A concrete security treatment of symmetric encryption. In: 38th Annual Symposium on Foundations of Computer Science, FOCS 1997, 19–22 October 1997, Miami Beach, Florida, USA, pp. 394–403. IEEE Computer Society (1997)
2. Berlekamp, E., McEliece, R., van Tilborg, H.: On the inherent intractability of certain coding problems. IEEE Trans. Inf. Theor. **24**(3), 384–386 (1978)
3. Biasi, F., Barreto, P., Misoczki, R., Ruggiero, W.: Scaling efficient code-based cryptosystems for embedded platforms. J. Crypt. Eng. **4**, 1–12 (2014)
4. Cayrel, P.-L., Hoffmann, G., Persichetti, E.: Efficient implementation of a CCA2-secure variant of McEliece using generalized Srivastava codes. In: Fischlin, M., Buchmann, J., Manulis, M. (eds.) PKC 2012. LNCS, vol. 7293, pp. 138–155. Springer, Heidelberg (2012)
5. Cramer, R., Shoup, V.: Design and analysis of practical public-key encryption schemes secure against adaptive chosen ciphertext attack. SIAM J. Comput. **33**(1), 167–226 (2003)
6. Eisenbarth, T., Güneysu, T., Heyse, S., Paar, C.: MicroEliece: McEliece for embedded devices. In: Clavier, C., Gaj, K. (eds.) CHES 2009. LNCS, vol. 5747, pp. 49–64. Springer, Heidelberg (2009)
7. Gallager, R.: Low-density parity-check codes. IRE Trans. Inf. Theor. **8**(1), 21–28 (1962)

8. Heyse, S.: Implementation of McEliece based on quasi-dyadic Goppa codes for embedded devices. In: Yang, B.-Y. (ed.) PQCrypto 2011. LNCS, vol. 7071, pp. 143–162. Springer, Heidelberg (2011)
9. Heyse, S., von Maurich, I., Güneysu, T.: Smaller keys for code-based cryptography: QC-MDPC McEliece implementations on embedded devices. In: Bertoni, G., Coron, J.-S. (eds.) CHES 2013. LNCS, vol. 8086, pp. 273–292. Springer, Heidelberg (2013)
10. Huffman, W.C., Pless, V.: Fundamentals of Error-Correcting Codes. Cambridge University Press, Cambridge (2010)
11. Kobara, K., Imai, H.: Semantically secure McEliece public-key cryptosystems-Conversions for McEliece. In: Kim, K. (ed.) PKC 2001. LNCS, vol. 1992, pp. 19–35. Springer, Heidelberg (2001)
12. von Maurich, I., Güneysu, T.: Lightweight code-based cryptography: QC-MDPC McEliece encryption on reconfigurable devices. In: DATE, pp. 1–6. IEEE (2014)
13. von Maurich, I., Güneysu, T.: Towards side-channel resistant implementations of QC-MDPC McEliece encryption on constrained devices. In: Mosca, M. (ed.) PQCrypto 2014. LNCS, vol. 8772, pp. 266–282. Springer, Heidelberg (2014)
14. von Maurich, I., Oder, T., Güneysu, T.: Implementing QC-MDPC McEliece encryption. ACM Trans. Embedded Comput. Syst. 14(3), 1–27 (2015)
15. McEliece, R.J.: A public-key cryptosystem based on algebraic coding theory. Deep Space Netw. Prog. Rep. 44, 114–116 (1978)
16. Misoczki, R., Tillich, J.-P., Sendrier, N., Barreto, P.S.L.M.: MDPC-McEliece: new McEliece variants from moderate density parity-check codes. In: ISIT, pp. 2069–2073. IEEE (2013)
17. Niederreiter, H.: Knapsack-type cryptosystems and algebraic coding theory. Probl. Control Inf. Theor./Problemy Upravlen. Teor Inform. 15(2), 159–166 (1986)
18. Nojima, R., Imai, H., Kobara, K., Morozov, K.: Semantic security for the McEliece cryptosystem without random oracles. Des. Codes Crypt. 49(1–3), 289–305 (2008)
19. Perlner, R.: Optimizing information set decoding algorithms to attack cyclosymmetric MDPC codes. In: Mosca, M. (ed.) PQCrypto 2014. LNCS, vol. 8772, pp. 220–228. Springer, Heidelberg (2014)
20. Persichetti, E.: Secure and anonymous hybrid encryption from coding theory. In: Gaborit, P. (ed.) PQCrypto 2013. LNCS, vol. 7932, pp. 174–187. Springer, Heidelberg (2013)
21. Shor, P.W.: Polynomial-time algorithms for prime factorization and discrete logarithms on a quantum computer. SIAM J. Comput. 26(5), 1484–1509 (1997)
22. STMicroelectronics: STM32F417VG High-performance foundation line, ARM Cortex-M4 core with DSP and FPU, 1 Mbyte Flash, 168 MHz CPU, ART Accelerator, Ethernet, FSMC, HW crypto - STMicroelectronics (2015). http://www.st.com/web/en/catalog/mmc/FM141/SC1169/SS1577/LN11/PF252139
23. Xu, N., Zhu, J., Lu, D., Zhou, X., Peng, X., Du, J.: Quantum factorization of 143 on a dipolar-coupling nuclear magnetic resonance system. Phys. Rev. Lett. 108, 130–501 (2012)

RankSynd a PRNG Based on Rank Metric

Philippe Gaborit[1], Adrien Hauteville[1,2(✉)], and Jean-Pierre Tillich[2]

[1] XLIM-DMI, Université de Limoges, 123, Avenue Albert Thomas,
87060 Limoges Cedex, France
adrien.hauteville@etu.unilim.fr
[2] Inria, Domaine de Voluceau, BP 105, 78153 Le Chesnay, France

Abstract. In this paper, we consider a pseudo-random generator based on the difficulty of the syndrome decoding problem for rank metric codes. We also study the resistance of this problem against a quantum computer. Our results show that with rank metric it is possible to obtain fast PRNG with small public data, without considering additional structure for public matrices like quasi-cyclicity for Hamming distance.

1 Introduction

Pseudo-random number generators (PRNG) are an essential tool in cryptography. They can be used for one-time cryptography or to generate random keys for cryptosystems. A long series of articles have demonstrated that the existence of a PRNG is equivalent to the existence of one-way functions [19,22,29]. Basically, a one-way function is a function which is easy to compute but hard to invert.

There are two types of PRNG in cryptography. The first one is based on block cipher schemes, like AES for instance, used in OFB mode. This gives in general very fast random generators. The second type includes PRNG proven to be secure by reduction to a hard problem. The problems considered can be based on classical problems from cryptography, like factorization or discrete logarithm, [5,6] or they may be based on linear algebra, like coding theory [11] or lattices [1] or multivariate quadratic systems [2].

Recent works [13,26] have proven that PRNG based on the syndrome decoding (SD) problem could be almost as fast as PRNG based on AES. However the PRNG based on the SD problem have to store huge matrices. This problem can be solved with the use of quasi-cyclic codes but there is currently no proof of the hardness of the SD problem for quasi-cyclic codes. Moreover recent quantum attacks on special ideal lattices [10], clearly raise the issue of the security of quasi-cyclic structures for lattices and codes, even if a straight generalization of this quantum attack from cyclic structures to quasi-cyclic structures seems currently out of reach.

Code-based cryptography has been studied for many years, since the proposal of the McEliece cryptosystem [25]. This type of cryptography relies on the difficulty of the SD problem for Hamming distance, which is proven NP-hard [3]. Besides this particular metric, other metrics may be interesting for cryptographic purposes. For instance, the rank metric leads to SD problems whose complexity grows very fast with the size of parameters. In particular, recent advances in

© Springer International Publishing Switzerland 2016
T. Takagi (Ed.): PQCrypto 2016, LNCS 9606, pp. 18–28, 2016.
DOI: 10.1007/978-3-319-29360-8_2

this field have shown that the problem of decoding general codes in rank metric is hard [15]. Moreover the best known attacks have an exponential complexity with a quadratic term in the exponent. In practice it means that it is possible to obtain cryptosystems with keysizes of only a few thousand bits and without additional structure such as cyclicity (or quasi-cyclicity). This is particularly interesting since it avoids relying on the hardness of structured problems whose security is less known than the security of general instances.

In this paper we study the case of a PRNG based on general instances of the Rank Syndrome Decoding problem. We build a PRNG based on the rank metric which has both a reasonable data size (a few thousand bits), which is reasonably fast and which is asymptotically better than PRNG based on the Hamming metric without cyclic structure. It is possible to optimize separately each of these aspects, like the size in constrained environments such as chip cards. We prove that breaking our PRNG is not easier than breaking the Fischer-Stern PRNG [11]. We also study how a quantum computer can be used to speed up the best known combinatorial attacks on the rank syndrome decoding problem. In the last section, we give parameters for our system, against classical and quantum attacks.

2   Generalities on the Rank Metric

First, let us define the central notion of this paper, namely matrix codes

Definition 1 (matrix code). *A matrix code $\mathcal{C}$ of length $m \times n$ over $\mathbb{F}_q$ is a subspace of the vector space of matrices of size $m \times n$ with entries in $\mathbb{F}_q$. If $\mathcal{C}$ is of dimension K, we say that $\mathcal{C}$ is an $[m \times n, K]_q$ matrix code, or simply an $[m \times n, K]$ code if there is no ambiguity.*

The difference between an $[m \times n, K]$ matrix code and a code of length mn and dimension K is that it allows to define another metric given by $d(A, B) \overset{\text{def}}{=} \text{Rank}(A - B)$. The weight of a word $\boldsymbol{c}$ is equal to $w_R(\boldsymbol{c}) \overset{\text{def}}{=} d(\boldsymbol{c}, 0)$. Linear codes over an extension field $\mathbb{F}_{q^m}$ give in a natural way matrix codes, and they have in this case a very compact representation which allows to decrease key sizes.

Definition 2 (matrix code associated to an $\mathbb{F}_{q^m}$-linear code). *Let $\mathcal{C}$ be an $[n, k]$ linear code over $\mathbb{F}_{q^m}$. Each word $\boldsymbol{c}$ of $\mathcal{C}$ can be associated to an $m \times n$ matrix over $\mathbb{F}_q$ by representing each coordinate $\boldsymbol{c}_i$ by a column vector $(c_{i1}, \ldots, c_{im})^T$ where $\boldsymbol{c}_i = \sum_{j=1}^{m} c_{ij}\beta_j$ with $\beta_1, \ldots, \beta_m$ being an arbitrary basis of $\mathbb{F}_{q^m}$ viewed as a vector space over $\mathbb{F}_q$ and $c_{ij} \in \mathbb{F}_q$. In other words the c_{ij}'s are the coordinates of $\boldsymbol{c}_i$ in this basis. The matrix code associated to $\mathcal{C}$ is of type $[m \times n, km]_q$.*

By definition, the weight of a word $\boldsymbol{c} \in \mathcal{C}$ is the rank of its associated matrix. It does not depend on the choice of the basis. Such matrix codes have a more compact representation than generic matrix codes. Indeed an $[n, k]$ $\mathbb{F}_{q^m}$-linear code can be described by a systematic parity-check matrix over $\mathbb{F}_{q^m}$, which requires $k(n-k)m \lceil \log q \rceil$ bits, whereas a representation of an $[m \times n, km]_q$ matrix code requires in general $km(mn - km)\lceil \log q \rceil = k(n-k)m^2 \lceil \log q \rceil$ bits. In other words we can reduce the size of the representation of such codes by a factor m if we consider the subclass of matrix codes obtained from $\mathbb{F}_{q^m}$-linear codes.

There is also a notion of Gilbert-Varshamov distance for the rank metric. For the Hamming metric, the Gilbert Varshamov distance for $[n,k]_q$ codes corresponds to the "typical" minimum distance of such codes. It is given by the smallest t for which $|B_t^{\mathrm{H}}| \geq q^{n-k}$ where B^{H} is the ball of radius t centered around 0 for the Hamming metric. The Gilbert-Varshamov distance for $[m \times n, km]_q$ matrix codes in the rank metric is given by the smallest t for which

$$|B_t^{\mathrm{R}}| \geq q^{m(n-k)}$$

where B^{R} is the ball of radius t centered around 0 for the rank metric (in other words it is the set of $m \times n$ matrices over $\mathbb{F}_q$ of rank $\leq t$). It is readily checked that (see [24])

$$|B_t^{\mathrm{R}}| \approx q^{t(m+n-t)}$$

which gives $d_{GV} \approx \frac{m+n-\sqrt{(m+n)^2-4m(n-k)}}{2}$.

3   Cryptography Based on Rank Metric

3.1   A Difficult Problem

Similarly to the syndrome decoding problem for the Hamming metric we can define the rank syndrome decoding (RSD) problem.

Problem 1 (Rank Syndrome Decoding). Let $\mathcal{C}$ be an $[n,k]$ $\mathbb{F}_{q^m}$-linear code, w an integer and $s \in \mathbb{F}_{q^m}^{n-k}$. Let $\boldsymbol{H}$ be a parity-check matrix of $\mathcal{C}$. The problem is to find a word $\boldsymbol{e} \in \mathbb{F}_{q^m}^n$ such that

$$\begin{cases} \boldsymbol{H}\boldsymbol{e}^T = s \\ w_R(\boldsymbol{e}) = w \end{cases}$$

Recently it was proven in [15] that this problem had a probabilistic reduction to the Syndrome Decoding problem for the Hamming distance which is known to be NP-complete. This substantiates claims on the hardness of this problem.

3.2   Complexity of Practical Attacks

The complexity of practical attacks grows quickly with the size of parameters, there is a structural reason for this: for the Hamming distance a key notion in the attacks is counting the number of words of length n and support size t, which corresponds to the notion of Newton binomial coefficient $\binom{n}{t}$, whose value is exponential in n for a fixed ratio t/n, since $\log_2 \binom{n}{t} = nh(t/n)(1+o(1))$ where $h(x) \overset{\text{def}}{=} -x\log_2 x - (1-x)\log_2(1-x)$. In the case of the rank metric, counting the number of possible supports of size w for a matrix code associated to an

$\mathbb{F}_{q^m}$-linear code of length n corresponds to counting the number of subspaces of dimension w in $\mathbb{F}_{q^m}$. This is given by the Gaussian binomial coefficient $\begin{bmatrix} m \\ r \end{bmatrix}_q$. In this case $\log_q \begin{bmatrix} m \\ r \end{bmatrix}_q = w(m-w)(1+0(1))$. Again this number behaves exponentially but the exponent is quadratic. This is of course to be compared to the "real" length of the matrix code which is also quadratic: $m \times n$.

The approaches that have been tried to solve this problem fall into two categories:

– **Combinatorial Approach:** This approach gives the best results for small values of q (typically $q = 2$) and for large values of n and k. When q becomes large, they become less efficient however. The first non-trivial combinatorial algorithm for the RSD problem was proposed in 1996 (see [8]), then in 2002 Ourivski and Johannson [27] improved it. However for both of the algorithms suggested in [27] the exponent of the complexity does not involve n. Recently these two algorithms were generalized in [14] by Gaborit et al. with a complexity in $\mathcal{O}\big((n - k)^3 m^3 q^{(w-1)\lceil \frac{(k+1)m}{n} \rceil}\big)$. Notice that the exponent involves now n and when $n > m$ the exponent becomes better than the one in [27].

– **Algebraic Approach:** The particular nature of rank metric makes it a natural field for algebraic system solving by Groebner bases. The complexity of these algorithms is largely independent of the value of q and in some cases may also be largely independent from m. These attacks are usually the most efficient ones when q becomes large. There exist different types of algebraic modeling for the rank metric decoding problem. The algebraic modeling proposed by Levy and Perret [23] in 2006 considers a quadratic system over $\mathbb{F}_q$ by taking as unknowns the support E of the error and the error coordinates regarding E. There are also other ways of performing the algebraic modeling: the Kernel attack [9,17], the Kipnis-Shamir modeling [21] or the minor approach (see [28] for the most recent results on this topic). The last one uses the fact that the determinant of minors of size greater than w is zero to derive algebraic equations of degree $w + 1$. All of these proposed algorithms can be applied to the RSD problem but they are based on an algebraic modeling in the base field $\mathbb{F}_q$ so that the number of unknowns is always quadratic in n (for $m = \Theta(n)$ and $w = \Theta(n)$), so that the general complexity for solving these algebraic equations with Groebner basis techniques is exponential in $\mathcal{O}(n^2)$.

More recently, a new algebraic modeling based on a annulator approach was proposed by Gaborit et al. in [14]. It yields multivariate sparse equations of degree q^{r+1} but on the extension field $\mathbb{F}_{q^m}$ rather than on the base field $\mathbb{F}_q$ and results in a drastic reduction of the number of unknowns. The latter attack is based on the notion of q-polynomial and is particularly efficient when w is small. Moreover all these attacks can be declined in a hybrid approach where some unknowns are guessed but asymptotically they are less efficient than other approaches.

Overall, all the known attacks for solving the RSD problem in the case where $m = \mathcal{O}(n), w = \mathcal{O}(n)$ have a complexity in $2^{\mathcal{O}(n^2)}$. Moreover because of the behavior of the Gaussian binomial coefficient and because of the number of unknowns for algebraic solving, it seems delicate to do better.

4   One-Way Functions Based on Rank Metric

We use here the hardness of the RSD problem to build a family of one-way functions based on this problem. Let us start by recalling the definition of a strongly one-way function (see [12, Definition 1]):

Definition 3. *A collection of functions $\{f_n : E_n \to \mathbb{F}_2^{k_n}\}$ is called strongly one way if:*

- *there exists a polynomial-time algorithm which computes $f_n(x)$ for all $x \in E_n$*
- *for every probabilistic polynomial-time algorithm A, for all $c > 0$ and for sufficiently large n, $Prob\big(A(f_n(x)) \in f_n^{-1}(f_n(x))\big) < \dfrac{1}{n^c}$*

We will consider the following family:
$$E_{n,k} = \{(\boldsymbol{H}, \boldsymbol{y}) : \boldsymbol{H} \in \mathbb{F}_{q^n}^{(n-k)\times n}, \boldsymbol{y} \in \mathbb{F}_{q^n}^n, w_R(\boldsymbol{y}) = w_n\}$$

$$f : \begin{array}{l} E_{n,k} \to \mathbb{F}_{q^n}^{(n-k)\times(n+1)} \\ (\boldsymbol{H}, \boldsymbol{y}) \mapsto (\boldsymbol{H}, \boldsymbol{H}\boldsymbol{y}^T) \end{array}$$

We take $m = n$ so that the first algorithm of [14] does not improve the complexity of [27]. These functions should be strongly one-way if we choose $w_n \approx d_{GV}(n, k)$ which corresponds to the range where there is basically in general a unique preimage.

5   A PRNG Based on Rank Metric Codes

5.1   Description of the Generator

Now that we have a family of one-way functions based on a hard problem, our goal is to use them to build a PRNG which will inherit of that hardness. We begin by letting $k = Rn$ and $w = \omega n$ for some constant R and ω. The security and the complexity of computing the pseudo-random sequence associated to this generator will then be expressed as a function of n, with R and ω as parameters.

First it is necessary to expand the size of the input, so that the number of syndromes becomes larger than the number of words of weight w_n. By definition, these two numbers are equal when $w = d_{GV}$ so that we can choose $\omega < \frac{d_{GV}}{n}$. The size of the input is $n(n-k)n \lceil \log q \rceil = n^3(1-R) \lceil \log q \rceil$ for $\boldsymbol{H}$ plus $w_n(2n - w_n) \lceil \log q \rceil = n^2(2\omega - \omega^2) \lceil \log q \rceil$ for $\boldsymbol{y}$ and the size of the output is $n^3(1 - R) \lceil \log q \rceil + n^2(1 - R) \lceil \log q \rceil$. So the function f_n expands the size of the input by $n^2(1 - R - 2\omega + \omega^2) \lceil \log q \rceil = \mathcal{O}(n^2)$ bits. To compute $f_n(\boldsymbol{H}, \boldsymbol{y})$ one has to perform a product matrix-vector in a field of degree n, which costs $\mathcal{O}(n^3)$ operations in $\mathbb{F}_q$.

Secondly we need an algorithm which computes a word $\boldsymbol{y} \in \mathbb{F}_{q^n}^n$ of weight ωn with $n^2(2\omega - \omega^2) \lceil \log q \rceil$ bits. This can be done very easily. According to Definition 2, $\boldsymbol{y}$ can be seen as an $n \times n$ matrix M over $\mathbb{F}_q$ of rank ωn. Let

$\beta = (\beta_1, \ldots, \beta_{\omega n})$ be a basis of the subspace generated by the rows of M. We can represent β by a matrix $B \in \mathbb{F}_q^{\omega n \times n}$. There exists a unique matrix $A \in \mathbb{F}_q^{nn}$ such that $M = AB$. In order to ensure the unicity of this representation, we need to take B in its echelon form B_{ech}, then $M = A'B_{ech}$ for some matrix A'. Unfortunately, it is not so easy to enumerate all the echelon matrices efficiently. To avoid this problem, we only generate words with a certain form, as it is done for SYND [13].

Definition 4 (Regular Rank Words). *A word* $y \in \mathbb{F}_{q^n}^n$ *of weight* r *is said regular if its associated matrix* $M \in \mathbb{F}_q^{n \times n}$ *is of the form*

$$M = A \begin{pmatrix} 1 & & \\ & \ddots & C \\ & & 1 \end{pmatrix}$$

with $A \in \mathbb{F}_q^{n \times r}$ *and* $C \in \mathbb{F}_q^{r \times (n-r)}$.

The probability that a word of weight r is regular is equal to the probability that a $r \times r$ matrix over $\mathbb{F}_q$ is invertible. This probability is greater than a constant $c > 0$ for all r and q. Thus it is not harder to solve the RSD problem in the general case than to solve the RSD problem by restraining it to the regular words, since if a polynomial algorithm could solve the RSD problem in the case of regular words then it would also give an algorithm solving the RSD problem with a probability divided by a constant, hence the RSD problem with regular words remains hard.

Algorithm 1. Expansion Algorithm

Input: $n^2(2\omega - \omega^2) \lceil \log q \rceil$ bits
Output: $y \in \mathbb{F}_{q^n}^n, w_R(y) = \omega n$
Data: A basis $(\beta_1, \ldots, \beta_n)$ of $\mathbb{F}_{q^n}/\mathbb{F}_q$
begin

> compute $x \in \mathbb{F}_q^{n^2(2\omega - \omega^2)}$ with the input bits;
> compute $A \in \mathbb{F}_q^{n \times \omega n}$ with the first ωn^2 coordinates of x;
> compute $B \in \mathbb{F}_q^{\omega n \times (n - \omega n)}$ with the last coordinates of x;
> $B \leftarrow (I_{\omega n}|B)$ /* this is the concatenation of two matrices */;
> $M \leftarrow AB$;
> $y \leftarrow (\beta_1, \ldots, \beta_n)M$;
> return y;

The most expensive step of this algorithm is the matrix product which takes ωn^3 operations in $\mathbb{F}_q$, so its overall complexity is $\mathcal{O}(n^3)$.

With these two functions, we can construct an iterative version of the generator which can compute as many bits as we want.

Algorithm 2. Our Pseudo-Random Generator

Input: a vector $x \in \mathbb{F}_q^K$ where K is the security parameter
Output: N pseudo-random bits
Data: a random matrix in systematic form $H \in \mathbb{F}_{q^n}^{(1-R)n \times n}$, an
   initialization vector $v \in \mathbb{F}_q^{n^2(2\omega-\omega^2)-K}$

begin
  $\quad y \leftarrow \text{Expansion}(x \| v)$;
  repeat
   $\quad\quad s \leftarrow Hy^T$;
   $\quad\quad$ split s into two strings of bits s_1 and s_2, with s_1 of length
    $\quad\quad n^2(2\omega - \omega^2) \lceil \log q \rceil$;
   $\quad\quad$ output s_2;
   $\quad\quad y \leftarrow \text{Expansion}(s_1)$;
  until *the number of bits generated* $> N$;

5.2 Security of the Generator

We recall that a distribution is pseudo-random if it is polynomial-time indistinguishable from a truly random distribution. If our generator were not pseudo-random, then there would exist a distinguisher D_R which distinguishes a sequence produced by our generator from a truly random sequence with a non-negligible advantage. We can use this distinguisher to build another distinguisher for the Fischer-Stern generator [11]. That generator is proven pseudo-random if syndrome decoding in the Hamming metric is hard [3]. It takes as input a parity-check matrix $M \in \mathbb{F}_2^{k \times n}$ of a random code and a vector $x \in \mathbb{F}_2^n$ of Hamming weight d, with d smaller than the Gilbert-Varshamov bound (in the Hamming metric) of the code and outputs (M, Mx^T).

We need a method to embed an $\mathbb{F}_q$-linear code into an $\mathbb{F}_{q^m}$-linear code. We use the same technique as in [15].

Definition 5. *Let $m \geqslant n$ and $\alpha = (\alpha_1, \ldots, \alpha_n) \in \mathbb{F}_{q^m}^n$. We define the embedding of $\mathbb{F}_q^n$ into $\mathbb{F}_{q^m}^n$ by:*

$$\psi_\alpha : \quad \begin{array}{ll} \mathbb{F}_q^n & \to \mathbb{F}_{q^m}^n \\ (x_1, \ldots, x_n) & \mapsto (\alpha_1 x_1, \ldots, \alpha_n x_n) \end{array} \tag{1}$$

For every $\mathbb{F}_q$-linear code $\mathcal{C}$, we denote by $\mathcal{C}(\mathcal{C}, \alpha)$ the $\mathbb{F}_{q^m}$-linear code generated by the set $\psi_\alpha(\mathcal{C})$.

Our distinguisher works as follow:

– it takes as input $M \in \mathbb{F}_2^{(n-k) \times n}$ and $s \in \mathbb{F}_2^{n-k}$.

– it chooses a vector $\boldsymbol{\alpha} \in \mathbb{F}_{2^m}^n$ at random until the coordinates of $\boldsymbol{\alpha}$ are $\mathbb{F}_2$-linearly independent.
– it gives to D_R the input $(\psi_{\boldsymbol{\alpha}}(M), s)$.
– it returns the same value as D_R.

If (M, s) is an output of the Fisher-Stern generator, then there exists an $\boldsymbol{x}$ such that $s = M\boldsymbol{x}^T$ and $w_H(\boldsymbol{x}) = d$. Hence $s = \psi_{\boldsymbol{\alpha}}(M)\psi_{\boldsymbol{\beta}}(\boldsymbol{x})^T$ with $\boldsymbol{\beta} = \boldsymbol{\alpha}^{-1} = (\alpha_1^{-1}, \ldots, \alpha_n^{-1})$.

Let $\mathcal{C}$ be the code of parity-check matrix M. Since $\mathcal{C}$ is a random code, its Hamming minimum distance d is on the Gilbert-Varshamov bound, so $d \approx d_{GV}$.

Note that $w_H(\psi_{\boldsymbol{\beta}}(\boldsymbol{x})) = d$. According to Theorem 8 of [15], if we choose $m > 8n$, the probability that the rank minimum distance d_R of $\mathcal{C}(\mathcal{C}, \boldsymbol{\alpha})$ is different from d decreases exponentially with n. According to Lemma 7 of [15], the rank weight of $\psi_{\boldsymbol{\beta}}(\boldsymbol{x})$ satisfies $w_R(\psi_{\boldsymbol{\beta}}(\boldsymbol{x})) = w_H(\boldsymbol{x}) = d$. This implies that the distinguisher D_R accepts (M, s) with a non-negligible advantage.

If (M, s) is purely random, D_R sees only a random distribution and accepts the inputs with probability $1/2$.

Thus the existence of a distinguisher for our generator implies the existence of a distinguisher for the Fisher-Stern generator, which contradicts Theorem 2 of [12]. This implies that our generator is pseudo-random.

6   Quantum Attacks

In this section we evaluate the complexity of solving the rank (metric) syndrome decoding problem with a quantum computer. We will use for that a slight generalization of Grover's quantum search algorithm [16, 18] given in [7] what we will use in the following form. We will use the NAND circuit model as in [4], which consists in a directed acyclic graph where each node has two incoming edges and computes the NAND of its predecessors.

Theorem 1. *[7] Let f be a Boolean function $f : \{0, 1\}^b \to \{0, 1\}$ that is computable by a NAND circuit of size S. Let p be the proportion of roots of the Boolean function*

$$p \overset{def}{=} \frac{\#\{x \in \{0, 1\}^b : f(x) = 0\}}{2^b}.$$

Then there is a quantum algorithm based on iterating a quantum circuit $\mathcal{O}\left(\frac{1}{\sqrt{p}}\right)$ many times that outputs with probability at least $\frac{1}{2}$ one of the roots of the Boolean function. The size of this circuit is $\mathcal{O}(S)$.

Basically this tool gives a quadratic speed-up when compared to a classical algorithm. Contrarily to what happens for the Hamming metric [4], where using this tool does not yield a quadratic speed-up over the best classical decoding algorithms, the situation is here much clearer: we can divide the exponential complexity of the best algorithms by two. The point is that the algorithms of [14, 20] can be viewed as looking for a linear subspace which has the right property, where linear spaces with appropriate parameters are drawn uniformly at random and this property can be checked in polynomial time. The exponential complexity of these algorithms is basically given by $\mathcal{O}\left(\frac{1}{p}\right)$ where p is the fraction of linear spaces that have this property. More precisley we have

$$\frac{1}{p} = \mathcal{O}\left(q^{(w-1)(k+1)}\right)$$

for $m > n$, (see [20]) and

$$\frac{1}{p} = \mathcal{O}\left(q^{(w-1)\lfloor \frac{(k+1)m}{n} \rfloor}\right)$$

when $m \leq n$, see [14]. Checking whether the linear space has the right property can be done by
(i) solving a linear system with $(n - k - 1)m$ equations and with about as many unknowns over $\mathbb{F}_q$,
(ii) checking whether a matrix over $\mathbb{F}_q$ of size $r \times r'$ is of rank equal to w where $(r, r') = (m - \lceil \frac{(k+1)m}{n} \rceil, n)$ in the case $m \leq n$ and $(r, r') = (n - k - 1, m)$ in the case $m > n$.

If we view q as a fixed quantity, there is a classical NAND circuit of size $\mathcal{O}\left((n-k)^3 m^3\right)$ that realizes these operations. In other words, by using Theorem 1 we obtain

Proposition 1. *For fixed q, there is a quantum circuit with $\mathcal{O}\left((n - k)^3 m^3\right)$ gates that solves the rank metric syndrome decoding problem in time $\mathcal{O}\left((n - k)^3 m^3\right)q^{(w-1)(k+1)/2}$ when $m > n$ and in time $\mathcal{O}\left((n - k)^3 m^3 q^{(w-1)\lceil \frac{(k+1)m}{n} \rceil}/2\right)$ when $m \leq n$.*

7   Conclusion

In this paper we give the first PRNG based on rank metric. The security if system relies on the hardness of solving general instances of the RSD problem, which permits to obtain small size of keys without considering additional structure like cyclicity or quasi-cyclicity. We give results and parameters which show that our system is a good trade-off between speed and data size when compared to other code-based PRNG in a context of PRNG provably as secure as known difficult problems. We also study the improvement of the complexity of the best known combinatorial attacks a quantum computer may bring. We give parameters both resistant to the best known classical and quantum attacks.

References

1. Banerjee, A., Peikert, C., Rosen, A.: Pseudorandom functions and lattices. In: Pointcheval, D., Johansson, T. (eds.) EUROCRYPT 2012. LNCS, vol. 7237, pp. 719–737. Springer, Heidelberg (2012)

2. Berbain, C., Gilbert, H., Patarin, J.: QUAD: a practical stream cipher with provable security. In: Vaudenay, S. (ed.) EUROCRYPT 2006. LNCS, vol. 4004, pp. 109–128. Springer, Heidelberg (2006)
3. Berlekamp, E., McEliece, R., van Tilborg, H.: On the inherent intractability of certain coding problems. IEEE Trans. Inform. Theor. **24**(3), 384–386 (1978)
4. Bernstein, D.J.: Grover vs. McEliece. In: Sendrier, N. (ed.) PQCrypto 2010. LNCS, vol. 6061, pp. 73–80. Springer, Heidelberg (2010)
5. Blum, L., Blum, M., Shub, M.: A simple unpredictable pseudo-random number generator. SIAM J. comput. **15**(2), 364–383 (1986)
6. Blum, M., Micali, S.: How to generate cryptographically strong sequences of pseudorandom bits. SIAM J. Comput. **13**(4), 850–864 (1984)
7. Boyer, M., Brassard, G., Høyer, P., Tapp, A.: Tight bounds on quantum searching. Fortsch. Phys. **46**, 493 (1998)
8. Chabaud, F., Stern, J.: The cryptographic security of the syndrome decoding problem for rank distance codes. In: Kim, K., Matsumoto, T. (eds.) ASIACRYPT 1996. LNCS, vol. 1163, pp. 368–381. Springer, Heidelberg (1996)
9. Courtois, N.T.: Efficient zero-knowledge authentication based on a linear algebra problem minrank. In: Boyd, C. (ed.) ASIACRYPT 2001. LNCS, vol. 2248, p. 402. Springer, Heidelberg (2001)
10. Cramer, R., Ducas, L., Peikert, C., Regev, O.: Recovering short generators of principal ideals in cyclotomic rings. Cryptology ePrint Archive, Report 2015/313 (2015). http://eprint.iacr.org/
11. Fiat, A., Shamir, A.: How to prove yourself: practical solutions to identification and signature problems. In: Odlyzko, A.M. (ed.) CRYPTO 1986. LNCS, vol. 263, pp. 186–194. Springer, Heidelberg (1987)
12. Fischer, J.-B., Stern, J.: An efficient pseudo-random generator provably as secure as syndrome decoding. In: Maurer, U.M. (ed.) EUROCRYPT 1996. LNCS, vol. 1070, pp. 245–255. Springer, Heidelberg (1996)
13. Gaborit, P., Lauradoux, C., Sendrier, N.: SYND: a fast code-based stream cipher with a security reduction. In: Proceedings of the IEEE International Symposium on Information Theory - ISIT, pp. 186–190, Nice (2007)
14. Gaborit, P., Ruatta, O., Schrek, J.: On the complexity of the rank syndrome decoding problem. CoRR (2013). arxiv.org/abs/1301.1026
15. Gaborit, P., Zémor, G.: On the hardness of the decoding and the minimum distance problems for rank codes. CoRR (2014). arxiv.org/abs/1404.3482
16. Gibson, J.K.: The security of the Gabidulin public key cryptosystem. In: Maurer, U.M. (ed.) EUROCRYPT 1996. LNCS, vol. 1070, pp. 212–223. Springer, Heidelberg (1996)
17. Goubin, L., Courtois, N.T.: Cryptanalysis of the TTM cryptosystem. In: Okamoto, T. (ed.) ASIACRYPT 2000. LNCS, vol. 1976, p. 44. Springer, Heidelberg (2000)
18. Grover, L.K.: Quantum mechanics helps in searching for a needle in a haystack. Phys. Rev. Lett. **79**, 325 (1997)
19. Håstad, J., Impagliazzo, R., Levin, L.A., Luby, M.: A pseudorandom generator from any one-way function. SIAM J. Comput. **28**(4), 1364–1396 (1999)
20. Hauteville, A., Tillich, J.-P.: New algorithms for decoding in the rank metric and an attack on the LRPC cryptosystem (2015). arxiv.org/abs/1504.05431
21. Kipnis, A., Shamir, A.: Cryptanalysis of the HFE public key cryptosystem by relinearization. In: Wiener, M. (ed.) CRYPTO 1999. LNCS, vol. 1666, p. 19. Springer, Heidelberg (1999)
22. Levin, L.A.: One way functions and pseudorandom generators. Combinatorica **7**(4), 357–363 (1987)

23. Lévy-dit-Vehel F., Perret, L.: Algebraic decoding of codes in rank metric. In: Proceedings of YACC06, Porquerolles, France (2006). http://grim.univ-tln.fr/YACC06/abstracts-yacc06.pdf
24. Lidl, R., Niederreiter, H.: Finite Fields, Volume 20 of Encyclopedia of Mathematics and its Applications, 2nd edn. Cambridge University Press, Cambridge (1997)
25. McEliece, R.J.: A public-key system based on algebraic coding theory. DSN Progress Report 44, pp. 114–116. Jet Propulsion Lab (1978)
26. Meziani, M., Cayrel, P.-L., Hoffmann, G.: Improving the performance of the SYND stream cipher. In: Mitrokotsa, A., Vaudenay, S. (eds.) AFRICACRYPT 2012. LNCS, vol. 7374, pp. 99–116. Springer, Heidelberg (2012)
27. Ourivski, A.V., Johansson, T.: New technique for decoding codes in the rank metric and its cryptography applications. Prob. Inf. Transm. **38**(3), 237–246 (2002)
28. Spaenlenhauer, P.-J.: Résolution de systèmes multi-homogènes et determinantiels. Ph.D. thesis, Univ. Pierre et Marie Curie- Paris 6 (2012)
29. Yao, A.C.: Theory and application of trapdoor functions. In: 23rd Annual Symposium on Foundations of Computer Science, SFCS 2008, pp. 80–91. IEEE (1982)

Applying Grover's Algorithm to AES: Quantum Resource Estimates

Markus Grassl[1,2], Brandon Langenberg[3], Martin Roetteler[4(✉)], and Rainer Steinwandt[3]

[1] Universität Erlangen-Nürnberg, Erlangen, Germany
[2] Max Planck Institute for the Science of Light,
Günther-Scharowsky-Straße 1, Bau 24, 91058 Erlangen, Germany
Markus.Grassl@fau.de
[3] Florida Atlantic University, 777 Glades Road, Boca Raton, FL 33431, USA
{blangenb,rsteinwa}@fau.edu
[4] Microsoft Research, One Microsoft Way, Redmond, WA 98052, USA
martinro@microsoft.com

Abstract. We present quantum circuits to implement an exhaustive key search for the Advanced Encryption Standard (AES) and analyze the quantum resources required to carry out such an attack. We consider the overall circuit size, the number of qubits, and the circuit depth as measures for the cost of the presented quantum algorithms. Throughout, we focus on Clifford+T gates as the underlying fault-tolerant logical quantum gate set. In particular, for all three variants of AES (key size 128, 192, and 256 bit) that are standardized in FIPS-PUB 197, we establish precise bounds for the number of qubits and the number of elementary logical quantum gates that are needed to implement Grover's quantum algorithm to extract the key from a small number of AES plaintext-ciphertext pairs.

Keywords: Quantum cryptanalysis · Quantum circuits · Grover's algorithm · Advanced Encryption Standard

1 Introduction

Cryptanalysis is an important area where quantum algorithms have found applications. Shor's seminal work invalidates some well-established computational assumptions in *asymmetric* cryptography [27], including the hardness of factoring and the computation of discrete logarithms in finite cyclic groups such as the multiplicative group of a finite field. On the other hand, regarding *symmetric* encryption, the impact of quantum algorithms seems less dramatic. While a quantum version of related key attacks [26] would be a threat for block ciphers provided that quantum access to the encryption function is given, as this requires the ability to generate quantum superpositions of related keys, this attack model is somewhat restrictive. In particular, the related key attack of [26] is not applicable to, say, a context where a small number of plaintext-ciphertext pairs are given and the goal is to identify the encryption key.

© Springer International Publishing Switzerland 2016
T. Takagi (Ed.): PQCrypto 2016, LNCS 9606, pp. 29–43, 2016.
DOI: 10.1007/978-3-319-29360-8_3

It has been known for some time that in principle Grover's search algorithm [15] can be applied to the problem of finding the key: the square root speed-up offered by Grover's algorithm over a classical exhaustive key search seems to be the most relevant quantum cryptanalytic impact for the study of block ciphers. To actually implement such an attack, the Boolean predicate that is queried in Grover's algorithm needs to be realized as a circuit. Perhaps interestingly, even for the most obvious target—the Advanced Encryption Standard [24], which in its 256-bit version has recently been suggested to be quantum-safe [5]—to the best of our knowledge no detailed logical level resource estimate for implementing Grover's algorithm is available. The seemingly simple task of implementing the AES function actually requires some analysis as the circuit implementation is required to be reversible, i.e., it must be possible to implement the operation via an embedding into a permutation. Once a reversible implementation is known, in principle also a quantum implementation can be derived as the set of permutations is a subset of all unitary operations.

Our contribution. We provide reversible circuits that implement the full Advanced Encryption Standard AES-k for each standardized key size (i.e., $k = 128, 192, 256$). We establish resource estimates for the number of qubits and the number of Toffoli gates, controlled NOT gates, and NOT gates. See [23] for basic definitions of quantum and reversible logic gates. Furthermore, we consider decompositions of the reversible circuits into a universal fault-tolerant gate set that can then be implemented as the set of logical gates. As underlying fault-tolerant gate set we consider the so-called set of Clifford+T gates.[1] This gate set is motivated, e.g., by the fact that this set of gates can be implemented fault-tolerantly on a large set of codes, including the surface code family [13,14] and concatenated CSS codes [25,28]. Clifford gates typically are much cheaper than the T-gate which commonly is implemented using state distillation. When breaking down the circuit to the level of T-gates we therefore pay attention to reducing the overall T-count. See also [3,4] for techniques how to optimize the T-count and [2] for techniques that allow to navigate the trade-space between T-depth and the number of qubits used. For the particular case of the Toffoli gate we use an implementation that requires 7 T-gates and several Clifford gates, see [3,23]. There is a probabilistic circuit known that implements the Toffoli gate with only 4 T-gates [16], however, as the architecture requirements will be stronger in that measurement and feed-forward of classical information is required, we focus on the purely unitary decomposition that requires 7 T-gates. We remark however, that the only source of T-gates in this paper are Toffoli gates, hence it is possible to use Jones' Toffoli factorization *mutatis mutandis* which leads to all given resource estimates for the T-count being multiplied by $4/7$ and the requirement of 1 additional ancilla qubit. In our resource estimates we do not to restrict interactions between qubits and leave the implementation, e.g., on a 2D nearest neighbor array for further study, including an investigation

---

[1] As is common, we do not distinguish between $T = \begin{pmatrix} 1 & 0 \\ 0 & \exp(i\pi/4) \end{pmatrix}$ and $T^\dagger$-gates.

of the remaining *quantum circuit placement* problems [21] that will have to be solved for the logical gate lists that are produced by our approach.

One of our main findings is that the number of logical qubits required to implement a Grover attack on AES is relatively low, namely between around $3,000$ and $7,000$ logical qubits. However, due to the large circuit depth of unrolling the entire Grover iteration, it seems challenging to implement this algorithm on an actual physical quantum computer, even if the gates are not error corrected. It is worth noting that much of the circuit cost within each Grover iteration originates from the key expansion, i.e., from deriving the round keys and that the overall depth is a direct result of the serial nature of Grover's algorithm.

2   Preliminaries: Grover's Algorithm

Before going into technicalities of how to implement AES as a quantum circuit, we briefly recall the interface that we need to provide to realize a key search, namely Grover's algorithm [15]. The Grover procedure takes as an input a quantum circuit implementing a Boolean function $f\colon \{0,1\}^k \longrightarrow \{0,1\}$ in the usual way, i.e., via a quantum circuit U_f that implements $|x\rangle|y\rangle \mapsto |x\rangle|y \oplus f(x)\rangle$, where $x \in \{0,1\}^n$ and $y \in \{0,1\}$. The basic Grover algorithm finds an element x_0 such that $f(x_0) = 1$. Denoting by H the 2×2 Hadamard transform, the Grover algorithm consists of repeatedly applying the operation G to the initial state $|\psi\rangle \otimes |\varphi\rangle$, where $|\psi\rangle = \frac{1}{\sqrt{2^k}}\sum_{x\in\{0,1\}^k}|x\rangle$, $|\varphi\rangle = \frac{1}{\sqrt{2}}(|0\rangle - |1\rangle)$, and where G is defined as

$$G = U_f \left((H^{\otimes k}(2|0\rangle\langle 0| - 1_{2^k})H^{\otimes k}) \otimes 1_2 \right), \tag{1}$$

where $|0\rangle$ denotes the all zero basis state of the appropriate size. Overall, G has to be applied a number of $O(\sqrt{N/M})$ times in order to measure an element x_0 such that $f(x_0) = 1$ with constant probability, where N is the total number of candidates, i.e., $N = 2^k$, and provided that there are precisely M solutions, i.e., $M = |\{x\colon f(x) = 1\}|$; see also [23, Sect. 6.1.2], [8] for an analysis. If we know that there is only one solution, i.e., $M = 1$, this means that we can find a solution by applying $H^{\otimes k+1}$ to the initial state $|0\rangle^{\otimes k} \otimes |1\rangle$ and then applying G^ℓ, where $\ell = \lfloor \frac{\pi}{4}\sqrt{N} \rfloor$, followed by a measurement of the entire quantum register which will yield a solution x_0 with high probability [23, Sect. 6.1.4], [8].

As we will show in the following section, we can indeed define a function f from the set of possible keys, i.e., $k \in \{128, 192, 256\}$ for the case of AES, such that there is (plausibly) precisely one solution to the problem of finding the correct key K that was used to encrypt a small set of given plaintext-ciphertext pairs, i.e., we can (plausibly) enforce the situation $M = 1$ by defining a suitable function f. We remark, however, that it is possible to modify Grover's algorithm in various ways so that it can cope with a larger (but known) number $M > 1$ of solutions or even with a completely unknown number of solutions: as mentioned above, if the number M of solutions is known, $O(\sqrt{N/M})$ iterations are enough, however, if the number is *unknown*, there is an issue that it is not possible to pick the right number of iterations a priori. Nonetheless, there is a variant of

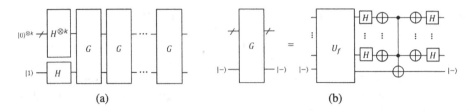

Fig. 1. (a) Quantum circuit to implement Grover's algorithm. The algorithm consists of creating the equal superposition $\sum_x |x\rangle$ in the upper register which for the case of AES has $k = 128, 192, 256$ qubits and a single qubit state $|-\rangle = |0\rangle - |1\rangle$ in the lower register. The operator G is the Grover iterate and is applied a total number of $\lfloor \frac{\pi}{4}\sqrt{2^k} \rfloor$ many times. (b) One round of Grover's algorithm. Shown is the operator $G = U_f \left((H^{\otimes k}(2|0\rangle\langle 0| - 1_{2^k})H^{\otimes k}) \otimes 1_2 \right)$ and its circuit decomposition. Note that the effect of the gates between the two layers of Hadamard gates is to invert the phase of the basis state $|0\rangle$ on the upper k bits (up to a global phase).

the algorithm which finds a solution in expected running time $O(\sqrt{N/M})$ even when the number M of solutions is unknown [8, Sect. 6].

There are several ways out of this dilemma which we mention briefly for completeness but point out that we did not implement these alternatives: one can first apply a quantum algorithm to count the number of solutions [8,10] or one can do an exponential search on the number of iterations [8,9], or one can employ an adaptive schedule in which the Grover operator is changed to an operator that rotates by different angles depending on the index of the iteration [30], thereby driving the oscillation of the quantum state into a bounded region (the "fixed point") which then yields a solution upon measurement.

Returning to the case of Grover's algorithm with a unique solution, we now study the number of gates and the space requirements needed in order to implement the algorithm. We consider the gates shown in Fig. 1, in particular we first focus on the circuit shown in part (b) of the figure and analyze its complexity. While H is a Clifford operation, besides the operation U_f which involves the classical computation of (several) AES functions, we also have to determine the cost κ for the operation $(2|0\rangle\langle 0| - 1)$ in Eq. (1). This reduces to the implementation of a k-fold controlled NOT gate, where for us $k \in \{128, 192, 256\}$. The resource estimates for this gates in terms of Toffoli gates can be obtained from [6] to be (as $n \geq 5$): $8k - 24$ Toffoli gates which evaluates to $1,000$, $1,512$, and $2,024$ Toffoli gates per phase operation $(2|0\rangle\langle 0| - 1_{2^k})$, respectively. For the number of Clifford+T gates (counting only Ts) one could directly apply an upper bound by multiplying κ with 7, however, one can derive a slightly better bound: as shown in [29] (see also [20]), one can employ phase cancellations and show an upper bound of $32k - 84$ for a k-fold controlled NOT gate, i.e., we obtain $4,012$, $6,060$, and $8,108$ for the T-count per phase operation for the three key sizes $k \in \{128, 192, 256\}$.

We spend the rest of the paper to obtain estimates for $f \colon \{0,1\}^k \to \{0,1\}$ which proceeds by first mapping $K \mapsto (\text{AES}_K(m_1), \ldots, \text{AES}_K(m_r))$ and then computing the equality function of the resulting vector with the given ciphertexts

$c_1, \ldots, c_r$, where $c_i \in \{0, 1\}^{128}$. In other words, we define the value of f on a given input key $K \in \{0, 1\}^k$ (where $k \in \{128, 192, 256\}$) as follows:

$$f(K) := (\mathrm{AES}_K(m_1) = c_1) \wedge \ldots \wedge (\mathrm{AES}_K(m_r) = c_r).$$

As argued below, it is plausible that $r = 3, 4, 5$ are sufficient for the three standardized AES key sizes. The equality function can be implemented by a multiply controlled NOT gate that has $128r$ (many controls where $r = 3, 4, 5$) and a single target. Using the above formulas this leads to Toffoli counts of $3,048$, $4,072$, and $5,096$, respectively, as well as T-counts of $12,204$, $16,300$, and $20,396$, respectively. We return to the question of providing exact quantum resource estimates for Grover's algorithm in Sect. 3.4 after the implementation details of the "oracle" function U_f have been derived in the subsequent sections.

3   Implementing the Boolean Predicate—Testing a Key

An essential component needed in Grover's algorithm is a circuit which on input a candidate key $|K\rangle$ indicates if this key is equal to the secret target key or not. To do so, the idea is to simply encrypt some (fixed) plaintext under the candidate key and compare the result with the (assumed to be known) corresponding ciphertext under the secret target key.

3.1   Ensuring Uniqueness of the Solution

As AES always operates on 128-bit plaintexts, at least for 192-bit and 256-bit keys we have to assume that fixing a single plaintext-ciphertext pair is not sufficient to determine a secret key uniquely.

Arguing with the strict avalanche criterion [11,19] exactly in the same way as in [26, Sect. 2.1], we can plausibly assume that for every pair of keys $(K, K') \in \{0, 1\}^{k \times k}$ with $K \neq K'$ the condition

$$(\mathrm{AES}_K(m_1), \ldots, \mathrm{AES}_K(m_r)) \neq (\mathrm{AES}_{K'}(m_1), \ldots, \mathrm{AES}_{K'}(m_r))$$

holds for some suitable collection of plaintexts $m_1, \ldots, m_r$. The reason for this is that, for a fixed plaintext, when flipping a bit in the secret key, then each bit of the corresponding ciphertext should change with probability $1/2$. Hence, for r simultaneous plaintext-ciphertext pairs that are encrypted under two secret keys $K' \neq K$ we expect to get different results with probability about $1 - 2^{-rn}$, if the plaintexts are pairwise different, where n denotes the length of the message. Hence out of a total of $2^{2k} - 2^k$ key pairs (K, K') with $K \neq K'$, about $(2^{2k} - 2^k) \cdot 2^{-rn} \leq 2^{2k-rn}$ keys $K' \neq K$ are expected to give the same encryptions. Hence it seems plausible to estimate that

$$r > \lceil 2k/n \rceil \tag{2}$$

plaintexts suffice to ensure that for every $K' \neq K$ at least one separating plaintext is available. As AES has 128-bit plaintexts we have that $n = 128$, i.e.,

Eq. (2) implies that for key length k the adversary has $r > \lceil 2k/128 \rceil$ plaintext-ciphertexts pairs $(m_1, r_1), \ldots, (m_r, c_r)$ for the target key available. In other words, to characterize the secret target key uniquely, we assume that $r = 3$ (AES-128), $r = 4$ (AES-192), and $r = 5$ (AES-256) suitable plaintext-ciphertext pairs are known by the adversary.

3.2 Reversible and Quantum Circuits to Implement AES

We assume that the reader is familiar with the basic components of AES. For a detailed specification of AES we refer to FIPS-PUB 197 [24]. To realize this round-oriented block cipher as a reversible circuit over the Toffoli gate set, respectively as a quantum circuit over the Clifford+T gate set, we need to take care of the *key expansion*, which provides all needed 128-bit round keys, as well as the individual rounds. While the number of rounds depends on the specific key length k, the four main functions—AddRoundKey, MixColumns, ShiftRows, and SubBytes— that are used to modify the 128-bit internal state of AES are independent of k.

First, we discuss the realization of these four functions, before going into details of combining them with the key expansion into complete round functions and a full AES. In our design choices, we tried to keep the number of qubits low, even when this results in a somewhat larger gate complexity. For instance, to implement the $\mathbb{F}_{256}$-multiplications within SubBytes, we opted for a multiplier architecture requiring less qubits, but more Clifford and more T-gates.

3.2.1 Circuits for the Basic AES Operations

The internal AES state consists of 128 bits, organized into a rectangular array of 4×4 bytes. We will devote 128 qubits to hold the current internal state.

AddRoundKey. In the implementation of the key expansion, we ensure that the current round key is available on 128 dedicated wires. Implementing the bit-wise XOR of the round key then reduces to 128 CNOT gates which can all be executed in parallel.

MixColumns. Since MixColumns operates on an entire column of the state or 32 (qu)bits at a time, the matrix specified in [24] was used to generate a 32×32 matrix. An LUP-type decomposition was used on this 32×32 matrix in order to compute this operation in place with 277 CNOT gates and a total depth of 39. Example 1 offers a similar but smaller version of an LUP-type decomposition as we used.

ShiftRows. As ShiftRows amount to a particular permutation of the current AES state, we do not have to add any gates to implement this operation as it corresponds to a permutation of the qubits. Instead, we simply adjust the position of subsequent gates to make sure that the correct input wire is used.

SubBytes. This operation replaces one byte of the current state with a new value. For a classical implementation, a look-up table can be an attractive implementation option, but for our purposes, explicitly calculating the result of this operation seems the more resource friendly option. Treating a state byte as element $\alpha \in \mathbb{F}_2[x]/(1+x+x^3+x^4+x^8)$, first the multiplicative inverse of α (leaving 0 invariant) needs to be found. This is followed by an affine transformation. To find α^{-1} we adopt the idea of [1] to build on a classical Itoh-Tsujii multiplier, but we work with in-place matrix multiplications. Specifically, we compute

$$\alpha^{-1} = \alpha^{254} = ((\alpha \cdot \alpha^2) \cdot (\alpha \cdot \alpha^2)^4 \cdot (\alpha \cdot \alpha^2)^{16} \cdot \alpha^{64})^2, \tag{3}$$

exploiting that all occurring exponentiations are $\mathbb{F}_2$-linear. Using again an LUP-type decomposition, the corresponding matrix-multiplication can be realized in-place, using CNOT gates only. And by adjusting the positions of subsequent gates accordingly, realizing the permutation is for free, no gates need to be introduced for this.

Example 1. Squaring in $\mathbb{F}_2[x]/(1+x+x^3+x^4+x^8)$ can be expressed as multiplying the coefficient vector from the left with

$$\begin{bmatrix} 1&0&0&0&1&0&1&0 \\ 0&0&0&0&1&0&1&1 \\ 0&1&0&0&0&1&0&0 \\ 0&0&0&0&1&1&1&1 \\ 0&0&1&0&1&0&0&1 \\ 0&0&0&0&0&1&1&0 \\ 0&0&0&1&0&1&0&0 \\ 0&0&0&0&0&0&1&1 \end{bmatrix} = \begin{bmatrix} 1&0&0&0&0&0&0&0 \\ 0&0&0&0&1&0&0&0 \\ 0&1&0&0&0&0&0&0 \\ 0&0&0&0&0&0&1&0 \\ 0&0&1&0&0&0&0&0 \\ 0&0&0&0&0&1&0&0 \\ 0&0&0&1&0&0&0&0 \\ 0&0&0&0&0&0&0&1 \end{bmatrix} \cdot \begin{bmatrix} 1&0&0&0&0&0&0&0 \\ 0&1&0&0&0&0&0&0 \\ 0&0&1&0&0&0&0&0 \\ 0&0&0&1&0&0&0&0 \\ 0&0&0&0&1&0&0&0 \\ 0&0&0&0&0&1&0&0 \\ 0&0&0&0&1&1&1&0 \\ 0&0&0&0&0&0&1&1 \end{bmatrix} \cdot \begin{bmatrix} 1&0&0&0&1&0&1&0 \\ 0&1&0&0&0&1&0&0 \\ 0&0&1&0&1&0&0&1 \\ 0&0&0&1&0&1&0&0 \\ 0&0&0&0&1&0&1&1 \\ 0&0&0&0&0&1&1&0 \\ 0&0&0&0&0&0&1&0 \\ 0&0&0&0&0&0&0&1 \end{bmatrix}.$$

From this, we see that in-place-squaring can be implemented with only twelve CNOT gates. The resulting circuit is shown in Fig. 2.

To realize the six multiplications in Eq. (3), we use a general purpose multiplier in the underlying binary field. We opted for a design by Maslov et al. [22], which requires less than 60 % of the number of qubits than a more recent design in [18]. This comes at the cost of an increased gate complexity, however, and a different design choice could be considered. For the specific polynomial basis representation of $\mathbb{F}_{256}$ at hand, Maslov et al.'s design, requires 64 Toffoli plus 21 CNOT gates, which with Amy et al. [3] translates into $64 \cdot 7 = 448$ T- plus $64 \cdot 8 + 21 = 533$ Clifford gates.

Noticing that three of the multiplications in Eq. (3) are actually duplicates, it turns out that four multiplications suffice in order to implement the inversion. Trying to reduce the number of total qubits required at each step, the actual calculation of computing α^{-1} fits into 40 qubits total, producing $|\alpha\rangle$, $|\alpha\rangle^{-1}$, and twenty-four reinitialized qubits as output. To do so, and reinitialize qubits, we invest twelve linear transformations and eight $\mathbb{F}_{256}$-multiplications, totalling 3584 T-gates and 4539 Clifford gates.

Once α^{-1} is found, the affine transformation specified in [24] must be computed, which can be done with an LUP-type decomposition; four uncontrolled NOT gates take care of the vector addition after multiplication with a matrix. In total one 8-bit S-box requires 3584 T-gates and 4569 Clifford gates.

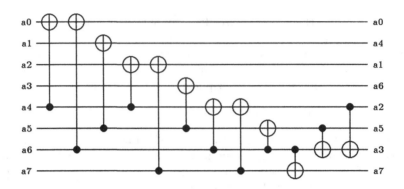

Fig. 2. Squaring in $\mathbb{F}_2[x]/(1 + x + x^3 + x^4 + x^8)$

SubBytes —an alternative implementation minimizing qubits. The inversion $\alpha \mapsto \alpha^{-1}$ (where 0 is mapped to 0) can be seen as a permutation on $\mathbb{F}_{256}$. This permutation is odd, while quantum circuits with NOT, CNOT, and Toffoli gates on $n > 3$ qubits generate the full alternating group A_{2^n} of even permutations. Hence we have to use one ancilla qubit, i.e., nine qubits in total. The task is then to express a permutation on 512 points in terms of the generators corresponding to the NOT, CNOT, and Toffoli gates. While computer algebra systems like Magma [7] have built-in functions for this, the resulting expressions will be huge. In order to find a short factorization, we compute a stabilizer chain and corresponding transversals using techniques similar to those described in [12]. We use a randomized search to find short elements in each transversal. As it is only relevant to implement the exact function when the ancilla qubit is in the state $|0\rangle$, we choose the first 256 points in the basis for the permutation group as those with the ancilla in the state $|0\rangle$, and the remaining 256 points as those with the ancilla in the state $|1\rangle$. This allows to compute a factorization modulo permutations of the last 256 points. With this approach, we found a circuit with no more than 9695 T-gates and 12631 Clifford gates, less than three times more gates than the version above, but using only 9 instead of 40 qubits in total.

3.2.2 Key Expansion

Standard implementation of the key expansion for AES-k ($k = 128, 192, 256$) separates the original k-bit key into 4, 6 or 8 *words* of length 32, respectively and must expand the k-bit key into forty-four *words* for $k = 128$, fifty-two *words* for $k = 192$ and sixty *words* for $k = 256$. Each AES key expansion uses the same operations and there are only slight differences in the actual round key construction. The operations are RotWord, a simple rotation, SubBytes, and Rcon[i], which adds $x^{i-1} \in \mathbb{F}_{256}$ to the first byte of each word.

While the three different versions of AES employ up to 14 rounds of computation, the key expansion is independent of the input. The *words* created by the key expansion were divided into two categories: the *words* needing SubBytes in their computation and those that do not. The *words* not involving SubBytes can be recursively constructed from those that do by a combination of XORings

Table 1. Quantum resource estimates for the key expansion phase of AES-k, where $k \in \{128, 192, 256\}$.

	#gates			Depth		#qubits	
	NOT	CNOT	Toffoli	T	Overall	Storage	Ancillae
128	176	21,448	20,480	5,760	12,636	320	96
192	136	17,568	16,384	4,608	10,107	256	96
256	215	27,492	26,624	7,488	16,408	416	96

making them simple to compute as needed, saving up to 75 % of the storage cost of the key expansion. The most expensive of these is *word 41* or w_{41} in AES-128 which is constructed by XORing 11 previous *words* costing 352 CNOT gates and a total depth of 11.

Since `SubBytes` is costly, the remaining *words* are stored as they are constructed. In a classical AES implementation, these *words* (every fourth or sixth) are produced by starting with the previous word, however in this construction the previous word must be constructed, and removed, as needed. For example, in AES-128, to construct w_8, first w_7 must be constructed as follows: $w_7 = w_4 \oplus w_3 \oplus w_2 \oplus w_1$.

This can be done on the previously constructed word (here w_4) saving qubits, gates, and depth. Since the construction of w_8 involves the use of w_4 the above process needs to be repeated to be removed before the end of construction of w_8. For the construction of these words, similar to `ShiftRows`, `RotWord` can be eliminated if the position of the gates is shifted to use the correct wires. Since `SubWord` applies `SubBytes` to each byte of the word independently, each of the four `SubBytes` computations can be done concurrently.

Example 2. Below is the construction of w_8. Notice that w_7 is constructed on top of w_4.

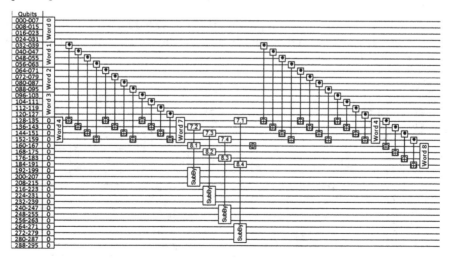

To allow each of the four SubBytes routines per round to perform simultaneously, 96 auxiliary qubits would be needed, along with the 32 needed to store the new word. With each word constructed requiring the previous word be constructed first, we did not reduce the depth further. Computation costs are listed in Table 1 (the listed qubit costs do not include storing the original key).

3.2.3   AES Rounds

AES starts with a simple whitening step—XORing the input with the first four words of the key. Since, in this case, the input is a fixed value, and adding a fixed value can be done by simply flipping bits, approximately 64 uncontrolled NOT gates are used on the first four key words to start round one. This can be reversed later when needed, but saves 128 qubits. If this is not the case, then 128 qubits are needed to store the input and 128 CNOT gates can be used to compute this step. While the 10, 12, or 14 rounds of AES all apply the same basic functions, the circuit structure differs slightly per round to reduce qubits and depth. SubBytes must be computed 16 times per round, requiring 384 auxiliary qubits for all to be done simultaneously or an increase in depth is needed. Using only the minimum 24 auxiliary qubits and the 128 qubits needed to store the result, it was noticed that all 16 SubBytes calculations per round could be done with a maximum depth of 8 SubBytes cycles.

Since SubBytes is not done in place, and AES-k requires 128 qubits per round, the computation takes 128 qubits times the number of rounds per AES, in addition to the number of qubits needed to store the original key. This number can be reduced by reversing steps between computations to clear qubits for future use. Once SubBytes has been applied, the input can be removed by reversing enough steps (but the output could not be removed as its counterpart (inverse) is gone). Since AES-128 employs 10 rounds, using 512 qubits for storage and 24 auxiliary qubits, allows the reverse process to be applied three times. For AES-192 and AES-256, we used 640 qubits for storage since we did not manage to have three rounds of reversing on 536 qubits.

Example 3. The reverse process representation for AES-128. Notice this method leaves Round 4, Round 7 and Round 9 with no way to be removed unless the entire process is reversed.

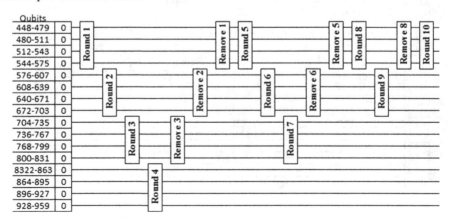

For AES-192 and AES-256 the reversing process is done after rounds five, nine and twelve, requiring only 128 qubits more than AES-128.

As stated, ShiftRows is for free and using an LUP-type decomposition for MixedColumns allows this process to be done in place using 277 CNOT gates with a maximum depth of 39. To compute all 10 rounds of AES-128, 536 qubits were needed, 664 qubits were used to compute the 12 rounds of AES-192 and 14 rounds of AES-256.

The XORing of the round keys can be done directly on top of the input for each round. If the round key needed is already constructed, 128 CNOT gates with a depth of 1 are used to complete the round. If the round key is not already constructed and thus a combination of constructed keys, then it only requires this process to be done multiple times. AES-128 requires this to be done 11 times (the most) in the case of w_{41}, increasing the depth and CNOT gate count by at most 11.

3.3   Resource Estimates: Reversible AES Implementation

The numbers listed in the three tables below show the costs in gates, depth and qubits to achieve the output of each AES-k system.

3.4   Resource Estimates: Grover Algorithm

From the discussion in the previous sections we obtain a reversible circuit for computing $AES_K(m_i)$, i.e., a circuit $\mathcal{C}$ that implements the operation $|K\rangle|0\rangle \mapsto |K\rangle|AES_K(m_i)\rangle$. The overall circuit to implement U_f is shown in Fig. 3. The AES layer can be applied in parallel, however, as the used ancilla qubits have to be returned clean after each round, we have to uncompute each AES box within each round. Hence the depth (and T-depth) increases by a factor of 2 within each invocation of U_f. The total number of gates (and T-gates) on the other hand increases by a factor of $2r$ as all boxes have now to be counted. The number of qubits is given by r times the number of qubits within each AES box.

Once the AES boxes have been computed, the result is compared with the given ciphertexts $c_1, \ldots, c_r$. Note that as AES operates on plaintexts/ciphertexts of length 128 we have that $c_i \in \{0,1\}^{128}$ throughout. The comparison is done

Table 2. Quantum resource estimates for the implementation of AES-128.

	#gates		Depth		#qubits
	T	Clifford	T	Overall	
Initial	0	0	0	0	128
Key Gen	143,360	185,464	5,760	12,626	320
10 Rounds	917,504	1,194,956	44,928	98,173	536
Total	1,060,864	1,380,420	50,688	110,799	984

Table 3. Quantum resource estimates for the implementation of AES-192. The lower gate count in Key Gen and the lower depth, when compared to AES-128, arises from using the additional available space to store intermediate results and to parallelize parts of the circuit.

	#gates		Depth		#qubits
	T	Clifford	T	Overall	
Initial	0	0	0	0	192
Key Gen	114,688	148,776	4,608	10,107	256
12 Rounds	1,089,536	1,418,520	39,744	86,849	664
Total	1,204,224	1,567,296	44,352	96,956	1,112

Table 4. Quantum resource estimates for the implementation of AES-256.

	#gates		Depth		#qubits
	T	Clifford	T	Overall	
Initial	0	0	0	0	256
Key Gen	186,368	240,699	7,488	16,408	416
14 Rounds	1,318,912	1,715,400	52,416	114,521	664
Total	1,505,280	1,956,099	59,904	130,929	1,336

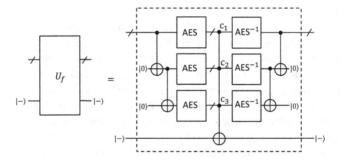

Fig. 3. The reversible implementation of the function U_f is shown in further detail. In this case the key size $k = 128$ is considered for which $r = 3$ invocations of AES suffice in order to make the target key unique. For the cases of $k = 192$ the number of parallel AES boxes increases to $r = 4$ and for $k = 256$ to $r = 5$, however, the overall structure of the circuit is common to all key sizes.

by a multiply controlled NOT gate and the controls are either 0 or 1 depending on the bits of c_i. This is denoted by the superscript c_i on top of the controls in Fig. 3. We can now put everything together to estimate the cost for Grover's algorithm based on the AES-k resource estimates given in the previous section: denoting by s_k the total number of qubits, t_k the total number of T-gates, c_k the total number of Clifford gates, δ_k the overall T-depth and Δ_k the overall depth,

Table 5. Quantum resource estimates for Grover's algorithm to attack AES-k, where $k \in \{128, 192, 256\}$.

k	#gates		Depth		#qubits
	T	Clifford	T	Overall	
128	$1.19 \cdot 2^{86}$	$1.55 \cdot 2^{86}$	$1.06 \cdot 2^{80}$	$1.16 \cdot 2^{81}$	2,953
192	$1.81 \cdot 2^{118}$	$1.17 \cdot 2^{119}$	$1.21 \cdot 2^{112}$	$1.33 \cdot 2^{113}$	4,449
256	$1.41 \cdot 2^{151}$	$1.83 \cdot 2^{151}$	$1.44 \cdot 2^{144}$	$1.57 \cdot 2^{145}$	6,681

where $k = 128, 192, 256$, then we obtain the following estimates for the overall Grover algorithm. The space requirements are $3s_{128} + 1$ qubits for AES-128, $4s_{192} + 1$ qubits for AES-192, and $5s_{256} + 1$ qubits for AES-256.

Regarding the time complexity, we obtain that per Grover iteration we need $6t_{128}$ many T-gates for AES-128 plus the number of T-gates needed for the 384-fold controlled NOT inside U_f and the 128-fold controlled NOT to implement the phase $(2|0\rangle\langle 0| - 1)$. We estimated the T-counts of these two operations earlier to be 12,204 and 1,000 respectively. Overall, we have to perform $\lfloor \frac{\pi}{4} 2^{k/2} \rfloor$ iterations, i.e., we obtain for the overall T-gate count for Grover on AES-128 the estimate of

$$\left\lfloor \frac{\pi}{4} 2^{64} \right\rfloor \cdot \left(6t_{128} + 13,204\right) = 9.24 \cdot 10^{25} = 1.19 \cdot 2^{86}$$

many T-gates. Similarly, we can estimate the number of Clifford gates which for simplicity we just assume to be $6c_{128}$, ignoring some of the Clifford gates used during the rounds. For AES-192 we have to perform $\lfloor \frac{\pi}{4} 2^{96} \rfloor$ iterations and for AES-256 we have to perform $\lfloor \frac{\pi}{4} 2^{128} \rfloor$ iterations. For the T-count of the controlled operations we obtained $16,300 + 1,512 = 17,812$ and $20,396 + 2024 = 22,420$ earlier. Overall, this gives for Grover on AES-192 the estimate of $3.75 \cdot 10^{36} = 1.81 \cdot 2^{114}$ many T-gates and for Grover on AES-256 the estimate of $4.03 \cdot 10^{45} = 1.41 \cdot 2^{151}$ many T-gates. For the overall circuit depth we obtain the number of rounds times 2 times δ_k, respectively Δ_k, ignoring some of the gates which do not contribute significantly to the bottom line. The overall quantum resource estimates are given in Table 5.

4 Conclusion

When realizing AES, only SubBytes involves T-gates. Moreover, SubBytes is called a minimum of 296 times as in AES-128 and up to 420 times in AES-256. As shown above, for all three standardized key lengths, this results in quantum circuits of quite moderate complexity. So it seems prudent to move away from 128-bit keys when expecting the availability of at least a moderate size quantum computer.

As mentioned in the context of the discussion about Grover's algorithm in the presence of an unknown number of solutions, the implementation of the algorithms in [10] for quantum counting, [9] for general amplitude amplifications, and

[30] for fixed-point quantum search might lead to space-time tradeoff implementations of the function f. This might in particular be beneficial for the circuit mentioned in [30] as this does not incur a space overhead and can deal with an unknown number of solutions, provided an upper bound on the number of solutions is known a priori. We leave the question of providing quantum resource estimations for attacking AES and other block ciphers by means of such fixed-point versions of Grover's algorithm for future work. Also an interesting area of future research is the resource cost estimation of recently proposed quantum linear and differential cryptanalysis [17].

Acknowledgments. BL and RS were supported by AFRL/RIKF Award No. FA8750-15-2-0047. RS was also supported by NATO's Public Diplomacy Division in the framework of "Science for Peace", Project MD.SFPP 984520. The authors thank Schloss Dagstuhl for hosting Seminar 15371, during which part of this work was done.

References

1. Amento, B., Rötteler, M., Steinwandt, R.: Efficient quantum circuits for binary elliptic curve arithmetic: reducing T-gate complexity. Quantum Inf. Comput. **13**, 631–644 (2013)
2. Amy, M., Maslov, D., Mosca, M.: Polynomial-time T-depth optimization of Clifford+T circuits via matroid partitioning. IEEE Trans. Comput. Aided Des. Integr. Circuits Syst. **33**(10), 1476–1489 (2014). arXiv:1303.2042
3. Amy, M., Maslov, D., Mosca, M., Roetteler, M.: A meet-in-the-middle algorithm for fast synthesis of depth-optimal quantum circuits. IEEE Trans. Comput. Aided Des. Integr. Circuits Syst. **32**(6), 818–830 (2013). For a preprint version see [4]
4. Amy, M., Maslov, D., Mosca, M., Roetteler, M.: A meet-in-the-middle algorithm for fast synthesis of depth-optimal quantum circuits (2013). arXiv:quant-ph/1206.0758v3, arxiv.org/abs/1206.0758v3
5. Augot, D., Batina, L., Bernstein, D.J., Bos, J., Buchmann, J., Castryck, W., Dunkelmann, O., Güneysu, T., Gueron, S., Hülsing, A., Lange, T., Mohamed, M.S.E., Rechberger, C., Schwabe, P., Sendrier, N., Vercauteren, F., Yang, B.-Y.: Initial recommendations of long-term secure post-quantum systems (2015). http://pqcrypto.eu.org/docs/initial-recommendations.pdf
6. Barenco, A., Bennett, C.H., Cleve, R., DiVincenzo, D.P., Margolus, N., Shor, P.W., Sleator, T., Smolin, J., Weinfurter, H.: Elementary gates for quantum computation. Phys. Rev. A **52**(5), 3457–3467 (1995)
7. Bosma, W., Cannon, J., Playoust, C.: The Magma algebra system. I. the user language. J. Symbolic Comput. **24**, 235–265 (1997)
8. Boyer, M., Brassard, G., Høyer, P., Tapp, A.: Tight bounds on quantum searching. Fortschritte der Physik **46**, 493–506 (1998). arxiv:quant-ph/9605034
9. Brassard, G., Høyer, P., Mosca, M., Tapp, A.: Quantum amplitude amplification and estimation. AMS Contemp. Math. **305**, 53–74 (2002). arxiv:quant-ph/0005055
10. Brassard, G., Høyer, P., Tapp, A.: Quantum counting. In: Larsen, K.G., Skyum, S., Winskel, G. (eds.) ICALP 1998. LNCS, vol. 1443, pp. 820–831. Springer, Heidelberg (1998)
11. Dawson, E., Gustafson, H., Pettitt, A.N.: Strict key avalanche criterion. Australas. J. Comb. **6**, 147–153 (1992)

12. Egner, S., Püschel, M.: Solving puzzles related to permutations groups. In: Proceedings of International Symposium on Symbolic and Algebraic Computation (ISSAC 1998), pp. 186–193 (1998)
13. Fowler, A.G., Mariantoni, M., Martinis, J.M., Cleland, A.N.: Surface codes: towards practical large-scale quantum computation. Phys. Rev. A **86**, 032324 (2012). arXiv:1208.0928
14. Fowler, A.G., Stephens, A.M., Groszkowski, P.: High threshold universal quantum computation on the surface code. Phys. Rev. A **80**, 052312 (2009)
15. Grover, L.K.: A fast quantum mechanical algorithm for database search. In: Miller, G.L. (ed.) Proceedings of the Twenty-Eighth Annual ACM Symposium on the Theory of Computing (STOC 1996), pp. 212–219. ACM (1996)
16. Jones, N.C.: Novel constructions for the fault-tolerant Toffoli gate. Phys. Rev. A **87**, 022328 (2013)
17. Kaplan, M., Leurent, G., Leverrier, A., Naya-Plasencia, M.: Quantum differential and linear cryptanalysis. arXiv:1510.05836
18. Kepley, S., Steinwandt, R.: Quantum circuits for $\mathbb{F}_{2^n}$ -multiplication with subquadratic gate count. Quantum Inf. Process. **14**(7), 2373–2386 (2015)
19. Konheim, A.G.: Crypt. A Primer. Wiley, Hoboken (1981)
20. Maslov, D.: On the advantages of using relative phase Toffolis with an application tomultiple control Toffoli optimization. arXiv:1508.03273
21. Maslov, D., Falconer, S.M., Mosca, M.: Quantum circuit placement: optimizing qubit-to-qubit interactions through mapping quantum circuits into a physical experiment. In: Proceedings of the 44th Design Automation Conference – DAC 2007, pp. 962–965. ACM (2007)
22. Maslov, D., Mathew, J., Cheung, D., Pradhan, D.K.: On the design and optimization of a quantum polynomial-time attack on elliptic curve cryptography (2009). arXiv:0710.1093v2, arxiv.org/abs/0710.1093v2
23. Nielsen, M.A., Chuang, I.L.: Quantum Computation and Quantum Information. Cambridge University Press, Cambridge (2000)
24. NIST: Specification for the Advanced Encryption Standard (AES). Federal Information Processing Standards Publication 197 (2001)
25. Reichardt, B.W.: Quantum universality by state distillation. Quantum Inf. Comput. **9**, 1030–1052 (2009)
26. Roetteler, M., Steinwandt, R.: A note on quantum related-key attacks. Inf. Process. Lett. **115**(1), 40–44 (2015)
27. Shor, P.W.: Polynomial-time algorithms for prime factorization and discrete logarithms on a quantum computer. SIAM J. Comput. **26**(5), 1484–1509 (1997)
28. Steane, A.M.: Overhead and noise threshold of fault-tolerant quantum error correction. Phys. Rev. A **68**, 042322 (2003). arXiv:quant-ph/0207119
29. Wiebe, N., Roetteler, M.: Quantum arithmetic and numerical analysis using Repeat-Until-Success circuits. arXiv:1406.2040
30. Yoder, T.J., Low, G.H., Chuang, I.L.: Fixed-point quantum search with an optimal number of queries. Phys. Rev. Lett. **113**, 210501 (2014)

Post-Quantum Security of the CBC, CFB, OFB, CTR, and XTS Modes of Operation

Mayuresh Vivekanand Anand[(✉)], Ehsan Ebrahimi Targhi, Gelo Noel Tabia, and Dominique Unruh

University of Tartu, Tartu, Estonia
mayuresh.anand@ut.ee

Abstract. We examine the IND-qCPA security of the wide-spread block cipher modes of operation CBC, CFB, OFB, CTR, and XTS (i.e., security against quantum adversaries doing queries in superposition). We show that OFB and CTR are secure assuming that the underlying block cipher is a standard secure PRF (a pseudorandom function secure under classical queries). We give counterexamples that show that CBC, CFB, and XTS are not secure under the same assumption. And we give proofs that CBC and CFB mode are secure if we assume a quantum secure PRF (secure under queries in superposition).

Keywords: Post-quantum cryptography · Block ciphers · Modes of operation · IND-qCPA security

1 Introduction

Block ciphers are one of the most fundamental primitives in cryptography. On its own, however, a block cipher is almost useless because it can only encrypt messages of a fixed (and usually very short) length. Therefore block ciphers are usually used in so-called "modes of operation": constructions whose goal it is to extend the message space of the block cipher, and possibly add other features or more security in the process. Since most encryption in practice uses at some level a mode of operation, the security of those modes of operation is of paramount importance for the security of many cryptographic systems.

In the light of the possible advent of quantum computers,[1] we have to ask: is existing classical cryptography also secure in the presence of attackers with quantum computers? In particular, does the security of common modes of operation break down?

---

[1] There seem to be no clear predictions as to when quantum computers will be available and strong enough to attack cryptography. But it seems daring to simply assume that they will not be available in the mid-term future, just because we do not have clear predictions.

© Springer International Publishing Switzerland 2016
T. Takagi (Ed.): PQCrypto 2016, LNCS 9606, pp. 44–63, 2016.
DOI: 10.1007/978-3-319-29360-8_4

In this paper, we study a number of common modes of operation, namely those listed in the 2013 ENISA[2] report on recommended encryption algorithms [9]: CBC, CFB, OFB, CTR, and XTS. We study whether those modes are secure in the quantum setting under comparable assumptions as in the classical setting, and if not, we construct counterexamples.

The aforementioned modes of operation (except ECB and XTS) are known to be IND-CPA secure in the classical setting, under the assumption that the underlying block cipher is a pseudo-random function (PRF).[3] ECB is known not to have reasonable security for most applications, while the security of XTS is an open question.

In the quantum case, there are two variants of the IND-CPA notion: "standard IND-CPA" and "IND-qCPA". While standard IND-CPA lets the quantum adversary perform only classical encryption queries, IND-qCPA (as defined by [6]) allows the adversary to perform quantum encryption queries (i.e., queries which are a superposition of different messages, to get a superposition of different ciphertexts). In other words, IND-qCPA additionally guarantees security when the encryption key is used to encrypt messages in superposition. (See below for a discussion on the relevance of this notion.)

Similarly, there are two variants of the notion of a classical PRF in the quantum setting: standard secure PRF and quantum secure PRF. In the first case, the function cannot be distinguished from a random function when making arbitrary classical queries to that function. In the second case, the function cannot be distinguished from random when making arbitrary quantum queries, i.e., when querying the function on a superposition of many inputs.

We can now ask the question: which variant of quantum PRFs is needed for which variant of IND-CPA. As it turns out, if we merely wish to get standard IND-CPA security, the answer is trivial: CBC, CFB, OFB, and CTR are secure assuming that the underlying block cipher is a standard PRF. In fact, the original security proofs of these schemes can be reused unmodified.[4] (We hence abstain from reproducing the original proofs in this paper and refer to the classical proofs instead.) And ECB is still trivially insecure, and for XTS we still do not know which security we achieve.

On the other hand, if we ask for IND-qCPA security, the picture changes drastically. OFB and CTR mode can be shown IND-qCPA secure based on a standard secure PRF. (The proof is relatively straightforward.)

---

[2] European Union Agency for Network and Information Security. We chose this list as a basis in order to investigate a practically relevant and industrially deployed set of modes of operations.

[3] If we want to be able to decrypt, then the block cipher should, of course, be a pseudo-random *permutation*. But for mere security, PRF is sufficient.

[4] Except that the set of adversaries we consider is, of course, that of quantum polynomial-time adversaries, instead of classical polynomial-time adversaries. Note that it is not always the case that a classical security proof goes through unchanged in the quantum case. (A typical example are zero-knowledge proof systems where rewinding is used in the classical proof. Rewinding-based proofs cannot be directly translated to the quantum setting [1,12,15]).

In contrast, we prove that CBC and CFB are *not* IND-qCPA secure based when based on a standard secure PRF. In fact, for CBC and CFB we show that the adversary can even recover the secret key using quantum queries. For XTS, we show that the adversary can recover the second half of a plaintext if he can provide the first half of the plaintext (and the adversary can get half of the key). Although this does not formally contradict IND-qCPA (because IND-qCPA does not allow the challenge query to be performed in superposition), it show that XTS does not satisfy the intuitive notion of CPA security under superposition attacks.

If, however, the block cipher is a quantum secure PRF, then CBC and CFB are IND-qCPA secure. The proof of this fact, however, is quite different from the classical security proof: since the block cipher is invoked in superposition, we are in a situation similar to the analysis of quantum random oracles, which are notoriously difficult to handle in the quantum case. (Note: this refers only to the difficulties encountered in our proof. Our results are in the standard model, not in the random oracle model.)

We summarize the results in Table 1. Our counter-examples are in the quantum random oracle model, but our positive results are in the standard model (no random oracle).

Table 1. Summary of our results. The superscripts refer to the bibliography or to theorem numbers. "No in spirit" means that there is an attack using superposition queries that does not formally violate IND-qCPA.

Mode of operation	Classical IND-CPA?	Standard (quantum) IND-CPA?	IND-qCPA? (with PRF)	(with qPRF)
ECB	no	no	no	no
CBC	yes [16]	yes	no (Lemma 2)	yes (Theorem 3)
CFB	yes [16]	yes	no (Lemma 3)	yes (Theorem 3)
OFB	yes [16]	yes	yes (Lemma 2)	yes (Theorem 2)
CTR	yes [16]	yes	yes (Lemma 2)	yes (Theorem 2)
XTS	unknown [10]	unknown	"no in spirit" (Lemma 4)	unknown

On the IND-qCPA Security Notion. The IND-qCPA security notion [6] models passive security against adversaries that have access to the encryption of (chosen) plaintexts in superposition. The obvious question is: do we need that?

- The most obvious reason is that in the future, we might want to encrypt messages in superposition for some legitimate purpose. E.g., the encryption scheme is used as part of a quantum protocol. (That is, a protocol that actively uses quantum communication, not just a classical protocol secure against quantum adversaries.)
- A second argument (made in [7]) is that with continuing miniaturization, supposedly classical devices may enter the quantum scale, and thus "accidentally"

encrypt messages in superposition. (Personally, we have doubts how realistic this case is, but we mention it for completeness.)

- There is, however, a reason why insecurity under notions such as IND-qCPA may affect the security of a purely classical system in the presence of a quantum attacker. If a classical protocol is proven secure (with respect to a quantum adversary), intermediate games in the security proof may actually contain honest parties that run in superposition. This happens in particular if zero-knowledge proof systems or similar are involved [12,15]. For example, in [13, Sect. 5], the security proof of a classical protocol did not go through because the signature scheme was not secure under quantum queries (they had to change the protocol considerably instead). Encryption schemes that are not just standard IND-CPA, but IND-qCPA might help in similar situations.

1.1 Our Techniques

We briefly summarize the techniques we use to prove or disprove the security of the various modes of operation.

IND-qCPA Security of OFB and CTR Mode Using a Standard PRF. Both OFB and CTR mode are stream ciphers. That is, in both cases, encryption can be represented as $\mathsf{Enc}_k(M) = G_k(|M|; r) \oplus M$, where G_k is a pseudorandom generator with key k for some randomness r. Thus, to encrypt a superposition $\sum_i \alpha_i |M_i\rangle$ of messages of length ℓ, all we need to do is to compute $c := \mathsf{Enc}_k(0) = G_k(\ell; r)$, and then to compute $\sum_i \alpha_i |\mathsf{Enc}_k(M_i; r)\rangle = \sum_i \alpha_i |M_i \oplus c\rangle$. Since computing $\mathsf{Enc}_k(0)$ can be done using a classical encryption query, it follows that superposition encryption queries can be simulated using classical encryption queries. Hence the IND-qCPA security of OFB and CTR can be directly reduced to the standard IND-CPA security of the same schemes. And standard IND-CPA security is shown exactly in the same way as in the classical setting.

IND-qCPA Security of CBC and CFB Mode Using a Quantum Secure PRF. To show security of CBC and CFB mode, we cannot directly follow the classical security proof since that one relies inherently on the fact that the block cipher (the PRF) is queried only classically. Instead, we use the following techniques to prove CBC security:

- Since the block cipher is a PRF, we can assume it to be a truly random function H (to which the adversary has no access, since he does not know the key). CBC encryption is thus performed as sketched in Fig. 1(a).
- We replace the challenge encryption (i.e., the encryption query where the adversary should distinguish between $\mathsf{Enc}(m_0)$ and $\mathsf{Enc}(m_1)$) step by step by randomness. That is, we consider a sequence of hybrid games, and in the i-th game, the first i blocks of the challenge ciphertext are replaced by uniformly random bitstrings. Once all ciphertext blocks are replaced by randomness, the probability of guessing whether m_0 or m_1 was encrypted is obviously $\frac{1}{2}$. Thus, all we need to show is that replacing one block of the challenge ciphertext by randomness leads to a negligible change in the advantage of the adversary. The situation is depicted in Fig. 1(b).

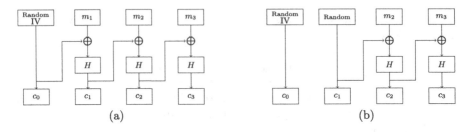

Fig. 1. (a) CBC mode (using a random function H instead of the block cipher). (b) Modified challenge ciphertext computation (c_1 replaced by randomness). We need to prove that replacing c_2 by a random value leads to an indistinguishable view.

– Say we want to show that $c_2 = H(m_2 \oplus c_1)$ is indistinguishable from random (the situation in Fig. 1(b). At a first glance, this seems simple: $m_2 \oplus c_1$ is uniformly random, so the probability that it collides with other H-queries is negligible, hence $H(m_2 \oplus c_1)$ is uniformly random. However, this argument does not hold in the quantum setting: since some encryption queries are performed in superposition, it can be that H was queries on all inputs simultaneously, hence we cannot say that H was not queried at $m_2 \oplus c_1$ before. Fortunately, we can use the "One-way to Hiding (O2H) Lemma" from [14] here. This lemma basically says: for a uniformly random x, to show that $H(x)$ is indistinguishable from random, we need to show: when running the adversary, and aborting at a randomly chosen H-query, and measuring the input to that query (disturbing the superposition), then the probability that the outcome is x is negligible.

In the present setting this means: if we measure a random H-query during the execution of the IND-qCPA game, the probability that the argument equals $m_2 \oplus c_1$ is negligible. For example, the probability that one of the h-queries before the challenge encryption equals $m_2 \oplus c_1$ is trivially negligible, because c_1 has not yet been chosen at that point.

– For the H-queries performed during the challenge query, we use the fact that H is indistinguishable from a random permutation [18]. In that case, the H-query inputs are uniformly random due to the fact that c_2 is chosen uniformly at random (remember that we replaced c_2 by a random value), hence they collide with $m_2 \oplus c_1$ only with negligible probability.

– For the H-queries performed after the challenge query, we cannot use the same argument, because those queries can be performed in superposition. However: if we only care whether the chosen H-query has input $m_2 \oplus c_1$, then, instead of just measuring the H-query input, we can measure in the computational basis all registers involved in the encryption. Then we observe that measuring all registers commutes with the operations performed during encryption, so equivalently we can assume that that measurement happens at the beginning of the encryption (and in particular measures the plaintext). And that means, for the purposes of bounding the probability of measuring H-query input

$m_2 \oplus c_1$, we can assume that we encrypt a classical plaintext. From here, the argument from the previous item applies.

- Altogether, the probability of measuring $m_2 \oplus c_1$ in any H-query is negligible. Then the O2H lemma implies that the $H(m_2 \oplus c_1)$ is indistinguishable from random. And by iterating this indistinguishably, we can replace the whole challenge ciphertext by randomness. And then the adversary has only probability $\frac{1}{2}$ of guessing which challenge plaintext was encrypted.

This shows that CBC mode is IND-qCPA secure if the block cipher is a quantum secure PRF. The security of CFB mode is shown very similarly.

Insecurity of CBC and CFB Mode Using a Standard Secure PRF. To show that CBC and CFB mode are insecure using a standard secure PRF, we first construct a specific block cipher BC as follows:

$$\mathsf{BC}_k(x) := E_{H(k)}\big(\mathsf{droplastbit}\,(x \oplus (k\|1) \cdot \mathsf{lastbit}(x))\big)$$

where E is a standard secure PRF and H refers to a random oracle. (This construction is not really a block cipher because it is not infective and hence not decrypt able. The definition of BC_k can be refined to make it decryptable, we omit this technicality in this proof overview, see Sect. 3.1.) This block cipher has the special property of being $k\|1$-periodic: $\mathsf{BC}_k(x) = \mathsf{BC}_k(x \oplus (k\|1))$. In particular, this it cannot be a quantum secure PRF, even if E is. Namely, given superposition access to BC_k, Simon's algorithm [11] allows us to recover $k\|1$ given quantum oracle access to BC_k.[5] This idea also allows us to break CBC mode when CBC mode uses BC_k as its underlying blockcipher. If we encrypt a single block message m using CBC, we get the ciphertext $(c_0, \mathsf{BC}_k(c_0 \oplus m))$. Although the message m is XORed with the random IV c_0, the period remains the same, namely $k\|1$. Thus, using what is basically Simon's algorithm, using superposition queries to CBC mode, we get $k\|1$ (more precisely, one bit of information about it for each superposition query). This reveals the key k completely and in particular shows that CBC is not IND-qCPA secure.

The question of course is whether BC_k is indeed a standard secure PRF. Even though the adversary has only classical access to BC_k, the proof cannot be purely classical: we use a random oracle H that the adversary can query in superposition. Instead, we use again the O2H lemma [14] mentioned above. This allows us to replace $H(k)$ by a random key y in the definition of BC_k. Now the analysis of BC_k becomes purely classical and basically amount to showing that the adversary cannot guess two inputs to BC_k that lead to the same input for E_y. (Using the actual, decryptable construction of BC_k, this proof becomes technically a bit more complex, but still follows the same ideas.)

In the case of CFB mode, the attack is similar, except that here we need to encrypt two-block messages in order to get a ciphertext that depends in a $k\|1$-periodic way on the plaintext. (Since the first message block is not fed through the block cipher in CFB mode.)

---

[5] A similar idea was already used in [17] to show that there is a standard secure PRF that is not quantum secure. However, their construction had a period with respect to $+$, not to $\oplus$, which makes it unsuitable for showing the insecurity of CBC mode.

Insecurity of XTS Mode Using a Standard Secure PRF. To attack XTS, we use the same basic idea as for CBC and CFB. However, there are some additional complications. In XTS, two keys k_1, k_2 are used. Each ciphertext block is computed as $c_i := \alpha^{i-1}L \oplus \mathsf{BC}_{k_2}(\alpha^{i-1}L \oplus m_i)$. Here $L := \mathsf{BC}_{k_1}(I)$ is a secret value that is derived from a nonce I (thus L stays fixed throughout one encryption operation, but changes from ciphertext to ciphertext). If we use the block cipher constructed above (when breaking CBC), we can easily derive k_2: since BC_{k_2} is k_2-periodic, so is $\mathsf{BC}_{k_2}(\alpha^{i-1}L \oplus m_i)$. Thus with one single block encryption we would be able to retrieve one bit of k_2 using Simon's algorithm. However, retrieving k_2 does not help us in decrypting XTS mode, since we do not know k_1, and hence cannot compute the value L. Also, the fact that $\mathsf{BC}_{k_1}(I)$ is k_1-periodic does not help us to retrieve k_1 since we do not have any control over I. Instead, we use the following trick. We construct

$$\mathsf{BC}_k(x, y) := E_{H(k)}(\mathsf{droplastbit}\,(x \oplus (k\|1) \cdot \mathsf{lastbit}(x)),$$
$$\mathsf{droplastbit}\,(y \oplus f_k(x) \cdot \mathsf{lastbit}(x))$$

where f_k is a suitable function depending on k (with the property that $\mathsf{lastbit}(f_k(\cdot)) = 1$). (We interpret message blocks are pairs x, y by splitting them in the middle.) Again we ignore in this proof overview that BC_k cannot be decrypted, the more involved construction given in the full version [2] avoids this problem.

Now BC_k is k-periodic in x, and $f_k(x)$-periodic in y for fixed first input x. Using this block cipher, we can first use the attack technique described for CBC mode to recover k_2 (by encrypting a number of one block messages). The main difference is that now we create a plaintext that is a superposition in the first half of the block (x), and fixes the second block ($y := 0$). Now, instead of recovering k_1 (which seems impossible), we can recover the message L used during a given encryption query: We encrypt a message where the x-part of each block is 0, and the y-part of each block is the superposition of all messages. Since BC_{k_2} is invoked with $\alpha^{i-1}L \oplus m_i$ when encrypting m_i, we have that the first half of the input to BC_{k_2} is the first half of $\alpha^{i-1}L$. Thus BC_{k_2} is $f_{k_2}(firsthalf(\alpha^{i-1}L))$-periodic. Thus from message block i, using Simon's algorithm, we get one bit of $f_{k_2}(firsthalf(\alpha^{i-1}L))$. Since we know k_2, this reveals one bit of information about $\alpha^{i-1}L$. Thus we get a bit each about many different $\alpha^{i-1}L$ (for different i), and this allows us to compute L. If our ciphertext, in addition to the superposition-message-blocks contains parts that are unknown, we can then decrypt those using our knowledge of L and k_2. (Note that we cannot use this knowledge to decrypt another ciphertext, since each ciphertext uses a different L.) Thus, we can decrypt ciphertexts whose plaintexts are partially under our control (and in superposition), and partially unknown.

1.2 Related Work

Boneh et al. [4] have argued the requirement of quantum-accessible random oracle model to prove post-quantum of BR encryption scheme introduced in [3]. They have proved the CCA security of hybrid encryption scheme introduced in [3] in the quantum random oracle model. Ebrahimi and Unruh in [8] prove the CCA security of Fujisaki-Okamoto transform in the quantum random oracle model. In [5] Boneh and Zhandry construct the first message authentication codes (MACs) that are existentially unforgeable against a quantum chosen message attack and show that quantum-secure PRF leads to quantum-secure MACs. In [7], Damgård *et al.* study secret sharing scheme and multiparty computation where the adversary make ask superposition queries. They also examine the zero knowledge protocols and use the secret sharing results to design zero knowledge proofs for all of NP in the common reference string model.

1.3 Organisation

In Sect. 2 we provide the various security definitions and lemmas used throughout the paper. Section 2.1 contains the definition of all the modes of operations discussed. In Sect. 3.1, we provide the a standard-secure construction of a PRF used in CBC the and CFB attack. Section 3 describes the attack on the CBC mode of operation based on that standard-secure PRF. (The insecurity of CFB and XTS are deferred to the full version [2].) Finally, in Sect. 4 we show how to achieve the IND-qCPA security for OFB, CTR, CBC, and CFB modes of operation.

2   Notation and Tools

Notation. By $x \leftarrow A(y)$ we denote an algorithm A that takes an input y outputs a value that is assigned to x. We write $x \leftarrow A^H(y)$ if A has access to an oracle H. By $(A \leftarrow B)$ we refer to the set of all functions from A to B. $x \xleftarrow{\$} A$ represents an x which is uniformly randomly chosen from the set A. $\{0,1\}^n$ represents the bit-strings of length n and $a\|b$ for strings a and b represents the concatenation of two strings. For two vectors a and b, $a \odot b$ denotes the dot product between two vectors. We use $\eta(t)$ to denote a function with a security parameter t. If we say a quantity is *negligible*(denoted *negl.*) we mean that it is in $o(\eta^c)$ or $1 - o(\eta^c)$ for all $c > 0$. We use the notation $A \approx B$ to say that quantity A has *negl.* difference with quantity B. For an $n-$bit string a and binary variable b, $a \cdot b = a$ if $b = 1$ otherwise $a \cdot b = 0^n$. For a string $x = x_1 x_2 x_3 \cdots x_n$ where x_i is the $i - th$ bit we use functions lastbit and droplastbit such that $\mathsf{lastbit}(x) = x_n$ and $\mathsf{droplastbit}(x) = x_i x_2 \cdots x_{n-1}$.

Definition 1 (IND-CPA). *A symmetric encryption scheme $\Pi = (\mathsf{Gen}, \mathsf{Enc}, \mathsf{Dec})$ is indistinguishable under chosen message attack (IND-CPA secure) if no classical poly-time adversary $\mathcal{A}$ can win in the $PrivK^{CPA}_{\mathcal{A},\Pi}(t)$ game, except with probability at most $1/2 + $ negl:*

> **PrivK$^{CPA}_{\mathcal{A},\Pi}(t)$ game:**
>   **Key Gen:** *The challenger picks a random key $k \leftarrow \mathsf{Gen}$ and a random bit b.*

Query: *Adversary $\mathcal{A}$ chooses two messages m_0, m_1 and sends them to the challenger. Challenger chooses $r \xleftarrow{\$} \{0,1\}^*$ and responds with $c^* = \mathsf{Enc}_k(m_b; r)$.*
Guess: *Adversary $\mathcal{A}$ produces a bit b', and wins if $b = b'$.*

Definition 2 (IND-qCPA [6]**).** *A symmetric encryption scheme $\Pi = (\mathsf{Gen}, \mathsf{Enc}, \mathsf{Dec})$ is indistinguishable under quantum chosen message attack (IND-qCPA secure) if no efficient adversary $\mathcal{A}$ can win in the $PrivK_{\mathcal{A},\Pi}^{qCPA}(t)$ game, except with probability at most $1/2 +$ negl:*

$PrivK_{\mathcal{A},\Pi}^{qCPA}(t)$ *game:*
   Key Gen: *The challenger picks a random key k and a random bit b.*
   Queries
      - Challenge Queries: *$\mathcal{A}$ sends two messages m_0, m_1 to which the challenger responds with $c^* = \mathsf{Enc}_k(m_b; r)$.*
      - Encryption Queries: *For each such query, the challenger chooses randomness r, and encrypts each message in the superposition using r as randomness:*

$$\sum_{m,c} \psi_{m,c} |m, c\rangle \rightarrow \sum_{m,c} \psi_{m,c} |m, c \oplus Enc_k(m; r)\rangle$$

   Guess: $\mathcal{A}$ produces a bit b', and wins if $b = b'$.

Definition 3 (Standard-Security [17]**).** *A function PRF is a standard-secure PRF if no efficient quantum adversary $\mathcal{A}$ making classical queries can distinguish between a truly random function and a function PRF_k for a random k. That is, for every such $\mathcal{A}$, there exists a negligible function $\epsilon = \epsilon(t)$ such that*

$$\Big| \Pr_{k \leftarrow \mathcal{K}}[A^{PRF_k}() = 1] - \Pr_{O \leftarrow \mathcal{Y}^{\mathcal{X}}}[A^O() = 1] \Big| < \epsilon.$$

Definition 4 (Quantum-Security [17]**).** *A function PRF is a quantum secure PRF if no poly-time quantum adversary $\mathcal{A}$ making quantum queries can distinguish between truly random function and the function PRF_k for a random k.*

Lemma 1 (One Way to Hiding (O2H) [14]**).** *Let $H : \{0,1\}^t \rightarrow \{0,1\}^t$ be a random oracle. Consider an oracle algorithm A_{O2H} that makes at most q_{o2h} queries to H. Let B be an oracle algorithm that on input x does the following: pick $i \xleftarrow{\$} \{1, \ldots, q_{o2h}\}$ and $y \xleftarrow{\$} \{0,1\}^t$, run $A_{O2H}^H(x, y)$ until (just before) the $i - th$ query, measure the argument of the query in the computational basis, output the measurement outcome. (When A_{O2H} makes less than i queries, B outputs $\perp \notin \{0,1\}^t$.) Let,*

$$P_{A_{O2H}}^1 := \Pr[b' = 1 : H \xleftarrow{\$} (\{0,1\}^t \rightarrow \{0,1\}^t), x \xleftarrow{\$} \{0,1\}^t, b' \leftarrow A_{O2H}^H(x, H(x))],$$

$$P_{A_{O2H}}^2 := \Pr[b' = 1 : H \xleftarrow{\$} (\{0,1\}^t \to \{0,1\}^t), x \xleftarrow{\$} \{0,1\}^t, y \xleftarrow{\$} \{0,1\}^t,$$
$$b' \leftarrow A_{O2H}^H(x, y)],$$

$$P_B := \Pr[x' = x : H \xleftarrow{\$} (\{0,1\}^t \to \{0,1\}^t), x \xleftarrow{\$} \{0,1\}^t, x' \leftarrow B^H(x, i)].$$

Then,

$$\left| P_{A_{O2H}}^1 - P_{A_{O2H}}^2 \right| \le 2q_{o2h} \sqrt{P_B}.$$

2.1 Modes of Operation

Definition 5 (ECB Scheme). *For a given permutation $E : \mathcal{K} \times \{0,1\}^t \to \{0,1\}^t$ we define the symmetric encryption scheme $\Pi_{ECB} = (\mathsf{Gen}, \mathsf{Enc}, \mathsf{Dec})$ as follows:*

Gen: *Pick a random key $k \xleftarrow{\$} \mathcal{K}$.*
Enc: *For a given message $M = m_1 m_2 \cdots m_n$, where n is a polynomial in t;*
$\mathsf{Enc}_k(M) := c_1 \cdots c_n$, *where $c_i = E(k, m_i)$ for $0 < i \le n$.*
Dec: *For a given cipher-text $C = c_1 \cdots c_n$ and key k; $\hat{m}_i := E^{-1}(k, c_i)$ for $0 < i \le n$.*

Definition 6 (CBC Scheme). *For a given permutation $E : \mathcal{K} \times \{0,1\}^t \to \{0,1\}^t$ we define the symmetric encryption scheme $\Pi_{CBC} = (\mathsf{Gen}, \mathsf{Enc}, \mathsf{Dec})$ as follows:*

Gen: *Pick a random key $k \xleftarrow{\$} \mathcal{K}$.*
Enc: *For a given message $M = m_1 m_2 \cdots m_n$, where n is a polynomial in t;*
$\mathsf{Enc}_k(M) := c_0 c_1 \cdots c_n$, *where $c_0 \xleftarrow{\$} \{0,1\}^t$ and $c_i = E(k, m_i \oplus c_{i-1})$ for $0 < i \le n$.*
Dec: *For a given cipher-text $C = c_0 c_1 \cdots c_n$ and key k; $\hat{m}_i := E^{-1}(k, c_i) \oplus c_{i-1}$ for $0 < i \le n$.*

Definition 7 (CFB Scheme). *For a given function $E : \mathcal{K} \times \{0,1\}^t \to \{0,1\}^t$ we define the symmetric encryption scheme $\Pi_{CFB} = (\mathsf{Gen}, \mathsf{Enc}, \mathsf{Dec})$ as follows:*

Gen: *Pick a random key $k \xleftarrow{\$} \mathcal{K}$.*
Enc: *For a given message $M = m_1 m_2 \cdots m_n$, where n is a polynomial in t;*
$\mathsf{Enc}_k(M) := c_0 c_1 \cdots c_n$, *where $c_0 \xleftarrow{\$} \{0,1\}^t$ and $c_i = E(k, c_{i-1}) \oplus m_i$ for $0 < i \le n$.*
Dec: *For a given cipher-text $C = c_0 c_1 \cdots c_n$ and key k; $\hat{m}_i := E(k, c_{i-1}) \oplus c_i$ for $0 < i \le n$.*

Definition 8 (OFB Scheme). *For a given function $E : \mathcal{K} \times \{0,1\}^t \to \{0,1\}^t$ we define the symmetric encryption scheme $\Pi_{OFB} = (\mathsf{Gen}, \mathsf{Enc}, \mathsf{Dec})$ as follows:*

Gen: *Pick a random key $k \xleftarrow{\$} \mathcal{K}$.*
Enc: *For a given message $M = m_1 m_2 \cdots m_n$, where n is a polynomial in t;*
$\mathsf{Enc}_k(M) := c_0 c_1 \cdots c_n$, *where $c_0 = r_0 \xleftarrow{\$} \{0,1\}^t$, $r_i = E(k, r_{i-1})$ and $c_i = r_i \oplus m_i$ for $0 < i \le n$.*
Dec: *For a given cipher-text $C = c_0 c_1 \cdots c_n$ and key k; $\hat{m}_i := E(k, c_{i-1}) \oplus c_i$ for $0 < i \le n$.*

Definition 9 (CTR Scheme). *For a given function $E : \mathcal{K} \times \{0,1\}^t \rightarrow \{0,1\}^t$ we define the symmetric encryption scheme $\Pi_{CTR} = (\mathsf{Gen}, \mathsf{Enc}, \mathsf{Dec})$ as follows:*

Gen: *Pick a random key $k \stackrel{\$}{\leftarrow} \mathcal{K}$.*

Enc: *For a given message $M = m_1 m_2 \cdots m_n$, where n is a polynomial in t;* $\mathsf{Enc}_k(M) := c_0 c_1 \cdots c_n$, *where $c_0 \stackrel{\$}{\leftarrow} \{0,1\}^t$ and $c_i = E(k, c_0 + i) \oplus m_i$ for $0 < i \leq n$.*

Dec: *For a given cipher-text $C = c_0 c_1 \cdots c_n$ and key k; $\hat{m}_i := E(k, c_0 + i) \oplus c_i$ for $0 < i \leq n$.*

Definition 10 (XTS Scheme). *For a given permutation $E : \mathcal{K} \times \{0,1\}^t \rightarrow \{0,1\}^t$ we define the symmetric encryption scheme $\Pi_{XTS} = (\mathsf{Gen}, \mathsf{Enc}, \mathsf{Dec})$ as follows:*

Gen: *Pick random keys k_1 and k_2 i.e., $k_1 \stackrel{\$}{\leftarrow} \mathcal{K}$ and $k_2 \stackrel{\$}{\leftarrow} \mathcal{K}$.*

Enc: *For a given message $M = m_1 m_2 \cdots m_n$, where n is a polynomial in t;* $\mathsf{Enc}_k(M) := c_0 c_1 \cdots c_n$, *where $c_i = E(k_1, m_i \oplus \Delta_i) \oplus \Delta_i$ for $0 < i \leq n$, $\Delta = \alpha^{i-1} L$, $L = E(k_2, I)$ and α is the primitive element of the field $\mathbb{F}_2^n$. Here I is a publicly known nonce that is agreed upon out of band (but that is different in different ciphertexts).*

Dec: *For a given cipher-text $C = c_1 \cdots c_n$; and key k; $\hat{m}_i := E(k, c_i \oplus \Delta_i) \oplus \Delta_i$ for $0 < i \leq n$.*

3   Quantum Attacks on CBC, CFB, and XTS Based on Standard Secure PRF

We show that CBC and CFB mode are not IND-qCPA secure in general when the underlying block cipher is only a standard secure PRF, and that XTS has a chosen-plaintext attack using superposition queries. For this, in Sect. 3.1 we first construct a block cipher that is a standard secure PRF (but are intentionally not quantum secure). Then, in Sect. 3.2 we show how to break CBC and CFB, respectively, when using that block cipher.

3.1   Construction of the Block Cipher for CBC

To show that a standard secure PRF is not sufficient for IND-qCPA security of CBC and XTS modes of operation we need a block cipher that is standard secure PRF but not quantum secure. Our first step is to construct such a block cipher and prove it to be standard secure. In this section we provide two such constructions of block cipher that would be later used to show insecurity of CBC and XTS against a quantum adversary respectively.

Construction 1:

$$\mathsf{BC}_k(x) = E_{H(k)_1}\big(\mathsf{droplastbit}(x \oplus (k\|1) \cdot \mathsf{lastbit}(x))\big)$$
$$\big\| t_{H(k)_2}\big(x \oplus (k\|1) \cdot \mathsf{lastbit}(x)\big) \oplus \mathsf{lastbit}(x),$$

where, $E : \{0,1\}^{n-1} \times \{0,1\}^{n-1} \to \{0,1\}^{n-1}$ is a standard secure PRF, $t : \{0,1\}^n \times \{0,1\}^n \to \{0,1\}$ is a standard secure PRF, $H : \{0,1\}^n \to \{0,1\}^n \times \{0,1\}^n$ is a random oracle and the key $k \xleftarrow{\$} \{0,1\}^{n-1}$.

Theorem 1. *Construction 1 is a standard secure PRF for any quantum adversary D given classical access to BC_k and quantum access to the random oracle H.*

We give the proof in the full version [2].

Thus, we have proved that the given construction is pseudo-random and hence a standard secure PRF.

3.2   Attack on CBC Mode of Operation

We choose a block cipher BC as in Construction 1 in Sect. 3.1 for the construction of the Π_{CBC} scheme (Definition 6). As proved, this block cipher is a standard secure PRF (i.e., if the quantum adversary has only classical access to it).

Lemma 2. *There exists a standard secure pseudo-random function such that Π_{CBC} is not IND-qCPA secure (in the quantum random oracle model).*

Proof. Let the Π_{CBC} scheme use the block cipher BC, we use one block message to attack the Π_{CBC} scheme. We know that the adversary has quantum access to the Π_{CBC} scheme, hence a quantum adversary can query the superposition of all messages of size equal to the block length of BC (i.e., n). The adversary prepares the quantum registers M and C to store quantum messages and receive quantum cipher-texts respectively. The adversary then stores the superposition of all the messages in M (i.e., $\sum_m 2^{-n/2}|m\rangle$) of size equal to block size of BC and string $|0^{2n-1}\rangle|+\rangle$ in C equal to twice the block size of BC respectively, and makes an encryption query. The corresponding reply is then stored in the quantum register C. The attack has been sketched in Fig. 2.

After application of encryption algorithm Enc of Π_{CBC} the message and cipher-text registers contain the following data

$$|M,C\rangle = \sum_m 2^{-n/2}|m\rangle\,|c_0\rangle\,|\mathsf{droplastbit}(\mathsf{BC}_k(m \oplus c_0))\rangle|+\rangle.$$

The adversary now XORs c_0 to the message register by using a CNOT gate. Hence, the quantum bits of the system changes to[6]

$$|M,C\rangle = \sum_m 2^{-n/2}|m \oplus c_0\rangle\,|c_0\rangle\,|\mathsf{droplastbit}(\mathsf{BC}_k(m \oplus c_0))\rangle|+\rangle.$$

Using $y = m \oplus c_0$ we have,

$$|M,C\rangle = \sum_m 2^{-n/2}|y\rangle\,|c_0\rangle\,|\mathsf{droplastbit}(\mathsf{BC}_k(y))\rangle|+\rangle.$$

---

[6] Here, k is the key for the block cipher BC.

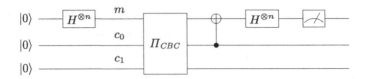

Fig. 2. Attack on 1 block CBC using Simon's algorithm

Also, we have that

$$|M, C\rangle = \sum_m 2^{-n/2} |y\rangle \, |c_0\rangle \, |\text{droplastbit}(\text{BC}_k(y \oplus (k\|1)))\rangle |+\rangle.$$

Hence,

$$|M, C\rangle = \sum_y 2^{-\frac{n+1}{2}} \frac{(|y\rangle + |y \oplus (k\|1)\rangle)}{\sqrt{2}} |c_0\rangle \, |\text{droplastbit}(\text{BC}_k(y))\rangle |+\rangle,$$

We now apply n Hadamard gate (*i.e.*, $H^{\otimes n}$) giving us the state

$$|M, C\rangle = \sum_y \sum_z 2^{-\frac{n+1}{2}} \frac{((-1)^{y \odot z} + (-1)^{(y \oplus (k\|1)) \odot z})}{\sqrt{2}} |z\rangle \, |c_0\rangle \, |\text{droplastbit}(\text{BC}_k(y))\rangle |+\rangle$$

As $(-1)^{(y \odot z)} = 1$ or -1 and doesn't affect the outcome of register (except in phase) we can remove y. Therefore, we have

$$|M, C\rangle = \sum_z 2^{-\frac{n+1}{2}} (-1)^{y \odot z} \frac{(1 + (-1)^{z \odot (k\|1)})}{\sqrt{2}} |z\rangle \, |c_0\rangle \, |\text{droplastbit}(\text{BC}_k(y))\rangle |+\rangle.$$

Hence, if $z \odot (k\|1) = 0$ we have (up to normalization)

$$2(-1)^{y \odot z} \sum_z |z\rangle \, |c_0\rangle \, |\text{droplastbit}(\text{BC}_k(y))\rangle |+\rangle$$

otherwise the superposition collapses to zero string. Now if the $n-$bits of message register is measured one gets a vector z such that $z \odot (k\|1) = 0$. Hence, to retrieve k we can repeat the same attack again and again until we get $n-1$ independent vectors v_i's (we know that the last bit of $(k\|1)$ is 1). Now using the gaussian elimination one can retrieve the $n-1$ bits of k, thereby breaking the Π_{CBC} scheme.

A very similar attack also breaks CBC mode:

Lemma 3. *There exists a standard secure pseudo-random function such that Π_{CFB} is not IND-qCPA secure (in the quantum random oracle model).*

And for XTS mode we get (using a more complex attack):

Lemma 4. *There exists a standard-secure pseudo-random function (in the random oracle model) such that Π_{XTS} admits an attack of the following form: The adversary first performs a number of superposition encryption queries. Then the adversary performs a superposition encryption query where the first half of the plaintext is an adversary chosen superposition of messages, and the second half is a bitstring m unknown to the adversary. Then the adversary can compute m.*

Details and proofs are given in the full version [2].

4   IND-qCPA Security of OFB and CTR Modes of Operation

In this section, we analyze the quantum security of OFB and CTR modes of operation. Our motive is to prove the security of these schemes against the quantum adversary based on IND-qCPA definition (Definition 2) in Sect. 2. These two modes of operation are similar in working thence similar proofs.

We provide a generic proof for any cryptographic-system with encryption function which XOR's the message with a random pad based on the length of message and random key. This proof shows that IND-qCPA security of the scheme reduces to the fact that it is IND-CPA secure.

Lemma 5. *Let $\Pi = (\mathsf{Gen}, \mathsf{Enc}, \mathsf{Dec})$ be an encryption scheme with encryption algorithm as $\mathsf{Enc}_k(M) = G_k(|M|; r) \oplus M$, for randomness r, given message M and key $k \leftarrow \mathsf{Gen}$. If Π is IND-CPA secure then it is IND-qCPA secure.*

Proof. Let $\Pr[PrivK_{\mathcal{A}_q,\Pi}^{qCPA}(t) = 1] = \varepsilon(t) + \frac{1}{2}$, for a poly-time quantum adversary $\mathcal{A}_q$. We construct an efficient quantum adversary $\mathcal{A}$ such that $\Pr[PrivK_{\mathcal{A},\Pi}^{CPA}(t) = 1] = \varepsilon(t) + \frac{1}{2}$. Adversary $\mathcal{A}^{\mathsf{Enc}_k}(1^t)$ works as follows:

1. $\mathcal{A}$ prepares two quantum registers M and C being message and ciphertext registers respectively.
2. Runs $\mathcal{A}_q$, whenever $\mathcal{A}_q$ queries encryption oracle on superposition of messages answer the queries in the following way:
   - the quantum message and $|0^{|M|}\rangle$ are stored in M and C respectively,
   - query $s := \mathsf{Enc}_k(0^{|M|}) = G_k(|M|; r)$, where r is the randomness.
   - apply unitary operator U to quantum register M and C where $U|M, C\rangle := |M, C \oplus M \oplus s\rangle$.
   - send the register $|M, C\rangle$ to the adversary $\mathcal{A}_q$.
3. When $\mathcal{A}_q$ asks the challenge query send it to the challenger and send received result back to $\mathcal{A}_q$.
4. Continue to answer any encryption oracle query as in step 2.
5. $\mathcal{A}_q$ outputs the result b', send b' to the challenger.

It is clear that $\Pr[PrivK_{\mathcal{A},\Pi}^{CPA}(t) = 1] = \Pr[PrivK_{\mathcal{A}_q,\Pi}^{qCPA}(t) = 1] = \frac{1}{2} + \varepsilon(t)$ and $\mathcal{A}$ is poly-time.

Theorem 2. *If E is a standard secure pseudo-random function then Π_{OFB} and Π_{CTR} schemes are* IND-qCPA *secure.*

Proof. Π_{OFB} and Π_{CTR} schemes are IND-CPA secure when E is standard secure pseudo-random function. Thus, result follows from Lemma 5.

5   IND-qCPA Security of CBC and CFB Mode of Operation

IND-qCPA security of CBC and CFB modes of operation are conditional on the existence of quantum secure primitives. We use the One-way to Hiding Lemma [14] (Lemma 1) to prove the bound for any quantum adversary that attacks the system.

We define $\mathsf{Enc}^{i,H}_{CBC}(M) := c_0 c_1 \cdots c_n$, where $c_j \xleftarrow{\$} \{0,1\}^t$ for $j \leq i$ and $c_j = H(m_j \oplus c_{j-1})$ for $i < j \leq n$. Similarly we define, $\mathsf{Enc}^{i,H}_{CFB}(M) := c_0 c_1 \cdots c_n$, where $c_j \xleftarrow{\$} \{0,1\}^t$ for $j \leq i$ and $c_j = H(c_{j-1}) \oplus m_j$ for $i < j \leq n$.

In the next lemma we prove that probability of distinguishing the output of CBC $\mathsf{Enc}^{i,H}_{CBC}$ from $\mathsf{Enc}^{i+1,H}_{CBC}$ by a quantum adversary having access to oracle $\mathsf{Enc}^{i,H}_{CBC}$ is negligible in t, where t is the security parameter. As the proof for $\mathsf{Enc}^{i,H}_{CBC}$ and $\mathsf{Enc}^{i+1,H}_{CBC}$ is similar we provide the instances for $\mathsf{Enc}^{i,H}_{CFB}$ in parentheses [] wherever there is a difference. Also, we use $\mathsf{Enc}^{i,H}$ to represent the encryption functions of $\mathsf{Enc}^{i,H}_{CBC}$ and $\mathsf{Enc}^{i,H}_{CFB}$ to generalize the proof.

Lemma 6. *For any i with $i : 0 \leq i \leq p(t) - 1$, and every quantum adversary $\mathcal{A}$ that makes at most q_A queries,*

$$\Big| \Pr[b = b' : H \leftarrow (\{0,1\}^t \to \{0,1\}^t), b \xleftarrow{\$} \{0,1\}; M_0, M_1 \leftarrow \mathcal{A}^{\mathsf{Enc}^{i,H}};$$

$$b' \leftarrow \mathcal{A}^{\mathsf{Enc}^{i,H}}(\mathsf{Enc}^{i,H}(M_b))] - \Pr[b = b' : H \leftarrow (\{0,1\}^t \to \{0,1\}^t), b \xleftarrow{\$} \{0,1\};$$

$$M_0, M_1 \leftarrow \mathcal{A}^{\mathsf{Enc}^{i,H}}; b' \leftarrow \mathcal{A}^{\mathsf{Enc}^{i,H}}(\mathsf{Enc}^{i+1,H}(M_b))] \Big| \leq O\left(\frac{p(t)^2 q_A{}^2}{2^{\frac{t}{2}}} \right),$$

where $p(t)$ is the maximum number of blocks in the message M and t is the length of each message block.

Proof.

$$\varepsilon(t) = \Big| \Pr[b = b' : H \leftarrow (\{0,1\}^t \to \{0,1\}^t), b \xleftarrow{\$} \{0,1\}; M_0, M_1 \leftarrow \mathcal{A}^{\mathsf{Enc}^{i,H}};$$

$$b' \leftarrow \mathcal{A}^{\mathsf{Enc}^{i,H}}(\mathsf{Enc}^{i,H}(M_b))] - \Pr[b = b' : H \leftarrow (\{0,1\}^t \to \{0,1\}^t), b \xleftarrow{\$} \{0,1\};$$

$$M_0, M_1 \leftarrow \mathcal{A}^{\mathsf{Enc}^{i,H}}; b' \leftarrow \mathcal{A}^{\mathsf{Enc}^{i,H}}(\mathsf{Enc}^{i+1,H}(M_b))] \Big|$$

For a given message $M = m_0 m_1 \cdots m_n$ let $\widetilde{\mathsf{Enc}}_H^i(M, c_0, \cdots, c_i) := \hat{c}_1 \hat{c}_2 \cdots \hat{c}_n$ where

$$\hat{c}_j = \begin{cases} c_j & 0 \leq j \leq i \\ H(\hat{c}_{j-1} \oplus m_j) & [= H(\hat{c}_{j-1}) \oplus m_j] & i < j \leq n \end{cases}$$

Then we have,

$$\varepsilon(t) = \Big| \Pr[b = b' : H \leftarrow (\{0,1\}^t \to \{0,1\}^t), b \xleftarrow{\$} \{0,1\}; M_0, M_1 \leftarrow \mathcal{A}^{\mathsf{Enc}^{i,H}};$$

$$c_0, \ldots, c_i \xleftarrow{\$} \{0,1\}^t; b' \leftarrow \mathcal{A}^{\mathsf{Enc}^{i,H}} (\widetilde{\mathsf{Enc}}_H^i(M_b, c_0, \ldots, c_i))] -$$

$$\Pr[b = b' : H \leftarrow (\{0,1\}^t \to \{0,1\}^t), b \xleftarrow{\$} \{0,1\}; M_0, M_1 \leftarrow \mathcal{A}^{\mathsf{Enc}^{i,H}};$$

$$c_0, \ldots, c_{i+1} \xleftarrow{\$} \{0,1\}^t; b' \leftarrow \mathcal{A}^{\mathsf{Enc}^{i,H}} (\widetilde{\mathsf{Enc}}_H^{i+1}(M_b, c_0, \ldots, c_{i+1}))] \Big| \quad (1)$$

We put $c_i := x \oplus m_b^{i+1} [= x]$ where m_b^{i+1} is the $(i+1)^{th}$ block of the message M_b and $x \xleftarrow{\$} \{0,1\}^t$. This means that c_i is uniformly random as x is randomly chosen. Therefore,

$$\varepsilon(t) = \Big| \Pr[b = b' : H \leftarrow (\{0,1\}^t \to \{0,1\}^t), b \xleftarrow{\$} \{0,1\}; M_0, M_1 \leftarrow \mathcal{A}^{\mathsf{Enc}^{i,H}};$$

$$c_0, \ldots, c_{i-1} \xleftarrow{\$} \{0,1\}^t, x \xleftarrow{\$} \{0,1\}^t, c_i := x \oplus m_b^{i+1} [:= x];$$

$$b' \leftarrow \mathcal{A}^{\mathsf{Enc}^{i,H}} (\widetilde{\mathsf{Enc}}_H^i(M_b, c_0, \ldots, c_i))] - \Pr[b = b' : H \leftarrow (\{0,1\}^t \to \{0,1\}^t), b \xleftarrow{\$} \{0,1\};$$

$$M_0, M_1 \leftarrow \mathcal{A}^{\mathsf{Enc}^{i,H}}; c_0, \ldots, c_{i-1} \xleftarrow{\$} \{0,1\}^t, x \xleftarrow{\$} \{0,1\}^t, c_i := x \oplus m_b^{i+1} [c_i := x],$$

$$y \xleftarrow{\$} \{0,1\}^t, c_{i+1} := y [:= y \oplus m_b^{i+1}]; b' \leftarrow \mathcal{A}^{\mathsf{Enc}^{i,H}} (\widetilde{\mathsf{Enc}}_H^{i+1}(M_b, c_0, \ldots, c_{i+1}))] \Big| \quad (2)$$

By definition of $\widetilde{\mathsf{Enc}}_H^i$, we have $\widetilde{\mathsf{Enc}}_H^i(M_b, c_0, \cdots, c_i) = \widetilde{\mathsf{Enc}}_H^{i+1}(M_b, c_0, \cdots, c_{i+1})$ with $c_{i+1} := H(x)$ $[:= H(x) \oplus m_b^{i+1}]$. Hence,

$$\varepsilon(t) = \Big| \Pr[b = b' : H \leftarrow (\{0,1\}^t \to \{0,1\}^t), b \xleftarrow{\$} \{0,1\}; M_0, M_1 \leftarrow \mathcal{A}^{\mathsf{Enc}^{i,H}};$$

$$c_0, \ldots, c_{i-1} \xleftarrow{\$} \{0,1\}^t, x \xleftarrow{\$} \{0,1\}^t, c_i := x \oplus m_b^i [:= x], c_{i+1} := H(x) [:= H(x) \oplus m_b^{i+1}];$$

$$b' \leftarrow \mathcal{A}^{\mathsf{Enc}^{i,H}} (\widetilde{\mathsf{Enc}}_H^{i+1}(M_b, c_0, \ldots, c_{i+1}))] - \Pr[b = b' : H \leftarrow (\{0,1\}^t \to \{0,1\}^t),$$

$$b \xleftarrow{\$} \{0,1\}; M_0, M_1 \leftarrow \mathcal{A}^{\mathsf{Enc}^{i,H}}; c_0, \ldots, c_{i-1} \xleftarrow{\$} \{0,1\}^t, x \xleftarrow{\$} \{0,1\}^t, y \xleftarrow{\$} \{0,1\}^t,$$

$$c_i := x \oplus m_b^i [:= x], c_{i+1} := y [:= y \oplus m_b^{i+1}]; b' \leftarrow \mathcal{A}^{\mathsf{Enc}^{i,H}} (\widetilde{\mathsf{Enc}}_H^{i+1}(M_b, c_0, \ldots, c_{i+1}))] \Big|$$

We define an adversary $\mathcal{A}_{O2H}$ that makes oracle queries to random function $H \xleftarrow{\$} (\{0,1\}^t \to \{0,1\}^t)$. $\mathcal{A}_{O2H}$ with given inputs x and y does the following:

Adversary $A_{O2H}^H(x, y)$:

$M_0, M_1 \leftarrow \mathcal{A}^{\mathsf{Enc}^{i,H}}$

$b \xleftarrow{\$} \{0,1\}$

$c_0, \ldots, c_{i-1} \xleftarrow{\$} \{0,1\}^t; c_i = x \oplus m_b^{i+1}[\![= x]\!]; c_{i+1} = y[\![= y \oplus m_b^{i+1}]\!];$

compute $C := \widetilde{\mathsf{Enc}}_H^i(M_b, c_0, c_1, \ldots, c_{i+1})$

$b' \leftarrow \mathcal{A}^{\mathsf{Enc}^{i,H}}(C)$

return $b' = b$

We note here that adversary A_{O2H} can answer the adversary $\mathcal{A}$'s query as it has oracle access to H. Let q_{o2h} be the number of H-queries made by A_{O2H}, it is clear that $q_{o2h} \leq 3p(t)q_A$. Let q_1, q_2 and q_3 denote the number of queries that A_{O2H} makes to H before the challenge query, during challenge query and after challenge query respectively.[7]

It is clear that:

$$\varepsilon(t) = \Big| \Pr[\tilde{b} = 1 : H \leftarrow (\{0,1\}^t \rightarrow \{0,1\}^t), x \xleftarrow{\$} \{0,1\}^t, \tilde{b} \leftarrow A_{O2H}^H(x, H(x))]$$

$$- \Pr[\tilde{b} = 1 : H \leftarrow (\{0,1\}^t \rightarrow \{0,1\}^t), x \xleftarrow{\$} \{0,1\}^t, y \xleftarrow{\$} \{0,1\}^t, \tilde{b} \leftarrow A_{O2H}^H(x, y)] \Big| \quad (3)$$

Let B be an oracle algorithm described in the O2H lemma (Lemma 1). Therefore, we have that $\varepsilon(t) \leq 2q_{o2h}\sqrt{P_B}$, where we have the probability P_B as

$$P_B = \Pr[x = x' : j \xleftarrow{\$} \{1, \ldots, q_{o2h}\}, x \xleftarrow{\$} \{0,1\}^t, H \xleftarrow{\$} (\{0,1\}^t \rightarrow \{0,1\}^t),$$
$$x' \leftarrow B^H(x, j)]$$

$$= \frac{1}{q_{o2h}} \cdot \underbrace{\Pr[x = x' : x \xleftarrow{\$} \{0,1\}^t, H \xleftarrow{\$} (\{0,1\}^t \rightarrow \{0,1\}^t), x' \leftarrow B^H(x, j)]}_{:=P_B^j}$$

To evaluate P_B^j we consider three cases depending whether the j-th H-query is before, during, or after the challenge query.

Case I $(j \leq q_1)$:

In this case, the j-th iteration query to the oracle H is computed before the challenge query is done. So adversary $\mathcal{A}$ does not get access to x while queries are done. Therefore, adversary $\mathcal{A}$'s queries are independent of x, as it never executes challenge query and beyond. As the adversary $\mathcal{A}$ never used the x for any query we can therefore say that fixing x to be any string should not affect argument of the query. Therefore, we fix input x as the null string 0^n.

$$P_B^j = \Pr[x = x' : x \xleftarrow{\$} \{0,1\}^t, H \xleftarrow{\$} (\{0,1\}^t \rightarrow \{0,1\}^t), x' \leftarrow B^H(0, j)] \leq 2^{-t}.$$

---

[7] We can assume without loss of generality that A_{O2H} performs exactly q_1, q_2, q_3 queries respectively. If it performs less, we simply add dummy queries.

Case II ($q_1 \leq j \leq q_1 + q_2$):

In this case the j-th iteration query to the oracle H is made during the challenge query (i.e, $q_1 < j \leq q_1 + q_2$). Therefore, oracle algorithm B can stop adversary $\mathcal{A}$ at any of the following queries:

$$H(m_b^{i+2} \oplus y), H(m_b^{i+3} \oplus H(m_b^{i+2} \oplus y)), \cdots, H(m_b^{p(t)} \oplus H(m_b^{p(t)-1} \oplus \cdots H(m_b^{i+2} \oplus y) \cdots))$$

$$[\![H(y) \oplus m_b^{i+2}, H(H(y) \oplus m_b^{i+2}) \oplus m_b^{i+3}, \cdots, H(H(H(\cdots H(y) \oplus m_b^{i+2}) \cdots)) \oplus m_b^{p(t)}]\!]$$

By using result from Zhandry [18] on distinguishing a random function from a random permutation we have,

$$P_B^j \leq \Pr[x = x' : H \xleftarrow{\$} \text{Perm}(), x \xleftarrow{\$} \{0,1\}^t, x' \leftarrow B^H(x,j)] + O\left(\frac{j^3}{2^t}\right)$$

Note that the argument of the j-th query is $s := m_b^{i+j-q_1+1} \oplus H(m_b^{i+j-q_1} \oplus \cdots \oplus H(m_b^{i+2} \oplus y) \cdots)$ $[\![s := H(\cdots H(H(y) \oplus m_b^{i+2}) \cdots \oplus m_b^{i+j-q_1}) \oplus m_b^{i+j-q_1+1}]\!]$. From the definition of O2H lemma we know that y is chosen independently at random from x and H. It is easy to see that for a fixed message M_b s would be assigned an output by a permutation that is independent of x but dependent on y since the input to first call to H is $m_b^{i+2} \oplus y$ $[\![y]\!]$. Therefore,

$$P_B^j \leq \Pr[x = x' : H \xleftarrow{\$} \text{Perm}(), x \xleftarrow{\$} \{0,1\}^t, x' = s] + O(\frac{j^3}{2^t}) \leq \frac{1}{2^t} + O\left(\frac{j^3}{2^t}\right) \approx O\left(\frac{j^3}{2^t}\right)$$

Case III ($j \geq q_1 + q_2$):

In this case, the j-th iteration query to the oracle H is computed after the challenge query is done. We have $j > q_1 + q_2$. Adversary $\mathcal{A}$ makes many encryption oracle queries and eventually measures the argument of one of the H oracle query and stops. Say it measures in the kth H oracle query of j-th encryption query.

$$P_B^j := \Pr[x = x' : x \xleftarrow{\$} \{0,1\}^t, H \xleftarrow{\$} (\{0,1\}^t \rightarrow \{0,1\}^t), x' \leftarrow B^H(x,j)]$$

The circuit diagram in Fig. 3 represents the working of adversary $\mathcal{A}_{O2H}$. $\mathcal{A}_{O2H}$ answers encryption queries using oracle access to H. Let the quantum message (possibly entangled) to be stored in the quantum register M and the corresponding ciphertext in the quantum register C. The encryption circuit is composed of the quantum gates $U_{IV}, U_H, CNOT$ and measurements. Where $U_{IV}|M\rangle = |M \oplus IV\rangle$, $U_H|M,C\rangle = |M, C \oplus H(M)\rangle$, $CNOT|M,C\rangle = |M, C \oplus M\rangle$, and the measurements are in the computational basis of the message space. Thus, in each case I,II,III we have $P_B^j \in O\left(\frac{q_{o2h}^3}{2^{-t}}\right)$.[8]

The unitary gates used to compose the circuits are diagonal in the computational basis and hence commute with the measurements. Therefore, moving

---

[8] Note that in Fig. 3 we measure all registers, not only the query register. This does not change P_B^j since the additional measurements are performed on registers that are not used further.

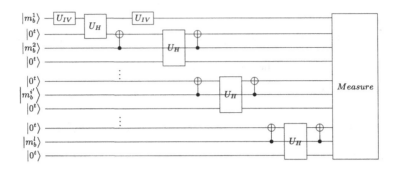

Fig. 3. Composition of Encryption Oracle using H oracle

the measurements prior to the unitary operations do not affect the probability distribution of the output. Hence, we can measure the message register M before performing the unitary operations. Thus, it is similar to the Case II where we have a query on a classical message.

Therefore, we have $P_B^j = O(\frac{j^3}{2^t})$.

Hence by the definition of P_B we have, $P_B \leq O(\frac{q_{o2h}^3}{2^t})$. Therefore, we have that $\varepsilon(t) \leq q_{o2h}\sqrt{P_B} \leq q_{o2h}\sqrt{O(\frac{q_{o2h}^3}{2^t})} = O(\frac{q_{o2h}^3}{2^t})$

Theorem 3. *If the function E is a quantum secure PRF then Π_{CBC} and Π_{CFB} is IND-qCPA secure.*

This follows now easily from Lemma 6 and the fact that $\mathsf{Enc}^{i,H}(M_b)$ is independent of its argument M_b for $i = p(t)$. We give the details in the full version [2].

References

1. Ambainis, A., Rosmanis, A., Unruh, D.: Quantum attacks on classical proof systems (the hardness of quantum rewinding). In: FOCS 2014, pp. 474–483. IEEE, October 2014. Preprint on IACR ePrint 2014/296
2. Anand, M.V., Targhi, E.E., Tabia, G.N., Unruh, D.: Post-quantum security of the CBC, CFB, OFB, CTR, and XTS modes of operation. IACR ePrint (2015). Full version of this paper
3. Bellare, M., Rogaway, P.: Random oracles are practical: a paradigm for designing efficient protocols. In: Denning, D.E., Pyle, R., Ganesan, R., Sandhu, R.S., Ashby, V. (eds.) Proceedings of the 1st ACM Conference on Computer and Communications Security, CCS 1993, Fairfax, Virginia, USA, 3–5 November, pp. 62–73. ACM (1993)
4. Boneh, D., Dagdelen, Ö., Fischlin, M., Lehmann, A., Schaffner, C., Zhandry, M.: Random oracles in a quantum world. In: Lee, D.H., Wang, X. (eds.) ASIACRYPT 2011. LNCS, vol. 7073, pp. 41–69. Springer, Heidelberg (2011)
5. Boneh, D., Zhandry, M.: Quantum-secure message authentication codes. In: Johansson, T., Nguyen, P.Q. (eds.) EUROCRYPT 2013. LNCS, vol. 7881, pp. 592–608. Springer, Heidelberg (2013)

6. Boneh, D., Zhandry, M.: Secure signatures and chosen ciphertext security in a quantum computing world (2013). https://eprint.iacr.org/2013/088, The definition of IND-qCPA only appear in this eprint, not in the conference version

7. Damgård, I., Funder, J., Nielsen, J.B., Salvail, L.: Superposition attacks on cryptographic protocols. In: Padró, C. (ed.) ICITS 2013. LNCS, vol. 8317, pp. 146–165. Springer, Heidelberg (2014)

8. Targhi, E.E., Unruh, D.: Quantum security of the fujisaki-okamoto transform. Technical report, Institute of Computer Science, University of Tartu (2015)

9. European Union Agency for Network and Information Security (ENISA). Algorithms, key sizes and parameters report - 2013 recommendations, October 2013. https://www.enisa.europa.eu/activities/identity-and-trust/library/deliverables/algorithms-key-sizes-and-parameters-report

10. Rogaway, P.: Evaluation of some blockcipher modes of operation. Evaluation carried out for the Cryptography Research and Evaluation Committees (CRYPTREC) for the Government of Japan (2011)

11. Simon, D.R.: On the power of quantum computation. SIAM J. Comput. **26**(5), 1474–1483 (1997)

12. Unruh, D.: Quantum proofs of knowledge. In: Pointcheval, D., Johansson, T. (eds.) EUROCRYPT 2012. LNCS, vol. 7237, pp. 135–152. Springer, Heidelberg (2012)

13. Unruh, D.: Everlasting multi-party computation. In: Canetti, R., Garay, J.A. (eds.) CRYPTO 2013, Part II. LNCS, vol. 8043, pp. 380–397. Springer, Heidelberg (2013)

14. Unruh, D.: Revocable quantum timed-release encryption. IACR Cryptology ePrint Archive, 2013:606 (2013)

15. Watrous, J.: Zero-knowledge against quantum attacks. SIAM J. Comput. **39**(1), 25–58 (2009)

16. Wooding, M.: New proofs for old modes. IACR Cryptology ePrint Archive, 2008:121 (2008)

17. Zhandry, M.: How to construct quantum random functions. In: 53rd Annual IEEE Symposium on Foundations of Computer Science, FOCS 2012, New Brunswick, NJ, USA, 20–23 October 2012, pp. 679–687. IEEE Computer Society (2012)

18. Zhandry, M.: A note on the quantum collision and set equality problems. Quantum Inf. Comput. **15**(7&8), 557–567 (2015)

Post-Quantum Security Models
for Authenticated Encryption

Vladimir Soukharev[1], David Jao[2](✉), and Srinath Seshadri[3]

[1] David R. Cheriton School of Computer Science, University of Waterloo,
Waterloo, ON N2L 3G1, Canada
vsoukhar@uwaterloo.ca

[2] Department of Combinatorics and Optimization, University of Waterloo,
Waterloo, ON N2L 3G1, Canada
djao@uwaterloo.ca

[3] Department of Mathematics and Computer Science,
Sri Sathya Sai Institute of Higher Learning, Prasanthi Nilayam, Puttaparthi,
Anantapur 515134, Andhra Pradesh, India
srinathms@sssihl.edu.in

Abstract. We propose a security model for evaluating the security of
authenticated encryption schemes in the post-quantum setting. Our security model is based on a combination of the classical Bellare-Namprempre
security model for authenticated encryption together with modifications
from Boneh and Zhandry to handle message authentication against quantum adversaries. We give a generic construction based on the Bellare-
Namprempre model for producing an authenticated encryption protocol
from any quantum-resistant symmetric-key encryption scheme together
with any authentication scheme (digital signature scheme or MAC)
admitting a classical security reduction to a quantum-computationally
hard problem. We give examples of suitable authentication schemes
under the quantum random oracle model using the Boneh-Zhandry transformation. We also provide tables of communication overhead calculations and comparisons for various choices of component primitives in
our construction.

Keywords: Authenticated encryption · Security models · Post-
quantum cryptography

1 Introduction

Authenticated encryption (AE) forms a critical component of our existing inter-
net infrastructure, with many widely used protocols such as TLS, SSH, and
IPsec depending on AE for their basic functionality. Despite this importance,
there is relatively little existing literature on the subject of combining post-
quantum authentication and encryption schemes in a provably secure way. A
few works [6,7,14] have dealt with the problem of post-quantum authenticated
key exchange, but do not provide any self-contained discussion of AE outside

© Springer International Publishing Switzerland 2016
T. Takagi (Ed.): PQCrypto 2016, LNCS 9606, pp. 64–78, 2016.
DOI: 10.1007/978-3-319-29360-8_5

of the (much) more complicated context of key exchange; moreover, [6,14] simply use RSA and DH respectively for long-term authentication keys, on the grounds that there is no immediate need for quantum-safe authenticity. In this work, we adopt a different goal: we propose security definitions for post-quantum AE with the goal of achieving authentication and confidentiality against fully quantum adversaries, and give examples of such AE schemes constructed from existing underlying symmetric-key and digital signature primitives, using the quantum random oracle for the latter. Although our definitions are technically new, they are largely based on combinations of existing ideas, allowing us to reuse security proofs from other settings in the present context.

Note that our emphasis in this work is on constructing generic compositions of confidentiality and authentication primitives, rather than specialized authenticated encryption modes of operation as in the CAESAR competition [13]. While specialized first-class primitives are certainly valuable, we feel that understanding composed primitives represents a natural first step.

2 Security Definitions

Bellare and Namprempre [2] showed that an IND-CPA encryption scheme combined with a SUF-CMA message authentication code under the Encrypt-then-MAC paradigm yields an IND-CCA authenticated encryption scheme. We wish to obtain a generalization of this construction which works against quantum adversaries. As a starting point, we review the security definitions of Boneh and Zhandry [5] for symmetric-key encryption schemes and digital signatures.

The most natural extension of IND-CPA security to the quantum setting consists of allowing full unrestricted quantum queries to the encryption oracle. However, Boneh and Zhandry showed [5, Theorems 4.2 and 4.4] that this definition is too powerful, in the sense that no encryption scheme satisfies this security definition. In place of full quantum queries, Boneh and Zhandry propose a definition in which challenge messages can only be encrypted classically [5, Definition 4.5]:

Definition 1 (IND-qCPA). *We say a symmetric-key encryption scheme $\mathcal{E} = $ (Enc, Dec) is indistinguishable under a quantum chosen message attack (IND-qCPA secure) if no efficient adversary $\mathcal{A}$ can win in the following game, except with probability at most $1/2 + \epsilon$:*

Key Generation: *The challenger picks a random key k and a random bit b.*
Queries: *$\mathcal{A}$ is allowed to make two types of queries:*
  Challenge Queries: *$\mathcal{A}$ sends two messages m_0, m_1, to which the challenger responds with $c* = \text{Enc}(k, m_b)$.*
  Encryption Queries: *For each such query, the challenger chooses randomness r, and encrypts each message in the superposition using r as randomness:*

$$\sum_{m,c} \psi_{m,c} |m, c\rangle \mapsto \sum_{m,c} \psi_{m,c} |m, c \oplus \text{Enc}(k, m; r)\rangle$$

Guess: *$\mathcal{A}$ produces a bit b', and wins if $b = b'$.*

Similarly, Boneh and Zhandry define the notion of quantum chosen ciphertext security [5, Definition 4.6]:

Definition 2 (IND-qCCA). *We say a symmetric-key encryption scheme $\mathcal{E} =$ (Enc, Dec) is indistinguishable under a quantum chosen ciphertext attack (IND-qCCA secure) if no efficient adversary $\mathcal{A}$ can win in the following game, except with probability at most $1/2 + \epsilon$:*

Key Generation: *The challenger picks a random key k and a random bit b. It also creates a list $\mathcal{C}$ which will store challenger ciphertexts.*

Queries: *$\mathcal{A}$ is allowed to make three types of queries:*

    Challenge Queries: *$\mathcal{A}$ sends two messages m_0, m_1, to which the challenger responds with $c* = \text{Enc}(k, m_b)$.*

    Encryption Queries: *For each such query, the challenger chooses randomness r, and encrypts each message in the superposition using r as randomness:*

$$\sum_{m,c} \psi_{m,c} |m, c\rangle \mapsto \sum_{m,c} \psi_{m,c} |m, c \oplus \text{Enc}(k, m; r)\rangle$$

Decryption Queries: *For each such query, the challenger decrypts all ciphertexts in the superposition, except those that were the result of a challenge query:*

$$\sum_{c,m} \psi_{c,m} |c, m\rangle \mapsto \sum_{c,m} \psi_{c,m} |c, m \oplus f(c)\rangle$$

    where

$$f(c) = \begin{cases} \perp & \text{if } c \in \mathcal{C} \\ \text{Dec}(k, c) & \text{otherwise.} \end{cases}$$

Guess: *$\mathcal{A}$ produces a bit b', and wins if $b = b'$.*

We now discuss Boneh and Zhandry's quantum security definition for signatures. It is assumed that the adversary can query for signatures of superpositions of messages. In this situation, the definition of existential unforgeability needs to be modified, since a naive reading of the definition would allow the adversary simply to measure a superposition and claim the resulting signature as an existential forgery. To solve this problem we simply require the adversary to produce $q + 1$ signatures from q queries [5, Definition 3.2]:

Definition 3 (SUF-qCMA). *A signature scheme $\mathcal{S} = $ (Gen, Sign, Ver) is strongly unforgeable under a quantum chosen message attack (SUF-qCMA secure) if, for any efficient quantum algorithm $\mathcal{A}$ and any polynomial q, the algorithm $\mathcal{A}$'s probability of success in the following game is negligible in λ:*

Key Generation: *The challenger runs $(sk, pk) \leftarrow \text{Gen}(\lambda)$, and gives pk to $\mathcal{A}$.*

Signing Queries: *$\mathcal{A}$ makes a polynomial q chosen message queries. For each query, the challenger chooses randomness r, and responds by signing each message in the query using r as randomness:*

$$\sum_{m,t} \psi_{m,t} |m, t\rangle \mapsto \sum_{m,t} \psi_{m,t} |m, t \oplus \text{Sign}(sk, m; r)\rangle$$

Forgeries: *$\mathcal{A}$ is required to produce $q + 1$ message-signature pairs. The challenger then checks that all the signatures are valid, and that all message-signature pairs are distinct. If so, the adversary wins.*

Definition 4 (WUF-qCMA). *A signature scheme $\mathcal{S}$ is weakly unforgeable under a quantum chosen message attack (WUF-qCMA secure) if it satisfies the same definition as SUF-qCMA, except that we require the $q+1$ message-signature pairs to have distinct messages.*

Note that our terminology differs slightly from Boneh and Zhandry [5], although the content of the definitions is identical: Boneh and Zhandry use the terms "strongly EUF-qCMA" and "weakly EUF-qCMA" instead of SUF-qCMA and WUF-qCMA. In addition, Boneh and Zhandry have similar definitions for SUF-qCMA and WUF-qCMA secure message authentication codes [4].

Finally, we give our definitions of INT-qCTXT and INT-qPTXT. We constructed these definitions by starting with the classical security definitions of INT-CTXT and INT-PTXT from Bellare and Namprempre [2, Sect. 2], and modifying them in a manner similar to Boneh and Zhandry's definition for digital signatures (Definition 3).

Definition 5 (INT-qCTXT). *An encryption scheme $\mathcal{E} = (\text{Enc}, \text{Dec})$ satisfies integrity of ciphertext under a quantum attack (INT-qCTXT security) if, for any efficient quantum algorithm $\mathcal{A}$ and any polynomial q, the probability of success of $\mathcal{A}$ in the following game is negligible in λ:*

Key Generation: *The challenger picks a random key k.*

Encryption Queries: *$\mathcal{A}$ makes a polynomial q such queries. For each such query, the challenger chooses and randomness r, and encrypts each message in the superposition using r as randomness:*

$$\sum_{m,c} \psi_{m,c} |m, c\rangle \mapsto \sum_{m,c} \psi_{m,c} |m, c \oplus \text{Enc}(k, m; r)\rangle$$

Decryption Queries: *For each such query, the challenger decrypts all ciphertexts in the superposition, except those that were the result of a challenge query:*

$$\sum_{c,m} \psi_{c,m} |c, m\rangle \mapsto \sum_{c,m} \psi_{c,m} |c, m \oplus f(c)\rangle$$

where

$$f(c) = \begin{cases} \bot & \text{if } c \in \mathcal{C} \\ Dec(k, c) & \text{otherwise.} \end{cases}$$

Forgeries: A *is required to produce* $q + 1$ *message-ciphertext pairs. The challenger then checks that all the ciphertexts are valid, and that all message-
ciphertexts pairs are distinct. If so, the adversary wins.*

Definition 6 (INT-qPTXT). *An encryption scheme* $\mathcal{E} = (\text{Enc}, \text{Dec})$ *satisfies the integrity of plaintext under a quantum attack (INT-qPTXT secure) if
it satifies the same definition as INT-qCTXT, except that we require the* $q + 1$
message-ciphertext pairs to have distinct messages.

3   Main Theorem

In this section, we prove that an IND-qCPA encryption scheme together with
a SUF-qCMA signature or MAC scheme yields an authenticated encryption
scheme via the Encrypt-then-MAC method, satisfying the respective privacy
and integrity guarantees of IND-qCCA (Definition 2) and INT-qCTXT (Definition 5), the quantum analogues of the classical notions of IND-CCA and INT-
CTXT security used in Bellare and Namprempre [2]. We begin by showing a
WUF-qCMA MAC implies INT-qPTXT security:

Theorem 1. *Let* $\mathcal{SE} = (\mathcal{K}_e, \mathcal{E}, \mathcal{D})$ *be a symmetric-key encryption scheme, let*
$\mathcal{MA} = (\mathcal{K}_m, \mathcal{T}, \mathcal{V})$ *be a message authentication scheme, and let* $\overline{\mathcal{SE}} = (\bar{\mathcal{K}}, \bar{\mathcal{E}}, \bar{\mathcal{D}})$
be the authenticated encryption scheme obtained from $\mathcal{SE}$ *and* $\mathcal{MA}$ *via the
Encrypt-then-MAC method. Given any adversary I against* $\overline{\mathcal{SE}}$*, we can construct
an adversary F such that*

$$\text{Adv}_{\overline{\mathcal{SE}}}^{\text{INT-qPTXT}}(I) \leq \text{Adv}_{\mathcal{SE}}^{\text{WUF-qCMA}}(F).$$

Proof. (Based on [2, Theorem 4.1]) We construct the adversary F as follows:

1. Use the key $\mathcal{K}_e$.
2. Run I.
3. On query Enc(M) (where M can be in superposition):

$$C' \leftarrow \mathcal{E}(K_e, M); \tau \leftarrow \text{Tag}(C'); \text{ Return } C' \parallel \tau \text{ to } I$$

4. On query Ver(C):

$$\text{Parse } C \text{ as } C' \parallel \tau'; v \leftarrow \text{Ver}(C', \tau'); \text{ Return } v \text{ to } I$$

until I halts.

Let $C_i = C_i' \parallel \tau_i$ for $i \in \{1, \ldots, q+1\}$ be the Ver queries of I that lead to
winning game INT-qPTXT$_{\overline{\mathcal{SE}}}$, after q queries to Enc. Let $M_i = \mathcal{D}(K_e, C_i')$. We
know that due to the property of INT-qPTXT of $\overline{\mathcal{SE}}$, at most q of them were
obtained from the q queries to Enc of I; hence C_i's were the result of at most q
queries of F to Tag, but we obtained $q + 1$ valid tags. Hence, F wins whenever
WUF-qCMA$_{\mathcal{MA}}$ I wins INT-qPTXT$_{\overline{\mathcal{SE}}}$.

Although our proof of Theorem 1 is for MACs, the same proof works for digital signatures (replacing the Tag oracle with the Sign oracle).

Next we show that a SUF-qCMA signature or MAC implies an INT-qCTXT authenticated encryption scheme.

Theorem 2. *Let $\mathcal{SE} = (\mathcal{K}_e, \mathcal{E}, \mathcal{D})$ be a symmetric-key encryption scheme, let $\mathcal{MA} = (\mathcal{K}_m, \mathcal{T}, \mathcal{V})$ be a message authentication scheme, and let $\overline{\mathcal{SE}} = (\bar{\mathcal{K}}, \bar{\mathcal{E}}, \bar{\mathcal{D}})$ be the authenticated encryption scheme obtained from $\mathcal{SE}$ and $\mathcal{MA}$ via encrypt-then-MAC composition method. Given any adversary I against $\overline{\mathcal{SE}}$, we can construct an adversary F such that*

$$\mathrm{Adv}_{\overline{\mathcal{SE}}}^{\text{INT-qCTXT}}(I) \leq \mathrm{Adv}_{\mathcal{SE}}^{\text{SUF-qCMA}}(F).$$

Proof. (Based on [2, Theorem 4.4]) Here we use the same adversary as in Theorem 1. Let $C_i = C_i' \parallel \tau_i$ for $i \in \{1, \ldots, q+1\}$ be the Ver queries of I that lead to winning game INT-qCTXT$_{\overline{\mathcal{SE}}}$, after q queries to Enc. If only at most q of the C_i's were returned to I by Enc, then at most q were queried by F with Tag (i.e., the corresponding $C_i's$). Hence, F wins whenever SUF-qCMA$_{\mathcal{MA}}$ I wins INT-qCTXT$_{\overline{\mathcal{SE}}}$.

Again, the proof of Theorem 2 carries over to digital signatures as well, replacing the Tag oracle with a Sign oracle.

We now show that the authenticated encryption scheme in Encrypt-then-MAC inherits the IND-qCPA property from the underlying encryption scheme:

Theorem 3. *Let $\mathcal{SE} = (\mathcal{K}_e, \mathcal{E}, \mathcal{D})$ be a symmetric-key encryption scheme, let $\mathcal{MA} = (\mathcal{K}_m, \mathcal{T}, \mathcal{V})$ be a message authentication scheme, and let $\overline{\mathcal{SE}} = (\bar{\mathcal{K}}, \bar{\mathcal{E}}, \bar{\mathcal{D}})$ be the authenticated encryption scheme obtained from $\mathcal{SE}$ and $\mathcal{MA}$ via the Encrypt-then-MAC composition method. Given any adversary $\mathcal{A}$ against $\overline{\mathcal{SE}}$, we can construct an adversary $\mathcal{A}_p$ such that*

$$\mathrm{Adv}_{\overline{\mathcal{SE}}}^{\text{IND-qCPA}}(\mathcal{A}) \leq \mathrm{Adv}_{\mathcal{SE}}^{\text{IND-qCPA}}(\mathcal{A}_p).$$

Furthermore, $\mathcal{A}_p$ uses the same resources as $\mathcal{A}$.

Proof. (Based on [2, Theorem 4.3]) We construct $\mathcal{A}_p$ as follows:

$$\mathcal{K}_m \leftarrow \mathcal{K}_m$$
Run $\mathcal{A}$
On query to Enc
$C \leftarrow Enc(M)$
$\tau \leftarrow \mathrm{Tag}(\mathcal{K}_m, C)$
Return $C \parallel \tau$ to $\mathcal{A}$
Until $\mathcal{A}$ halts and returns b
Return b.

We can see that if $\mathcal{A}$ wins, then so does $\mathcal{A}_p$, since a winning output for $\mathcal{A}$ is a winning output for $\mathcal{A}_p$; the tag can be ignored.

Finally, we prove that INT-qCTXT and IND-qCPA security imply IND-qCCA security (Theorem 4). The proof relies on three games G_0, G_1, and G_2 as defined in Fig. 1. These games are based on the corresponding three games from Fig. 7 of [2], except that we modify the games mutadis mutandis to conform to our quantum definitions (Definitions 1 and 2).

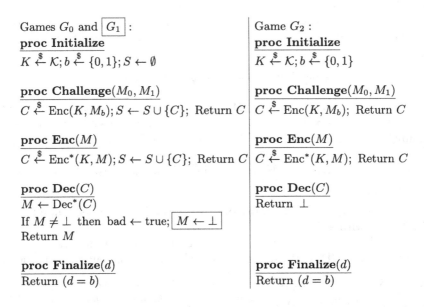

Fig. 1. Games G_0, G_1, and G_2. Game G_1 contains the code in the box while G_0 does not. The functions Enc* and Dec* refer to the encryption and decryption oracle functions from Definition 2.

The proof of Theorem 4 uses the identical until bad lemma [2, Lemma 2.1]:

Lemma 1. *(Identical until bad lemma) Let G_i and G_j be identical until bad games, and $\mathcal{A}$ an adversary. Then for any y: $Pr[G_i^{\mathcal{A}} \implies y] - Pr[G_j^{\mathcal{A}} \implies y] \leq Pr[G_j \text{ sets bad}]$.*

It is not immediately clear (to us, anyway) that the identical until bad lemma holds for quantum adversaries. Fortunately, in Theorem 4, we only need the special case $i = 0, j = 1$, and $y = \text{true}$, and in this case we can prove the result for quantum adversaries. We use the following lemma of Shoup [15, Lemma 1].

Lemma 2. *Let E, E', and F be events defined on a probability space such that $Pr[E \wedge \neg F] = Pr[E' \wedge \neg F]$. Then we have $|Pr[E] - Pr[E']| \leq Pr[F]$.*

This lemma holds regardless of whether or not the adversary is classical or quantum, as it is a mathematical statement. Define the event E to be $[G_0^{\mathcal{A}} \implies \text{true}]$ and E' to be $[G_1^{\mathcal{A}} \implies \text{true}]$. Define F to be $[G_1^{\mathcal{A}} \text{sets bad}]$. Observe that in this case $E \wedge \neg F$ corresponds to the outcome $M = \bot$ in the game G_0, meaning that A wins the game. Similarly, $E' \wedge \neg F$ corresponds to the outcome $M = \perp$ in G_1, meaning that A wins the game. Note that for $M = \perp$, both G_0 and G_1 return the same responses, and hence have the same probability of winning. Hence, $Pr[E \wedge \neg F] = Pr[E' \wedge \neg F]$, which means Lemma 1 of [15] can be applied to obtain $|Pr[E] - Pr[E']| \leq Pr[F]$. Finally, we need to remove the absolute values, to obtain $Pr[E'] \leq Pr[E]$. It is easy to see that we can do so, because for G_0 we sometimes return the message, while for G_1, we always return $M = \perp$, so that the success probability of G_0 is at least that of G_1. Hence the identical until bad lemma holds for quantum adversaries in the special case where $i = 0$, $j = 1$, and $y = \text{true}$.

We recall Definition (1) in [2]:

$$\text{Adv}_{\mathcal{SE}}^{\text{IND-CCA}}(\mathcal{A}) = 2 \cdot \Pr[\text{IND-CCA}_{\mathcal{SE}}^{\mathcal{A}} \implies 1] - 1.$$

The quantum version of this definition is:

$$\text{Adv}_{\mathcal{SE}}^{\text{IND-qCCA}}(\mathcal{A}) = 2 \cdot \Pr[\text{IND-qCCA}_{\mathcal{SE}}^{\mathcal{A}} \implies 1] - 1.$$

Theorem 4. *Let $\mathcal{SE} = (\mathcal{K}, \mathcal{E}, \mathcal{D})$ be an encryption scheme. Let $\mathcal{A}$ be an IND-qCCA adversary against $\mathcal{SE}$ running in time t and making q_e Enc queries and q_d Dec queries. Then, we can construct an INT-qCTXT adversary $\mathcal{A}_c$ and IND-qCPA adversary $\mathcal{A}_p$ such that*

$$\text{Adv}_{\mathcal{SE}}^{\text{IND-qCCA}}(\mathcal{A}) \leq 2 \cdot \text{Adv}_{\mathcal{SE}}^{\text{INT-qCTXT}}(\mathcal{A}_c) + \text{Adv}_{\mathcal{SE}}^{\text{IND-qCPA}}(\mathcal{A}_p).$$

Furthermore, $\mathcal{A}_c$ runs in time $O(t)$ and makes q_e Enc queries and q_d Ver queries, while $\mathcal{A}_p$ runs in time $O(t)$ and makes q_e queries of target messages M_i.

Proof. We have:

$$\Pr[\text{IND-qCCA}_{\mathcal{SE}}^{\mathcal{A}} \implies \text{true}] = \Pr[G_0^{\mathcal{A}} \implies \text{true}]$$
$$= \Pr[G_1^{\mathcal{A}} \implies \text{true}]+$$
$$(\Pr[G_0^{\mathcal{A}} \implies \text{true}] - Pr[G_1^{\mathcal{A}} \implies \text{true}])$$
$$\leq \Pr[G_1^{\mathcal{A}} \implies \text{true}] + \Pr[G_1^{\mathcal{A}} \text{ sets bad}] \qquad (1)$$

The last inequality follows from the identical until bad lemma in the special case $i = 0$, $j = 1$, and $y = \text{true}$ (which we proved above). Now, observe that for Dec, G_1 always returns $\perp$, and hence

$$\Pr[G_1^{\mathcal{A}} \implies \text{true}] = \Pr[G_2^{\mathcal{A}} \implies \text{true}]. \qquad (2)$$

Let us now define the adversary $\mathcal{A}_p$. It simply runs $\mathcal{A}$, answering $\mathcal{A}$'s challenge and encryption queries with its own queries, and answering $\mathcal{A}$'s queries for decryption with $\perp$. It outputs whatever $\mathcal{A}$ outputs. Hence, we get:

$$\Pr[G_2^{\mathcal{A}} \implies \text{true}] \leq \Pr[\text{IND-qCPA}_{\mathcal{SE}}^{\mathcal{A}_p} \implies \text{true}]. \qquad (3)$$

Next, we define the adversary $\mathcal{A}_c$. The adversary $\mathcal{A}_c$ picks a random bit b, then runs $\mathcal{A}$ and answers its queries as follows. For challenge and encryption queries, $\mathcal{A}_c$ submits challenge and encryption queries and returns the results to $\mathcal{A}$. For the Dec query, $\mathcal{A}_c$ submits it to the Ver oracle, and, regardless of the response, returns $\perp$ to $\mathcal{A}$. Hence, we get:

$$\Pr[G_1^{\mathcal{A}} \text{ sets bad}] \leq \Pr[\text{INT-qCTXT}_{\mathcal{SE}}^{\mathcal{A}_c} \implies \text{true}]. \tag{4}$$

Combining the definition

$$\text{Adv}_{\mathcal{SE}}^{\text{IND-qCCA}}(\mathcal{A}) = 2 \cdot \Pr[\text{IND-qCCA}_{\mathcal{SE}}^{\mathcal{A}} \implies 1] - 1$$

with Eqs. (1), (2), (3), and (4), we obtain

$$\text{Adv}_{\mathcal{SE}}^{\text{IND-qCCA}}(\mathcal{A}) \leq 2 \cdot \text{Adv}_{\mathcal{SE}}^{\text{INT-qCTXT}}(\mathcal{A}_c) + \text{Adv}_{\mathcal{SE}}^{\text{IND-qCPA}}(\mathcal{A}_p).$$

Combining Theorems 2, 3, and 4, we obtain our main theorem:

Theorem 5. *Let $\mathcal{SE} = (\mathcal{K}_e, \mathcal{E}, \mathcal{D})$ be a symmetric-key encryption scheme, let $\mathcal{MA} = (\mathcal{K}_m, \mathcal{T}, \mathcal{V})$ be a message authentication scheme, and let $\overline{\mathcal{SE}} = (\bar{\mathcal{K}}, \bar{\mathcal{E}}, \bar{\mathcal{D}})$ be the authenticated encryption scheme obtained from $\mathcal{SE}$ and $\mathcal{MA}$ via the Encrypt-then-MAC composition method. Given that $\mathcal{SE}$ is IND-qCPA and $\mathcal{MA}$ is SUF-qCMA, then the resulting $\overline{\mathcal{SE}}$ is IND-qCCA.*

Proof. By Theorem 2, since $\mathcal{MA}$ is SUF-qCMA, we get that $\overline{\mathcal{SE}}$ is INT-qCTXT. Also, by Theorem 3, since $\mathcal{SE}$ is IND-qCPA, we get that $\overline{\mathcal{SE}}$ is also IND-qCPA. Finally, because $\overline{\mathcal{SE}}$ is INT-qCTXT and IND-qCPA, by Theorem 4, we get that it is IND-qCCA.

As with Theorems 1, 2 and 5 also holds with digital signature schemes used in place of MACs.

4   Quantum-Resistant Strongly Unforgeable Signature Schemes

In this section we examine some concrete choices of strongly unforgeable signature/MAC schemes which could be suitable for our AE construction. We limit ourselves to only a few representative examples to illustrate the general idea. We focus on signature schemes as in our view they are somewhat more interesting, but similar ideas apply to MACs [4]. We begin with a review of the Boneh-Zhandry transformation [5, Construction 3.12] for transforming any classically strongly secure digital signature scheme into a SUF-qCMA scheme:

Construction 6. *Let $S_c = (\text{Gen}_c, \text{Sign}_c, \text{Ver}_c)$ be a be a signature scheme, H be a hash function, and $\mathcal{Q}$ be a family of pairwise independent functions mapping messages to the randomness used by Sign_c, and k some polynomial in λ. Define $S = (\text{Gen}, \text{Sign}, \text{Ver})$ where:*

- $\text{Gen}(\lambda) = \text{Gen}_c(\lambda)$
- $\text{Sign}(sk, m)$:
    - *Select $Q \in \mathcal{Q}$, $r \in \{0, 1\}^k$ at random.*
    - *Set $s = Q(m)$, $h = H(m, r)$, $\sigma = \text{Sign}_c(sk, h; s)$. Output (r, σ).*
- $\text{Ver}(pk, m, (r, \sigma))$:
    - *Set $h = H(m, r)$. Output $\text{Ver}_c(pk, h, \sigma)$.*

If the original signature scheme S_c is SUF-CMA against a classical chosen message attack performed by a quantum adversary, then by [5, Corollary 3.17] the transformed scheme S is SUF-qCMA in the quantum random oracle model.

Furthermore, if the verification function in the signature scheme S_c involves independently deriving the value of σ and checking whether or not the derived value matches the value which was originally sent, a further optimization is possible: one can hash σ to reduce its length to a minimum. We employ this optimization in our examples.

4.1   Strong Designated Verifier Signatures from Isogenies

A strong designated verifier signature (SDVS) scheme [10] is a digital signature scheme in which only a designated party (specified at the time of signing) can verify signatures, and verification requires that party's private key. Note that an SDVS is enough for AE, since only the two parties participating in the AE protocol need to be able to verify signatures.

Sun, Tian, and Wang in [17] present an isogeny-based SDVS scheme, and give a classical security reduction to the SSDDH problem [11], which is believed to be infeasible on quantum computers. This reduction qualifies as a straight-line reduction in the sense of the security framework of Song [16], and hence remains valid for quantum adversaries. However, the reduction only establishes SUF-CMA security, not SUF-qCMA security. Applying the Boneh-Zhandry transformation (Construction 6), we obtain the following SDVS scheme, which is SUF-qCMA:

Setup: Fix a prime $p = \ell_A^{e_A} \ell_B^{e_B} \cdot f \pm 1$, a supersingular base curve E over $\mathbb{F}_{p^2}$, generators $\{P_A, Q_A\}$ of $E[\ell_A^{e_A}]$, and generators $\{P_B, Q_B\}$ of $E[\ell_B^{e_B}]$. Let $H_1, H_2 : \{0, 1\}^* \to \{0, 1\}^k$ be independent secure hash functions (with parameter k), and $\mathcal{Q}$ a family of pairwise independent functions mapping messages to the randomness used in signing.

Key Generation: A signer selects at random $m_S, n_S \in \mathbb{Z}/\ell_A^{e_A}\mathbb{Z}$, not both divisible by ℓ_A, and then computes an isogeny $\phi_S : E \to E_S = E/\langle[m_S]P_A + [n_S]Q_A\rangle$ and the values $\phi_S(P_B)$ and $\phi_S(Q_B)$. The private key is (m_S, n_S) and the public key is the curve E_S and the points $\phi_S(P_B)$ and $\phi_S(Q_B)$. A designated verifier selects at random $m_V, n_V \in \mathbb{Z}/\ell_B^{e_B}\mathbb{Z}$, not both divisible by ℓ_B, and then computes an isogeny $\phi_V : E \to E_V = E/\langle[m_V]P_B + [n_V]Q_B\rangle$ and the values $\phi_V(P_A)$ and $\phi_V(Q_A)$. The private key is (m_V, n_V) and the public key is the curve E_V and the points $\phi_V(P_A)$ and $\phi_V(Q_A)$.

Signing: Select at random $Q \in \mathcal{Q}, r \in \{0,1\}^k$ for use in the Boneh-Zhandry transformation. Compute $s = Q(m)$, $h = H_1(m,r)$, and $\phi'_S \colon E_V \to E_{SV} = E_V/\langle[m_S]\phi_V(P_A) + [n_S]\phi_V(Q_A)\rangle$. Set $\sigma = H_2(h||j(E_{SV})||s)$. The signature is (r, σ).

Verification: Compute $\phi'_V \colon E_S \to E_{SV} = E_S/\langle[m_V]\phi_S(P_B) + [n_V]\phi_S(Q_B)\rangle$ and $h = H_1(m,r)$. Set $\sigma' = H_2(h||j(E_{SV})||Q(m))$. Verify that $\sigma' \stackrel{?}{=} \sigma$.

4.2 Ring-LWE Signatures

As another example, we combine the Ring-LWE signature scheme of Güneysu et al. [8] with Construction 6 from [5] to obtain a SUF-qCMA signature scheme based on Ring-LWE:

Setup: Set $R = \mathbb{F}_q/\langle x^n + 1\rangle$ where n is a power of 2. Let $H_1 \colon \{0,1\}^* \to \{0,1\}^k$ and $H_3 \colon \{0,1\}^* \to R$ be independent secure hash functions (with parameter k) and $\mathcal{Q}$ a family of pairwise independent functions mapping messages to the randomness used in the signing function. Choose a bound B on the maximum coefficient size.

Key Generation: A signer generates two small polynomials $s_1(x), s_2(x) \in R$, selects $a(x) \in R$ at random, and computes the public key $t(x) = as_1(x) + s_2(x)$.

Signing: Select $Q \in \mathcal{Q}$, $r \in \{0,1\}^k$ at random for the Boneh-Zhandry transformation, and $y_1(x), y_2(x) \in R$ at random for the signature scheme. Compute $s = Q(m)$, $h = H_1(m,r)$, and $c(x) = H_3(\text{BitString}(a(x)y_1(x) + y_2(x))||h||s)$. Finally, compute $z_1(x) = s_1(x)c(x) + y_1(x)$ and $z_2(x) = s_2(x)c(x) + y_2(x)$. Check that the coefficients of the polynomials $z_1(x), z_2(x)$ are within the bound B; if not, restart. The signature is $(r, z_1(x), z_2(x), c(x))$

Verification: Check that the coefficients of the polynomials $z_1(x), z_2(x)$ are within the bound B; if not, reject. Compute x $h = H_1(m,r)$, and check whether $c(x) \stackrel{?}{=} H_3(a(x)z_1(x) + z_2(x) - t(x)c(x)||h||Q(m))$. If so, accept; otherwise reject.

5 Quantum-Resistant Authenticated Encryption Schemes

We give a generic construction of authenticated encryption schemes which are provably quantum-resistant in the sense of IND-qCTXT and IND-qCCA. For the underlying encryption scheme, we assume that a classical symmetric-key block cipher $\mathcal{E}$ in a suitable block cipher mode of operation with random IVs will suffice to provide quantum security, taking care to use 2ℓ key sizes to obtain ℓ bits of security. We refer to [1] for a discussion of the choice of the mode of operation. For the MAC/signature scheme we can employ the Boneh-Zhandry transformation on any SUF-CMA scheme secure against quantum adversaries as described in Sect. 4. Combining those two components, we obtain an IND-qCCA and IND-qCTXT authenticated encryption scheme as follows:

Setup:
1. Choose parameters for the underlying encryption and signature schemes.
2. Let $H: \{0,1\}^* \to \{0,1\}^k$ be a secure hash function (with security parameter k).
3. Let $\mathcal{Q}$ be a family of pairwise independent functions mapping messages to the randomness used in the signature scheme.

Key generation:
1. Alice chooses her private parameters for the encryption and signature schemes. If required, she produces and publishes the corresponding public keys.
2. Bob chooses his private parameters for the encryption and signature schemes. If required, he produces and published the corresponding public keys.

Encryption: Suppose Bob wants to send a message $m \in \{0,1\}^*$ to Alice.
1. Using the common encryption key e that he shares with Alice, encrypt the message using the underlying symmetric-key encryption scheme to obtain $c = \mathcal{E}(e, m)$.
2. Select $Q \in \mathcal{Q}$, $r \in \{0,1\}^k$ at random.
3. Compute $t = Q(m)$.
4. Computes the value $h = H(c, r)$.
5. Using h and his private signing key s, Bob computes the authentication tag $\sigma = \text{Sign}(s, h; t)$.
6. The ciphertext is $\{c, r, \sigma\}$.

Decryption: Suppose Alice receives ciphertext $\{c, r, \sigma\}$ from Bob.
1. Compute the value $h = H(c, r)$.
2. Using h and Bob's public signing key p, compute the verification function $\text{Ver}(s, h, r, \sigma)$, if it returns true, continue; if not, stop.
2. Using the common encryption key e that she shares with Bob, decrypt the message and obtain $m = \mathcal{D}(e, c)$.

Again, in the case where the verification function in the signature scheme involves independently deriving the value of σ and checking that the derived value matches the value which was originally sent, we can hash σ prior to transmission to reduce its length to a minimum.

6 Overhead Calculations and Comparisons

In this section we study the communication costs of our AE scheme, from the point of view of both per-message communication overhead and key transmission overhead.

6.1 Communication Overhead

Recall that the ciphertext which Bob sends to Alice consists of the triplet (c, r, σ), where c is the underlying ciphertext content, r is a k-bit nonce, and σ is the signature tag. In the case where the verification function in the signature scheme involves independently deriving the value of σ, we can hash σ down to k bits as well. For a security level of ℓ bits, the minimum value of k required for collision resistance is 2ℓ bits in the quantum setting [3]. The per-message communication overhead of the scheme is thus 4ℓ bits in the case where the signature tag can be hashed, and $2\ell+|\sigma|$ bits otherwise. Note that in the former case the per-message communications overhead is always the same, independent of which component schemes are chosen.

6.2   Public Key Overhead

For the overhead involved in transmitting the public keys to be used for the signature scheme, we use the table of Fujioka et al. [7], augmented with some more recent results as described below. Although [7] deals with the case of post-quantum authenticated key exchange, the same key sizes apply to the AE setting.

With the exception of Ring-LWE as explained below, we aim for 128-bit quantum security. For Ring-LWE, we use the numbers from [8]. Since the scheme in [8] is based on power-of-2 cyclotomic rings, there is a large jump in parameter size between $n = 2^9$ and $n = 2^{10}$, with the former providing 80 bits of security and the latter 256 bits of security. There is no intermediate power of 2 that would provide 128 bits of security. For this reason, we list both 80-bit and 256-bit security levels in our table. The numbers for NTRU are from Schanck et al. [14]. For isogeny-based SDVS schemes we use the recent results of [12]. Note that SDVS schemes require two-way transmission of public keys even if the encrypted communication is one-way, whereas standard signature schemes require two-way transmission of public keys only for two-way communication (Table 1).

Table 1. Key transmission overhead

Signature scheme	Bits
Ring-LWE (80-bit security) [8]	11600
Ring-LWE (256-bit security) [8]	25000
NTRU [14]	5544
Code-based [7]	52320
Multivariate polynomials [9] (via [7])	7672000
Isogeny-based [12]	3073

7   Conclusion

We propose a security model for authenticated encryption against fully quantum adversaries, based on the classical security model of Bellare and Namprempre together with the Boneh and Zhandry framework for modeling quantum adversaries. We provide concrete examples of authenticated encryption schemes satisfying our security model along with estimates of overhead costs for such schemes.

Acknowledgments. This work was supported by the CryptoWorks21 NSERC CRE-ATE Training Program in Building a Workforce for the Cryptographic Infrastructure of the 21st Century, and the Indian Space Research Organization (ISRO) through the Sponsored Research (RESPOND) program.

References

1. Anand, M.V., Targhi, E.E., Tabia, G.N., Unruh, D.: Post-quantum security of the CBC, CFB, OFB, CTR, and XTS modes of operation. PQCrypto (to appear, 2016)
2. Bellare, M., Namprempre, C.: Authenticated encryption: relations among notions and analysis of the generic composition paradigm. J. Cryptol. **21**(4), 469–491 (2008)
3. Bernstein, D.J.: Cost analysis of hash collisions: will quantum computers make SHARCS obsolete? In: Workshop Record of SHARCS 2009: Special-Purpose Hardware for Attacking Cryptographic Systems, pp. 51–82 (2009)
4. Zhandry, M., Boneh, D.: Quantum-secure message authentication codes. In: Johansson, T., Nguyen, P.Q. (eds.) EUROCRYPT 2013. LNCS, vol. 7881, pp. 592–608. Springer, Heidelberg (2013)
5. Boneh, D., Zhandry, M.: Secure signatures and chosen ciphertext security in a quantum computing world. In: Canetti, R., Garay, J.A. (eds.) CRYPTO 2013, Part II. LNCS, vol. 8043, pp. 361–379. Springer, Heidelberg (2013)
6. Bos, J.W., Costello, C., Naehrig, M., Stebila, D.: Post-quantum key exchange for the TLS protocol from the ring learning with errors problem. Cryptology ePrint Archive, Report 2014/599 (2014). http://eprint.iacr.org/
7. Fujioka, A., Suzuki, K., Xagawa, K., Yoneyama, K.: Practical and post-quantum authenticated key exchange from one-way secure key encapsulation mechanism. In: Proceedings of the 8th ACM SIGSAC Symposium on Information, Computer and Communications Security, ASIA CCS 2013, pp. 83–94. ACM, New York (2013)
8. Güneysu, T., Lyubashevsky, V., Pöppelmann, T.: Lattice-based signatures: optimization and implementation on reconfigurable hardware. IEEE Trans. Comput. **64**(7), 1954–1967 (2015)
9. Yang, B.-Y., Liu, F.-H., Huang, Y.-J.: Public-key cryptography from new multivariate quadratic assumptions. In: Fischlin, M., Buchmann, J., Manulis, M. (eds.) PKC 2012. LNCS, vol. 7293, pp. 190–205. Springer, Heidelberg (2012)
10. Jakobsson, M., Sako, K., Impagliazzo, R.: Designated verifier proofs and their applications. In: Maurer, U.M. (ed.) EUROCRYPT 1996. LNCS, vol. 1070, pp. 143–154. Springer, Heidelberg (1996)
11. De Feo, L., Jao, D.: Towards quantum-resistant cryptosystems from supersingular elliptic curve isogenies. In: Yang, B.-Y. (ed.) PQCrypto 2011. LNCS, vol. 7071, pp. 19–34. Springer, Heidelberg (2011)
12. Jao, D., Kalach, K., Leonardi, C.: Key compression for isogeny-based cryptography. (in preparation)
13. Maimut, D., Reyhanitabar, R.: Authenticated encryption: toward next-generation algorithms. IEEE Secur. Priv. **12**(2), 70–72 (2014)
14. Schanck, J., Whyte, W., Zhang, Z.: A quantum-safe circuit-extension handshake for tor. Cryptology ePrint Archive, Report 2015/287 (2015). http://eprint.iacr.org/
15. Shoup, V.: OAEP reconsidered. In: Kilian, J. (ed.) CRYPTO 2001. LNCS, vol. 2139, pp. 239–259. Springer, Heidelberg (2001)

16. Song, F.: A note on quantum security for post-quantum cryptography. Cryptology ePrint Archive, Report 2014/709 (2014). http://eprint.iacr.org/
17. Sun, X., Tian, H., Wang, Y.: Toward quantum-resistant strong designated verifier signature from isogenies. In: Xhafa, F., Barolli, L., Pop, F., Chen, X., Cristea, V. (eds.) INCoS, pp. 292–296. IEEE (2012)

Quantum Collision-Resistance of Non-uniformly Distributed Functions

Ehsan Ebrahimi Targhi[✉], Gelo Noel Tabia, and Dominique Unruh

University of Tartu, Tartu, Estonia
Ehsan.Ebrahimi.Targhi@ut.ee

Abstract. We study the quantum query complexity of finding a collision for a function f whose outputs are chosen according to a distribution with min-entropy k. We prove that $\Omega(2^{k/9})$ quantum queries are necessary to find a collision for function f. This is needed in some security proofs in the quantum random oracle model (e.g. Fujisaki-Okamoto transform).

Keywords: Quantum · Collision · Non-uniform distribution · Query complexity

1 Introduction

Let D be a distribution with min-entropy k over set Y and f be a function whose outputs are drawn according to the distribution D. In this paper, we study the difficulty of finding a collision for unknown function f in the quantum query model. Recall that a collision for function f consists of two distinct inputs x_1 and x_2 such that $f(x_1) = f(x_2)$. Classically, by application of the birthday attack it is easy to observe that $\Theta(2^{k/2})$ queries are necessary and sufficient to find a collision with constant probability. However, in quantum query model this number of queries may be high for the reason that one quantum query may contain the whole input-output values of the function.

Zhandry [Zha15] shows that $\Theta(2^{k/3})$ quantum queries are necessary and sufficient to find a collision for the function f when D is a uniform distribution. However, he leaves the non-uniform case as an open problem. One motivation for studying the quantum collision problem for a non-uniform distribution is the interest in proving the security of classical cryptographic schemes against quantum adversaries. Hash functions are crucial cryptographic primitives that are used to construct many encryption schemes and cryptographic schemes. They are usually modeled as random functions and they are used inside other functions. Therefore the output of combination of a function f and a random function H may not be distributed uniformly and finding a collision for this non-uniformly distributed $f \circ H$ may break the security of the scheme. For example the well-known Fujisaki-Okamoto construction [FO99] uses a random function H to produce the randomness for an encryption scheme f. The security relies on the fact that the adversary can not find two inputs of the random function that lead to the same ciphertext. This is roughly equivalent to saying that $f \circ H$

© Springer International Publishing Switzerland 2016
T. Takagi (Ed.): PQCrypto 2016, LNCS 9606, pp. 79–85, 2016.
DOI: 10.1007/978-3-319-29360-8_6

is collision-resistant. In fact, our result is a crucial ingredient for analyzing a variant of Fujisaki-Okamoto construction in the quantum setting [ETU15].

We prove an $\Omega(2^{k/9})$ lower bound for the quantum query complexity of the function f and leave as an open problem to verify whether or not Zhandry's bound applies to the function f. The proof procedure is as follows. We apply the Leftover Hash Lemma [HILL93] to the function f to extract the number of bits that are indistinguishable from uniformly random bits. After applying the Leftover Hash Lemma, the output distribution of $h \circ f$, where h is a universal hash function, is indistinguishable from the uniform distribution over a set. Note that a collision for function f is a collision for $h \circ f$. Let A be a quantum adversary that has quantum access to f and finds a collision for $h \circ f$. Using the existence of A, we show that there exists a quantum algorithm B that has quantum access to $h \circ f$ and finds a collision for $h \circ f$ with the same probability and the same number of queries as algorithm A. Theorem 1.1 by Zhandry [Zha12] shows that two distribution are indistinguishable if and only if they are oracle-indistinguishable. Therefore, $h \circ f$ is indistinguishable from a random function (recall that the output of $h \circ f$ is indistinguishable from the uniform distribution by Leftover Hash Lemma) and as a result any quantum algorithm B is unable to differentiate between $h \circ f$ and a random function. By using an existing result for finding a collision for a random function presented by Zhandry [Zha15, Theorem 7], we obtain an upper bound for the probability of finding a collision for function $h \circ f$. Therefore, we get an upper bound for the probability of success for the quantum collision problem applied to the function f.

The quantum collision problem has been studied in various previous works. In the following, we mention the existing results on the number of queries that are necessary to find a collision. An $\Omega(N^{1/3})$ lower bound for function f is given by Aaronson and Shi [AS04] and Ambainis [Amb05] where f is a two-to-one function with the same domain and co-domain and N is the domain size. Yuen [Yue14] proves an $\Omega(N^{1/5}/\text{polylog}N)$ lower bound for the quantum collision problem for a random function f with same domain and co-domain. He reduces the distinguishing between a random function and a random permutation problem to the distinguishing between a function with r-to-one part and a function without r-to-one part. His proof is a merger of using the r-to-one lower bound from [AS04] and using the quantum adversary method [Amb00]. Zhandry [Zha15] improves Yuen's bound to the $\Omega(N^{1/3})$ and also removes the same size domain and co-domain constraint. He uses the existing result from [Zha12] to prove his bound.

The sufficient number of quantum queries to find a collision is given in the following works. A quantum algorithm that requires $O(N^{1/3})$ quantum queries and finds a collision for any two-to-one function f with overwhelming probability is given by Brassard, Høyer and Tapp [BHT97]. Ambainis [Amb07] gives a quantum algorithm that requires $O(N^{2/3})$ queries to find two equal elements among N given elements and therefore it is an algorithm for finding a collision in an arbitrary function f given the promise that f has at least one collision. Yuen [Yue14] shows that the collision-finding algorithm from [BHT97] is able to produce a collision for a random function with same domain and co-domain using $O(N^{1/3})$ queries. Zhandry shows that $O(M^{1/3})$ queries are adequate to find a collision for a random function $f : [N] \rightarrow [M]$ where $N = \Omega(M^{1/2})$. He uses Ambainis's element distinctness algorithm [Amb07] as a black box in his proof. Zhandry's bound also implies that we can not expect a lower bound for the query complexity of finding a collision for a non-uniform function better than $O(2^{k/3})$.

2   Preliminaries

In this section, we present some definitions and existing results that are needed in this paper. Notation $x \overset{\$}{\leftarrow} X$ shows that x is chosen uniformly at random from set X. If D is a distribution over X, then notation $x \leftarrow D$ shows that x is chosen at random according to the distribution D. $\Pr[P : G]$ is the probability that the predicate P holds true where free variables in P are assigned according to the program in G. We say that the quantum algorithm A has quantum access to the oracle $O : \{0,1\}^{n_0} \rightarrow \{0,1\}^{n_1}$, denoted by A^O, where A can submit queries in superposition and the oracle O answers to the queries by a unitary transformation that maps $|x, \, y\rangle$ to $|x, \, y \oplus O(x)\rangle$.

Definition 1. *Let D_1 and D_2 be distributions on a set X. The statistical distance between D_1 and D_2 is*

$$\mathrm{SD}(D_1, D_2) = \frac{1}{2} \sum_{x \in X} \big| \Pr[D_1(x)] - \Pr[D_2(x)] \big|.$$

Definition 2. *Let D be a distribution on a set X. The min-entropy of this distribution is defined as*

$$H_\infty(D) = -\log \max_{x \in X} \Pr[D(x)].$$

Definition 3. *We say that function $f : \{0,1\}^{n_1} \rightarrow \{0,1\}^{n_2}$ has min-entropy k if,*

$$-\log \max_{y \in \{0,1\}^{n_2}} \Pr[y = f(x) : x \overset{\$}{\leftarrow} \{0,1\}^{n_1}] = k.$$

Definition 4 (Universal Hash Function [CW79]). *A family of functions $H = \{h : \{0,1\}^n \rightarrow \{0,1\}^m\}$ is called a universal family if for all distinct $x, y \in \{0,1\}^n$:*

$$\Pr[h(x) = h(y) : h \overset{\$}{\leftarrow} H] \leq 1/2^m.$$

Lemma 1 (Leftover Hash Lemma [HILL93]). *Let D be a distribution with min-entropy k and e be a positive integer. Let $h : \{0,1\}^m \times \{0,1\}^n \rightarrow \{0,1\}^{k-2e}$ be a universal hash function. Then,*

$$\mathrm{SD}\left(\big(h(y,x), y\big), \big(z, y\big) \right) \leq 2^{-e-1}$$

where $x \overset{D}{\leftarrow} \{0,1\}^n, y \overset{\$}{\leftarrow} \{0,1\}^m$ and $z \overset{\$}{\leftarrow} \{0,1\}^{k-2e}$.

Lemma 2 ([Zha12]). *Let D_1 and D_2 be efficiently sampleable distributions over some set Y, and let X be some other set. For $i = 1$, 2, let D_i^X be the distributions of functions F_i from X to Y where for each $x \in X$, $F_i(x)$ is chosen at random according to the distribution D_i. Then if A be a quantum algorithm that makes q queries and distinguish D_1^X from D_2^X with non-negligible probability ϵ, we can construct a quantum algorithm B that distinguishes samples from D_1 and D_2 with probability at least $\frac{3\epsilon^2}{64\pi^2 q^3}$.*

Lemma 3 (Theorem 7 [Zha15]). *Let $h : \{0,1\}^n \rightarrow \{0,1\}^m$ be a random function. Then any quantum algorithm making q number of queries to h outputs a collision for h with probability at most $\frac{C(q+2)^3}{2^m}$ where C is a universal constant.*

3   Main Result

Let $\Pr[\mathsf{Coll}(O; A^O) : O \leftarrow D]$ be the probability of finding a collision in function O that is drawn according to the distribution D using a quantum algorithm A with quantum access to the function O.

Lemma 4. *Let D be a distribution over $\{0,1\}^{n_1}$. Let $f : \{0,1\}^{n_1} \rightarrow \{0,1\}^{n_2}$ be a public function and $X = \{0,1\}^{n_0}$. If A is a quantum algorithm that makes q queries to function O drawn from distribution D^X and finds a collision for $f \circ O$ with some probability, then there exists a quantum algorithm B that makes q queries to $f \circ O$ and outputs a collision for $f \circ O$ with the same probability.*

Proof. Let $S_y = f^{-1}(\{y\})$ for $y \in \mathrm{Im}\, f$. We define distribution D_y over S_y as

$$\Pr[D_y(z)] := \frac{\Pr[D(z)]}{\sum_{z \in S_y} \Pr[D(z)]}.$$

Let D' be the distribution of functions F from $\{0,1\}^{n_0} \times \mathrm{Im}\, f$ to $\{0,1\}^{n_1}$ where for each $x \in \{0,1\}^{n_0}$ and $y \in \mathrm{Im}\, f$, $F(x,y)$ is chosen at random in S_y according to the distribution D_y. Let $(F \odot g)(x) := F(x, g(x))$. We show that output of O and output of $F \odot (f \circ O)$ have the same distribution when F is chosen according to distribution D'. For every $x \in \{0,1\}^{n_0}$ and $z \in \{0,1\}^{n_1}$:

$$\Pr[(F \odot (f \circ O))(x) = z : O \leftarrow D^X, F \leftarrow D']$$
$$= \Pr[F(x, f(O(x))) = z : O \leftarrow D^X, F \leftarrow D']$$
$$= \Pr[F(x, f(z')) = z : z' \leftarrow D, F \leftarrow D']$$
$$= \Pr[z'' = z : z' \leftarrow D, z'' \leftarrow D_{f(z')}]$$
$$\overset{(*)}{=} \Pr[z'' = z \wedge z' \in S_{f(z)} : z' \leftarrow D, z'' \leftarrow D_{f(z')}]$$
$$\overset{(**)}{=} \Pr[z' \in S_{f(z)} : z' \leftarrow D] \Pr[z'' = z : z'' \leftarrow D_{f(z)}]$$
$$= \left(\sum_{z' \in S_{f(z)}} \Pr[D(z')] \right) \cdot \frac{\Pr[D(z)]}{\sum_{z' \in S_{f(z)}} \Pr[D(z')]} = \Pr[D(z)],$$

where $(*)$ holds for the reason that if $z'' = z$ be true, then z' will be in the set $S_{f(z)}$ and $(**)$ uses the conditional probability. As a result:

$$\Pr[\mathsf{Coll}(f \circ O; A^O) : O \leftarrow D^X] = \Pr[\mathsf{Coll}(f \circ O; A^{F \odot f \circ O}) : O \leftarrow D^X, F \leftarrow D'].$$

Now, we construct quantum algorithm B. Algorithm B runs A and answers to its query as follows: (i) query $(f \circ O)(x) := y$, (ii) pick $z \leftarrow D_y$, and (iii) set $O(x) := z$. That is, B runs $A^{F \odot f \circ O}$ with $F \leftarrow D'$. Let $\overline{O} = f \circ O$. The way that quantum algorithm B handles quantum queries is shown in the following circuit.

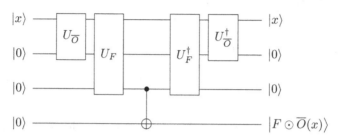

Algorithm B returns the output of A after q queries. Therefore, we prove the existence of quantum algorithm B stated in the lemma.

Theorem 1. *Let D be a distribution with $H_\infty(D) \geq k$ over set $\{0,1\}^{n_1}$. Let O be a function drawn from distribution D^X. Then any quantum algorithm A making q queries to O returns a collision for O with probability at most $\frac{C'(q+2)^{9/5}}{2^{k/5}}$ where C' is a universal constant. That is,*

$$\Pr[\mathsf{Coll}(O; A^O) : O \leftarrow D^X] \leq \frac{C'(q+2)^{9/5}}{2^{k/5}}.$$

Let $h : \{0,1\}^m \times \{0,1\}^{n_1} \to \{0,1\}^{k-2e}$ be a universal hash function. Lemma 1 implies that:

$$SD(h_y(x), z) \leq 2^{-e-1} \tag{1}$$

where $h_y(x) := h(y,x)$, $x \leftarrow D$, $y \overset{\$}{\leftarrow} \{0,1\}^m$ and $z \overset{\$}{\leftarrow} \{0,1\}^{k-2e}$.

The upper bound can be concluded by following steps:

$\Pr[\mathsf{Coll}(O; A^O) : O \leftarrow D^X]$

$\overset{(i)}{\leq} \Pr[\mathsf{Coll}(h_y \circ O; A^O) : O \leftarrow D^X]$

$\overset{(ii)}{=} \Pr[\mathsf{Coll}(h_y \circ O; B^{h_y \circ O}) : O \leftarrow D^X]$

$\overset{(iii)}{\leq} \Pr[\mathsf{Coll}(O^*; B^{O^*}) : O^* \overset{\$}{\leftarrow} (\{0,1\}^{n_1} \to \{0,1\}^{k-2e})] + \sqrt{64\pi^2 q^3 2^{-e-1}/3}$

$\overset{(iv)}{\leq} \frac{C(q+2)^3}{(2^{k-2e})} + \sqrt{\frac{64\pi^2 q^3}{3(2^{e+1})}}$

where

(i) follows from the fact that collisions for O will also be collisions for $h_y \circ O$, and that $h_y \circ O$ can have other collisions;

(ii) follows from Lemma 4 that implies the existence of quantum algorithm B;

(iii) can be seen as follows: Let D_1 be output distribution of $h_y \circ O$ and D_2 be uniform distribution over $\{0,1\}^{k-2e}$. Equation 1 implies that for every adversary A,

$$|\Pr[A(y) = 1 : y \leftarrow D_1] - \Pr[A(y) = 1 : y \leftarrow D_2]| \leq 2^{-e-1}.$$

Using Lemma 2, we can conclude that

$$\left| \Pr[\mathsf{Coll}(h_y \circ O; B^{h_y \circ O}) : O \leftarrow D^X] - \right.$$
$$\left. \Pr[\mathsf{Coll}(O^*; B^{O^*}) : O^* \overset{\$}{\leftarrow} (\{0,1\}^{n_1} \to \{0,1\}^{k-2e})] \right| \leq \sqrt{64\pi^2 q^3 2^{-e-1}/3};$$

and finally

(iv) follows from applying Lemma 3 to the random function O^*.

So far, we have the upper bound

$$\eta_e := \frac{2^{2e}\mu}{2^k} + \frac{\nu}{2^{e/2}}, \qquad \text{where } \mu := C(q+2)^3 \text{ and } \nu := \frac{8\pi q^{3/2}}{\sqrt{6}}.$$

It is minimized by choosing

$$e = \frac{2}{5}k + \frac{2}{5}\log\frac{\nu}{4\mu}.$$

Substituting this value of e gives us

$$\Pr[\mathsf{Coll}(O; A^O) : O \leftarrow D^X] \leq \frac{2^{2/5}\mu^{1/5}\nu^{4/5}}{2^{k/5}} \leq \frac{C'(q+2)^{9/5}}{2^{k/5}}.$$

Corollary 1. *Let* $f : \{0,1\}^{n_1} \to \{0,1\}^{n_2}$ *be a function with min-entropy* k. *Let* $O : \{0,1\}^* \to \{0,1\}^{n_1}$ *be a random function. Then any quantum algorithm* A *making* q *queries to* O *returns a collision for* $f \circ O$ *with probability at most* $O\left(\frac{q^{9/5}}{2^{k/5}}\right)$.

We apply Lemma 4 to obtain the quantum algorithm B that has access to $f \circ O$ and finds a collision for $f \circ O$ with the same number of queries and the same probability as the quantum algorithm A. Then the result follows by Theorem 1 for the reason that the output distribution of $f \circ O$ has min-entropy k.

Acknowledgments. We would like to thank the anonymous reviewers for their comments. This work was supported by the Estonian ICT program 2011–2015 (3.2.1201.13-0022), the European Union through the European Regional Development Fund through the sub-measure "Supporting the development of R&D of info and communication technology", by the European Social Fund's Doctoral Studies and Internationalisation Programme DoRa, by the Estonian Centre of Excellence in Computer Science, EXCS.

References

[Amb00]   Ambainis, A.: Quantum lower bounds by quantum arguments. In: Yao, F.F., Luks, E.M. (eds.) Proceedings of the Thirty-Second Annual ACM Symposium on Theory of Computing, May 21–23, Portland, OR, USA, pp. 636–643. ACM (2000)

[Amb05]   Ambainis, A.: Polynomial degree and lower bounds in quantum complexity: Collision and element distinctness with small range. Theor. Comput. **1**(1), 37–46 (2005)

[Amb07]   Ambainis, A.: Quantum walk algorithm for element distinctness. SIAM J. Comput. **37**(1), 210–239 (2007)

[AS04]   Aaronson, S., Shi, Y.: Quantum lower bounds for the collision and the element distinctness problems. J. ACM **51**(4), 595–605 (2004)

[BHT97]   Brassard, G., Høyer, P., Tapp, A.: Quantum algorithm for the collision problem. ACM SIGACT News (Cryptology Column) **28**, 14–19 (1997)

[CW79]   Carter, L., Wegman, M.N.: Universal classes of hash functions. J. Comput. Syst. Sci. **18**(2), 143–154 (1979)

[ETU15]   Targhi, E.E., Unruh, D.: Quantum security of the Fujisaki-Okamoto transform (2015). http://2015.qcrypt.net/wp-content/uploads/2015/09/Poster10_Ehsan-Ebrahimi.pdf

[FO99]   Fujisaki, E., Okamoto, T.: Secure integration of asymmetric and symmetric encryption schemes. In: Wiener, M. (ed.) CRYPTO 1999. LNCS, vol. 1666, pp. 537–554. Springer, Heidelberg (1999)

[HILL93]   Håstad, J., Impagliazzo, R., Levin, L.A., Luby, M.: Construction of a pseudorandom generator from any one-way function. SIAM J. Comput. **28**, 12–24 (1993)

[Yue14]   Yuen, H.: A quantum lower bound for distinguishing random functions from random permutations. Quantum Inf. Comput. **14**(13–14), 1089–1097 (2014)

[Zha12]   Zhandry, M.: How to construct quantum random functions. In: 53rd Annual IEEE Symposium on Foundations of Computer Science, FOCS , New Brunswick, NJ, USA, October 20–23, 2012, pp. 679–687. IEEE Computer Society (2012)

[Zha15]   Zhandry, M.: A note on the quantum collision and set equality problems. Quantum Inf. Comput. **15**(7–8), 557–567 (2015)

An Efficient Attack on a Code-Based Signature Scheme

Aurélie Phesso[2] and Jean-Pierre Tillich[1][(✉)]

[1] SECRET Project - INRIA Rocquencourt, Domaine de Voluceau,
B.P. 105, 78153 Le Chesnay Cedex, France
jean-pierre.tillich@inria.fr
[2] Université Bordeaux, Talence, France
aurelie.phesso@gmail.com

Abstract. Baldi et al. have introduced in [BBC+13] a very novel code based signature scheme. However we will prove here that some of the bits of the signatures are correlated in this scheme and this allows an attack that recovers enough of the underlying secret structure to forge new signatures. This cryptanalysis was performed on the parameters which were devised for 80 bits of security and broke them with $100,000$ signatures originating from the same secret key.

1 Introduction

It is a long standing open problem to build an efficient and secure signature scheme based on the hardness of decoding a linear code which could compete in all respects with DSA or RSA. Such schemes could indeed give a quantum resistant signature for replacing in practice the aforementioned signature schemes that are well known to be broken by quantum computers. The first answer to this question was given in [CFS01]. They adapted the Niederreiter scheme [Nie86] for this purpose. This requires a linear code for which there exists an efficient complete decoding algorithm. This means that if H is a $r \times n$ parity-check matrix of the code, there exists for any $s \in \{0,1\}^r$ an efficient way to find a word e of smallest Hamming weight such that $He^T = s^T$. To sign a message m, a hash function $\mathcal{H}$ is first applied to the message (say that the output of the hash function is a binary string of length r). Then the complete decoding algorithm of the code with parity-check matrix H is used to produce the signature of m which is a word e of smallest weight such that

$$He^T = \mathcal{H}(m)^T.$$

The authors of [CFS01] noticed that very high rate Goppa codes are able to fulfill this task, and their scheme can indeed be considered as the first practical solution to the aforementioned problem. Moreover they gave a security proof of their scheme relying only on the assumption that two problems were hard, namely (i) decoding a generic linear code and (ii) distinguishing a Goppa code from a random linear code with the same parameters. However, afterwards it was

© Springer International Publishing Switzerland 2016
T. Takagi (Ed.): PQCrypto 2016, LNCS 9606, pp. 86–103, 2016.
DOI: 10.1007/978-3-319-29360-8_7

realized that the parameters proposed in [CFS01] can be attacked by an unpublished attack of Bleichenbacher, which despite its exponential complexity gives an attack which is probably implementable in practice nowadays. Subsequently, it was shown in [Fin10] that there is a slight variation called Parallel-CFS which avoids the significant increase of parameters needed to thwart the Bleichenbacher attack on the original system. However, even this modified scheme shares the same nice features as the original scheme, that is very short signature sizes and reasonably fast software implementation for 80 bits of security [LS12] it has also some drawbacks, such as for instance:

(i) a lack of security proof in light of the distinguisher of high rate Goppa codes found in [FGO+11] (see also [FGO+13] for more details) which shows that the hypotheses used in [CFS01] to give a security proof of the signature scheme were not met,

(ii) and poor scaling of the parameters when security has to be increased. This comes from the following behavior. The [CFS01] scheme uses t-error correcting Goppa codes of length 2^m. The public key is of size $K = tm2^m$ whereas decoding attacks take about $\lambda = 2^{tm/2}$ operations whereas obtaining signature needs about $t!t^2m^3$ operations. If we want to stick to a reasonable signature cost, this needs that we fix t to a small value (say smaller than 12). In this case the security parameter λ is basically only a polynomial function of the key size K: $\lambda \approx K^{t/2}$.

Other signature schemes based on codes were also given in the literature such as for instance the KKS scheme [KKS97,KKS05] or its variant [BMS11]. But they can be considered at best to be one-time signature schemes in light of the attack given in [COV07] and great care has to be taken to choose the parameters of this scheme as shown by [OT11] which broke all the parameters proposed in [KKS97,KKS05,BMS11].

Recently, there has been some revival in the CFS strategy [CFS01], by choosing other code families (or by replacing the Hamming metric by another metric). The new code families that were used are LDGM codes in [BBC+13], i.e. codes with a Low Density Generator Matrix, LRPC codes in [GRSZ14], or (essentially) convolutional codes [GSJB14]. While there are still some doubts that there is a way to choose the parameters of the scheme [GSJB14] in order to avoid the attack [LT13] on the McEliece cryptosystem based on convolutional codes [LJ12], there was no clear indication that the two other schemes are insecure. In particular, the LRPC-based scheme comes with a security proof that obtaining a fairly large amount of message-signature pairs does not simplify the work of an attacker (and obtaining a feasable attack on the parameters proposed in [GRSZ14] is a completely open question). Both schemes are based on two very original ideas for decoding in the rank metric case for LRPC codes and decoding in the Hamming metric for the [BBC+13] scheme.

The [BBC+13] scheme builds upon the following idea. It is namely easy to find an error e of low weight which has some specific syndrome s (i.e. $s^T = He^T$) of low weight when the parity-check matrix H is systematic, i.e. it has the form $H = (P\ I)$, where I is the identity matrix and P is arbitrary. Here is enough to take $e = 0||s$ where $||$ stands for concatenation and 0 is the all-zero vector that has as many entries as there are columns in P. Basically the authors of [BBC+13] choose a hash function $\mathcal{H}$, such that the result of the hash function is a word of low weight for which the aforementioned decoding procedure works. Of course, an attacker can also perform the same task and it is the purpose of the [BBC+13] scheme to hide the structure that allows this way of signing. This is obtained by taking LDGM codes whose low weight codewords will be used to hide the structure of the signature and by multiplying H by appropriate matrices.

However, contrarily to [GRSZ14] the LDGM code based scheme does not come with a security proof that message-signature pairs do not leak information. It is the purpose of this paper to show that indeed there is an efficient attack for breaking this scheme when the attacker has at her/his disposal enough signatures obtained from the same secret key. It is based on the fact that in this scheme some of the bits of the signature are correlated. These correlations can be used to recover an equivalent secret key which can be used to forge new signatures. This cryptanalysis was performed on the parameters which were devised for 80 bits of security and broke them with $100,000$ signatures originating from the same secret key in about one hour.

Notation: In the whole paper, the sum between bits is always performed as the sum over $\mathbb{F}_2$ (that is always modulo 2) and the sum between binary words $x = (x_i)_i$ and $y = (y_i)_i$ of the same length is performed componentwise $x + y = (x_i + y_i)_i$. We use bold letters for matrices and vectors, A, x and so on and so forth. Vectors are understood as row vectors and we use the transpose notation to denote column vectors, for instance when x is a (row)-vector, x^T denotes this vector written in column form.

2   Description of the LDGM Code Based Signature Scheme Proposed in [BBC+13]

This scheme can be described as follows.

Private key

- a full rank $k \times n$ binary matrix G with rows of some small and constant weight w_G which is a generator matrix of a binary LDGM code $\mathscr{C}$ of length n and dimension k. It is assumed that the square $k \times k$ submatrix formed by the k first columns of G is invertible. In this case $\mathscr{C}$ admits an $(n-k) \times n$ parity-check matrix H of the form $H = (P\ I)$ where I is the identity matrix of size $(n-k) \times (n-k)$.
- an $n \times n$ matrix S that is sparse and non-singular of average row and column weight m_S.
- an invertible $(n-k) \times (n-k)$ transformation matrix Q of the form $Q = R+T$ where R is of very low rank z (say 1 or 2) and T is sparse with row and column weight m_T. R can be written as $R = a^T b$ where a and b are two $z \times (n-k)$ matrices.

Public key

$$H' = Q^{-1}HS^{-1}.$$

Moreover this scheme also uses two fixed functions, a hash function $\mathcal{H}$ and a map $\mathcal{F}$ mapping any hash to a binary string of length $n - k$ and Hamming weight w.

Signature Generation

1. To sign a message m, the signer computes $s = \mathcal{F}(\mathcal{H}(m))$ which is an element of $\{0,1\}^{n-k}$ of weight w. He checks whether $bs^T = 0$. If this is the case, he goes to the next step. If not, he appends a counter l to $\mathcal{H}(m)$ to obtain $\mathcal{H}(m)\|l$ [1] and computes $\mathcal{F}$ applied to $\mathcal{H}(m)\|l$ until getting a syndrome s of weight w that satisfies $bs^T = 0$ (for more details see [BBC+13, §3.2]). This requires $O(2^z)$ attempts on average.
2. The signer computes the private syndrome $s'^T = Qs^T$. This syndrome has weight $\leq m_T w$.
3. The signer appends k zeros in front of s': $e = \mathbf{0}_k\|s'$ where $\mathbf{0}_k = \underbrace{00\cdots0}_{k}$.
4. The signer selects m_G rows of G at random where m_G is some fixed and small constant and adds these rows to obtain a codeword c of $\mathscr{C}$ of weight $\leq w_c \overset{\text{def}}{=} m_G w_G$.
5. The signature is then equal to

$$\sigma = (e + c)S^T. \tag{1}$$

Signature Verification

1. The verifier checks that the weight of the signature σ is less than $(m_T w + w_c)m_S$. If this is not the case the signature is discarded.
2. He computes $s^* \overset{\text{def}}{=} \mathcal{F}(\mathcal{H}(m))$ and checks whether $H'\sigma^T = s^{*T}$. If this is not the case he appends a counter l to $\mathcal{H}(m)$ and checks whether $H'\sigma^T = \mathcal{F}(\mathcal{H}(m)\|l)^T$. If after $O(2^z)$ verification attempts no such equality is found, the signature is eventually discarded.

The point behind the verification process is the following chain of equalities

$$\begin{aligned}
H'\sigma^T &= Q^{-1}HS^{-1}S(e^T + c^T) \\
&= Q^{-1}H(e^T + c^T) \\
&= Q^{-1}He^T \\
&= Q^{-1}s'^T \\
&= Q^{-1}Qs^T \\
&= s^T.
\end{aligned}$$

Note that this is a general description of the scheme. Now in order to have reasonable key sizes, quasi-cyclic LDGM codes and quasi-cyclic matrices Q and

---

[1] Here $\|$ stands for the concatenation of strings.

S are actually chosen in [BBC+13]. More precisely G is chosen as a $k_0p \times n_0p$ matrix formed by sparse and circulant blocks $C_{i,j}$ of size p (and such that all the rows of G have weight w_G)

$$G = \begin{pmatrix} C_{0,0} & C_{0,1} & C_{0,2} & \cdots & C_{0,n_0-1} \\ C_{1,0} & C_{1,1} & C_{1,2} & \cdots & C_{1,n_0-1} \\ C_{2,0} & C_{2,1} & C_{2,2} & \cdots & C_{2,n_0-1} \\ \vdots & \vdots & \vdots & \ddots & \vdots \\ C_{k_0-1,0} & C_{k_0-1,1} & C_{k_0-1,2} & \cdots & C_{k_0-1,n_0-1} \end{pmatrix}.$$

Moreover in all the parameters suggested in [BBC+13], m_T was chosen to be equal to 1, that is T is a permutation matrix. Furthermore it is assumed in [BBC+13] that T is also formed by circulant blocks of size $p \times p$ (that is T is a quasi-cyclic permutation). R is also chosen to have a block circulant form. This is obtained by choosing R as follows.

$$R = (a_{r_0}^T b_{r_0}) \otimes 1_{p \times p}$$

where $r_0 \overset{\text{def}}{=} n_0 - k_0$, a_{r_0} and b_{r_0} are two binary matrices of size $z \times r_0$, $1_{p \times p}$ is the all-one $p \times p$ matrix and $\otimes$ stands for the Kronecker product. This implies that Q is formed by circulant blocks of size $p \times p$. S is also chosen in this way, namely formed by circulant blocks of size $p \times p$.

3   The Idea Underlying the Attack

3.1   Correlations Between Bits of the Signature

The creation of a signature can be summarized as follows. It is obtained by first obtaining a binary word s of small weight from the message m that has to be signed and then computing the product

$$((0_k||sQ^T) + c)S^T$$

where c is a codeword of small weight $\leq w_c$ of the LDGM code chosen for this scheme. From the fact that $Q = T + R$ and $Rs^T = 0$ where T is a permutation matrix (this choice is made in all the parameters proposed in [BBC+13]), it turns out that the signature σ can be written as

$$\sigma = ((0_k||s') + c)S^T$$

where s' is a word of (small) weight w. To simplify the discussion we will make this assumption from now on, i.e. T is a permutation matrix. We wish to emphasize that this assumption is just here to simplify the discussion a little bit, and that our attack will also work in a more general setting where the weight of s' stays sufficiently small. Let us bring in the quantities

$$x = (x_1 \ldots x_n) \overset{\text{def}}{=} (0_k||s') + c.$$

Here we have

$$\sigma = x S^T.$$

Roughly speaking, the idea of the attack is to look for correlations between bits of σ by using a bunch of signatures that will allow to compute such statistics. These correlations will give a lot of useful information about S that allows to recover a column permuted version S_p of S and later on from the knowledge of $Q^{-1}HS^{-1}$ recover a possible matrix Q_p that allows to forge signatures.

Before we explain where these correlations come from, let us first observe that each bit σ_i of σ is a linear combination of a small number of bits x_j:

$$\sigma_i = \sum_{j:S_{ij}=1} x_j \tag{2}$$

where S_{ij} denotes the entry of S at row i and column j and the bits of x are highly biased, as we have

$$\mathbf{prob}(x_i = 1) = \frac{w_c}{n} \text{ for } i \in \{1, \cdots, k\}. \tag{3}$$

$$\mathbf{prob}(x_i = 1) = \frac{w_c}{n} + \frac{w}{n-k} - 2\frac{ww_c}{n(n-k)} \approx \frac{w_c}{n} + \frac{w}{n-k} \text{ for } i \in \{k+1, \cdots, n\}. \tag{4}$$

This already allows to find for a given position i the number of x_j's for j in $\{1, \ldots, k\}$ and the number of x_j's for $j \in \{k+1, \ldots, n\}$ that appear in the linear combination (2) defining σ_i. For this we assume that the x_j's are independent and that their distribution is given by (3) and (4). This can be obtained by computing estimates of $\mathbf{prob}(\sigma_i = 1)$ and the piling up lemma [Mat93]

Proposition 1. *Assume that the x_j's are independent Benoulli random variables and that their distribution is given by (3) and (4). Let*

$$l_i \stackrel{def}{=} \#\{j \in \{1, \ldots, k\} : S_{ij} = 1\}.$$
$$r_i \stackrel{def}{=} \#\{j \in \{k+1, \ldots, n\} : S_{ij} = 1\}.$$

Then

$$\mathbf{prob}(\sigma_i = 1) = \frac{1 - (1 - 2w_c/n)^{l_i+r_i}(1 - 2w/(n-k))^{r_i}}{2}$$

Computing an estimate for $\mathbf{prob}(\sigma_i = 1)$ by using a bunch of signatures allows to recover for each position the numbers l_i and r_i. This gives all of the row weights of S, but we can go beyond this by taking advantage of the correlations between the bits of σ.

If σ_i and σ_j do not share a common bit in the associated linear combination (for instance $\sigma_i = x_1 + x_{3000}$ whereas $\sigma_j = x_{1300} + x_{2780} + x_{4000}$) then we may expect that σ_i and σ_j are independent and there is no significant statistical correlation between them. On the other hand, when σ_i and σ_j share a same bit x_t in their associated linear combination (for instance $\sigma_i = x_1 + x_{3000}$ whereas

$\sigma_j = x_{1300} + x_{3000} + x_{4000})$ σ_i and σ_j are clearly correlated as explained by the following proposition.

Proposition 2. *Let* X_1, X_2, X_3 *be independent Bernoulli variables such that* $\mathbf{prob}(X_i = 1) = p_i$, $\sigma_1 \overset{def}{=} X_1 + X_3$ *and* $\sigma_2 \overset{def}{=} X_2 + X_3$. *Then if* $p_3 \notin \{0, 1\}$, $p_1, p_2 \neq \frac{1}{2}$, *we have that* σ_1 *and* σ_2 *are correlated with*

$$\mathrm{Cov}(\sigma_1, \sigma_2) \overset{def}{=} \mathbb{E}(\sigma_1 \sigma_2) - \mathbb{E}(\sigma_1)\mathbb{E}(\sigma_2) = p_3(1 - p_3)(1 - 2p_1)(1 - 2p_2).$$

This proposition is proved in Sect. A of the appendix. By computing estimates for all $\mathrm{Cov}(\sigma_i, \sigma_j)$ we know if the associated linear combinations (2) corresponding to σ_i and σ_j share a common x_t. From this information we easily obtain $\boldsymbol{S}$ up to a column permutation as shown in Sect. 4.

3.2   An Additional Source of Correlations

This method works as long as the low codewords of the LDGM code do not introduce another source of correlations that competes with the aforementioned correlations. These correlations are in essence a consequence of a rather subtle interplay between these codewords and the rows of $\boldsymbol{S}$. To explain this new source of correlations let us introduce some notation.

Notation 1. *Let* (i, j) *be a pair of signature positions. We denote by* $n(i, j)$ *the number of rows of* $\boldsymbol{G}' = \boldsymbol{G}\boldsymbol{S}^T$ *whose support contains both* i *and* j. *We will also use the notation* n_i *for the number of rows of* $\boldsymbol{G}'$ *whose support contains position* i. *Finally, we denote by* $\boldsymbol{g}'_i$ *the* i-*th row of* $\boldsymbol{G}'$.

Roughly speaking, large values of $n(i, j)$ explain the correlations between positions i and j. To understand this link, let us first observe that from (1) we know that a signature $\boldsymbol{\sigma}$ can be written as $\boldsymbol{\sigma} = (\boldsymbol{e} + \boldsymbol{c})\boldsymbol{S}^T$ where $\boldsymbol{c}$ is a sum of m_G rows of the matrix $\boldsymbol{G}$. This implies that

$$\boldsymbol{\sigma} = \sum_{s=1}^{m_G} \boldsymbol{g}'_{i_s} + \boldsymbol{e}\boldsymbol{S}^T \tag{5}$$

Here it should be noticed that the weight of the rows $\boldsymbol{g}'_i$ is rather small compared to the length n of these rows (think of about 180 for the parameters proposed for 80 bits of security in [BBC+13] whereas the length is 9600). Moreover the weight of $\boldsymbol{e}\boldsymbol{S}^T$ is approximately of the same order as the weight of the $\boldsymbol{g}'_i$'s. This means that if σ_i is equal to 1, this is generally due to the fact that one of these rows $\boldsymbol{g}'_{i_s}$ has a 1 in the i-th position. Moreover since the weight of the $\boldsymbol{g}'_i$'s is small compared to the length of these vectors, their intersection is in general very small, meaning that if σ_i is equal to 1, this is generally due to the fact that there is exactly one of the $\boldsymbol{g}'_{i_j}$ that has an i-th coordinate equal to 1. Here (positive) correlations appear precisely when $n(i, j)$ is unusually large, that is larger than we would expect if the $\boldsymbol{g}'_i$ behaved at random. In such a case when σ_i and σ_j are both equal to 1, this is rather often due to one of those $n(i, j)$ rows

g'_u that appears in both linear combinations (5) defining σ_i and σ_j (and whose i-th and j-th coordinates are both equal to 1).

To put things on a more quantitive level, we would expect that

$$\mathbb{E}(n(i,j)) = k\frac{\binom{n-2}{m_S w_G - 2}}{\binom{n}{m_S w_G}} \approx \frac{km_S^2 w_G^2}{n^2}.$$

If $n(i,j)$ is greater than this quantity, then positive correlations appear.

Large values of $n(i,j)$ appear either because

(i) of the aforementioned phenomenon: the linear combinations (2) defining σ_i and σ_j share a common x_t. This happens when the support of the i-th row of S and the support of the j-th row of S share a common position (i.e. position t here). In such a case we denote by $n_1(i,j)$ the Hamming weight of the t-th column of G.

(ii) or a certain interplay between the rows of G and the rows of S that occurs when there are rows of G whose support contains an element of the support of the i-th row of S and an element of the support of the j-th row of S. We let $n_2(i,j)$ be the number of such rows.

We clearly have that the second case is more general than the first one and a row of G' is non zero in position i and position j is such that the row of the same index in G has a support that has to intersect both the support of the i-th row and the j-th row of S. In other words:

$$n_2(i,j) \geq n_1(i,j) \tag{6}$$
$$n(i,j) \leq n_2(i,j). \tag{7}$$

Notice that we generally have $n(i,j) = n_2(i,j)$ and if $n_1(i,j) \neq 0$ then we generally have $n(i,j) = n_1(i,j) = n_2(i,j)$.

Correlations between σ_i and σ_j allow to detect large values of $n(i,j)$. In case (i) we obtain directly information on the rows of S, however the second case does not seem to give direct information on S since it involves both G' (that we do not know) and S. There is however a way to distinguish between the cases $n_1(i,j) \neq 0$ and $n_1(i,j) = 0$. This comes from the following phenomenon in the first case.

Fact 2. *Consider a column of index t of S and denote by $\{i_1, \ldots, i_s\}$ the set of rows where this column has a 1 at that position. Then all possible pairs (i_a, i_b) are correlated because σ_{i_a} and σ_{i_b} share a common x_t.*

Let us define a graph with vertex set the set of positions $\{1, \ldots, n\}$ and where two positions are linked together with an edge if they are sufficiently correlated. Of course this graph depends on the threshold we choose for deciding whether two positions are sufficiently correlated or not. Correlations of the first kind give rise to cliques associated to columns of S where the size of the clique is the weight of the column. Recall that a clique of a graph is a subset of vertices which are linked together with edges of the graph (every two distinct vertices in the clique are adjacent). The second source of correlations is unlikely to yield such cliques and this phenomenon is used in the next section to distinguish between both sources of correlations. It will be essential to recognize the first source of correlation in order to recover S up to a column permutation.

3.3 Obtaining Low Weight Codewords of the Code with Parity-Check Matrix H'

Correlations also allow to obtain codewords of the code with parity-check matrix H'. Note that this code is known to an attacker since H' is public. It will be handy to introduce the following notation

Definition 1 (public code $\mathscr{C}_{\text{pub}}$). *The code with parity-check matrix H' is denoted by $\mathscr{C}_{pub}$.*

We can also observe that the matrix $G' = GS^T$ is a generator matrix of this code. It can be used to "perturb" signatures (by changing their Hamming weight), without changing the syndrome $H'\sigma^T$ of the signature. It is actually used exactly in this way in the signature scheme. Note that this is also an LDGM code since G' has rows of weight $\leq m_S w_G$. Such rows allow to add small perturbations to the signature and they are used later on in our attack.

Some of these rows can be recovered in the following fashion. Assume that we have obtained a set of valid signatures S and that i and j are two positions that are correlated. Consider in this case the following subset of S:

$$\Sigma(i,j) \stackrel{\text{def}}{=} \{\text{signatures } \sigma \in S : \sigma_i = \sigma_j = 1\}. \tag{8}$$

When σ_i and σ_j are significantly correlated it turns out that a non negligible fraction of elements of $\Sigma(i,j)$ are of the form $\sum_{s=1}^{m_G} g'_{i_s} + eS^t$ where exactly one of those g'_{i_s} has a "1" in the i-th position and the j-th position. This means that such a g'_{i_s} is precisely one of the $n(i,j)$ rows of G' that have a 1 in the i-th and the j-th positions.

Such a phenomenon implies that if we consider the intersection of the supports of the pairs of elements σ^s and σ^t of $\Sigma(i,j)$, a fraction of order $\frac{1}{n(i,j)}$ of these intersections has an unusually large size which is precisely due to the pairs (σ^s, σ^t) that correspond to a pair of linear combinations $(\sum_{a=1}^{m_G} g'_{i_a} + e^s S^t, \sum_{b=1}^{m_G} g'_{i_b} + e^t S^t)$ that share a common g'_u that belongs to one of the $n(i,j)$ rows of G' that have a 1 in position i and j.

This phenomenon clearly points to an algorithm arranging signatures of $\Sigma(i,j)$ in $n(i,j)$ groups such that all the elements in a group have an unusual large intersection with each other. Each group corresponds here to one of the rows g'_l of G' that has a "1" in position i and j and the signatures in this group have an unusual large intersection precisely because they share this common g'_l in the linear combination (5) which defines them.

Roughly speaking, the idea of considering this set $\Sigma(i,j)$ is that it acts as a filter that gives signatures for which an unusual number of them has a large intersection, and this because a non negligible fraction of them uses one of the rows g'_l of G' that has a "1" in position i and j in the linear combination (5) that defines them.

To filter inside the set $\Sigma(i,j)$ the signatures that are of this form, it suffices to compute for each signature σ in this set the number $N(\sigma)$ of signatures in $\Sigma(i,j)$ different from σ that have an unusually large intersection with σ and to keep only those signatures for which $N(\sigma)$ is large. Setting up the threshold for deciding that two signatures have a large intersection is easily achieved by plotting the histogram of those intersections as shown by Fig. 1. Choosing the signatures σ of $\Sigma(i,j)$ for which $N(\sigma)$ is above this threshold yields a set that we denote by $\Sigma'(i,j)$. Then we form inside $\Sigma'(i,j)$ groups consisting of signatures which have all with each other a large intersection. This is done by considering the graph with vertices the elements of $\Sigma'(i,j)$ and putting an edge between two signatures if their intersection is sufficiently large (say greater than some threshold) and by looking for large cliques in this graph.

Once we have such groups we can recover from them some of the rows of G'. Indeed, for each of those groups we can recover the common element g'_u in the linear combination (5) corresponding to these signatures. The support of g'_u is easily obtained by counting for each position i the number N_i of signatures of the group that have a 1 in this position. The support of g'_u corresponds to the positions i for which N_i is unusually large.

4 Recovering S up to a Column Permutation

Computing the correlations between bits of the signature reveals pairs (i,j) of rows of S that have a "1" at the same position. Consider a function Θ whose purpose is to give the threshold for deciding whether a pair of position (i,j) is sufficiently correlated or not. It takes five inputs: x a real number that gives the computed correlation of the pair and four nonnegative integers that represent l_i, r_i, l_j and r_j respectively:

$$\Theta : \mathbb{R} \times \mathbb{N} \times \mathbb{N} \times \mathbb{N} \times \mathbb{N} \to \{0,1\}$$
$$(x, l_i, r_i, l_j, r_j) \mapsto \Theta(x, l_i, r_i, l_j, r_j)$$

In practice, it has been enough to suggest a relevant function for the "degree" $l_i + r_i$ of a position i, that is we chose a function $\Theta(x, l_i, r_i, l_j, r_j)$ depending only on $x, l_i + r_i$ and $l_j + r_j$. We associate to such a threshold function Θ a graph $\mathcal{G}_\Theta$ defined as follows

Definition 2 (Threshold graph). *The threshold graph $\mathcal{G}_\Theta$ associated to the threshold function is the graph with*

- *vertex set the set of signature positions,*
- *there is an edge between i and j if and only if $\Theta(\text{empCov}(\sigma_i, \sigma_j), l_i, r_i, l_j, r_j) = 1$, where $\text{empCov}(\sigma_i, \sigma_j)$ denotes the empirical covariance between σ_i and σ_j that is computed from the available set of signatures.*

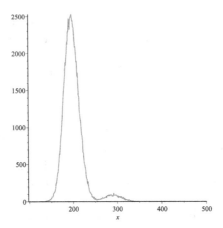

Fig. 1. Distribution of the weights of the intersections of every pair of signatures in $\Sigma(i, j)$. Here the threshold is set at a weight of about 250.

Let $\mathcal{G}_{\text{sec}}$ be the graph with the same set of vertices and there is an edge between i and j if and only if the i-th row and j-th row of S have a "1" in common. Our aim is to recover $\mathcal{G}_{\text{sec}}$ by using $\mathcal{G}_{\Theta}$. Note that cliques in $\mathcal{G}_{\text{sec}}$ (that is subset of vertices of $\mathcal{G}_{\text{sec}}$ that are all linked together by edges of $\mathcal{G}_{\text{sec}}$) correspond to columns of S, the clique correspond to all the rows of S where this column has a "1" entry. Recovering S up to a column permutation amounts to recover the cliques of $\mathcal{G}_{\text{sec}}$.

This is easily achieved by considering two different threshold functions Θ_1 and Θ_2. The first one is chosen in a conservative manner. More precisely, we choose Θ_1 such that whenever $\Theta_1(\text{empCov}(\sigma_i, \sigma_j), l_i, r_i, l_j, r_j) = 1$ there is an edge between i and j in $\mathcal{G}_{\text{sec}}$ (i.e. this threshold is chosen in such a way, that if we declare that there is a correlation between i and j it always corresponds to two rows of S that have a "1" in common). To put it differently, $\mathcal{G}_{\Theta_1}$ is a subgraph of $\mathcal{G}_{\text{sec}}$. The second threshold is chosen in a much less conservative way so that we never miss an edge of $\mathcal{G}_{\text{sec}}$, i.e. when there is an edge between i and j in $\mathcal{G}_{\text{sec}}$, then $\Theta_2(\text{empCov}(\sigma_i, \sigma_j), l_i, r_i, l_j, r_j) = 1$. In other words, $\mathcal{G}_{\text{sec}}$ is a subgraph of $\mathcal{G}_{\Theta_2}$ this time. In our experiments, we have always been able to choose Θ_1 and Θ_2 in this way.

Cliques of $\mathcal{G}_{\text{sec}}$ are found by adding edges to $\mathcal{G}_{\Theta_1}$ and finding cliques in the "augmented" graph by closing triangles in $\mathcal{G}_{\Theta_1}$ whenever there was such a triangle in $\mathcal{G}_{\Theta_2}$. More precisely, we add an edge between i and k in $\mathcal{G}_{\Theta_1}$ when there was a j for which there are edges between i and j and between j and k in $\mathcal{G}_{\Theta_1}$ and $\{i, j, k\}$ forms a triangle in $\mathcal{G}_{\Theta_2}$ meaning that there are edges between i and j, between i and k and between j and k in $\mathcal{G}_{\Theta_2}$. We have been able to recover all cliques in $\mathcal{G}_{\text{sec}}$ by this simple algorithm in all cases when the columns of S were of weight at least 3, meaning that all vertices of $\mathcal{G}_{\text{sec}}$ are involved in at least one clique which contains a triangle. We ended up here with a matrix

S_p that is equal to S up to a column permutation.

$$S_p = S\Pi$$

where Π is a permutation matrix for which we can assume that it is formed by circulant blocks of size p (by reordering S_p in such a way that it is formed only by circulant blocks of size p).

5   Recovering Q up to a Column Permutation

The previous attack lead to find S up to a column permutation. This will lead us to recover Q up to a permutation too. We will need for this the following proposition.

Proposition 3. *Let $M_{r_0 \times r_0}$ be the ring of $r_0 p \times r_0 p$ matrices formed by circulant blocks of size $p \times p$ and let $A_{r_0 \times r_0}$ be the subset of matrices of $M_{r_0 \times r_0}$ which are formed only by 0 blocks $\boldsymbol{0}_{p \times p}$ or by all-ones blocks $\boldsymbol{1}_{p \times p}$. $A_{r_0 \times r_0}$ is a subring of $M_{r_0 \times r_0}$ which is stable by multiplication*

$$A_{r_0 \times r_0} M_{r_0 \times r_0} = M_{r_0 \times r_0} A_{r_0 \times r_0} = A_{r_0 \times r_0}.$$

The inverse of Q is of the form $T^{-1} + A$ where A belongs to $A_{r_0 \times r_0}$.

The proof of this proposition is given in the appendix. Recall now that we have a matrix S_p which up to a column permutation is equal to S, that is

$$S_p = S\Pi \tag{9}$$

Recall now the following relation between the public parity-check matrix H' and the secret one H:

$$H' = Q^{-1} H S^{-1}.$$

We also have $H = (P \,|\, I)$. By putting all these equations together and by multiplying H' on the right by S_p we obtain

$$\begin{aligned}
H' S_p &= Q^{-1} H S^{-1} S_p \\
&= Q^{-1} (P \,|\, I) S^{-1} S\Pi \\
&= Q^{-1} (P \,|\, I) \Pi \\
&= (Q^{-1} P \,|\, Q^{-1}) \Pi
\end{aligned}$$

By using Proposition 3, we obtain

$$H' S_p = ((T^{-1} + A)P \,|\, (T^{-1} + A)) \Pi \tag{10}$$

for some A that belongs to $A_{r_0 \times r_0}$. We claim that we can find in $H' S'_p$ the columns that correspond to $T^{-1} + A$. Indeed in the matrix A the columns that belong to the same circulant block of size p are equal. Adding T^{-1} which is a permutation matrix just changes one entry per column. In other words columns belonging to the same circulant block of $T^{-1} + A$ are all at Hamming distance 2 from each other. Such groups of columns can easily be detected and we can find a permutation matrix Π' in $M_{n_0 \times n_0}$ such that

$$H'S_p\Pi' = \left(Q^{-1}P\Pi_l \mid Q^{-1}\Pi_r\right) \tag{11}$$

for some permutation matrices Π_l and Π_r in $M_{k_0 \times k_0}$ and $M_{r_0 \times r_0}$ respectively. Then we set

$$S'_p = S_p\Pi'$$
$$Q_p = (Q^{-1}\Pi_r)^{-1} = \Pi_r^{-1}Q$$

6   Forging New Signatures

We are ready now to put all the pieces together. Forging is performed by using the pair of matrices (Q_p, S'_p) instead of the pair (Q, S). To sign a message m we proceed as follows

1. The forger computes $s = \mathcal{F}(\mathcal{H}(m))$ which is an element of $\{0,1\}^{n-k}$ of weight w. He checks whether $bs^T = 0$. If this is the case he goes to the next step. If not, he appends a counter l to $\mathcal{H}(m)$ to obtain $\mathcal{H}(m)\|l$ and computes $\mathcal{F}$ applied to $\mathcal{H}(m)\|l$ until getting a syndrome s of weight w that satisfies $bs^T = 0$
2. He computes $s'^T = Q_p s^T$. This syndrome has weight $\leq m_T w$
3. The forger sets $e = \underbrace{00\cdots0}_{k}\|s'$
4. The forged signature is then computed as $\sigma = eS'_p{}^T$.

It can be verified that σ is a valid signature since

(i) $H'\sigma^T = s^T$, because

$$H'\sigma^T = H'S'_p e^T$$
$$= H'S_p\Pi' e^T$$
$$= \left(Q^{-1}P\Pi_l \mid Q^{-1}\Pi_r\right)\left(0_k \; s'\right)^T \quad \text{(follows from (11))}$$
$$= \left(Q^{-1}P\Pi_l \mid Q_p^{-1}\right)\begin{pmatrix} 0_k^T \\ Q_p s^T \end{pmatrix}$$
$$= s^T$$

(ii) It is readily verified that the signature σ has Hamming weight at most $m_T m_S w$ which is smaller than $(m_T w + w_c)m_S$.

It could be argued that this weight is significantly smaller than the weight of a genuine signature which should be typically slightly less than $(m_T w + w_c)m_S$ and that this could be detected. This attack can be improved in order to achieve the "right" weight of $(m_T w + w_c)m_S$ as follows. During the recovery process of $\boldsymbol{S}$ we have found rows of $\boldsymbol{G}'$. These rows have weight of about $w_G m_S$. Since such rows are in the public code $\mathscr{C}_{\text{pub}}$ which has parity-check matrix $\boldsymbol{H}'$ we can add m_G of them to $\boldsymbol{\sigma}$ without changing the syndrome $\boldsymbol{H}'\boldsymbol{\sigma}^T$. However this adds a Hamming weight of about $m_G w_G m_S = w_c m_S$ to the signature which is precisely the weight we want to achieve.

7 Experimental Results

Running the whole attack was performed on the parameters suggested for 80 bits of security of [BBC+13] namely (Table 1)

Table 1. Parameters for 80 bits of security.

n	k	p	w	w_g	w_c	z	m_T	m_s
9800	4900	50	18	20	160	2	1	9

We used $100,000$ signatures to perform the attack which was implemented in Sage and took about one hour on a 6-core Intel® Xeon® running at 3.20 GHz. It was performed on matrices $\boldsymbol{S}$ which were either regular (constant column and row weight equal to w_S) or irregular.

8 Conclusion

We have demonstrated here that correlations between some of the bits of the signature that can be observed in the signature scheme proposed in [BBC+13] can be used to recover enough of the secret information to be able to forge new signatures. Our attack was performed on the parameters devised for 80 bits of security, used $100,000$ signatures for this task and took about one hour. The real reason why this attack was possible comes from these correlations and has not to be attributed to other features of the parameters proposed in [BBC+13] (for instance $\boldsymbol{T}$ was chosen as a permutation matrix, the way $\boldsymbol{S}$ is chosen is not completely specified in [BBC+13] –we chose it to be either regular or irregular). Arguably, there is one place where our attack used a particular feature of the matrix $\boldsymbol{S}$, namely that its columns were at least of weight 3 –see Fact 2 where cliques in the threshold graph were used to detect correlations of type (i) (see Subsect. 3.2). When $\boldsymbol{S}$ has columns of weight 1 or 2, the strategy outlined in Sect. 4 does not work anymore and this might require more elaborate strategies to break the scheme in such a case. It is unlikely that such a modification is able to avoid attacks using these correlations. For all these reasons, it seems to us that the scheme proposed in [BBC+13] could only be used in one-time (or few-times) signature schemes.

Acknowledgment. The authors would like to thank the anonymous reviewers for their valuable comments and suggestions which were very helpful for improving the quality of the paper.

A   Proof of Proposition 2

Recall this proposition first.

Proposition. *Let* X_1, X_2, X_3 *be independent Bernoulli variables such that* $\mathbf{prob}(X_i = 1) = p_i$, $\sigma_1 \stackrel{\text{def}}{=} X_1 + X_3$ *and* $\sigma_2 \stackrel{\text{def}}{=} X_2 + X_3$. *Then if* $p_3 \notin \{0, 1\}$, $p_1, p_2 \neq \frac{1}{2}$, *we have that* σ_1 *and* σ_2 *are correlated with*

$$\mathrm{Cov}(\sigma_1, \sigma_2) \stackrel{\text{def}}{=} \mathbb{E}(\sigma_1\sigma_2) - \mathbb{E}(\sigma_1)\mathbb{E}(\sigma_2) = p_3(1 - p_3)(1 - 2p_1)(1 - 2p_2).$$

Proof. Let us compute the probability that σ_1 and σ_2 are both equal to 1. We have

$$\begin{aligned}
\mathbf{prob}(\sigma_1 = 1, \sigma_2 = 1) &= \mathbf{prob}(X_3 = 1)\mathbf{prob}(X_1 = 0)\mathbf{prob}(X_2 = 0) \\
&\quad + \mathbf{prob}(X_3 = 0)\mathbf{prob}(X_1 = 1)\mathbf{prob}(X_2 = 1) \\
&= p_3(1 - p_1)(1 - p_2) + (1 - p_3)p_1p_2
\end{aligned}$$

On the other hand by using Proposition 1 we have

$$\begin{aligned}
\mathbf{prob}(\sigma_1 = 1) &= p_1 + p_3 - 2p_1p_3 \\
\mathbf{prob}(\sigma_2 = 1) &= p_2 + p_3 - 2p_2p_3
\end{aligned}$$

A straighforward computation leads now to

$$\begin{aligned}
\mathrm{Cov}(\sigma_1, \sigma_2) &= \mathbf{prob}(\sigma_1 = 1, \sigma_2 = 1) - \mathbf{prob}(\sigma_1 = 1)\mathbf{prob}(\sigma_2 = 1) \\
&= p_3(1 - p_1)(1 - p_2) + (1 - p_3)p_1p_2 \\
&\quad -(p_1 + p_3 - 2p_1p_3)(p_2 + p_3 - 2p_2p_3) \\
&= p_3\left[(1 - p_1)(1 - p_2) - p_1p_2 - (1 - 2p_1)p_2 - (1 - 2p_2)p_1 \right. \\
&\quad \left. -(1 - 2p_1)(1 - 2p_2)p_3\right] + p_1p_2 - p_1p_2 \\
&= p_3\left[1 - p_1 - p_2 + p_1p_2 - p_1p_2 - p_2 + 2p_1p_2 - p_1 \right. \\
&\quad \left. +2p_1p_2 - (1 - 2p_1)(1 - 2p_2)p_3\right] \\
&= p_3\left[1 - 2p_1 - 2p_2 + 4p_1p_2 - (1 - 2p_1)(1 - 2p_2)p_3\right] \\
&= p_3\left[(1 - 2p_1)(1 - 2p_2) - (1 - 2p_1)(1 - 2p_2)p_3\right] \\
&= p_3(1 - p_3)(1 - 2p_1)(1 - 2p_2)
\end{aligned}$$

B   Proof of Proposition 3

Before we prove this proposition it will be very convenient to recall the following ring isomorphism Ψ between the ring of circulant binary matrices $\mathcal{M}_p$ of size

$p \times p$ and $\mathbb{F}_2[X]/(1 + X^p)$ which is given by

$$\Psi : \mathcal{M}_p \to \mathbb{F}_2[X]/(1 + X^p)$$

$$\begin{pmatrix} a_0 & a_1 & \dots & a_{p-1} \\ a_{p-1} & a_0 & \dots & a_{p-2} \\ \dots & \dots & \ddots & \dots \\ a_1 & a_2 & \dots & a_0 \end{pmatrix} \mapsto a_0 + a_1 X + \dots + a_{p-1} X^{p-1}$$

With this isomorphism we can view a $r_0 p \times r_0 p$ binary matrix formed by circulant blocks of size $p \times p$ as a $r_0 \times r_0$ matrix over $\mathbb{F}_2[X]/(1 + X^p)$ by replacing each of these circulant blocks by its image by the isomorphism Ψ to them.

We will also use the following property of the set $C_p \stackrel{\text{def}}{=} \{0, 1 + X + \dots + X^{p-1}\}$ of $\mathbb{F}_2[X]/(X^p - 1)$

Lemma 1. C_p is an ideal of $\mathbb{F}_2[X]/(X^p - 1)$.

Proof. This is just a straighforward use of the well known theory of cyclic codes: $1 + X + \dots + X^{p-1}$ divides $1 + X^p$ and C_p is nothing but the cyclic code generated by $1 + X + \dots + X^{p-1}$, see [MS86] (it is in fact a way of viewing the repetition code as a cyclic code). From this theory it follows that C_p is an ideal of $\mathbb{F}_2[X]/(X^p - 1)$.

Proposition 3 can now be rephrased as

Proposition 4. *Let $M^{\psi}_{r_0 \times r_0}$ be the ring of $r_0 \times r_0$ matrices over $\mathbb{F}_2[X]/(X^p - 1)$ and let $A^{\psi}_{r_0 \times r_0}$ be the ring of $r_0 \times r_0$ matrices over C_p. $A^{\psi}_{r_0 \times r_0}$ is a subring of $M^{\psi}_{r_0 \times r_0}$ which is stable by multiplication*

$$A^{\psi}_{r_0 \times r_0} M^{\psi}_{r_0 \times r_0} = M^{\psi}_{r_0 \times r_0} A^{\psi}_{r_0 \times r_0} = A^{\psi}_{r_0 \times r_0}.$$

The inverse of Q^{ψ} is of the form $(T^{\psi})^{-1} + A^{\psi}$ where A belongs to $A^{\psi}_{r_0 \times r_0}$, where we denote for a matrix M in $A_{r_0 \times r_0}$ by M^{ψ} the matrix where we have replaced every circulant block M_{ij} by $\psi(M_{ij})$.

Proof. The first part follows immediately from Lemma 1. T^{ψ} is invertible and therefore

$$(Q^{\psi})^{-1} = (T^{\psi} + R^{\psi})^{-1}$$
$$= (T^{\psi})^{-1}(I + (T^{\psi})^{-1} R^{\psi})^{-1}$$

We use now the first part of the proposition to deduce that $A^{\Psi} \stackrel{\text{def}}{=} (T^{\psi})^{-1} R^{\psi}$ belongs to $A^{\psi}_{r_0 \times r_0}$. Now it easy to prove that $(I + A^{\Psi})^{-1} = I + B^{\Psi}$ for some matrix B^{Ψ} in $A^{\Psi}_{r_0 \times r_0}$. This follows immediately from the formula

$$(I + A^{\Psi})^{-1} = \frac{1}{\det(I + A^{\psi})} C^T$$

where C is the cofactor matrix of $I + A^\Psi$, namely the matrix where the entry c_{ij} is equal to the (i,j)-minor, that is the determinant of the $(r_0 - 1) \times (r_0 - 1)$ matrix that results from deleting row i and column j of $I + A^\Psi$. Here Lemma 1 is used to conclude that any product that contains an element of C_p yields an element in C_p. We also use the fact that any product of the form $(1 + a)(1 + b)$ where a and b belong to C_p is of the form $1 + c$ where c belongs to C_p.

References

[BBC+13] Baldi, M., Bianchi, M., Chiaraluce, F., Rosenthal, J., Schipani, D.: Using LDGM codes and sparse syndromes to achieve digital signatures. In: Gaborit, P. (ed.) PQCrypto 2013. LNCS, vol. 7932, pp. 1–15. Springer, Heidelberg (2013)

[BMS11] Barreto, P.S.L.M., Misoczki, R., Simplicio Jr., M.A.: One-time signature scheme from syndrome decoding over generic error-correcting codes. J. Syst. Softw. **84**(2), 198–204 (2011)

[CFS01] Courtois, N.T., Finiasz, M., Sendrier, N.: How to achieve a McEliece-based digital signature scheme. In: Boyd, C. (ed.) ASIACRYPT 2001. LNCS, vol. 2248, pp. 157–174. Springer, Heidelberg (2001)

[COV07] Cayrel, P.-L., Otmani, A., Vergnaud, D.: On kabatianskii-krouk-smeets signatures. In: Carlet, C., Sunar, B. (eds.) WAIFI 2007. LNCS, vol. 4547, pp. 237–251. Springer, Heidelberg (2007)

[FGO+11] Faugère, J.-C., Gauthier, V., Otmani, A., Perret, L., Tillich, J.-P.: A distinguisher for high rate McEliece cryptosystems. In: Proceedings of IEEE Information Theory Workshop- ITW 2011, pp. 282–286, Paraty, Brasil, October 2011

[FGO+13] Faugère, J.-C., Gauthier, V., Otmani, A., Perret, L., Tillich, Jean-Pierre: A distinguisher for high rate McEliece cryptosystems. IEEE Trans. Inform. Theor. **59**(10), 6830–6844 (2013)

[Fin10] Finiasz, M.: Parallel-CFS. In: Biryukov, A., Gong, G., Stinson, D.R. (eds.) SAC 2010. LNCS, vol. 6544, pp. 159–170. Springer, Heidelberg (2011)

[GRSZ14] Zémor, G., Ruatta, O., Schrek, J., Gaborit, P.: RankSign: an efficient signature algorithm based on the rank metric. In: Mosca, M. (ed.) PQCrypto 2014. LNCS, vol. 8772, pp. 88–107. Springer, Heidelberg (2014)

[GSJB14] Gligoroski, D., Samardjiska, S., Jacobsen, H., Bezzateev, S.: McEliece in the world of Escher. IACR Cryptology ePrint Archive, Report 2014/360 (2014). http://eprint.iacr.org/

[KKS97] Kabatianskii, G., Krouk, E., Smeets, B.: A digital signature scheme based on random error-correcting codes. In: Darnell, Michael J. (ed.) Cryptography and Coding 1997. LNCS, vol. 1355. Springer, Heidelberg (1997)

[KKS05] Kabatianskii, G., Krouk, E., Smeets, B.J.M.: Error Correcting Coding and Security for Data Networks: Analysis of the Superchannel Concept. Wiley, New York (2005)

[LJ12] Löndahl, C., Johansson, T.: A new version of McEliece PKC based on convolutional codes. In: Chim, T.W., Yuen, T.H. (eds.) ICICS 2012. LNCS, vol. 7618, pp. 461–470. Springer, Heidelberg (2012)

[LS12] Landais, G., Sendrier, N.: Implementing CFS. In: Galbraith, S., Nandi, M. (eds.) INDOCRYPT 2012. LNCS, vol. 7668, pp. 474–488. Springer, Heidelberg (2012)

[LT13] Landais, G., Tillich, J.-P.: An efficient attack of a McEliece cryptosystem variant based on convolutional codes. In: Gaborit, P. (ed.) PQCrypto 2013. LNCS, vol. 7932, pp. 102–117. Springer, Heidelberg (2013)

[Mat93] Matsui, M.: Linear cryptanalysis method for DES cipher. In: Helleseth, T. (ed.) EUROCRYPT 1993. LNCS, vol. 765, pp. 386–397. Springer, Heidelberg (1994)

[MS86] MacWilliams, F.J., Sloane, N.J.A.: The Theory of Error-Correcting Codes, 5th edn. North-Holland, Amsterdam (1986)

[Nie86] Niederreiter, H.: Knapsack-type cryptosystems and algebraic coding theory. Probl. Control Inf. Theor. $15(2)$, 159–166 (1986)

[OT11] Otmani, A., Tillich, J.-P.: An efficient attack on all concrete KKS proposals. In: Yang, B.-Y. (ed.) PQCrypto 2011. LNCS, vol. 7071, pp. 98–116. Springer, Heidelberg (2011)

Vulnerabilities of "McEliece in the World of Escher"

Dustin Moody and Ray Perlner[(⊠)]

National Institute of Standards and Technology, Gaithersburg, MD, USA
{dustin.moody,ray.perlner}@nist.gov

Abstract. Recently, Gligoroski et al. proposed code-based encryption and signature schemes using list decoding, blockwise triangular private keys, and a nonuniform error pattern based on "generalized error sets." The general approach was referred to as *McEliece in the World of Escher*. This paper demonstrates attacks which are significantly cheaper than the claimed security level of the parameters given by Gligoroski et al. We implemented an attack on the proposed 80-bit parameters which was able to recover private keys for both encryption and signatures in approximately 2 hours on a single laptop. We further find that increasing the parameters to avoid our attack will require parameters to grow by (at least) two orders of magnitude for encryption, and may not be achievable at all for signatures.

Keywords: Information set decoding · Code-based cryptography · McEliece PKC · McEliece in the World of Escher

1 Introduction

The McEliece cryptosystem [McE78] is one of the oldest and most studied candidates for a postquantum cryptosystem. McEliece's original scheme used Goppa codes, but other families of codes have been proposed, such as moderate density parity check codes [MTSB12] and low rank parity check codes [GMRZ13, GRSZ14]. Recently, Gligoroski et al. [GSJB14, Gli] proposed a new approach to designing a code-based cryptosystem. Their approach uses a blockwise-triangular private key to enable decryption and signatures through a list decoding algorithm. The error vector in both cases is characterized, not by a maximum Hamming weight t, as is typical for code-based cryptosystems, but by an alphabet of allowed ℓ-bit substrings known as the *generalized error set*. Claimed advantages of this approach include a straightforward signature scheme and the ability to analyze security by using the tools of algebraic cryptanalysis.

The concept of information set decoding originates with Prange [Pra62]. Further optimizations were subsequently proposed by Lee and Brickell [LB88], Leon [Leo88], Stern [Ste89], and several others [FS09, BLP11, MMT11, BJMM12]. Information set decoding techniques can be used to attack code-based cryptosystems in several ways. They can be used to search for a low-weight error vector

© Springer International Publishing Switzerland 2016
T. Takagi (Ed.): PQCrypto 2016, LNCS 9606, pp. 104–117, 2016.
DOI: 10.1007/978-3-319-29360-8_8

directly, or they can be used to detect hidden structure in the public generator or parity check matrices by finding low weight code words in the row space of the generator matrix or parity check matrix. All of these applications of information set decoding are relevant to the scheme of Gligoroski et al. We will refer to their scheme as *McEliece Escher*, since it was introduced in their paper *McEliece in the World of Escher* [GSJB14, Gli]. We demonstrate that information set decoding techniques are much more effective against the McEliece Escher scheme than suggested by the authors' original security analysis.

Gligoroski et al. were aware of both categories of information set decoding attacks on their scheme, but their analysis of these attacks was incomplete. Most seriously, they believed that information set decoding only produced a distinguisher on the private key, rather than a full key recovery, and they failed to consider the application of information set decoding to find a valid error vector in the signature setting. Landais and Tillich [LT13] applied similar techniques to convolutional codes, which have similar structure to the private keys used by McEliece Escher. We offer improvements to the existing approaches, including showing how to take advantage of the structured permutation used by McEliece Escher to disguise the private generator matrix.

Furthermore, we show our attacks are practical. Using the proposed parameters for 80-bits of security, we were able to recover private keys for both encryption and signatures in less than 2 h on a single laptop. We find that increasing the parameters to avoid our attack will require parameters to grow by (at least) two orders of magnitude for encryption, and may not be practical at all for signature.

2   Background: McEliece Schemes

2.1   Public and Private Keys

Gligoroski et al. construct their scheme along the lines of the original McEliece cryptosystem. The public key is a $k \times n$ generator matrix G_{pub} for a linear code over $\mathbb{F}_2$. To encrypt a message, the sender encodes a k-bit message m as an n bit codeword and then intentionally introduces errors by adding an error vector e. The ciphertext is then given by:

$$c = mG_{pub} + e.$$

Gligoroski et al. also introduce a signature scheme by applying the decoding algorithm to a hashed message. A signature σ is verified by checking

$$\mathcal{H}(m) = \sigma G_{pub} + e,$$

for a suitably chosen hash function $\mathcal{H}$.

Similar to the ordinary McEliece scheme, G_{pub} is constructed from a structured private generator matrix G, an arbitrary $k \times k$ invertible matrix S, and an $n \times n$ permutation matrix P.

$$G_{pub} = SGP. \tag{1}$$

For encryption, G_{pub} must be chosen in such a way that the private key allows unique decoding of a properly constructed ciphertext. For signatures, on the other hand, G_{pub} must be constructed to allow some decoding (not necessarily unique) of a randomly chosen message digest.

It will sometimes be helpful to characterize the public and private codes by their parity check matrices. The private parity check matrix, H is a $(n - k) \times n$ matrix, related to the private generator matrix G by the relation

$$GH^T = 0.$$

Similarly, it is easy to construct a public parity check matrix H_{pub} from G_{pub}, characterized by the relation $G_{pub}H_{pub}^T = 0$. This will be related to the private parity check matrix as

$$H_{pub} = S'HP,$$

where S' is an $(n - k) \times (n - k)$ invertible matrix and P is the same permutation matrix as in Eq. (1).

2.2   Private Generator and Parity Check Matrices

To construct the binary (n, k) code used in the McEliece Escher scheme, the (private) generator matrix is of the form illustrated in Fig. 1. Each block B_i is a random binary matrix of dimension $(\sum_{j=1}^{i} k_j) \times n_i$, so that $k = k_1 + k_2 + \cdots + k_w$ and $n = k + n_1 + n_2 + \cdots + n_w$. The corresponding private parity check matrix is depicted in Fig. 2, and has a similar block-wise structure. For ease of notation, we will let $K = (k_1, k_2, .., k_w)$ and $N = (n_1, n_2, .., n_w)$.

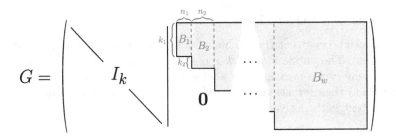

Fig. 1. The private generator matrix

2.3   Error Sets

In the McEliece Escher scheme, the error vector is broken up into n/ℓ segments, each ℓ-bits. The value ℓ is called the *granularity* of the scheme, and for all proposed parameter sets, ℓ is set to 2. While the original McEliece scheme restricted the error vectors to having a low Hamming weight t, the McEliece Escher scheme instead restricts the error space by choosing each ℓ-bit subsegment from a limited

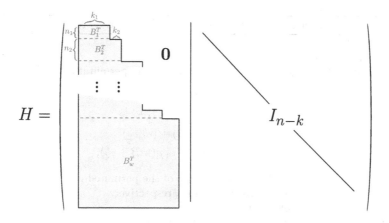

Fig. 2. The private parity check matrix

alphabet, called an *error set*. Error sets may be analyzed in terms of a density parameter ρ given by the formula

$$\rho = |E|^{1/\ell}.$$

For the proposed parameters, the error set is always $E = \{00, 01, 10\}$. This error set has granularity $\ell = 2$ and density $\rho = \sqrt{3}$.

Since public key operations require the encrypter or verifier to distinguish between valid and invalid error vectors, the permutation P used to disguise the private generator and parity check matrices must necessarily be of a special form. The action of P needs to rearrange ℓ-bit segments of the rows, but leave the segments themselves intact. In other words, P must consist of $\ell \times \ell$ blocks which are either 0 or the identity matrix I_ℓ.

3 Improving Information Set Decoding for the Error Vector

Information set decoding may be used to recover m and e from the ciphertext $c = mG_{pub} + e$. The basic strategy involves guessing k bits of the error vector and recovering the rest by linear algebra. One of the simplest information set decoding algorithms is given in Algorithm 1.

It should be clear that the number of iterations this algorithm requires is inversely proportional to the probability that an attacker can guess k bits of the error vector. As in the case of standard McEliece, the most probable guess for these k bits is the all zero vector. However, since McEliece Escher uses a nonuniform error pattern, the choice of the permutation P' has a significant effect on the probability of success. In their security analysis, Gligoroski et al. assumed that P' would be of similar form to the secret permutation matrix P used to disguise the private key. This has the effect of forcing the adversary to

---

Algorithm 1. Information set decoding for the error vector

Input: ciphertext c, and a parameter k

Output: message m, error e

  1. Permute the bits of the ciphertext by a random permutation matrix P':

$$c' = (mG_{pub} + e)P'$$
$$= mG_{pub}P' + eP'$$
$$= m(A|B) + (e'_1|e'_2)$$
$$= (mA + e'_1)|(mB + e'_2),$$

  where A and e'_1 are the first k columns of the permuted generator matrix $G_{pub}P'$ and permuted error vector eP', respectively.
  2. If A is not invertible, go to step 1.
  3. Guess e'_1. If correct the message can be reconstructed as

$$m = ((mA + e'_1) - e'_1)A^{-1}.$$

  The error vector is then $e = c - mG_{pub}$.
  4. If the error vector is properly formed (i.e., the Hamming weight is less than t for standard McEliece, or composed of ℓ-bit substrings from the proper generalized error set in McEliece Escher), return m and e. Otherwise go back to step 1 and start over with a new permutation P'.

---

guess all the bits in each ℓ-bit block chosen from a generalized error set. Thus the probability of each guess is ρ^{-k}. However, an attacker can do better by choosing a permutation that always separates the bits of an ℓ-bit block. For example, each bit is 0 two-thirds of the time when the error set is $E = \{00, 01, 10\}$, but both bits are 0 only one-third of the time. By guessing one bit within each 2-bit block, an attacker achieves a success probability of $(2/3)^k$, which is a significant improvement over the value $(1/\sqrt{3})^k$ assumed by Gligoroski et al.'s security analysis. Concretely, when used against Gligoroski et al.'s claimed 80-bit secure code with parameters $(n, k) = (1160, 160)$, the probability of a single guess of k bits of the error vector improves from 2^{-127} to 2^{-94}.

Similar improvements are available for more sophisticated decoding algorithms. In Sect. 5.1 of their paper [GSJB14], Gligoroski et al. analyze modifications to several information set decoding algorithms [LB88, Ste89, FS09, BLP11, MMT11, BJMM12], including several that use meet-in-the-middle strategies to try several guesses at once, and apply them to the case where $k = 256$. For our purposes these algorithms may be characterized by the number of bits $k + \lambda$ which are guessed, along with the Hamming weight p of those guesses. Whenever $p \cdot \log_2(\sqrt{3}) < (k + \lambda) \log_2(\frac{2}{\sqrt{3}})$, the modification described above decreases the complexity of decoding by a factor of at least $2^{(k+\lambda) \log_2(\frac{2}{\sqrt{3}}) - p \cdot \log_2(\sqrt{3})}$. This is true for some of the algorithms analyzed by Gligoroski et al. For example, Stern's algorithm is quoted as having a complexity of 2^{197} when applied to $k = 256$, however, with our modification, Stern's algorithm with $p = 2$ has a probability of success per iteration of approximately 2^{-136} corresponding to a complexity somewhere around 2^{150}. It does not however appear that a direct application of our modification improves the most efficient algorithm analyzed by Gligoroski et al., since p is apparently too large. This algorithm, adapted from the BJMM algorithm [BJMM12], is quoted as achieving a complexity of 2^{123}. It is possible that some sort of hybrid approach will provide an improvement. Nonetheless, for the remainder of this paper, we will assume that Gligoroski et al.'s analysis of the complexity of attacking the encryption algorithm, by direct search for a unique patterned error vector, is correct.

Algorithm 1, modified so that as many ℓ-bit blocks as possible of the error are spit between e_1' and e_2', is however an extremely effective method for signature forgery. For the error set $E = \{00, 01, 10\}$, when a 2-bit block is split between e_1' and e_2', the bit in e_1' may be forced to 0, and the pair of bits will remain within the error set, whether the corresponding bit in e_2' is set to 0 or 1. If all the bits of e_1' are set to 0, then the probability for the resultant error vector e to be a valid error vector is $(\frac{\sqrt{3}}{2})^{n-2k}$. For the claimed 80-bit secure signature code with parameters $(n, k) = (650, 306)$, this probability is approximately 2^{-8}.

4   Information Set Decoding for the Private Key

Information set decoding techniques can also be used to find low weight elements in the row spaces of matrices. In our case, we are interested in the public generator and parity check matrices, G_{pub} and H_{pub}. Note that elements of these public row spaces are related to the elements of the row spaces of the private generator and parity check matrices by the permutation P used in the construction of the public key:

$$vG_{pub} = ((vS)G)P,$$

$$v'H_{pub} = ((v'S')H)P,$$

where v and v' are k and $(n - k)$-bit row vectors respectively. Consequently, the result of an information set decoding attack on G_{pub} or H_{pub} will simply be the image under P of a low weight element of the row space of G or H. We thus examine the space of low weight vectors for encryption and signatures.

Recall the description of the private generator and parity check matrices given in Sect. 2.2. For encryption, the private key operation requires maintaining a list of at least ρ^{k_1} entries. This means that k_1 must be small in order for the scheme to be efficient. The first n_1 rows of H are forced by construction to have nonzero bits only in the $(n_1 + k_1)$ columns $C_j(H)$, with $1 \leq j \leq k_1$ or $k+1 \leq j \leq k+n_1$. Linear combinations of these rows will then produce approximately $\binom{n_1+k_1}{t}2^{-k_1}$ distinct row vectors of weight t. The general attack strategy will be to seek to sample from the images under P of this space of low weight row vectors, which are constrained to only contain nonzero bits in columns C_j, with the same bounds on j as above. We thereby learn the images of those columns, and once learned they can be removed from H_{pub}. The row space of the matrix formed by the remaining columns of H is the same as for the parity check matrix of a code of the same structure with $w' = w - 1$, $N' = (n_2, .., n_w)$, $K' = (k_2, .., k_w)$. Applying this strategy recursively will allow us to identify the underlying block structure and construct a new private key of the same form.

For signatures, the private key operation requires maintaining a list of at least $(2/\rho)^{n_w}$ entries. In order for the scheme to be efficient, n_w must be small. The last k_w rows of G have zero bits everywhere, except possibly in the $(k_w + n_w)$ columns $C_j(G)$, indexed by $(k - k_w + 1) \le j \le k$ and $(n - n_w + 1) \le j \le n$. Linear combinations of the rows will produce approximately $\binom{k_w + n_w}{t} 2^{-n_w}$ distinct row vectors of weight t. Similarly as done for encryption, the strategy for signatures will be to seek to sample from the images under P of this space of low weight row vectors, learning the images of the aforementioned columns. Once the columns have been learned, they can be removed from G_{pub} and the process recursively repeated since the row space of the matrix formed by the remaining columns of G is that of a parity check matrix for a code of the same form with $w' = w - 1$, $N' = (n_1, .., n_{w-1})$, $K' = (k_1, .., k_{w-1})$. See Fig. 3 for an illustration of the strategy for both encryption and signatures.

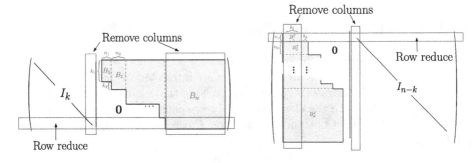

Fig. 3. Removing columns and row-reducing leaves a smaller code of the same form.

It should be noted that the space of short vectors with support on the target columns is not the only source of low weight vectors that can be obtained by information set decoding algorithms. However, for realistic parameters, it is generally advantageous to simply choose t to maximize the rate at which vectors from the target space are produced. This is because there is an efficient way to use a list of vectors, some of which are from the target space and some of which are not, to produce a full list of the target columns. The algorithm that does this uses a subroutine which is applied to a small subset of the list of vectors, and which will usually produce the full list of target columns if the chosen vectors are all from the target space. This subroutine will not only terminate quickly on correct inputs, but also if one of the vectors is not from the target space. In the latter case the algorithm will recognizably fail, by identifying too many columns. The first obtained list of vectors, required to recover the full target set of columns, will generally be small enough that trying the subroutine on all appropriately sized subsets of the list will be of insignificant cost compared to the information set decoding steps.

The subroutine proceeds as follows (see Algorithm 2). The input is a list of target columns, containing at least $(k_1 + 1)$ of the target columns for encryption (or at least $(n_w + 1)$ of the target columns for signatures). These columns may generally be obtained by combining the nonzero positions of a small number (e.g. two) of the target vectors produced by an information set decoding algorithm, such as Stern's algorithm.

Algorithm 2. Subroutine to complete the list of target columns

---

Input: A set S of columns

Output: A set of columns S' $\supseteq$ S, and a flag "Success" or "Failure"

1. Check whether removing the columns of S from the public matrix reduces the rank.
   - If all of the columns are from the target set, then removing the columns in S will likely reduce the rank of the public matrix by $|S| - k_1$ for encryption (or $|S| - n_w$ for signatures).
2. For each column C not in S, check whether the rank of the public matrix is decreased when C is removed in addition to those already in S.
   (a) if the rank is decreased, add C to S and repeat step 2.
   (b) if the rank stays the same for each $C \notin S$, return $S' = S$ and go to the last step to determine success.
3. The algorithm succeeds if the rank stops decreasing at $n - k - n_1$ for encryption (or $k - k_w$ for signatures). Otherwise output failure.

4.1   Using the Nonrandom P

The attack outlined in the previous section does not take into account the constraints on the permutation P used to disguise the private key G (or H). In particular, the permutation leaves blocks of ℓ consecutive columns intact. Thus, there is additional information about the location of our target columns that we did not use. In particular, if the column C_j is in our target set, we can be confident that all the columns $C_{\lfloor \frac{i-1}{\ell} \rfloor + 1}, ..., C_{\lfloor \frac{i-1}{\ell} \rfloor + \ell}$ are also in the target set. We modify Stern's algorithm to take advantage of this by choosing our random permutation P' in such a way as to leave ℓ-bit blocks of columns intact, just as the private matrix P does. We will also count the number of nonzero ℓ-bit blocks within a row vector as a substitute for Hamming weight, wherever Hamming weight is used by Stern's algorithm. We will refer to this altered weight as *block-weight*. Taking into account the special form of P also has other beneficial effects for the attacker. In particular, Algorithm 2 has a higher probability of success when the rank effects of the inclusion of blocks of ℓ columns (instead of individual columns) are considered, since it is much less likely for these blocks to be totally linearly dependent on each other, for reasons other than the overall block structure of the matrix.

The modified version of Stern's algorithm proceeds as shown in Algorithm 3. Note the Stern's algorithm window size will be denoted L, instead of the standard l, to avoid confusion with the granularity.

Algorithm 3. Modified Stern's Algorithm

Input: a matrix G_{pub}, parameters p, t, L, ℓ
Output: a vector in the row space of G_{pub} which has block-weight t

1. Permute the columns of G_{pub} :

$$G'_{pub} = G_{pub} P',$$

where P' is a permutation matrix consisting of $\ell \times \ell$ blocks which are either zero or the identity, but otherwise chosen randomly.

2. Check that the first k columns of the new matrix G'_{pub} form an invertible matrix A. If A is not invertible, go back to step 1.

3. Left-multiply by A^{-1}, resulting in a matrix of the form

$$M = A^{-1} G'_{pub} = [I_k \mid Q].$$

4. Search for low-weight row-vectors among linear combinations involving small subsets
   of the rows of M:

   (a) Divide the rows of M into two equal length lists, i.e.,
   for $0 < i \leq \frac{k}{2\ell}$, and for $B = (b_1, .., b_\ell) \in \mathbb{F}_2^\ell$

$$x_{i,B} = \sum_{r=1}^{\ell} b_r \mathrm{row}_{i\ell+r}(M).$$

   Similarly, for $\frac{k}{2\ell} < j \leq \frac{k}{\ell}$

$$y_{j,B} = \sum_{r=1}^{\ell} b_r \mathrm{row}_{j\ell+r}(M).$$

   (b) Compute each possible sum of all subsets of size p of the $x_{i,B}$, as well as for all possible sums of p of the $y_{j,B}$. Check for collisions on bits $(k+1), \ldots, (k+L)$:

$$\mathrm{bits}_{k+1,\ldots,k+L\ell}(x_{i_1,B_1} + \cdots + x_{i_p,B_p}) = \mathrm{bits}_{k+1,\ldots,k+L\ell}(y_{j_1,B_1} + \cdots + y_{j_p,B_p}).$$

   (c) When such a collision is found, compute the sum s of the $2p$ colliding row vectors
$$s = x_{i_1} + \ldots + x_{i_p} + y_{j_1} + \ldots + y_{j_p}.$$
   If the block-weight of any such s is equal to t return sP'. Otherwise, go back to step 1.

We now give an analysis of the complexity of obtaining the full list of target columns using this modified Stern's algorithm. Note that this analysis is only approximate, a tighter analysis may be possible using techniques similar to those outlined in Sect. 5 of [OT11]. For each block-weight t target vector g, the search will succeed if and only if gP' has block-weight p on its first $\frac{k}{2}$ bits, block-weight p on the next $\frac{k}{2}$ bits, and block-weight 0 on the next L bits. For a randomly chosen P' this probability is

$$\text{Prob}(n, k, p, \ell, L, t) = \binom{n/\ell}{t}^{-1} \binom{k/(2\ell)}{p}^2 \binom{(n-k-L)/\ell}{t-2p},$$

and the equivalent probability for an attack on H_{pub} is

$$\text{Prob}(n, n-k, p, \ell, L, t) = \binom{n/\ell}{t}^{-1} \binom{(n-k)/(2\ell)}{p}^2 \binom{(k-L)/\ell}{t-2p}.$$

The approximate number $\mathcal{D}$ of distinct target vectors of a given weight t is

$$\mathcal{D}_{sig} \approx \binom{(k_w + n_w)/\ell}{t} (2^\ell - 1)^t \cdot 2^{-n_w},$$

for signature, and for encryption

$$\mathcal{D}_{enc} \approx \binom{(n_1 + k_1)/\ell}{t} (2^\ell - 1)^t \cdot 2^{-k_1}.$$

The expected number $\mathcal{E}$ of target vectors required for a successful attack is

$$\mathcal{E}_{sig} \approx \left\lceil \frac{\log\left(\frac{k_w}{k_w + n_w}\right)}{\log\left(\frac{k_w + n_w - t\ell}{k_w + n_w}\right)} \right\rceil,$$

for signature, and for encryption

$$\mathcal{E}_{enc} \approx \left\lceil \frac{\log\left(\frac{n_1}{n_1 + k_1}\right)}{\log\left(\frac{n_1 + k_1 - t\ell}{n_1 + k_1}\right)} \right\rceil.$$

The total number of iterations of the modified Stern's algorithm is therefore

$$i_{sig} \approx \left\lceil \frac{\log(\frac{k_w}{k_w + n_w})}{\log(\frac{k_w + n_w - t\ell}{k_w + n_w})} \right\rceil \cdot \binom{(k_w + n_w)/\ell}{t}^{-1} (2^\ell - 1)^{-t} 2^{n_w}$$
$$\cdot \binom{n/\ell}{t} \binom{k/(2\ell)}{p}^{-2} \binom{(n-k-L)/\ell}{t-2p}^{-1},$$

and

$$i_{enc} \approx \left\lceil \frac{\log(\frac{n_1}{n_1 + k_1})}{\log(\frac{n_1 + k_1 - t\ell}{n_1 + k_1})} \right\rceil \cdot \binom{(n_1 + k_1)/\ell}{t}^{-1} (2^\ell - 1)^{-t} 2^{k_1}$$
$$\cdot \binom{n/\ell}{t} \binom{(n-k)/(2\ell)}{p}^{-2} \binom{(k-L)/\ell}{t-2p}^{-1}.$$

5   Experimental Results

We implemented the attacks described in the previous section on a standard laptop with a 2.2 GHZ Intel core i7 processor. We used the parameters suggested by Gligoroski et al. for 80 bits of security. Concretely, for encryption $n = 1160$, $k = 160, \ell = 2, w = 17$, with $K = (32, 8, 8, ..., 8)$ and $N = (32, 32, ..., 32, 488)$. We used parameters $(t, p, L) = (11, 1, 9)$ for the modified Stern's algorithm, which needed approximately 1000 iterations in our trials. The predicted value from the analysis in the previous section was 2500. The total wall time for the computation to recover a private key was on average less than 2 h.

For signatures, we have $n = 650, k = 306, \ell = 2, w = 6$, with $K = (84, 48, 48, 48, 48, 30)$ and $N = (48, 48, 48, 48, 48, 104)$. The modified Stern parameters we used were $(t, p, L) = (40, 1, 7)$. With such a high value for t, a higher number of iterations were needed, usually less than 10000 (the predicted value was around 4900). The total wall time was again less than 2 h on average.

6   Countermeasures

Attempts to increase the security of McEliece Escher by altering the parameters are severely constrained by the requirement that ρ^{k_1} be small for encryption and that $(2/\rho)^{n_w}$ be small for signatures.

One possiblility would be to try to decrease ρ (or $2/\rho$), as appropriate, to allow k_1 or n_w to increase. This, however, turns out to be counterproductive. Due to the attack in Sect. 4.1, we see what really matters for security is that k_1/ℓ be large for encryption, or n_w/ℓ be large for signatures. Asymptotically, there will be 2^ℓ vectors in the row space of H_{pub} of block-weight no more than $k_1/\ell + 1$ and 2^ℓ vectors in the row space of G_{pub} of block-weight no more than $n_w/\ell + 1$. The factor of 2^ℓ will make up for the increased cost per iteration of the modified Stern's algorithm with $p = 1$, but the probability of success per iteration will remain at approximately $(\frac{k}{n})^{k_1/\ell}$ for encryption and $(\frac{n-k}{n})^{n_w/\ell}$ for signatures. Encryption requires $(\rho^\ell)^{k_1/\ell}$ to be small for efficiency and k_1/ℓ to be large for security. Thus the ideal value for ρ and ℓ would minimize ρ^ℓ. Likewise, the signature scheme requires $((\frac{2}{\rho})^\ell)^{n_w/\ell}$ to be small for efficiency and n_w/ℓ to be large for security. Hence, the ideal value for ρ and ℓ would minimize $(\frac{2}{\rho})^\ell$.

While it is possible to decrease ρ (or $\frac{2}{\rho}$) by increasing ℓ, the consequence is that ρ^ℓ and $(\frac{2}{\rho})^\ell$ both increase at least linearly in ℓ for error sets of the proper form (for security, the generalized error set cannot impose linear constraints on the error vector, e.g. by forcing a bit of the error vector to always be 0). Thus, fixing $\frac{n}{k}$ and the security level, we find that the cost of decryption increases when we increase ℓ.

A better idea is to greatly increase n_w for encryption and k_w for signatures. This works by making $\frac{k}{n}$ very small for encryption and $\frac{n-k}{n}$ very small for signatures. In the context of an information set decoding attack, this has the effect of decreasing the probability that a given nonzero bit (or ℓ-bit block) of a target vector will be placed outside the information set by a randomly chosen (block) permutation. This is a much better solution for signatures than for encryption. For typical parameters, the modified Stern's algorithm requires ~ 30 nonzero blocks to fall outside the information set when attacking a signature. Thus, bringing the cost of the attack from $\sim 2^{30}$ to $\sim 2^{80}$ should only require $\frac{n-k}{n}$ to fall from about 0.5 to about 0.15. That is, the size of the 80-bit-secure code increases from a 650×304 bit generator matrix to a 2000×1654 bit generator matrix. For attacking typical encryption parameters, the modified Stern's algorithm only requires ~ 6 nonzero blocks to fall outside the information set. This means $\frac{k}{n}$ needs to fall from about 0.15 to 0.0005. The result is that for an 80-bit-secure code, the size would increase from 1160×160 to $300,000 \times 160$.

There is however an additional complication created by the above countermeasure for signatures. A code with error set $E = \{00, 01, 10\}$ can be trivially broken whenever $\frac{n-k}{n} < 0.5$ due to the attack described at the end of Sect. 3. This attack may be generalized to apply to other error sets, whenever there is a linear projection from $\mathbb{F}_2^\ell \to \mathbb{F}_2^{\ell'}$ with $\ell' \leq \frac{k}{n}\ell$ such that an element of $\mathbb{F}_2^\ell$ with a certain fixed projection onto $\mathbb{F}_2^{\ell'}$ is a member of the error set with very high probability. Thus in order to avoid attack, the error set must be chosen so that there is no such projection. We have not found any way to do this that makes the honest party's signing operation (list decoding for signatures) asymptotically more efficient than both attacks (ISD for the error vector and ISD for the private key.)

7   Conclusion

We demonstrate practical attacks on the proposed parameters of McEliece Escher. The poor choice of parameters is a demonstration of the general principle that code-based schemes should be designed in such a way as to avoid all practical distinguishers on the public key, since distinguishers can often be modified, at little cost, to create private-key recovery attacks. Additionally, our cryptanalysis demonstrates that information set decoding techniques can be modified to take advantage of code-based schemes whose private keys are disguised by a structured, rather than a completely random, permutation matrix. The recent cryptanalysis of cyclosymmetric-MDPC McEliece by Perlner [Per14] is another example of this general principle. This technique is especially effective in creating signature forgeries.

For encryption, it appears the above pitfalls can be compensated for, by simply making the parameters of McEliece Escher larger. However, this requires making the keys at least two orders of magnitude larger. This is a major burden on an already inefficient scheme. Asymptotically, these modifications can only make the complexity of a key-recovery attack quasi-polynomially worse than the complexity of decryption by the honest party.

References

[BJMM12] Becker, A., Joux, A., May, A., Meurer, A.: Decoding random binary linear codes in $2^{n/20}$: how $1 + 1 = 0$ improves information set decoding. In: Pointcheval, D., Johansson, T. (eds.) EUROCRYPT 2012. LNCS, vol. 7237, pp. 520–536. Springer, Heidelberg (2012)

[BLP11] Bernstein, D.J., Lange, T., Peters, C.: Smaller decoding exponents: ball-collision decoding. In: Rogaway, P. (ed.) CRYPTO 2011. LNCS, vol. 6841, pp. 743–760. Springer, Heidelberg (2011)

[FS09] Finiasz, M., Sendrier, N.: Security bounds for the design of code-based cryptosystems. In: Matsui, M. (ed.) ASIACRYPT 2009. LNCS, vol. 5912, pp. 88–105. Springer, Heidelberg (2009)

[Gli] Gligoroski, D.: A new code based public key encryption and signature scheme based on list decoding. Presented at Workshop on Cybersecurity in a Post-Quantum World, NIST, Gaithersburg MD, USA (2015)

[GMRZ13] Gaborit, P., Murat, G., Ruatta, O., Zemor, G.: Low rank parity check codes and their application to cryptography. In: Parker, M.G., Budaghyan, L., Helleseth, T. (eds.) The International Workshop on Coding and Cryptography (WCC 2013), Bergen, Norway, p. 13, April 2013. ISBN: 978-82-308-2269-2

[GRSZ14] Gaborit, P., Ruatta, O., Schrek, J., Zémor, G.: RankSign: an efficient signature algorithm based on the rank metric. In: Mosca, M. (ed.) PQCrypto 2014. LNCS, vol. 8772, pp. 88–107. Springer, Heidelberg (2014)

[GSJB14] Gligoroski, D., Samardjiska, S., Jacobsen, H., Bezzateev, S.: McEliece in the World of Escher. Cryptology ePrint Archive, Report 2014/360 (2014). http://eprint.iacr.org/

[LB88] Lee, P.J., Brickell, E.F.: An observation on the security of McEliece's public-key cryptosystem. In: Barstow, D., et al. (eds.) EUROCRYPT 1988. LNCS, vol. 330, pp. 275–280. Springer, Heidelberg (1988)

[Leo88] Leon, J.: A probabilistic algorithm for computing minimum weights of large error-correcting codes. IEEE Trans. Inf. Theory **34**(5), 1354–1359 (1988)

[LT13] Landais, G., Tillich, J.-P.: An efficient attack of a McEliece cryptosystem variant based on convolutional codes. In: Gaborit, Philippe (ed.) PQCrypto 2013. LNCS, vol. 7932, pp. 102–117. Springer, Heidelberg (2013)

[McE78] McEliece, R.J.: A Public-Key Cryptosystem Based On Algebraic Coding Theory. Deep Space Network Progress Report 44, pp. 114–116 (1978)

[MMT11] May, A., Meurer, A., Thomae, E.: Decoding random linear codes in $\tilde{O}(2^{0.054n})$. In: Lee, D.H., Wang, Xiaoyun (eds.) ASIACRYPT 2011. LNCS, vol. 7073, pp. 107–124. Springer, Heidelberg (2011)

[MTSB12] Misoczki, R., Tillich, J.-P., Sendrier, N., Barreto, P.S.L.M.: MDPC-McEliece: New McEliece Variants from Moderate Density Parity-Check Codes. Cryptology ePrint Archive, Report 2012/409 (2012). http://eprint.iacr.org/

[OT11] Otmani, A., Tillich, J.-P.: An efficient attack on all concrete KKS proposals. In: Yang, Bo-Yin (ed.) PQCrypto 2011. LNCS, vol. 7071, pp. 98–116. Springer, Heidelberg (2011)

[Per14] Perlner, R.: Optimizing information set decoding algorithms to attack cyclosymmetric MDPC codes. In: Mosca, M. (ed.) PQCrypto 2014. LNCS, vol. 8772, pp. 220–228. Springer, Heidelberg (2014)

[Pra62] Prange, E.: The use of information sets in decoding cyclic codes. IRE Tran. Inf. Theory **8**(5), 5–9 (1962)

[Ste89] Stern, J.: A method for finding codewords of small weight. In: Cohen, G., Wolfmann, J. (eds.) Coding Theory and Applications. LNCS, vol. 388, pp. 106–113. Springer, Heidelberg (1989)

Cryptanalysis of the McEliece Public Key Cryptosystem Based on Polar Codes

Magali Bardet[1], Julia Chaulet[2], Vlad Dragoi[1], Ayoub Otmani[1][(✉)], and Jean-Pierre Tillich[2]

[1] UR, LITIS, Normandie Université, 76821 Mont-Saint-Aignan, France
{magali.bardet,vlad.dragoi1,ayoub.otmani}@univ-rouen.fr
[2] SECRET Project, Inria, 78153 Le Chesnay Cedex, France
{julia.chaulet,jean-pierre.tillich}@inria.fr

Abstract. Polar codes discovered by Arikan form a very powerful family of codes attaining many information theoretic limits in the fields of error correction and source coding. They have in particular much better decoding capabilities than Goppa codes which places them as a serious alternative in the design of both a public-key encryption scheme *à la* McEliece and a very efficient signature scheme. Shrestha and Kim proposed in 2014 to use them in order to come up with a new code-based public key cryptosystem. We present a key-recovery attack that makes it possible to recover a description of the permuted polar code providing all the information required for decrypting any message.

1 Introduction

The concept of *post-quantum* cryptography appeared after Peter Shor showed in [Sho97] that all cryptosystems which base their security on the hardness of the factoring problem or the discrete logarithm problem can be attacked in polynomial time with a quantum computer (see [BBD09] for an extensive report). This threatens most if not all public-key cryptosystems deployed in practice, such as RSA [RSA78] or DSA [Kra91]. Cryptography based on the difficulty of decoding a linear code, on the other hand, is believed to resist quantum attacks and is therefore considered as a viable replacement for those schemes in future applications. Yet, independently of their so-called "post-quantum" nature, code-based cryptosystems offer other benefits even for present-day applications due to their excellent algorithmic efficiency.

The first code-based cryptosystem is the McEliece cryptosystem [McE78], originally proposed using binary Goppa codes. Afterwards, several code families have been suggested to replace them: generalized Reed–Solomon codes (GRS) [Nie86] or subcodes of them [BL05], Reed–Muller codes [Sid94], algebraic geometry codes [JM96], LDPC codes [BC07,BBC08], a certain kind of non binary Goppa codes (called wild Goppa codes or wild Goppa codes incognito) [BLP10,BLP11], MDPC codes [MTSB12], convolutional codes [LJ12], and more recently polar codes [SK14] or subcodes of them [HSEA14]. Some of these schemes allow to reduce the public key size compared to the original McEliece

© Springer International Publishing Switzerland 2016
T. Takagi (Ed.): PQCrypto 2016, LNCS 9606, pp. 118–143, 2016.
DOI: 10.1007/978-3-319-29360-8_9

cryptosystem while presumably keeping the same level of security against generic decoding algorithms.

However, for many of the aforementioned schemes it has been shown that a description of the underlying code suitable for decoding can be obtained which breaks the corresponding scheme. This has been achieved for GRS codes in [SS92], subcodes of GRS codes in [Wie10], Reed-Muller codes in [MS07]. Algebraic geometry codes based on (very) low genus hyperelliptic curves were broken in [FM08], whereas the general case was broken in [CMCP14]. A first version of the scheme based on LDPC codes proposed in [BC07] has been successfully attacked in [OTD08] (but the new scheme proposed in [BBC08] seems to be immune to this kind of attack). Some of the parameters that can be found in [BLP10, BLP11] have been successfully cryptanalyzed with a polynomial time attack in [COT14] or with an exponential time attack in [FPdP14], and finally the convolutional scheme of [LJ12] was successfully cryptanalyzed in [LT13].

All of these attacks (with the exception of [LT13]) pinpoint algebraic properties of the codes which raises the issue of looking for alternative code families with little or no algebraic structure. In this respect the proposals of [SK14, HSEA14] might be very attractive. Moreover, polar codes enjoy another feature that only few other codes have: they enjoy a decoding algorithm that can also be used to produce for any binary word a codeword that is essentially as close as possible as announced by the information theoretic upper bounds [CT91, Theorem 13.2.1 and 13.3.1] (see [KU10] for a proof of this result). This would make such codes perfect candidates in a signature scheme [OT12] based on the Niederreiter scheme [Nie86]. In particular, this would give a much more efficient signature than the CFS scheme [CFS01].

A McEliece scheme based on (binary) polar codes also raises some other interesting issues. There is basically no large choice for such codes and there is essentially only one polar code (up to permutation of the coordinates) of a given rate. Generally it is advocated that one should take a large code family in the McEliece cryptosystem, because if there is only one code up to permutation of the coordinates, then attacking the scheme amounts to solve the code equivalence problem [PR97]. For most codes, this is generally easy to do by using the support splitting algorithm [Sen00]. However, this algorithm requires in a crucial way that the code has a small hull (which is the intersection of the code with its dual) and a small permutation group, both of them being precisely the opposite for polar codes. Interestingly enough, polar codes are known to be related to the Reed-Muller code family [Ari09]. These two code families behave exactly in the same way with respect to these properties: they have very large hull and permutation group and there is also only one (or zero) Reed-Muller code for a given rate. Note that when a McEliece scheme based on Reed-Muller codes was proposed in [Sid94], its security relied precisely on the assumption that it could be possible in theory to use a single code (up to permutation of the coordinates) by using codes with a large hull and a large permutation group that would defeat attacks based on the support splitting algorithm. It took thirteen years [MS07] to break this McEliece scheme and the attack used many algebraic properties of the Reed-Muller codes, that are presumably absent for polar codes.

However, we will show that despite the fact that polar codes seem to be immune against a plain use of the support splitting algorithm, it can nevertheless be cryptanalyzed successfully. We will show here how to recover from the public generator matrix a description of the code that is suitable for decoding. Our attack uses several ingredients:

(i) polar codes have rather low weight codewords which can be found by standard low weight codeword searching algorithms [Ste88, Dum91];

(ii) shortening the code with respect to these low weight codewords and taking the dual also gives a code with low weight codewords which can be recovered with the aforementioned algorithms;

(iii) by characterizing the permutation group of polar codes together with the low-weight codewords found in Step (ii), it is possible to find among the codewords found in Step (i) a subset of codewords which up to equivalence by the permutation group can be considered as codewords whose support are very specific affine spaces;

(iv) Puncturing the code with respect to the support of an element of minimum weight in this last subset of codewords gives a code of small length (typically 16 or 32) whose structure is known up to code equivalence. The code equivalence problem is then solved in this case and is used to recover step by step the underlying polar codes.

Steps (i) and (ii) are directly inspired from the Minder-Shokrollahi attack [MS07] on the McEliece cryptosystem based on Reed-Muller codes, however Steps (iii) and (iv) are new and very specific to polar codes. Basically, the fact that the whole affine group is the permutation group of Reed-Muller code simplifies a great deal the attack of [MS07]. This is not the case anymore for polar codes and the crux for being able to mount this attack is to understand which subgroup of the affine group is part of the permutation group of a polar code and then to use this structure in a relevant way. Amazingly enough, it turns out that a rather large subgroup is the answer to this problem and that polar codes are much more symmetric than could be guessed from their definition. This result is of independent interest and might be used to improve the decoding algorithms of polar codes.

In a general way, in order to understand the structure of polar codes for breaking this cryptosystem we have introduced here new concepts. In particular we suggest here a new code construction, that we call decreasing monomial codes which contains both the Reed-Muller code family and the polar code family and which has a large subgroup of the affine group as permutation group. This construction explains why polar codes have such a large permutation group, but again this new code construction could be of independent interest in coding theory. We also introduce in Step (iv) a novel iterative way of solving the code equivalence problem that could be interesting for solving the code equivalence problem for codes obtained from the $(u|u + v)$ construction.

2   Basic Facts

In this section we recall a few facts about the McEliece cryptosystem, polar codes, the code equivalence problem, and code operations like shortening or puncturing.

Polar Codes. Polar codes were discovered by Arikan [Ari09] and form a very powerful family of codes that gave a nice constructive way of attaining many information theoretic limits in error correction and source coding. In particular, they allow to attain the capacity of any symmetric memoryless channel with a low complexity decoding algorithm (namely the successive cancellation decoder of Arikan). Since they have much better decoding capabilities than Goppa codes, it is reasonable to study whether they can be used in a McEliece scheme. Due to their better correction capacity, this allows for instance to decrease the key sizes of the scheme. Decoding such codes is also faster than decoding Goppa codes and this can also be used to speed up the decryption process.

They can be described as codes of length $n = 2^m$, where m is an arbitrary integer. They may take any dimension between 0 and 2^m. The polar code of length $n = 2^m$ and dimension k is obtained through a generator matrix which picks a specific subset of k rows of the $2^m \times 2^m$ matrix:

$$G_m \overset{\text{def}}{=} \underbrace{\begin{pmatrix} 1 & 1 \\ 0 & 1 \end{pmatrix} \otimes \cdots \otimes \begin{pmatrix} 1 & 1 \\ 0 & 1 \end{pmatrix}}_{m \ \text{times}}.$$

Note that we depart here slightly from the usual convention for polar codes which is to use in the Kronecker product the matrix $\begin{pmatrix} 1 & 0 \\ 1 & 1 \end{pmatrix}$. The two definitions (ours and the standard one) are easily seen to be equivalent, they just amount to order the code positions differently. Our convention presents the advantage of simplifying the polynomial formalism that follows.

The specific choice of rows that are picked depends (a little bit) on the noisy channel for which the code is devised. For a given noise model, there is a way to compute the k rows which are used to define the generator matrix of the code. Roughly speaking these rows are chosen in such a way that it gives good performances for the successive cancellation decoder.

McEliece Cryptosystem. The (binary) McEliece public-key scheme [McE78] can be described as follows. The key generation algorithm picks a random $k \times n$ generator matrix G of a binary linear code $\mathscr{C}$ which is itself randomly picked in a family of codes for which t errors can be efficiently corrected. The *secret* key is the decoding algorithm $\mathcal{D}$ associated to $\mathscr{C}$ and the *public* key is G. To encrypt $u \in \mathbb{F}_2^k$, the sender chooses a random vector e in $\mathbb{F}_2^n$ of Hamming weight less than or equal to t and computes the ciphertext $c = uG + e$. The receiver then recovers the plaintext by applying $\mathcal{D}$ on c.

Code Equivalence Problem. In the McEliece scheme based on polar codes [SK14], since there is in essence a single (binary) polar code of a given dimension and length, breaking the scheme amounts to find for a permuted version of the polar code a permutation that gives the original polar code. In other words, we face here as for the McEliece scheme based on Reed-Muller codes the code equivalence problem. To give a formal definition of this problem we will use the following notation and definition.

Notation 1 (Permutation of a Word and a Code). *The symmetric group of degree n is denoted by S_n. Let $\boldsymbol{x} = (x_i)_{0 \leqslant i < n} \in \mathbb{F}_2^n$ and π be a permutation of $\{0, 1, \ldots, n-1\}$. We denote by $\boldsymbol{x}^\pi = (x_{\pi(i)})_{0 \leqslant i < n}$ the vector $\boldsymbol{x}$ permuted by π and for a binary code $\mathscr{C}$ of length n, its permutation by π is defined by*

$$\mathscr{C}^\pi \overset{\text{def}}{=} \{ \boldsymbol{c}^\pi \mid \boldsymbol{c} \in \mathscr{C} \}.$$

Definition 1 (Permutation Group of a Code). *The permutation group of a code $\mathscr{C}$ is the set of permutations π such that $\mathscr{C}^\pi = \mathscr{C}$.*

The code equivalence problem can be stated as follows:

Problem 1 (Code Equivalence Search Problem). Given $\mathscr{C}$ and $\mathscr{C}^\pi$ where $\mathscr{C}$ is a code of length n and π belongs to S_n, find $\hat{\pi}$ in S_n such that $\mathscr{C}^{\hat{\pi}} = \mathscr{C}^\pi$.

Note that we do not necessarily have $\hat{\pi} = \pi$ when the permutation group of the code is non trivial. It is namely immediate to prove that:

Proposition 1. *For any $\boldsymbol{x} = (x_i)_{0 \leqslant i < n}$ in $\mathbb{F}_2^n$ and all permutations π and π' in S_n we have*

$$(\boldsymbol{x}^\pi)^{\pi'} = \boldsymbol{x}^{\pi \pi'}.$$

Let $\mathscr{C}$ be a code of length n with permutation group $\mathcal{G}$ and π be a permutation of the same length as $\mathscr{C}$ (i.e. a permutation in S_n). We have

$$\left\{ \hat{\pi} \in S_n \mid \mathscr{C}^{\hat{\pi}} = \mathscr{C}^\pi \right\} = \mathcal{G}\pi$$

If $\mathscr{C}$ has permutation group $\mathcal{G}$, then $\mathscr{C}^\pi$ has permutation group $\pi^{-1}\mathcal{G}\pi$.

Proof. The first part of the proposition can be proved by bringing in $\boldsymbol{x}' \overset{\text{def}}{=} \boldsymbol{x}^\pi$ and observing that:

(i) for any i in $\{0, \ldots, n-1\}$ we have $x_i = x'_{\pi^{-1}(i)}$ since $x'_j = x_{\pi(j)}$ for $j = \pi^{-1}(i)$.

(ii) $(\boldsymbol{x}^\pi)^{\pi'} = \boldsymbol{x}'^{\pi'} = (x'_{\pi'(i)})_{0 \leqslant i < n} = (x'_{\pi^{-1}(\pi(\pi'(i)))})_{0 \leqslant i < n} = (x_{\pi(\pi'(i))})_{0 \leqslant i < n} = \boldsymbol{x}^{\pi \pi'}.$

From this we deduce that for any σ in $\mathcal{G}$, we have $\mathscr{C}^{\sigma\pi} = (\mathscr{C}^\sigma)^\pi = \mathscr{C}^\pi$. Conversely if $\mathscr{C}^{\hat{\pi}} = \mathscr{C}^\pi$, then $(\mathscr{C}^{\hat{\pi}})^{\pi^{-1}} = \mathscr{C}$ and therefore $\hat{\pi}\pi^{-1}$ is in $\mathcal{G}$, meaning that $\hat{\pi}$ is in $\mathcal{G}\pi$.

To prove the last part we observe that if γ is a permutation that leaves $\mathscr{C}$ invariant, then $\pi^{-1}\gamma\pi$ is a permutation that leaves $\mathscr{C}^\pi$ invariant, since $(\mathscr{C}^\pi)^{\pi^{-1}\gamma\pi} = \mathscr{C}^{\gamma\pi} = (\mathscr{C}^\gamma)^\pi = \mathscr{C}^\pi$. Conversely if γ' is a permutation of $\mathscr{C}^\pi$, then the same kind of computation shows that $\gamma \overset{\text{def}}{=} \pi\gamma'\pi^{-1}$ is a permutation of $\mathscr{C}$.

What makes the equivalence problem difficult for polar codes is that the standard algorithm for solving it, namely the support splitting algorithm of [Sen00] is too complex to be used in this context due to the very large size of the hull of the polar code. What makes the problem even more intricate is the fact that a polar code turns out to have a very large permutation group which complicates the task significantly.

Operations on Codes. One of the basic operations used in the support splitting algorithm for solving the code equivalence problem is to consider shortened and punctured codes. For a given code $\mathscr{C}$ and a subset $\mathcal{J} \subseteq \{0, \ldots, n-1\}$ the *punctured* code $\mathcal{P}_{\mathcal{J}}(\mathscr{C})$ and *shortened* code $\mathcal{S}_{\mathcal{J}}(\mathscr{C})$ are defined as:

$$\mathcal{P}_{\mathcal{J}}(\mathscr{C}) \stackrel{\text{def}}{=} \left\{ (c_i)_{i \notin \mathcal{J}} \mid \boldsymbol{c} \in \mathscr{C} \right\};$$

$$\mathcal{S}_{\mathcal{J}}(\mathscr{C}) \stackrel{\text{def}}{=} \left\{ (c_i)_{i \notin \mathcal{J}} \mid \exists \boldsymbol{c} = (c_i)_i \in \mathscr{C} \text{ such that } \forall i \in \mathcal{J},\ c_i = 0 \right\}.$$

Instead of writing $\mathcal{P}_{\{j\}}(\mathscr{C})$ and $\mathcal{S}_{\{j\}}(\mathscr{C})$ when $\mathcal{J} = \{j\}$ we rather use the notation $\mathcal{P}_j(\mathscr{C})$ and $\mathcal{S}_j(\mathscr{C})$. These codes are used in the following way to solve the code equivalence problem: $\mathscr{C}$ is punctured in a position i whereas $\mathscr{C}^\pi$ is punctured in some position j. If we have a quick way to check that two codes are not equivalent, then we can use this tool to check whether the two punctured codes may be equivalent or not (in the support splitting algorithm this is done by computing the weight enumerator of the hull which is obviously invariant by permutation). If the two punctured codes are not equivalent, then we know for sure that i and j can not correspond to each other via the permutation of position π. The same idea works also for the shortened code.

3 Decreasing Monomial Codes

The purpose of this section is to introduce a novel algebraic framework that sheds some light about the structure of polar codes. We will in particular give a new class of codes, that we call *decreasing monomial codes* that contains as a particular case, polar codes and Reed-Muller codes. The dual of a decreasing monomial code is a decreasing monomial code and under a very mild condition, such codes turn out to be weakly self-dual (i.e. the hull of the code is the code itself). We will then prove that this general construction has a very large permutation group and both facts put together will explain why polar codes have such a large permutation group and hull. We will use here the polynomial formalism that is generally used to describe Reed-Muller codes. It turns out that this polynomial formalism is also very handy for describing polar codes.

Reed-Muller Codes. It is well known that Reed-Muller codes of length 2^m can be obtained as evaluation codes of polynomials in $\mathbb{F}_2[x_0, \ldots, x_{m-1}]$. Polar codes can also be described through this formalism. Since we are interested in evaluations of such polynomials over entries in $\mathbb{F}_2^m$ we will identify x_i with x_i^2 and work in the ring $\mathbb{R}_2[x_0, \ldots, x_{m-1}] = \mathbb{F}_2[x_0, \ldots, x_{m-1}]/(x_0^2 - x_0, \ldots, x_{m-1}^2 -$

x_{m-1}). It will be convenient with this formalism to associate to a polynomial $g \in \mathbb{R}_2[x_0, \ldots, x_{m-1}]$ the binary vector denoted by $\mathsf{ev}(g)$ in $\mathbb{F}_2^n$ with $n = 2^m$ which is the evaluation of the polynomial in all the binary entries $(u_0, \ldots, u_{m-1}) \in \mathbb{F}_2^m$. In other words

$$\mathsf{ev}(g) = \big(g(u_0, \ldots, u_{m-1})\big)_{(u_0, \ldots, u_{m-1}) \in \mathbb{F}_2^m}$$

With this notation, we will view the indices of a vector as elements of $\mathbb{F}_2^m$. This notation does not specify the order we use for the elements of $\mathbb{F}_2^m$. We actually use the natural order by viewing $(u_0, \ldots, u_m)$ as the integer $\sum_{i=0}^{m-1} u_i 2^i$. With this notation at hand, the Reed-Muller code $\mathscr{R}(r, m)$ is defined as

$$\mathscr{R}(r, m) \overset{\text{def}}{=} \big\{ \mathsf{ev}(P) \mid \deg P \leqslant r \big\}$$

Obviously this code is generated by the codewords $\mathsf{ev}(g)$ where g is a monomial of degree less than or equal to r. Recall that a *monomial* is any product of variables of the form $x_0^{g_0} \cdots x_{m-1}^{g_{m-1}}$ where $g_0, \ldots, g_{m-1}$ are binary. The set of all monomials is denoted by:

$$\mathcal{M} \overset{\text{def}}{=} \{1, x_0, \ldots, x_{m-1}, x_0 x_1, \ldots, x_0 \cdots x_{m-1}\}.$$

Reed-Muller codes have a very large permutation group which is isomorphic to the affine group over $\mathbb{F}_2^m$. Indeed, it can be checked immediately that:

(i) any bijective affine transformation A over $\mathbb{F}_2^m$ can be viewed as a permutation of the code positions by mapping $(u_0, \ldots, u_{m-1})$ to $A(u_0, \ldots, u_{m-1})$;

(ii) this permutation leaves the code invariant since $P(A(x_0, \ldots, x_{m-1}))$ is a polynomial of degree at most the degree of P and therefore if $\mathsf{ev}(P) \in \mathscr{R}(r, m)$ then $\mathsf{ev}(P \circ A) \in \mathscr{R}(r, m)$.

Monomial Codes. It is straightforward to check that the rows of $\boldsymbol{G}$ are all possible evaluations of monomials. This fact is easily proved by induction on m by observing that $(1, 1)$ is the evaluation of the constant monomial 1 and that $(0, 1)$ is the evaluation of the monomial x_0. From this, we easily see that a polar code is a *monomial code*, meaning codes generated by evaluations of monomials (see the formal definition below).

It will also be very convenient to introduce the following partial order $\preceq$ on monomials

Definition 2 (Monomial Order). *The monomials of the same degree are ordered as*

$$x_{i_1} \ldots x_{i_s} \preceq x_{j_1} \ldots x_{j_s} \text{ if and only if for any } \ell \in \{1, \ldots, s\}, \ i_\ell \leqslant j_\ell$$

where we assume that $i_1 < \cdots < i_s$ and $j_1 < \cdots < j_s$.

This order is extended to other monomials through divisibility, namely: $f \preceq g$ if and only if there is a divisor g^* of g such that $f \preceq g^*$.

Obviously for any monomial f of $\mathcal{M}$ the constant polynomial 1 satisfies the inequality $1 \preceq f$. The *interval* $[f; h]$ where f and h are in $\mathcal{M}$ with $f \preceq h$ is the set of monomials $g \in \mathcal{M}$ such that $f \preceq g \preceq h$. We will also need the following definition

Definition 3 (Decreasing Set). *A set $I \subseteq \mathcal{M}$ is* decreasing *if and only if ($f \in I$ and $g \preceq f$) implies $g \in I$.*

With these definitions, we define monomial and decreasing monomial codes as follows.

Definition 4 (Monomial and Decreasing Monomial Codes). *Let I be a finite set of multivariate polynomials in m variables and set $n \stackrel{def}{=} 2^m$. The linear code defined by I is the vector subspace $\mathscr{C}(I) \subseteq \mathbb{F}_2^n$ generated by $\{\mathrm{ev}(f) \mid f \in I\}$. It is called the* polynomial code *associated to I.*

1. *When $I \subseteq \mathcal{M}$, $\mathscr{C}(I)$ is called a* monomial code.
2. *When $I \subseteq \mathcal{M}$ is a decreasing set, $\mathscr{C}(I)$ is called a* decreasing monomial code.

The dimension of monomial codes is easily derived.

Lemma 1. *For all $I \subseteq \mathcal{M}$ the dimension of the monomial code $\mathscr{C}(I)$ is equal to $|I|$.*

Proof. This comes from the linear independence of the monomials in $\mathbb{R}_2[x_0, \ldots, x_{m-1}]$.

Example 1. The r-th order Reed-Muller code is the decreasing monomial code defined by the interval $[1; x_{m-r} \ldots x_{m-1}]$ since:

$$\mathscr{R}(r, m) = \mathscr{C}\left([1; x_{m-r} \ldots x_{m-1}]\right).$$

The dimension $1 + m + \cdots + \binom{m}{r}$ comes directly from Lemma 1.

It turns out that it can be proved, but this is beyond the scope of this article, that polar codes devised for the erasure channel are also decreasing monomial codes. The point is that if we take a row of $\boldsymbol{G}_m$ to be a row of the generator matrix (and view this row as a monomial - since as we have explained before - all these rows correspond to an evaluation of a particular monomial) all the rows that are "smaller" (in the sense of the monomial order defined before) will also be chosen to be part of the generator matrix of the polar code. This fact can be proved by studying the polarization process [Ari09] which is at the heart of choosing the relevant rows of $\boldsymbol{G}_m$. Simple heuristics can be invoked that this also holds for other channel models and we have experimental evidence showing that this seems to hold in particular for polar codes devised for the binary symmetric channel (which are the polar codes used here). This fact can be simply checked for the polar codes that we have attacked here.

Duality and Permutation Group of Decreasing Monomial Codes. Duals of decreasing monomial codes have a very simple description and it will turn out that under certain very weak conditions, they are weakly self-dual. It is readily seen that the dual of a monomial code is a polynomial code, but it is not necessarily a monomial code. However the dual of a decreasing monomial code turns out to be a decreasing monomial code. To describe this dual we will use the following notion of *(multiplicative) complement* of a monomial g and denote it by $\check{g}$.

Definition 5 (Complement). *For any $g \in \mathcal{M}$ we define the complement of g as*

$$\check{g} = \frac{x_0 \ldots x_{m-1}}{g}.$$

With this notion, we have the following proposition whose proof is in Sect. A of the appendix.

Proposition 2. *Let $\mathscr{C}(I)$ be a decreasing monomial code, then its dual is a decreasing monomial code given by*

$$\mathscr{C}(I)^{\perp} = \mathscr{C}(\mathcal{M} \setminus \check{I}).$$

Notice that this proposition yields the well known result about the dual of a Reed-Muller code $RM(r,m) = \mathscr{C}([1; x_{m-r} \ldots x_{m-1}])$ where we have

$$
\begin{aligned}
RM(r,m)^{\perp} &= \mathscr{C}(\mathcal{M} \setminus [x_0 \ldots x_{m-r-1}; x_0 \ldots x_{m-1}]) \\
&= \mathscr{C}([1; x_{r+1} \ldots x_{m-1}]) \\
&= \mathscr{R}(m - r - 1, m).
\end{aligned}
$$

A straightforward consequence of this is that under some conditions, any decreasing monomial code is weakly self-dual.

Corollary 1. *Let $\mathscr{C}(I)$ be a decreasing monomial code with $|I| \leqslant \frac{1}{2} 2^m$. Then*

$$\mathscr{C}(I) \subseteq \mathscr{C}(I)^{\perp} \text{ if and only if for any } f \in I, \ \check{f} \notin I.$$

Polar codes of rate (sufficiently) smaller than $1/2$ generally satisfy this assumption and in the case of rate greater than $\frac{1}{2}$ it is the dual of the polar code that satisfies this assumption. This can be explained by looking at the polarization process that is used to choose the monomials defining the polar code, but explaining this point is beyond the scope of this article. We just wish to add that this assumption is satisfied for the polar codes used in the McEliece cryptosystem that we have attacked in this article. This corollary explains why such codes are weakly self-dual and why the support splitting is of unreasonable complexity in such a case for recovering the unknown permutation between a known permuted polar code and a polar code.

Polynomial codes and monomial codes may have a trivial permutation group. Applying an affine permutation to a monomial code yields a polynomial code, but it is not necessarily a monomial code. To understand the action of a permutation π which is also an affine transformation on $\mathbb{F}_2^m$ we can notice that for any monomial f in $\mathbb{R}_2[x_0, \ldots, x_{m-1}]$ we have

$$\mathsf{ev}(f)^{\pi} = \mathsf{ev}(f \circ \pi) \tag{1}$$

where on the lefthand side we view π as a permutation on the coordinates (viewed as elements of $\mathbb{F}_2^m$) whereas on the righthand side we view π as an affine permutation. This equation explains why a monomial code may not be a monomial code after applying an affine permutation and it is rather straightforward to come up with examples of monomial codes that have a trivial permutation group. However by considering the subclass of decreasing monomial codes we obtain codes with a very large permutation group which is the *lower triangular affine group*, that is:

Definition 6 (Lower Triangular Affine Group). *The* lower triangular affine group $\mathbb{LTA}_m$ *on* $\mathbb{F}_2^m$ *is defined as the set of affine transformations over* $\mathbb{F}_2^m$ *of the form* $\boldsymbol{x} \mapsto \boldsymbol{A}\boldsymbol{x} + \boldsymbol{b}$ *where* $\boldsymbol{A}$ *is a lower triangular binary matrix with "1"'s on the diagonal and* $\boldsymbol{b}$ *is arbitrary in* $\mathbb{F}_2^m$.

Theorem 1. *The permutation group of a decreasing monomial code in m variables contains* $\mathbb{LTA}_m$.

This theorem is proved in Sect. A of the appendix. This theorem explains why polar codes have a large subgroup of the permutation group of Reed-Muller codes as permutation group. This fact is one of the keys for the cryptanalysis which follows.

Minimum Distance of Decreasing Codes. We first recall some well known facts about the minimum distance of Reed-Muller codes (see for instance [MS86, Chap. 13, Sect. 4]):

Theorem 2. *The minimum distance of the Reed-Muller code* $\mathscr{R}(r,m)$ *is* 2^{m-r}. *There is a one to one correspondance between the affine subspaces of* $\mathbb{F}_2^m$ *of dimension* $m-r$ *and the minimum codeword of* $\mathscr{R}(r,m)$: *all minimum codewords are obtained as* $\mathrm{ev}(x_0' \ldots x_{r-1}')$ *where* $x_0', \ldots, x_{r-1}'$ *are obtained from* $x_0, \ldots, x_{r-1}$ *by a bijective affine change of coordinates.*

In other words, "up to action of the permutation group there is only one codeword of minimum weight". All these facts have simplified significantly the attack of the McEliece cryptosystem based on Reed-Muller codes in [MS07]. We will see in what follows that polar codes behave differently with this respect.

To understand the minimum distance of a decreasing monomial code, and of a polar code in particular, the following notion is very useful.

Definition 7. *Let* $\mathscr{C}(I)$ *be a decreasing monomial code over m variables. We let*

$$r_-(\mathscr{C}(I)) \overset{def}{=} \max\left\{ r \mid \mathscr{R}(r,m) \subseteq \mathscr{C}(I) \right\}$$

$$r_+(\mathscr{C}(I)) \overset{def}{=} \min\left\{ r \mid \mathscr{C}(I) \subseteq \mathscr{R}(r,m) \right\}$$

It is readily checked that another way of defining these quantities is that r_- is the largest r for which the monomial $x_{m-r} \ldots x_{m-1}$ is in I. On the other hand r_+ is the largest integer r for which $x_0 \ldots x_{r-1}$ is in I. These quantities are related to the minimum distance of a decreasing monomial code and its dual through the following result

Proposition 3. *Let $\mathscr{C}(I)$ be a decreasing monomial code over m variables. We have the following properties:*

(i) The minimum distance of $\mathscr{C}(I)$ is equal to $2^{m-r_+(\mathscr{C}(I))}$.
(ii) $r_-(\mathscr{C}(I)^\perp)$ and $r_+(\mathscr{C}(I)^\perp)$ satisfy the equalities:

$$r_-(\mathscr{C}(I)^\perp) = m - 1 - r_+(\mathscr{C}(I))$$
$$r_+(\mathscr{C}(I)^\perp) = m - 1 - r_-(\mathscr{C}(I))$$

(iii) The minimum distance of $\mathscr{C}(I)^\perp$ is equal to $2^{r_-(\mathscr{C}(I))+1}$

This proposition is proved in appendix Sect. A. A straightforward corollary of these propositions is that the minimum distance of a polar code is always smaller than or equal to the minimum distance of the Reed-Muller code of the same dimension (if it exists) and this is already a strong indication that this minimum distance is rather small (at most the square root of the length for codes of rate greater than $\frac{1}{2}$ for instance). For the polar codes we are interested in this study, we will be able to find minimum weight codewords in the polar code and its dual with standard algorithms for finding low weight codewords [Ste88, Dum91], since both minimum distances turn out to be rather small.

For Reed-Muller codes there is only one orbit of the permutation group inside the set of minimum codewords. The case of decreasing monomial codes is more complicated. However, and this will be very helpful for classifying these codewords, we have:

Theorem 3. *Each orbit under the action of $\mathbb{LTA}_m$ contained in the set of minimum codewords of the decreasing monomial code $\mathscr{C}(I)$ contains a monomial of I.*

This theorem is proved in Sect. A of the appendix.

4   Cryptanalysis

We will explain here how we solve the code equivalence problem for a decreasing monomial code $\mathscr{C}(I)$. This can be applied to any polar code and yields an attack that breaks the McEliece scheme based on polar codes proposed in [SK14]. In this section, we use the simplified notation r_- for $r_-(\mathscr{C}(I))$ and r_+ for $r_+(\mathscr{C}(I))$. We also use the notion of signature formalized as follows.

Definition 8 (Signature). *Let $\mathscr{C}$ be a code of length n. Let $\mathcal{G}$ be a subgroup of permutations of $\mathscr{C}$ and W be a subset of $\mathscr{C}$ globally invariant under $\mathcal{G}$. We say that a function $\Sigma(\mathbf{c}, \mathscr{C})$ where $\mathbf{c}$ belongs to $\mathscr{C}$ is a signature for the action of $\mathcal{G}$ on W if and only if:*

(i) $\Sigma(\mathbf{c}, \mathscr{C}) = \Sigma(\mathbf{c}^\pi, \mathscr{C}^\pi)$ for π from S_n (i.e. Σ is invariant by permutation),
(ii) $\Sigma(\mathbf{c}, \mathscr{C}) \neq \Sigma(\mathbf{c}', \mathscr{C})$ if $\mathbf{c}$ and $\mathbf{c}'$ both belong to W but are not in the same orbit under $\mathcal{G}$ (i.e. Σ takes distinct values for each orbit).

Notice here that a signature always takes the same value on an orbit under $\mathcal{G}$ since if we take c in W and γ is an element of $\mathcal{G}$, then $\Sigma(c, \mathscr{C}) = \Sigma(c^\gamma, \mathscr{C}^\gamma) = \Sigma(c^\gamma, \mathscr{C})$ since γ belongs to the permutation group of the code.

The algorithm for performing the attack can now be summarized as follows:

Step 1. (Minimum weight codewords searching) Search the non-zero minimum weight vectors of $\mathscr{C}(I)$ and $\mathscr{C}(I)^\pi$. We denote these two sets by $W_{\min}$ and $W_{\min}^\pi$ respectively. Note that $W_{\min} = \{c \in \mathscr{C}(I) : |c| = 2^{m-r+}\}$, $W_{\min}^\pi = \{c \in \mathscr{C}(I)^\pi : |c| = 2^{m-r+}\}$ and the codeword $c_{\min} \overset{\text{def}}{=} \mathrm{ev}(x_0 \cdots x_{r_+ - 1})$ belongs to $W_{\min}$.

Step 2. (Signature of orbits in $W_{\min}$) Compute the orbits of $W_{\min}$ under the lower triangular subgroup LTA_m of the affine group and find a signature for these orbits. This signature is based on shortening the dual $\mathscr{C}(I)^\perp$ on the support of c (where c belongs to $W_{\min}$) and computing the dimension of this code and the number of codewords of minimum weight in it.

Step 3. (Computation of orbits in $W_{\min}^\pi$) Use this signature to decompose $W_{\min}^\pi$ into distinct orbits under the group $\pi^{-1}\mathrm{LTA}_m\pi$ and use it to find the orbit of $c_{\min}^\pi$.

Step 4. (Identification of affine spaces) Without loss of generality, we may take any codeword in the orbit of $c_{\min}^\pi$ and declare that it is equal to $c_{\min}^\pi$. Let $\mathcal{I}$ be the support of $c_{\min}$, and $\mathcal{J}$ be the complementary set (that is the set of position for which $c_{\min}$ takes the value 0). Note that with the way we identify positions as elements of $\mathbb{F}_2^m$, $\mathcal{I}$ can be viewed as the affine space $x_0 = x_1 = \cdots = x_{r_+ - 1} = 1$. The structure of the orbit of $c_{\min}$ is such that the supports of all the codewords in this orbit are affine spaces of the form $x_0 = \varepsilon_0$, $x_1 = \varepsilon_1, \ldots, x_{r_+ - 1} = \varepsilon_{r_+ - 1}$, where the ε_i's are arbitrary elements in $\mathbb{F}_2$. Denote this affine space by $A(\varepsilon_0, \ldots, \varepsilon_{r_+ - 1})$ and let $c_{\min}(\varepsilon_0, \ldots, \varepsilon_{r_+ - 1})$ be the corresponding codeword. Up to a permutation of $\mathscr{C}^\pi$, we identify all the elements $c_{\min}(\varepsilon_0, \ldots, \varepsilon_{r_+ - 1})^\pi$. This gives all the affine spaces permuted by π, that is $A(\varepsilon_0, \ldots, \varepsilon_{r_+ - 1})^\pi \overset{\text{def}}{=} \{\pi^{-1}(i) \mid i \in A(\varepsilon_0, \ldots, \varepsilon_{r_+ - 1})\}$.

Step 5. (Equivalence problem for a short code) Let $\mathcal{J}$ be the set of positions where $c_{\min}$ takes zero values. Notice that the set of positions for which $c_{\min}^\pi$ takes zero values is $\mathcal{J}^\pi$. Then we compute the codes $\mathscr{D} \overset{\text{def}}{=} \mathcal{P}_{\mathcal{J}}(\mathscr{C})$ and $\mathscr{D}^\pi \overset{\text{def}}{=} \mathcal{P}_{\mathcal{J}^\pi}(\mathscr{C}^\pi)$. We solve the code equivalence problem for $\mathscr{D}$ and $\mathscr{D}^{\pi'}$ where π' is the restriction of the permutation π to the affine space $\mathcal{I}$. Notice that this problem is solved for much shorter codes than the original system.

Step 6. (Induction step) Let $c^i = \mathrm{ev}(x_0 \ldots, x_{i-1})$ with c^0 being $\mathrm{ev}(1)$, that is the all-one codeword. Notice that $c_{\min} = c^{r_+}$, and let $\mathcal{J}^i$ be the set of positions for which c^i takes the value 0. Denote by $\mathscr{D}^i = \mathcal{P}_{\mathcal{J}^i}(\mathscr{C})$. Solve for $i = r_+ - 1, \ldots, 0$ the code equivalence problem for the pair $(\mathscr{D}^i, (\mathscr{D}^i)^{\pi^i})$ by using the solution to the code equivalence problem $(\mathscr{D}^{i+1}, (\mathscr{D}^{i+1})^{\pi^{i+1}})$ where π^i is the restriction of π to the set of positions of $\mathscr{D}^i$.

The last code equivalence problem we solve here (namely for $i = 0$) is just a solution to the original code equivalence problem.

4.1 Step 1 – Minimum Weight Codewords Searching

Finding the codewords of $\mathscr{C}(I)^\pi$ can be performed by applying Dumer's algorithm [Dum91]. The complexity of this algorithm for finding a codeword of weight w in a code of rate R can be estimated as $O\left(e^{-w\ln(1-R)(1+o(1))}\right)$ when w is a sublinear function of the length (see [CTS15] for more details) and the length n of the code goes to infinity. For monomial codes it can be readily checked that codes with rate greater than some constant $\varepsilon > 0$ have minimum distance at most $O(\sqrt{n})$ (this comes from straightforward and well known results about the minimum distance of Reed-Muller codes and Proposition 3). This is clearly achievable for the polar codes we have considered in this article.

On the other hand, all the minimum codewords of $\mathscr{C}(I)$ are easily obtained by using Theorem 3: $W_{\min}$ decomposes into orbits under the action of LTA_m where each orbit contains one of the monomials of I of degree r_+.

4.2 Step 2 – Signature of Orbits in $W_{\min}$

To distinguish between the codewords of $W_{\min}$ we have first chosen a monomial in each of the orbits under LTA_m that decompose $W_{\min}$. For each of such monomials g we have computed the dual of the shortened code $\mathscr{D} \overset{\mathrm{def}}{=} \left(\mathcal{S}_{\mathcal{J}}\left(\mathscr{C}(I)\right)\right)^\perp$ with respect to the support $\mathcal{J}$ of $\mathrm{ev}(g)$. It has turned out that, for the polar codes we have considered, the pair (number of codewords of weight 2^{r_-} in $\mathscr{D}$, dimension of $\mathscr{D}$) was discriminant enough to yield a signature of the orbit. This critical quantity 2^{r_-} occurs because we have

Theorem 4. *Let* $g = x_{i_1} \ldots x_{i_{r_+}}$ *be a monomial of degree r_+ in I. Denote by* $\mathrm{supp}(g)$ *the support of* $\mathrm{ev}(g)$, *then the minimum distance of* $\left(\mathcal{S}_{\mathrm{supp}(g)}\left(\mathscr{C}(I)\right)\right)^\perp$ *is equal to 2^{r_-} if and only if there exists a monomial h in $\mathcal{M} \setminus \check{I}$ such that:*

(i) the number of variables of h that are also variables of g is $r_+ - 1$,
(ii) the number of variables of h that are also variables of $\check{g}$ is $m - r_- - r_+$.

This theorem is proved in Sect. B of the appendix.

4.3 Step 3 – Computation of orbits in $W_{\min}^\pi$

The signature Σ that has been found in the previous step is now applied to $W_{\min}^\pi$. It gives the orbits of $W_{\min}^\pi$ with respect to the conjugate group $\pi^{-1}\mathcal{G}\pi$. Indeed, it can be verified that

Proposition 4. $W_{\min}^\pi$ *is invariant by the action of $\pi^{-1}\mathrm{LTA}_m\pi$ and if Σ is a signature for $W_{\min}$ under the action of LTA_m, then it is also a signature for the action of $\pi^{-1}\mathrm{LTA}_m\pi$ on $W_{\min}^\pi$.*

We use this signature for finding the orbit of c_{min}. This orbit has a particularly nice structure:

Proposition 5. *The orbit of c_{min} under LTA_m consists of 2^{r_+} codewords that are of the form $c_{min}(\varepsilon_0, \ldots, \varepsilon_{r_+-1})$ where the ε_i's are arbitrary elements of $\mathbb{F}_2$. The orbit of c_{min}^π under $\pi^{-1}\mathrm{LTA}_m\pi$ is given by 2^{r_+} codewords of weight 2^{m-r_+} that have disjoint supports which are the permuted versions $A(\varepsilon_0, \ldots, \varepsilon_{r_+-1})^\pi$ of the affine spaces $A(\varepsilon_0, \ldots, \varepsilon_{r_+-1})$.*

In other words, finding this orbit in W_{min}^π and looking at the support of the codewords that we have found in this way allows us to find the support of the permuted versions $A(\varepsilon_0, \ldots, \varepsilon_{r_+-1})^\pi$ of the affine spaces $A(\varepsilon_0, \ldots, \varepsilon_{r_+-1})$.

4.4   Step 4 – Identification of Affine Spaces

There are several ways to identify the permuted versions of the affine spaces we are interested in. One of the simplest way, which worked for the $[2048, 614]$ polar code that we studied, is by computing the dimensions of certain spaces. First we take any codeword in the orbit of c_{min}. Such codeword is of the form $c_{min}^{\gamma\pi}$ where γ is a permutation leaving $\mathscr{C}(I)$ invariant. In other words, up to applying the permutation group, we can safely declare that this codeword is c_{min}^π. Let I_0 be the support of $c_{min} = c(1, \ldots, 1)$. We choose I_0' be the support of the codeword $c(\underbrace{1, \ldots, 1}_{(r_+-1) \text{ times}}, 0)$. Notice that $I \overset{\text{def}}{=} I_0 \cup I_0'$ is the support of the codeword $\mathrm{ev}(x_0 \ldots x_{r_+-2})$. We compute the dimension of the code $\mathcal{P}_I(\mathscr{C}(I))$. Now, we let $J_0, \ldots, J_{2^{r_+}-1}$ be the supports of the codewords that are in the orbit of c_{min}^π, with J_0 being the support of the codeword $c_{min}^{\gamma\pi}$ that has been chosen. We compute the dimensions of the codes $\mathcal{P}_{J_0 \cup J_i}(\mathscr{C}(I)^\pi)$ for $i = 1, \ldots, 2^{r_+} - 1$. It turns out that there is generally a single space J_i such that $\dim\left(\mathcal{P}_{J_0 \cup J_i}(\mathscr{C}(I)^\pi)\right) = \dim\left(\mathcal{P}_I(\mathscr{C}(I))\right)$. We pair these two spaces J_0 and J_i together. This process can be used to pair together all the spaces $A(\varepsilon_0, \ldots, \varepsilon_{r_+-2}, 0)^{\gamma\pi}$ and $A(\varepsilon_0, \ldots, \varepsilon_{r_+-2}, 1)^{\gamma\pi}$ by pairing together J_i and J_j when J_j is the only space for a given i such that

$$\dim\left(\mathcal{P}_{J_i \cup J_j}(\mathscr{C}(I)^\pi)\right) = \dim\left(\mathcal{P}_I(\mathscr{C}(I))\right).$$

In such a case, J_i and J_j necessarily correspond to $A(\varepsilon_0, \ldots, \varepsilon_{r_+-2}, 0)^{\gamma\pi}$ and $A(\varepsilon_0, \ldots, \varepsilon_{r_+-2}, 1)^{\gamma\pi}$ for a certain $(\varepsilon_0, \ldots, \varepsilon_{r_+-2}) \in \mathbb{F}_2^{r_+-1}$. In other words, we know after this process all the spaces $A(\varepsilon_0, \ldots, \varepsilon_{r_+-2})^{\gamma\pi} = A(\varepsilon_0, \ldots, \varepsilon_{r_+-2}, 0)^{\gamma\pi} \cup A(\varepsilon_0, \ldots, \varepsilon_{r_+-2}, 1)^{\gamma\pi}$. We can carry on this process with the codeword $c = \mathrm{ev}(x_0 \ldots x_{r_+-1})$ instead of c_{min} and recover all the permuted affines spaces $A(1)^{\gamma\pi}, A(1, 1)^{\gamma\pi}, \ldots, A(\underbrace{1, 1, \ldots, 1}_{r_+ \text{ times}})^{\gamma\pi}$ for some permutation γ leaving $\mathscr{C}(I)$ invariant.

4.5   Step 5 – Equivalence Problem for a Short Decreasing Monomial Code

We now have to solve the code equivalence problem for $\mathscr{D}$ which is a code of length 2^{m-r+} which is much shorter than the original code. It is also straightforward to check that it is a decreasing monomial code. We can for instance carry out the process again that we saw before. For the $[2048, 614]$ polar code that we studied, we can even compute the whole permutation group of the code which is much closer to the whole affine group. It is here a code of length 32 that contains $\mathscr{R}(2, 5)$ and is contained in $\mathscr{R}(3, 5)$. We do not detail this point here, since there are many ways to actually solve the problem.

4.6   Step 6 – Induction Step

The idea here is to reconstruct the permutation $\hat{\pi}$ given that we already know its action on the support of $c_{\min}$. More precisely, the code equivalence problem that we solve here is:

Problem 2 (Code Equivalence Search Problem with Side Information). Given $(\mathscr{C}, \mathscr{C}^{\pi})$ and t pairs of code positions $(i_0, j_0), (i_1, j_1), \ldots, (i_{t-1}, j_{t-1})$, find $\hat{\pi}$ such that $\mathscr{C}^{\hat{\pi}} = \mathscr{C}^{\pi}$ and $\hat{\pi}(i_s) = j_s$ for all $s \in \{0, 1, \ldots, t-1\}$

We use the following algorithm for solving this problem (we let here $\mathcal{I} \overset{\text{def}}{=} \{i_0, \ldots, i_{t-1}\}$ and $\mathcal{J} \overset{\text{def}}{=} \{j_0, \ldots, j_{t-1}\}$)

1. We pick a certain number ℓ of codewords $c(0), \ldots, c(\ell - 1)$ of $\mathscr{C}$.
2. Let $\mathscr{C}(j)$ the set of codewords of $\mathscr{C}$ which coincide with $c(j)$ on the positions belonging to $\mathcal{J}$. We also define $\mathscr{C}(i)^{\pi}$ as the set of codewords of $\mathscr{C}^{\pi}$ that coincide with $c(i)^{\pi}$ on $\mathcal{I}$.
3. We compute for all i in $0, 1, \ldots, \ell - 1$ and all positions j which are not in $\mathcal{J}$, the number $\Sigma(i, j)$ which is the number of codewords of minimum weight in $\mathcal{P}_j(\mathscr{C}(i))$, and similarly for all all positions j that are not in $\mathcal{I}$, the number $\Sigma^{\pi}(i, j)$ which is the number of codewords of minimum weight in $\mathcal{P}_j(\mathscr{C}(i)^{\pi})$.
4. We declare for u which is not in $\mathcal{I}$ that $\hat{\pi}(u) = v$ if there exists a unique v which does not belong to $\mathcal{J}$ such that $\Sigma(i, v) = \Sigma^{\pi}(i, u)$ for all i in $\{0, 1, \ldots, \ell - 1\}$.

It is straightforward to verify that this algorithm outputs the unique $\hat{\pi}$ solving the problem in this case. We have also encountered cases, where even with the knowledge we have on $\hat{\pi}$, we have different solutions. In such a case, we were able to compute how many solutions we had and add to the set of pairs (i_s, j_s) an additional pair (or additional pairs) which gives a unique solution.

5   Implementation of the Attack on a $[2048, 614]$-Polar Code

We implemented the $[2048, 614]$-polar code as follows. The Shannon limit for the noise on a binary symmetric channel of crossover probability p that a code of rate $\frac{614}{2048}$ is able to sustain is about $p = 0.19$. We devised the polar code for a slightly smaller error rate of $p = 0.17$ and chose the 614 best rows of G_{11} which give the best performances for the successive cancellation decoder. Such a code is able to correct more than 200 errors with a small error probability- this should be compared to the 130 errors that a Goppa code of the same rate is able to tolerate. In the case of a Goppa code we have about 70 bits of security against message attacks based on generic linear codes decoding algorithms, whereas we have more than 105 bits of security for the polar code.

We first checked that this code $\mathscr{C}$ and its dual $\mathscr{C}^{\perp}$ are both decreasing monomial codes and computed all the minimum weight codewords by using Theorem 3. The conditions of Corollary 1 were met and the code was weakly self-dual $\mathscr{C} \subset \mathscr{C}^{\perp}$. The minimum distance of $\mathscr{C}$ turned out to be equal to 32 and there were 42176 codewords of this weight, whereas the minimum distance of $\mathscr{C}^{\perp}$ was 8 and there were 6912 codewords of this weight in the dual. The same number of codewords were found by Dumer's algorithm in $\mathscr{C}^{\pi}$ and in $(\mathscr{C}^{\pi})^{\perp}$. It tooks 27 seconds to find these codewords in $\mathscr{C}^{\pi}$ and 3 seconds to find these codewords in $(\mathscr{C}^{\pi})^{\perp}$ on a 8-core XEON E3-1240 running at 3.40 GHz.

But the most time consuming part was Step 6 of the attack when we have to compute the various $\Sigma(i,j)$'s that are needed. This is done again by using Dumer's algorithm. The difference with obtaining codewords of minimum weight of the polar code is that in the polar case we know beforehand the number of minimum weight codewords by using a counting procedure based on Theorem 3 and we can stop the search procedure once we have the right amount of different codewords. However when we compute $\Sigma(i,j)$ we do not know beforehand the number of minimum weight codewords in $\mathcal{P}_j(\mathscr{C}(i))$ and we use a probabilistic procedure based on the coupon collector problem : once we have found n different minimal codewords, where on average we have found each codeword $\alpha \ln n$ times we stop the procedure for a certain value of α greater than 1. Here we have taken α to be equal to 3. In this case, to speed up the computation we chose the $c(i)$'s to be minimum weight codewords of $\mathscr{C}$. More than 80 % of the total computation is actually taken for the last step of induction where we recover a permutation for the whole $[2048, 614]$ code from the partial permutation acting on half its positions. This takes about 227 hours and the total computation time is about 280 hours. This part of the attack is very likely to be improved significantly if need be.

6   Conclusion

Despite the fact that the code equivalence problem for binary polar codes is a hard instance for the Support Splitting Algorithm, we have shown in this paper that it can nevertheless be solved rather efficiently by a more sophisticated algorithm consisting in (i) looking for minimum weight codewords, (ii) classifying them by using our knowledge of the automorphism group of the polar code to find a particular minimum weight codeword, (iii) use this particular codeword to partition the code positions into affine spaces, (iv) puncture the set of positions with respect to all these affine spaces but one, and solve the code equivalence problem on this reduced problem. We use this to solve the code equivalence problem by induction on increasing affine spaces.

This allows to break the McEliece cryptosystem for the parameters proposed in [SK14]. It is likely that the only way to avoid this kind of attack (or possible improvements on it) is to look for polar code parameters for which we are unable to find minimum weight codewords either in the code or in its dual. This would require to change significantly the parameters proposed in [SK14] that would make such polar codes much less attractive for a use in a McEliece cryptosystem.

To obtain this attack we have proposed a new code family, that we call decreasing monomial codes containing as a particular subcase Reed-Muller codes and binary polar codes. These decreasing monomial codes have a very large permutation group that gives some insight about the permutation group of polar codes. This knowledge on the permutation group of polar codes we obtained could also be used in other settings, for instance to improve the decoding performances of polar codes.

This attack can be considered as a first step towards studying the polar code based McEliece scheme proposed in [HSEA14]. Our attack does not apply directly to this scheme since it is based on taking a particular kind of random subcode of the polar code. In such a case, the system does not consist in solving the code equivalence problem (or we have to solve as many instances as the number of possible subcodes of this kind which becomes unfeasible in this case). However it seems that some of the tools provided here, and a particular property of polar codes, might also be used to attack such a scheme. Indeed, taking the square of the polar code or the square of its dual (with the definition of a square code given in [CGG+14]) gives a code which is not the full space in many cases. If the subcode of a polar code was chosen uniformly at random among the spaces of some prescribed codimension inside the code, then the square of such codes would be almost always equal to the square of the polar code when the codimension is large enough. This would give an attack since the square of a polar code which is a decreasing monomial code is readily seen to be a decreasing monomial code itself. From there we can solve the code equivalence problem on the square of this code by using the tools given in this paper. This reveals the secret permutation and breaks the system. With the way the subcodes are chosen in [HSEA14] this does not happen, but still the square of the subcode is a very large subcode of the square of the polar code itself and this looks highly suspicious.

A   Proofs of the Results of Section 3

A.1   Proof of Proposition 2

In order to prove this result, we first prove a few lemmas about the partial order we introduced.

Lemma 2. *For all f and g in $\mathcal{M}$, $f \preceq g$ if and only if $\check{f} \succeq \check{g}$.*

Proof. Let $f = x_{i_1} \ldots x_{i_s}$ and $g = x_{j_1} \ldots x_{j_t}$ with $s \leqslant t$ and $i_1 < \cdots < i_s$, $j_1 < \cdots < j_t$. Then we have two cases:

- if $\deg f = \deg g$ then by definition of the order we have $i_\ell \leqslant j_\ell$ for all $j = 1, \ldots, s$. Consider the ℓ-th variable $x_{i'_\ell}$ in the monomial $\check{f}$ and the ℓ-th variable $x_{j'_\ell}$ in the monomial $\check{g}$. Let us define

$$\varphi(u) \stackrel{\text{def}}{=} \ell - 1 + \#\{i_a : i_a \leqslant u\}$$
$$\gamma(u) \stackrel{\text{def}}{=} \ell - 1 + \#\{j_a : j_a \leqslant u\}$$

Observe now that

(i) since $\varphi(u+1)$ is either equal to $\varphi(u)$ or to $\varphi(u) + 1$ and since $\varphi(0) \geqslant 0$, $\varphi(m-1) \leqslant m-1$, there exists at least one u such that $\varphi(u) = u$,

(ii) when $\varphi(u) = u$ this means that there exist exactly ℓ variables x_b for b in $\{0, 1, \ldots, u\}$ that belong to the monomial $\check{f}$.

All this implies that i'_ℓ is the smallest index u such that $\varphi(u) = u$ (or what amounts to the same it is the smallest index u such that $\varphi(u) \leqslant u$). A similar property holds for j'_ℓ. In other words

$$i'_\ell = \min\{u : \varphi(u) \leqslant u\} \tag{2}$$
$$j'_\ell = \min\{u : \gamma(u) \leqslant u\} \tag{3}$$

From the fact that $j_a \geqslant i_a$ for all a in $\{1, \ldots, s\}$ we have that for all indices u

$$\varphi(u) \geqslant \gamma(u) \tag{4}$$

On the other hand, we know that $i'_\ell = \varphi(i'_\ell)$, where the righthand term is larger than or equal to $\gamma(i'_\ell)$ by using (4). Therefore $\gamma(i'_\ell) \leqslant i'_\ell$, and by using (3) we deduce that $j'_\ell \leqslant i'_\ell$.

- if $\deg f < \deg g$ then by definition of the order: $f \preceq g \Leftrightarrow \exists g_1 \in \mathcal{M}$ s.t. $g = g_1 g_2$ with $\deg g_1 = \deg f$ and $f \preceq g_1$. From the first case we deduce that $\check{f} \succeq \check{g_1}$. On the other hand one checks immediately that $\check{g_1} \succeq \check{g}$. From these two inequalities we deduce $\check{f} \succeq \check{g}$.

Corollary 2. *Let $I \subseteq \mathcal{M}$ be a decreasing set then $\mathcal{M} \setminus \check{I}$ is a decreasing set.*

Proof. Let h be a monomial that belongs to $\mathcal{M} \setminus \check{I}$, and let g be a monomial such that $g \preceq h$. If $g \notin \mathcal{M} \setminus \check{I}$ then it would mean that there exists $f \in I$ such that $g = \check{f}$. This means that $\check{f} \preceq h$ and by using Lemma 2 we would get $\check{h} \preceq \check{\check{f}} = f$. Since I is a decreasing set, $\check{h} \in I$, that is to say, $\check{\check{h}} = h \in \check{I}$ which contradicts the assumption. Therefore $\mathcal{M} \setminus \check{I}$ is a decreasing set.

These lemmas can now be used to prove Proposition 2 that we recall below.

Proposition. *Let $\mathscr{C}(I)$ be a decreasing monomial code, then its dual is a decreasing monomial code given by*

$$\mathscr{C}(I)^\perp = \mathscr{C}(\mathcal{M} \setminus \check{I}).$$

Proof. As $|\check{I}| = |I|$, we have $\dim \mathscr{C}(\mathcal{M} \setminus \check{I}) = |\mathcal{M}| - |\check{I}| = |\mathcal{M}| - |I| = 2^m - \dim \mathscr{C}(I) = \dim \mathscr{C}(I)^{\perp}$, so we need to prove only one inclusion.

Let $f \in \mathcal{M} \setminus \check{I}$ and consider $g \in I$. Notice that

$$< \mathsf{ev}(f), \mathsf{ev}(g) > = < \mathsf{ev}(fg), \mathsf{ev}(1) >$$

where $< ., . >$ stands for the standard inner product in $\{0,1\}^{2^m}$: $< \boldsymbol{x}, \boldsymbol{y} > = \sum_i x_i y_i$. Observe now that fg is a monomial and that the only monomial whose evaluation is not orthogonal (with respect to $<, >$) to the all 1 vector is the "full" monomial $x_1 \ldots x_m$. Assume now that we are in such a case: $fg = x_1 \cdots x_m$. This means that $\check{g}$ is a divisor of f. A divisor of a monomial is always smaller than or equal to this monomial with our definition of order. Therefore $\check{g} \preceq f$. From Corollary 2 we know that $\mathcal{M} \setminus \check{I}$ is a decreasing set and that this would imply $\check{g} \in \mathcal{M} \setminus \check{I}$. This would imply that $\check{\check{g}} = g$ would belong to $\check{\mathcal{M}} \setminus \check{I} = \mathcal{M} \setminus I$. This would contradict the assumption that g belongs to I. Therefore we proved by contradiction that $\mathscr{C}(\mathcal{M} \setminus \check{I}) \subseteq \mathscr{C}(I)^{\perp}$.

A.2   Proof of Theorem 1

Let us recall this theorem:

Theorem. *The permutation group of a decreasing monomial code in m variables contains* LTA_m.

Proof. Let $\mathscr{C}(I)$ be a decreasing monomial code and let π be in LTA_m. Consider $\boldsymbol{x}$ in $\mathbb{F}_2^m$. Let $\boldsymbol{x}' \stackrel{\text{def}}{=} \pi(\boldsymbol{x})$. There exist binary numbers a_{ij} and ε_i such that for any i in $\{0, \ldots, m-1\}$ we have

$$x_i' = x_i + \sum_{j<i} a_{ij} x_j + \varepsilon_i.$$

An affine permutation π acts also in a natural way on monomials, with its action being defined by

$$\pi(x_{i_1} \ldots x_{i_s}) \stackrel{\text{def}}{=} x_{i_1}' \ldots x_{i_s}'.$$

In other words the action of an affine permutation π on a monomial f is given by $f \circ \pi$. Observe that this action is such that

$$\mathsf{ev}(f)^{\pi} = \mathsf{ev}(f \circ \pi).$$

Choose now a monomial f in I and use the observation above. We can expand $f \circ \pi$ and verify that it is a sum of monomials that are smaller than f with respect to the order $\preceq$ that we introduced. Since I is a decreasing set, then all these monomials belong to I as well and therefore we obviously have that $\mathsf{ev}(f \circ \pi)$ is also in $\mathscr{C}(I)$. $\mathscr{C}(I)$ is therefore invariant by π.

A.3   Proof of Proposition 3

Let $\mathscr{C}(I)$ be a decreasing monomial code. Let us start by proving Point (i), namely that *the minimum distance of $\mathscr{C}(I)$ is equal to* $2^{m-r_+(\mathscr{C}(I))}$. This follows on the spot by noticing that r_+ is also the largest degree of a monomial in I. If we consider the evaluation of this monomial we obtain a codeword of weight $2^{m-r_+(\mathscr{C}(I))}$. This implies that the minimum distance of $\mathscr{C}(I)$ is smaller than or equal to this quantity. On the other hand, the minimum distance of $\mathscr{C}(I)$ is larger than or equal to the minimum distance of $\mathscr{R}(r_+, m)$ which is equal to $2^{m-r_+(\mathscr{C}(I))}$ by using Theorem 2. This implies our claim.

Consider now the second point that we recall below

$$r_-(\mathscr{C}(I)^\perp) = m - 1 - r_+(\mathscr{C}(I)) \tag{5}$$
$$r_+(\mathscr{C}(I)^\perp) = m - 1 - r_-(\mathscr{C}(I)) \tag{6}$$

This follows immediately from Proposition 2: $\mathscr{C}(I)^\perp = \mathscr{C}(\mathcal{M} \setminus \check{I})$ and the alternative definitions of $r_-(\mathscr{C}(I)^\perp)$ and of $r_+(\mathscr{C}(I)^\perp)$ which are respectively the largest degree r such that all monomials of degree r are monomials in $\mathcal{M} \setminus \check{I}$ and the largest degree of a monomial that belongs to $\mathcal{M} \setminus \check{I}$.

The third point, namely that *the minimum distance of $\mathscr{C}(I)^\perp$ is equal to* $2^{r_-(\mathscr{C}(I))+1}$ is a straightforward of Point(i) applied to the monomial code $\mathscr{C}(I)^\perp$ and by using (6).

A.4   Proof of Proposition 3

Here we want to prove that any minimum weight codeword c in a decreasing monomial code $\mathscr{C}(I)$ can be written as $c = \mathrm{ev}(f)^\pi$ where f is a monomial in I and π an element of $\mathbb{LTA}_m$.

Note that from Proposition 3 we know that a minimum weight codeword of $\mathscr{C}(I)$ is also a minimum codeword of $\mathscr{R}(r_+(\mathscr{C}(I)), m)$. For simplicity we will simply write r_+ for $r_+(\mathscr{C}(I))$ from now on. By using Theorem 2, we know that c can be written as the evaluation of the product of r_+ independent affine forms $x'_0 \overset{\mathrm{def}}{=} \varepsilon_0 + \sum_j a_{0j} x_j, \cdots, x'_{r_+-1} \overset{\mathrm{def}}{=} \varepsilon_{r_+-1} + \sum_j a_{r_+-1,j} x_j$ where the ε_i's are elements of the binary field $\mathbb{F}_2$. We claim now that there are r_+ independent affine forms $x''_0, \ldots, x''_{r_+-1}$ such that:

(i) $\mathrm{ev}(x'_0 \ldots x'_{r_+-1}) = \mathrm{ev}(x''_0 \ldots x''_{r_+-1})$,
(ii) for all $i \in \{0, \ldots, r_+ - 1\}$ we have that the x''_i's can be written as $\varepsilon'_i + \sum_{j<\varphi(i)} a'_{\varphi(i),j} x_j$, where φ is some permutation of $\{0, 1, \ldots, m-1\}$ and the ε'_i's and $a'_{\varphi(i),j}$ are binary.

This is easy to check by considering the affine form x'_i that involves the "largest" variable x_j (the one consisting of the largest index j). Let x_{j_0} be this variable. We may assume without loss of generality that this is x'_0. We can check now that

$$\mathrm{ev}(x'_0 x'_1 \ldots x'_{r_+-1}) = \mathrm{ev}(x'_0 x'''_1 \ldots x'''_{r_+-1}),$$

where $x_i''' = x_i' - x_0' - 1$ if x_i' involves the variable x_{j_0} and $x_i''' = x_i'$ otherwise. Observe now that the $r_+ - 1$ affine forms $x_1''', \ldots, x_{r_+-1}'''$ involve only variables x_j which are such that $j < j_0$. We can carry on this process with these
$r_+ - 1$ (independent) affine forms $x'''1, \ldots, x_{r_+-1}'''$ by considering the variable
x_j which is the largest among the variables that are involved in these affine
forms and so on and so forth. We end up with r_+ affine forms $x_0'', \ldots, x_{r_+-1}''$
which have exactly the aforementioned properties (i) and (ii). Consider the
monomial $x_{j_0} \ldots x_{j_{r_+-1}}$ which is the product of the "largest" variable x_j in
each of these x''_i's. This monomial has to belong to I and we obviously have
$\mathsf{ev}(x''_0 \ldots x''_{r_+-1}) = \mathsf{ev}(\pi(x_{j_0} \ldots x_{j_{r_+-1}}))$ for some π in $\mathbb{LTA}_m$. This proves our
theorem.

B   Proof of the Results of Section 4

B.1   Proof of Theorem 4

We will first begin this proof by proving a general result about the dual of
shortened monomial codes.

Lemma 3. *Let $\mathscr{C}(I)$ be a decreasing monomial code and $g \in I$. Let $\mathsf{supp}(g)$ be
the support of $\mathsf{ev}(g)$. We denote by $E\left(\mathcal{S}_{\mathsf{supp}(g)}\left(\mathscr{C}(I)\right)\right)^{\perp}$ the dual of the shortened
code in $\mathsf{supp}(g)$ that we have extended by zeros in the positions in which we have
shortened the code. Then*

$$E\left(\mathcal{S}_{\mathsf{supp}(g)}\left(\mathscr{C}(I)\right)\right)^{\perp} = \{\mathsf{ev}((1+g)f) : f \in \mathcal{M} \setminus \check{I}\}$$

Proof. Recall that we have

$$\left(\mathcal{S}_{\mathsf{supp}(g)}\left(\mathscr{C}(I)\right)\right)^{\perp} = \mathcal{P}_{\mathsf{supp}(g)}\left(\mathscr{C}(I)^{\perp}\right)$$

We know that $\mathscr{C}(I)^{\perp} = \mathscr{C}(\mathcal{M} \setminus \check{I})$. The lemma follows from this and the fact the
$\mathsf{ev}(1+g)$ takes value 1 on the complementary of $\mathsf{supp}(g)$ and 0 on $\mathsf{supp}(g)$.

The following notation turns out to be convenient.

Notation 2. *For a monomial $g = x_{i_1} \ldots x_{i_s}$, its set of indices $Ind(g)$ is given
by $\{i_1, \ldots, i_s\}$ and its intersection $g \wedge h$ with a monomial h is given by*

$$g \wedge h \overset{def}{=} \Pi_{i \in Ind(g) \cap Ind(h)} x_i.$$

We will also need the following result that is only a slight generalization of
[Mn07, Proposition 6, p. 69] (and our proof will follow closely the proof of this
proposition).

Lemma 4. *Let g be some monomial of degree $s \geqslant 1$. Denote by $\mathsf{supp}(g)$ the
support of $\mathsf{ev}(g)$, then the minimum distance of $\left(\mathcal{S}_{\mathsf{supp}(g)}\left(\mathscr{C}(I)\right)\right)^{\perp}$ is greater
than or equal to 2^{r_-}. If the minimum distance is equal to 2^{r_-} then there exists
a monomial h in $\mathcal{M} \setminus \check{I}$ such that*

(i) the number of variables of $h \wedge g$ is $s - 1$,
(ii) the number of variables of $h \wedge \check{g}$ is $m - r_- - s$.

Proof. Let us take a nonzero codeword of $\mathscr{C}(I)^{\perp}$, say that is the evaluation of some polynomial f, which is in this case of degree at most $m - 1 - r_-$. Write $f = \sum_j m_j$ as a sum of monomials. Then $\tilde{f} \stackrel{\text{def}}{=} \sum_{j: g \nmid m_j} m_j$ is defined as the polynomial where we have removed from the monomial expression of f all monomials that are divisible by g. Since $(\mathcal{S}_{\mathsf{supp}(g)}(\mathscr{C}(I)))^{\perp} = \mathcal{P}_{\mathsf{supp}(g)}(\mathscr{C}(I)^{\perp})$, we want to prove that the evaluation of f on $\{0,1\}^m \setminus \mathsf{supp}(g)$ is either zero or of weight $\geqslant 2^{r_-}$. Notice that the evaluation on $\{0,1\}^m \setminus \mathsf{supp}(g)$ coincides with the evaluation of $\tilde{f}$.

Let us assume that $g = x_0 \ldots x_{s-1}$. With this choice, let us pick a monomial of $\tilde{f}$ that has maximum degree in $x_s, \ldots, x_{m-1}$. Let d be this degree (in $x_s, \ldots, x_{m-1}$). $\tilde{f}$ can be written as

$$\tilde{f} = m u(x_0, \ldots, x_{s-1}) + v(x_0, \ldots, x_{m-1}),$$

where m is a monomial of degree d in $x_s, \ldots, x_{m-1}$. We take here in the monomials whose sum is equal to $\tilde{f}$ all monomials that are divisible by m and u is just the sum of these monomials divided by m. Let d' be the degree of u which is necessarily smaller than s since $\tilde{f}$ does not contain any monomial divisible by g.

Notice that $u(x_0 \ldots x_{s-1})$ is non zero in at least $2^{s-d'} - 1$ entries if we do not count the $(1, \ldots, 1)$ entry, since its evaluation is a codeword of $\mathscr{R}(d', s)$.

Call a "block" the set of points $(x_0, \ldots, x_{m-1})$ which take a prescribed value on $x_0, \ldots, x_{s-1}$. The support $\mathsf{supp}(g)$ of g corresponds to the block $x_0 = 1, \ldots, x_{s-1} = 1$. Notice that the weight of $\mathsf{ev}(\tilde{f})$ restricted to a block (with the exception of the block $x_0 = 1, \ldots, x_{s-1} = 1$) is at least 2^{m-s-d}, since this restriction is a codeword of $\mathscr{R}(d, m-s)$. In other words the weight of $\mathsf{ev}(\tilde{f}(1+g))$ is lower-bounded by

$$|\mathsf{ev}(\tilde{f})(1+g)| \geqslant 2^{m-s-d}(2^{s-d'} - 1) \geqslant 2^{m-s-d} 2^{s-d'} \frac{1}{2} = 2^{m-d-d'-1}.$$

Notice that we have $d + d' \leqslant m - r_- - 1$ and therefore we finally obtain

$$|\mathsf{ev}(\tilde{f})| \geqslant 2^{m-(m-r_--1)-1} = 2^{r_-}.$$

This proves the statement about the minimum distance in this case. A quick inspection of this proof shows that the only fact we used on g was that is is different from 1 (the particular form of g was only here to simplify notation), and therefore it also holds for all monomials g different from 1.

Assume now that the minimum distance of $(\mathcal{S}_{\mathsf{supp}(g)}(\mathscr{C}(I)))^{\perp}$ is equal to 2^{r_-}. By a quick inspection of this proof this means that $\deg u = s - 1$ and $\deg m = m - r_- - 1 - (s - 1) = m - r_- - s$. Write u as a set of monomials $u = \sum_j m'_j$ and choose m' as any monomial in this sum that is of degree $s - 1$. Obviously $h \stackrel{\text{def}}{=} m m'$ is a monomial of degree $s - 1 + m - r_- - s = m - r_- - 1$ that appears as a monomial in the sum $f = \sum_j m_j$. Therefore h is in $\mathcal{M} \setminus \check{I}$. Such an h has the aforementioned form.

We will now use this to prove Theorem 4. We recall its statement below.

Theorem. *Let* $g = x_{i_1} \ldots x_{i_{r_+}}$ *be a monomial of degree* r_+ *in* I. *Denote by* $\mathsf{supp}(g)$ *the support of* $\mathsf{ev}(g)$, *then the minimum distance of* $\left(\mathcal{S}_{\mathsf{supp}(g)}\left(\mathscr{C}(I)\right)\right)^{\perp}$ *is equal to* 2^{r_-} *if and only if there exists a monomial* h *in* $\mathcal{M} \setminus \check{I}$ *such that:*

(i) the number of variables of h *that are also variables of* g *is* $r_+ - 1$,
(ii) the number of variables of h *that are also variables of* $\check{g}$ *is* $m - r_- - r_+$.

Proof. First of all let us notice that the minimum distance of $E\left(\mathcal{S}_{\mathsf{supp}(g)}\left(\mathscr{C}(I)\right)\right)^{\perp}$ is the same as the minimum distance of $\left(\mathcal{S}_{\mathsf{supp}(g)}\left(\mathscr{C}(I)\right)\right)^{\perp}$. From Lemma 3 we know that any codeword in the first code can be written as $\mathsf{ev}((1+g)f))$ where f is polynomial which is a linear combination of monomials in $\mathcal{M} \setminus \check{I}$. Consider now that there is a monomial h satisfying the conditions above. Let us prove that the weight of $\mathsf{ev}((1+g)h)$ is equal to 2^{r_-}. Let i_0 be the only index that is in $\mathrm{Ind}(g)$ but not in $\mathrm{Ind}(g \wedge h)$. Observe now that

$$(1+g)h = (1 + x_{i_1} \ldots x_{i_{r_+}}) \prod_{i \in \mathrm{Ind}g \wedge h} x_i \prod_{i \in \mathrm{Ind}(\check{g} \wedge h)} x_i$$

$$= (1 + x_{i_0}) \prod_{i \in \mathrm{Ind}g \wedge h} x_i \prod_{i \in \mathrm{Ind}(\check{g} \wedge h)} x_i$$

$$= (1 + x_{i_0})h.$$

Thus
$$|\mathsf{ev}((1+g)h))| = |(\mathsf{ev}((1+x_{j_0})h)| = 2^{m-(m-r_--1+1)} = 2^{r_-}.$$

By using the lower-bound on the minimum distance coming from Lemma 4 we obtain that the minimum distance of $\left(\mathcal{S}_{\mathsf{supp}(g)}\left(\mathscr{C}(I)\right)\right)^{\perp}$ is equal to 2^{r_-}.

Assume now that the minimum distance of $\left(\mathcal{S}_{\mathsf{supp}(g)}\left(\mathscr{C}(I)\right)\right)^{\perp}$ is equal to 2^{r_-}, then we can use Lemma 4 and obtain the aforementioned claim.

B.2   Proof of Proposition 4

Proposition. $W^{\pi}_{\min}$ *is invariant by the action of* $\pi^{-1}\mathrm{LTA}_m\pi$ *and if* Σ *is a signature for* $W_{\min}$ *under the action of* LTA_m, *then it is also a signature for the action of* $\pi^{-1}\mathrm{LTA}_m\pi$ *on* $W^{\pi}_{\min}$.

Proof. The invariance of $W^{\pi}_{\min}$ follows from the fact that (i) LTA_m is a subgroup of the permutation group of $\mathscr{C}(I)$ by Theorem 1 and (ii) this implies that $\pi^{-1}\mathrm{LTA}_m\pi$ is a subgroup of the permutation group of $\mathscr{C}(I)^{\pi}$ by Proposition 1. For the second part, it suffices to prove that Σ takes different values on the orbits of $W^{\pi}_{\min}$ under the action of $\pi^{-1}\mathrm{LTA}_m\pi$. Consider two elements $\boldsymbol{x}^{\pi}$ and $\boldsymbol{y}^{\pi}$ that belong to two different orbits. They are the permuted versions of $\boldsymbol{x}$ and $\boldsymbol{y}$ which belong to different orbits of $W_{\min}$. If this were not the case we would have $\boldsymbol{x} = \boldsymbol{y}^{\gamma}$ for γ in LTA_m. However this would imply that $\boldsymbol{x}^{\pi} = \boldsymbol{y}^{\gamma\pi} = \boldsymbol{y}^{\pi\pi^{-1}\gamma\pi} = (\boldsymbol{y}^{\pi})^{\pi^{-1}\gamma\pi}$ and this would imply that $\boldsymbol{x}^{\pi}$ and $\boldsymbol{y}^{\pi}$ would be in the same orbit under the action of $\pi^{-1}\mathrm{LTA}_m\pi$. We finish the proof by observing that

$$\Sigma(\boldsymbol{x}^\pi, \mathscr{C}(I)^\pi) = \Sigma(\boldsymbol{x}, \mathscr{C}(I))$$
$$\Sigma(\boldsymbol{y}^\pi, \mathscr{C}(I)^\pi) = \Sigma(\boldsymbol{y}, \mathscr{C}(I))$$

Therefore $\Sigma(\boldsymbol{x}^\pi, \mathscr{C}(I)^\pi)$ and $\Sigma(\boldsymbol{y}^\pi, \mathscr{C}(I)^\pi)$ are different since $\Sigma(\boldsymbol{x}, \mathscr{C}(I))$ and $\Sigma(\boldsymbol{y}, \mathscr{C}(I))$ are different.

B.3   Proof of Proposition 5

Proposition. *The orbit of $\boldsymbol{c}_{\min}$ under LTA_m consists of 2^{r_+} codewords that are of the form $\boldsymbol{c}_{\min}(\varepsilon_0, \ldots, \varepsilon_{r_+-1})$ where the ε_i's are arbitrary element of $\mathbb{F}_2$. The orbit of $\boldsymbol{c}_{\min}^\pi$ under $\pi^{-1}\mathrm{LTA}_m\pi$ is given by 2^{r_+} codewords of weight 2^{m-r_+} that have disjoint supports which are the permuted versions $A(\varepsilon_0, \ldots, \varepsilon_{r_+-1})^\pi$ of the affine spaces $A(\varepsilon_0, \ldots, \varepsilon_{r_+-1})$.*

Proof. Let f be the monomial $x_0 \ldots x_{r_+-1}$ (i.e. $\boldsymbol{c}_{\min} = \mathsf{ev}(f)$). Under the action of π in LTA_m this monomial is transformed into $x_0' \ldots x_{r_+-1}'$ where $x_i' = \varepsilon_i + x_i + \sum_{j<i} a_{ij}x_j$ where the ε_i's and the a_{ij}'s are binary. The support of such a monomial is given by the affine space $x_0' = 1, \ldots, x_{r_+-1}' = 1$, but this is readily seen to be an affine space of the form $x_0 = \varepsilon_0', \ldots, x_{r_+-1} = \varepsilon_{r_+-1}'$ where the ε_i''s are binary. This implies the first claim. The claim on the orbit of $\boldsymbol{c}_{\min}^\pi$ follows from the fact that for any $\gamma \in \mathrm{LTA}_m$ we have

$$(\boldsymbol{c}_{\min}^\pi)^{\pi^{-1}\gamma\pi} = (\boldsymbol{c}_{\min}^\gamma)^\pi.$$

References

[Ari09] Arikan, E.: Channel polarization: a method for constructing capacity-achieving codes for symmetric binary-input memoryless channels. IEEE Trans. Inform. Theory **55**(7), 3051–3073 (2009)

[BBC08] Bodrato, M., Chiaraluce, F., Baldi, M.: A new analysis of the McEliece cryptosystem based on QC-LDPC codes. In: Ostrovsky, R., De Prisco, R., Visconti, I. (eds.) SCN 2008. LNCS, vol. 5229, pp. 246–262. Springer, Heidelberg (2008)

[BBD09] Bernstein, D.J., Buchmann, J., Dahmen, E. (eds.): Post-Quantum Cryptography. Springer-Verlag, Heidelberg (2009)

[BC07] Baldi, M., Chiaraluce, F.: Cryptanalysis of a new instance of McEliece cryptosystem based on QC-LDPC codes. In: Proceedings of IEEE International Symposium Information Theory - ISIT, Nice, France, pp. 2591–2595 (2007)

[BL05] Thierry, P.: Berger and Pierre Loidreau.: how to mask the structure of codes for a cryptographic use. Des. Codes Cryptogr. **35**(1), 63–79 (2005)

[BLP10] Bernstein, D.J., Lange, T., Peters, C.: Wild McEliece. In: Biryukov, A., Gong, G., Stinson, D.R. (eds.) SAC 2010. LNCS, vol. 6544, pp. 143–158. Springer, Heidelberg (2011)

[BLP11] Lange, T., Peters, C., Bernstein, D.J.: Wild McEliece incognito. In: Yang, B.-Y. (ed.) PQCrypto 2011. LNCS, vol. 7071, pp. 244–254. Springer, Heidelberg (2011)

[CFS01] Courtois, N.T., Finiasz, M., Sendrier, N.: How to achieve a McEliece-Based digital signature scheme. In: Boyd, C. (ed.) ASIACRYPT 2001. LNCS, vol. 2248, pp. 157–174. Springer, Heidelberg (2001)

[CGG+14] Couvreur, A., Gaborit, P., Gauthier-Umaña, V., Otmani, A., Tillich, J.-P.: Distinguisher-based attacks on public-key cryptosystems using Reed-Solomon codes. Des. Codes Cryptogr. **73**(2), 641–666 (2014)

[CMCP14] Couvreur, A., Márquez-Corbella, I., Pellikaan, R.: A polynomial time attack against algebraic geometry code based public key cryptosystems. In: Proceedings of IEEE International Symposium Information Theory - ISIT 2014, pp. 1446–1450, June 2014

[COT14] Couvreur, A., Tillich, J.P., Otmani, A.: Polynomial time attack on wild McEliece over quadratic extensions. In: Nguyen, P.Q., Oswald, E. (eds.) EUROCRYPT 2014. LNCS, vol. 8441, pp. 17–39. Springer, Heidelberg (2014)

[CT91] Cover, T.M., Thomas, J.A.: Information Theory. Wiley Series in Telecommunications. Wiley, New York (1991)

[CTS15] Canto-Torres, R., Sendrier, N.: Analysis of information set decoding for a sub-linear error weight (2015) (preprint)

[Dum91] Dumer, I.: On minimum distance decoding of linear codes. In: Proceedings of the 5th Joint Soviet-Swedish International Workshop Information Theory, Moscow, pp. 50–52 (1991)

[FM08] Faure, C., Minder, L.: Cryptanalysis of the McEliece cryptosystem over hyperelliptic curves. In: Proceedings of the Eleventh International Workshop on Algebraic and Combinatorial Coding Theory, Pamporovo, Bulgaria, pp. 99–107, June 2008

[FPdP14] Perret, L., de Portzamparc, F., Faugère, J.-C.: Algebraic attack against variants of McEliece with goppa polynomial of a special form. In: Sarkar, P., Iwata, T. (eds.) ASIACRYPT 2014. LNCS, vol. 8873, pp. 21–41. Springer, Heidelberg (2014)

[HSEA14] Hooshmand, R., Shooshtari, M.K., Eghlidos, T., Aref, M.R.: Reducing the key length of McEliece cryptosystem using polar codes. In: 2014 11th International ISC Conference on Information Security and Cryptology (ISCISC), pp. 104–108. IEEE (2014)

[JM96] Janwa, H., Moreno, O.: McEliece public key cryptosystems using algebraic-geometric codes. Des. Codes Cryptogr. **8**(3), 293–307 (1996)

[Kra91] David Kravitz.: Digital signature algorithm. US patent 5231668, July 1991

[KU10] Korada, S.B., Urbanke, R.: Polar codes are optimal for lossy source coding. IEEE Trans. Inform. Theory **56**(4), 1751–1768 (2010)

[LJ12] Johansson, T., Löndahl, C.: A new version of McEliece PKC based on convolutional codes. In: Chim, T.W., Yuen, T.H. (eds.) ICICS 2012. LNCS, vol. 7618, pp. 461–470. Springer, Heidelberg (2012)

[LT13] Landais, G., Tillich, J.-P.: An efficient attack of a McEliece cryptosystem variant based on convolutional codes. In: Gaborit, P. (ed.) PQCrypto 2013. LNCS, vol. 7932, pp. 102–117. Springer, Heidelberg (2013)

[McE78] McEliece, R.J.: A public-key system based on algebraic coding theory, pp. 114–116. Jet Propulsion Lab, 1978. DSN Progress Report 44

[Mn07] Minder, L.: Cryptography based on error correcting codes. Ph.D thesis, Ecole Polytechnique Fédérale de Lausanne (2007)

[MS86]   MacWilliams, F.J., Sloane, N.J.A.: The Theory of Error-Correcting Codes, 5th edn. North- Holland Publishing, Amsterdam (1986)

[MS07]   Minder, L., Shokrollahi, M.A.: Cryptanalysis of the sidelnikov cryptosystem. In: Naor, M. (ed.) EUROCRYPT 2007. LNCS, vol. 4515, pp. 347–360. Springer, Heidelberg (2007)

[MTSB12] Misoczki, R., Tillich, J.-P., Sendrier, N., Barreto, P.S.L.M.: MDPC-McEliece: New McEliece variants from moderate density parity-check codes. IACR Cryptology ePrint Archive, Report 2012/409, 2012 (2012)

[Nie86] Niederreiter, H.: Knapsack-type cryptosystems and algebraic coding theory. Probl. Control Inf. Theory **15**(2), 159–166 (1986)

[OT12]   Otmani, A., Tillich, J.-P.: On the design of code-based signatures. In: Code-based Cryptography Workshop (CBC 2012), Lyngby, Denmark, May 2012

[OTD08] Otmani, A., Tillich, J.-P., Dallot, L.: Cryptanalysis of McEliece cryptosystem based on quasi-cyclic LDPC codes. In: Proceedings of First International Conference on Symbolic Computation and Cryptography, Beijing, China, April 28–30 2008, pp. 69–81. LMIB Beihang University (2008)

[PR97]   Petrank, E., Roth, R.M.: Is code equivalence easy to decide? IEEE Trans. Inform. Theory **43**(5), 1602–1604 (1997)

[RSA78] Rivest, R.L., Shamir, A., Adleman, L.M.: A method for obtaining digital signatures and public-key cryptosystems. Commun. ACM **21**(2), 120–126 (1978)

[Sen00] Sendrier, N.: Finding the permutation between equivalent linear codes: the support splitting algorithm. IEEE Trans. Inform. Theory **46**(4), 1193–1203 (2000)

[Sho97] Shor, P.W.: Polynomial-time algorithms for prime factorization and discrete logarithms on a quantum computer. SIAM J. Comput. **26**(5), 1484–1509 (1997)

[Sid94] Sidelnikov, V.M.: A public-key cryptosytem based on Reed-Muller codes. Discrete Math. Appl. **4**(3), 191–207 (1994)

[SK14]   Shrestha, S.R., Kim, Y.-S.: New McEliece cryptosystem based on polar codes as a candidate for post-quantum cryptography. In: 2014 14th International Symposium on Communications and Information Technologies (ISCIT), pp. 368–372. IEEE (2014)

[SS92]   Sidelnikov, V.M., Shestakov, S.O.: On the insecurity of cryptosystems based on generalized Reed-Solomon codes. Discrete Math. Appl. **1**(4), 439–444 (1992)

[Ste88] Stern, J.: A method for finding codewords of small weight. In: Cohen, G.D., Wolfmann, J. (eds.) Coding Theory and Applications. LNCS, vol. 388, pp. 106–113. Springer, Heidelberg (1998)

[Wie10] Wieschebrink, C.: Cryptanalysis of the niederreiter public key scheme based on GRS subcodes. In: Sendrier, N. (ed.) PQCrypto 2010. LNCS, vol. 6061, pp. 61–72. Springer, Heidelberg (2010)

Analysis of Information Set Decoding
for a Sub-linear Error Weight

Rodolfo Canto Torres[1,2]([✉]) and Nicolas Sendrier[1]

[1] Inria, Rocquencourt, France
{rodolfo.canto-torres,nicolas.sendrier}@inria.fr
[2] Inria, 2 rue Simone IFF, Paris, France

Abstract. The security of code-based cryptography is strongly related to the hardness of generic decoding of linear codes. The best known generic decoding algorithms all derive from the Information Set Decoding algorithm proposed by Prange in 1962. The ISD algorithm was later improved by Stern in 1989 (and Dumer in 1991). Those last few years, some significant improvements have occurred. First by May, Meurer, and Thomae at Asiacrypt 2011, then by Becker, Joux, May, and Meurer at Eurocrypt 2012, and finally by May and Ozerov at Eurocrypt 2015. With those methods, correcting w errors in a binary linear code of length n and dimension k has a cost $2^{cw(1+o(1))}$ when the length n grows, where c is a constant, depending of the code rate k/n and of the error rate w/n. The above ISD variants have all improved that constant c when they appeared.

When the number of errors w is sub-linear, $w = o(n)$, the cost of all ISD variants still has the form $2^{cw(1+o(1))}$. We prove here that the constant c only depends of the code rate k/n and is the same for all the known ISD variants mentioned above, including the fifty years old Prange algorithm. The most promising variants of McEliece encryption scheme use either Goppa codes, with $w = O(n/\log(n))$, or MDPC codes, with $w = O(\sqrt{n})$. Our result means that, in those cases, when we scale up the system parameters, the improvement of the latest variants of ISD become less and less significant. This fact has been observed already, we give here a formal proof of it. Moreover, our proof seems to indicate that any foreseeable variant of ISD should have the same asymptotic behavior.

1 Introduction

Code-based cryptography is among the most promising solutions for designing cryptosystems safe against a quantum computer. In particular the McEliece public-key encryption scheme [1], based on binary Goppa codes, has so far successfully resisted to all cryptanalysis effort. Let us also mention a recent compact key variant [2] based on quasi-cyclic moderate density parity check codes. The effective security of those schemes is based on the hardness of decoding in a binary linear code. Thus, the improvement and the understanding of the best generic decoding technique is of great interest to select secure parameters for

© Springer International Publishing Switzerland 2016
T. Takagi (Ed.): PQCrypto 2016, LNCS 9606, pp. 144–161, 2016.
DOI: 10.1007/978-3-319-29360-8_10

code-based cryptosystems. Typically, when the amount of error to correct w is proportional to the code length n, the last variant of generic decoding, proposed by May and Ozerov [3] improves the asymptotic exponent (*i.e.* decreases the number of security bits) by about 20 % to 30 % compared with the elementary Prange algorithm [4]. This gain decreases relatively for a smaller amount of errors. Here we prove that when the error rate w/n tends to zero, the relative gain collapses completely.

The (Computational) Syndrome Decoding Problem. $CSD_{n,k,w}$ consists in correcting w errors (bit flips) that have occurred on a binary word belonging to a binary linear $[n, k]$ code (*i.e.* a k-dimensional subspace of $\mathbf{F}_2^n$). This problem is hard [5,6] and is central to assess the security of code-based cryptosystems.

Information Set Decoding. (ISD) was introduced by Prange in 1962 [4]. It is a generic decoding algorithm: it solves CSD taking only as inputs a basis of the code and a noisy codeword. We refer to this algorithm as Pra-ISD. There has been numerous works improving and analyzing ISD [3,7–14]. The variants which have improved the asymptotic behavior are chronologically due to: Stern [8] and Dumer [9][1], referred to as SD-ISD; May, Meurer, and Thomae [13], referred to as MMT-ISD; Becker, Joux, May, and Meurer [14], referred to as BJMM-ISD; May and Ozerov [3], referred to as Nearest Neighbors or NN-ISD. If $\mathcal{A}$ is one of the above algorithms, we denote $WF_{\mathcal{A}}(n, k, w)$ its workfactor, that is its average algorithmic cost, when addressing a (solvable) instance of $CSD_{n,k,w}$.

Asymptotic Analysis of Information Set Decoding. The usual setting for the asymptotic analysis of ISD variants is to consider, for growing n, a family of problems $CSD_{n,Rn,\tau n}$, with two positive constants: R, $0 < R < 1$, the code rate and τ, $0 < \tau \leq h^{-1}(1 - R)$, the error rate[2]. Any known variant $\mathcal{A}$ of ISD solves this family of problems for a cost

$$WF_{\mathcal{A}}(n, Rn, w = \tau n) = 2^{c'n(1+o(1))} = 2^{cw(1+o(1))}$$

when n grows, where the constants c' and $c = c'/\tau$ depend of R, τ, and of the variant. The various improvements of ISD have gradually improved the constant c. For instance, in Fig. 1 we give the value of c for $R = 0.5$ and τ varying from 0 to $h^{-1}(0.5) \approx 0.11$. We remark in the figure that the constant c does not vary very much with the error rate τ, moreover, when this rate tends to zero, all algorithms seem to have the same value for c.

---

[1] The results have been obtained independently, Dumer's variant is slightly better than Stern's, though by a very small amount.

[2] $h^{-1}(1 - R)$ is the asymptotic Gilbert-Varshamov bound, $h(x) = -x \log_2 x - (1 - x) \log_2(1 - x)$ is the binary entropy.

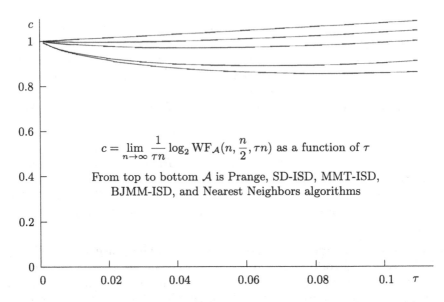

Fig. 1. Asymptotic exponent of ISD variants for binary codes of rate $1/2$

Our Contribution. We prove that if we consider a family of problems $\mathrm{CSD}_{n,Rn,w}$ with $\lim_{n\to\infty} w/n = 0$, we still have

$$\mathrm{WF}_{\mathcal{A}}(n, Rn, w) = 2^{cw(1+\mathbf{o}(1))}$$

when n grows, with a constant $c = -\log_2(1-R)$ regardless of the variant. There are many situations where $w = \mathbf{o}(n)$. The two most promising variants of McEliece encryption scheme for applications are based on binary Goppa codes [1] and on binary MDPC (Moderate Density Parity Check) codes [2]. Those codes correct respectively $w = \mathbf{O}(n/\log(n))$ and $w = \mathbf{O}(\sqrt{n})$ and thus they fall into the category we are considering here.

The paper is organized as follows. We first present a framework in which the known variants of ISD all fit. This framework allows us to give bounds on the algorithmic complexity. In the next section, we use those bounds to prove that asymptotically, when the error rate tends to zero, the complexity exponent is the same for all those variants. Finally we confront this asymptotic result to what we observe when computing the non asymptotic workfactors of decoding problems corresponding to the main McEliece-like code-based encryption schemes.

2   Generic Decoding

The (computational) syndrome decoding problem is stated as follows

Problem 1 (Computational Syndrome Decoding - CSD).
  input: $H \in \mathbf{F}_2^{(n-k)\times n}$, $s \in \mathbf{F}_2^{n-k}$, and an integer $w > 0$
 problem: Find $e \in \mathbf{F}_2^n$ of Hamming weight $\leq w$ such that $eH^T = s$.

It was proven NP-complete [5] and is conjectured hard on average [6,15]. It is equivalent to the decoding of w errors in a binary $[n, k]$ code of parity check matrix H. Solving this problem is often the best known attack against code-based cryptosystem, thus being able to accurately analyze the cost of the best CSD solvers is of great importance to select secure parameters and to understand how to scale up the security.

Our purpose is to solve $\text{CSD}(H_0, s_0, w)$ for some $H_0 \in \mathbf{F}_2^{(n-k)\times n}$ and $s_0 \in \mathbf{F}_2^{n-k}$. We will restrict the instance as follows.

Assumption 1 (on the instance (H_0, s_0, w) of CSD).

1. H_0 is chosen uniformly at random in $\mathbf{F}_2^{(n-k)\times n}$
2. s_0 is chosen uniformly at random in $\{eH_0^T \mid \text{wt}(e) = w\}$
3. w is smaller than the Gilbert-Varshamov distance, i.e. $\binom{n}{w} < 2^{n-k}$.

When this holds $\text{CSD}(H_0, s_0, w)$ has exactly one solution with high probability.

2.1   Information Set Decoding and Some Variants

We give in Fig. 2 a framework for many variants of ISD (all but the last one NN-ISD). This framework includes two additional integer parameters, p and ℓ, which will be chosen to minimize the cost of the algorithm. The optimal values of p and ℓ will depend on how instruction "1:" is implemented. The Prange algorithm corresponds to the degenerate case $p = \ell = 0$.

Proposition 1. *Within Assumption 1 on the input, we run the* generic_isd *procedure until the* SUCCESS *condition is met. The following holds on average up to a small constant factor:*

- *the instruction "1:" is executed at least* $\dfrac{\binom{n}{w}}{\binom{n-k-\ell}{w-p}\binom{k+\ell}{p}}$ *times,*
- *the instruction "2:" is executed at least* $\dfrac{\binom{n}{w}}{\binom{n-k-\ell}{w-p}2^{\ell}}$ *times.*

Proof is given in appendix.

Short Description of ISD Variants. We do not mean to be exhaustive nor self-contained here. We just give indications to estimate the cost of the algorithms. We refer the reader to the corresponding papers for a more detailed description. More specifically, we are interested in finding a lower bound on the cost L of one execution of instruction "1:" in Fig. 2. We will use the notation of that Figure.

The Stern-Dumer Variant: The instruction "1:" is performed by a birthday paradox. In that case, two lists of size $\binom{(k+\ell)/2}{p/2}$ are built then joined. We have $L \geq \binom{(k+\ell)/2}{p/2}$.

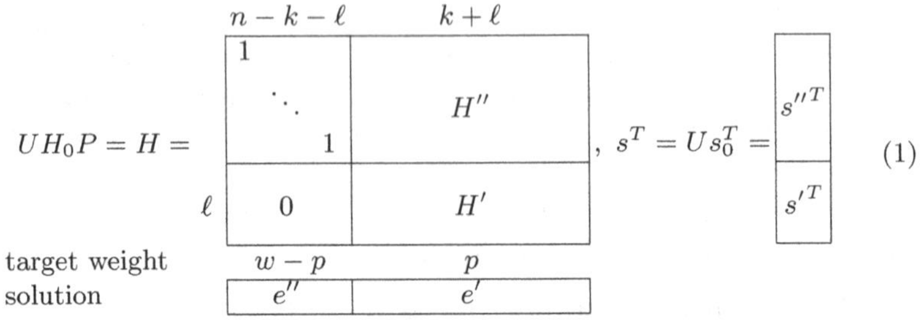

$$UH_0P = H = \begin{array}{c} \\ \ell \end{array} \begin{array}{|ccc|c|} \hline 1 & & & \\ & \ddots & & H'' \\ & & 1 & \\ \hline 0 & & & H' \\ \hline \end{array} \quad , \quad s^T = Us_0^T = \begin{array}{|c|} \hline s''^T \\ \hline s'^T \\ \hline \end{array} \quad (1)$$

target weight $\quad w-p \qquad p$

solution $\qquad \boxed{e'' \mid e'}$

procedure generic_isd
input: $H_0 \in \mathbf{F}_2^{(n-k)\times n}$, $s_0 \in \mathbf{F}_2^{n-k}$
repeat *(main loop)*
    $P \leftarrow$ random $n \times n$ permutation matrix
    $(H', H'', s', s'') \leftarrow \text{PartialGaussElim}(H_0P, s_0)$ // as in (1) above
1:   *Somehow compute* $\mathcal{E} \subset \{e' \in \mathbf{F}_2^{k+\ell} \mid \text{wt}(e') = p, e'H'^T = s'\}$
    for all $e' \in \mathcal{E}$
2:      $e'' \leftarrow e'H''^T + s''$; **if** $\text{wt}(e'') = w - p$ **then** SUCCESS

Fig. 2. A generic framework for most ISD variants

The MMT Variant: Four lists are joined in a two level tree structure. Four initial lists are joined pairwise to obtain two lists which are joined to produce $\mathcal{E}$. The four initial lists have size $\binom{(k+\ell)/2}{p/4}$, therefore $L \geq \binom{(k+\ell)/2}{p/4}$.

The BJMM Variant: The tree structure to join the lists has three levels and we initially build 8 lists of size $\binom{(k+\ell)/2}{p_2/2}$ with $p_2 = p/8 + \varepsilon_1/4 + \varepsilon_2/2$ where ε_1 and ε_2 are positive additional parameters. It follows that $L \geq \binom{(k+\ell)/2}{p_2/2} \geq \binom{(k+\ell)/2}{p/8}$. We remark in addition that we should also have $\binom{(k+\ell)/2}{p_2/2} \leq \binom{k+\ell}{p}$ else the algorithm would not perform better than a mere enumeration, in particular not better than SD-ISD, which cannot happen since SD-ISD is a particular case of BJMM-ISD in which some optimization parameters are restricted. It follows that the optimal value of p_2 is proportional to p with a ratio somewherebetween 0.25 and 2. Because $p_2 = p/8 + \varepsilon_1/4 + \varepsilon_2/2$, it also follows that $\varepsilon_1 = \mathbf{O}(p)$ and $\varepsilon_2 = \mathbf{O}(p)$.

The Nearest Neighbors Variant: This most recent variant does not fit exactly into the framework of Fig. 2. Still, we have the two parameters p and ℓ and the same *"main loop"* starting with same partial Gaussian elimination. Next, it starts as the BJMM variants by building 8 lists of size $\binom{(k+\ell)/2}{p_2/2}$ (with $p_2 = p/8 + \varepsilon_1/4 + \varepsilon_2/2$ as in BJMM-ISD). The tree structure to join the lists is the same as BJMM except for the last join which is replaced by a "nearest neighbors" search. We do not need the analyze further to find a lower bound.

The algorithm has the same *main loop* which succeeds with probability at most $\frac{\binom{n-k-\ell}{w-p}\binom{k+\ell}{p}}{\binom{n}{w}}$ and because it starts as BJMM, the total cost of an execution of the algorithm is at least

$$\mathrm{WF}_{\mathrm{NN-ISD}}(n,k,w) \geq \min_{p,\ell} \frac{\binom{n}{w}\binom{(k+\ell)/2}{p/8}}{\binom{n-k-\ell}{w-p}\binom{k+\ell}{p}} \geq \min_{p,\ell} \frac{\binom{n}{w}}{\binom{n-k-\ell}{w-p}\binom{k+\ell}{\frac{7}{8}p}} \qquad (2)$$

for large enough n,k (see proof of Corollary 1 in appendix for a proof of the rightmost inequality above). Moreover, from the algorithm description [3] the optimal value of ℓ verifies

$$2^\ell = \binom{p}{p/2}\binom{k+\ell-p}{\varepsilon_1}.$$

Finally note that, as in BJMM-ISD, we must have p_2 proportional to p, else the algorithm is outperformed by simpler variants. In particular, this means that $\varepsilon_1 = \mathbf{O}(p)$.

Lower Bound for ISD Variants. The cost L of one execution of instruction "1:" depends of the variants, from above we easily obtain the following bounds:

- for the SD-ISD variant we have $L \geq \binom{(k+\ell)/2}{p/2}$,
- for the MMT-ISD variant we have $L \geq \binom{(k+\ell)/2}{p/4}$,
- for the BJMM-ISD variant we have $L \geq \binom{(k+\ell)/2}{p/8}$.

Except for SD-ISD, the above bounds are loose. Nevertheless they are sufficient to serve our purpose, that is to prove the following statement.

Corollary 1. *For sufficiently large values of n,k, we have*

$$\mathrm{WF}_{\mathcal{A}}(n,k,w) \geq \min_{p,\ell} \frac{\binom{n}{w}}{\binom{n-k-\ell}{w-p}}\left(\frac{1}{\binom{k+\ell}{ap}} + \frac{1}{2^\ell}\right)$$

where a equals to $1/2$, $3/4$, and $7/8$ when $\mathcal{A}$ is respectively SD-ISD, MMT-ISD, and BJMM-ISD.

Proof is given in appendix.

Lower Bound for the Nearest Neighbors Variant. A lower bound is given above in Eq. (2). If we add to this bound that for an optimal choice of parameters we have $2^\ell = \binom{p}{p/2}\binom{k+\ell-p}{\varepsilon_1}$ and $\varepsilon_1 = \mathbf{O}(p)$, we have enough for our analysis in the next section.

3   Asymptotic Analysis

Our key result comes next and states that if the error weight w is negligible compared with n, then if we write the workfactors in the form 2^{cw}, then, when n grows, c tends to a constant which only depends of the code rate k/n.

Proposition 2. *Let k and w be two functions of n such that $\lim_{n \to \infty} k/n = R$, $0 < R < 1$, and $\lim_{n \to \infty} w/n = 0$. For any algorithm $\mathcal{A}$ among Pra-ISD, SD-ISD, MMT-ISD, BJMM-ISD, and NN-ISD, we have*

$$\mathrm{WF}_{\mathcal{A}}(n, k, w) = 2^{cw(1+o(1))}, c = \log_2 \frac{1}{1 - R}$$

when n tends to infinity.

The rest of this section is devoted to a proof of the above statement.

3.1   Main Theorem

We will divide the proof of the last proposition into two of cases: when $\mathcal{A}$ is among Pra-ISD, SD-ISD, MMT-ISD or BJMM-ISD and, finally, when $\mathcal{A}$ is NN-ISD. The first case is solved by the next theorem. We will prove the second case differently but with similar techniques. The proofs of the theorem and of the lemmas can be found in Appendix B.

Theorem 1. *Let k and w be two functions of n such that $\lim_{n \to \infty} k/n = R$, $0 < R < 1$, and $\lim_{n \to \infty} w/n = 0$. For any real number a, $0 \le a < 1$, we have*

$$\lim_{n \to \infty} c_a(n, k, w) = \log_2 \frac{1}{1 - R}$$

where

$$c_a(n, k, w) = \min_{p, \ell} \frac{1}{w} \log_2 \left(\frac{\binom{n}{w}}{\binom{n-k-\ell}{w-p}} \left(\frac{1}{\binom{k+\ell}{ap}} + \frac{1}{2^\ell} \right) \right) \tag{3}$$

We will first show a series of properties about the following expression, related to the workfactors of the various algorithms,

$$B_a(\ell, p) = \frac{\binom{n}{w}}{\binom{n-k-\ell}{w-p}} \left(\frac{1}{\binom{k+\ell}{ap}} + \frac{1}{2^\ell} \right).$$

The next lemma describes useful properties of the optimal arguments of B_a.

Lemma 1. *Let $\mathcal{D}$ the domain of definition of B_a and $a \in \,]0, 1[$. If $w < \frac{n-k}{2}$ then*

$$\min_{(\ell, p) \in \mathcal{D}} B_a(\ell, p) = \min_{(\ell, p) \in \mathcal{V}} B_a(\ell, p) \quad \text{where} \quad \mathcal{V} = \left\{ (\ell, p) \in \mathcal{D}, 2^\ell = \binom{k + \ell}{ap} \right\}.$$

Now, we will use this lemma to analyze the asymptotic behavior of parameter ℓ with respect n when we know asymptotic behavior of w and k with respect n.

Lemma 2. *If* $\lim\limits_{n\to\infty} \dfrac{w}{n} = 0$, $\lim\limits_{n\to\infty} \dfrac{k}{n} = R$ *and* $2^\ell = \binom{k+\ell}{ap}$, *then* $\lim\limits_{n\to\infty} \dfrac{\ell}{n} = 0$.

The above lemma will allow us to "remove" ℓ from ours formulae as stated in the following lemma.

Lemma 3. *If* $\lim\limits_{n\to\infty} \dfrac{w}{n} = 0$, $\lim\limits_{n\to\infty} \dfrac{k}{n} = R$ *and* $\ell = \mathbf{o}(n)$, *then*

$$\frac{\binom{n}{w}}{\binom{n-k-\ell}{w-p}\binom{k+\ell}{ap}} \geq 2^{\mathbf{o}(w)} b_a(p) \quad \text{where } b_a(p) = \frac{\binom{n}{w}}{\binom{n-k}{w-p}\binom{k}{ap}}.$$

Finally, this new bound allows us to predict the asymptotic behavior of p with respect w.

Lemma 4. *If* $w = \mathbf{o}(n)$ *and* $\hat{p} = \operatorname*{argmin}\limits_{p} b_a(p)$ *then we have* $\dfrac{\hat{p}}{w} = \mathbf{O}\left(\left(\dfrac{w}{n}\right)^{1-a}\right)$.

Those lemmas tell us that if $w = \mathbf{o}(n)$ then the optimal values of the parameters ℓ and p will be such that $\ell = \mathbf{o}(n)$ and $p = \mathbf{o}(w)$. This will allow us the prove the main theorem (in Appendix) and the corollaries of the next section.

3.2   Asymptotic Behaviour of the Workfactors

Now, we have all the elements to show the first case of proposition 2.

Corollary 2. *For all* $\mathcal{A}$ *among SD-ISD, MMT-ISD, and BJMM-ISD, and for any code rate* R, $0 < R < 1$, *if* w *is a function of* n *such that* $w(n) = \mathbf{o}(n)$, *then, when* n *grows, we have*

$$\mathrm{WF}_{\mathcal{A}}(n, Rn, w) = 2^{cw(1+\mathbf{o}(1))} \quad \text{where } c = \log_2 \frac{1}{1-R}$$

Proof. First recall that we have

$$\mathrm{WF}_{\mathrm{Pra-ISD}}(n, Rn, w) \geq \mathrm{WF}_{\mathcal{A}}(n, Rn, w),$$

for all $\mathcal{A}$ among SD-ISD, MMT-ISD, and BJMM-ISD. The workfactor of Prange is equal to $\binom{n}{w}/\binom{n}{w-k} = B_a(0,0)$ (for any $a \in\,]0,1[$). So, when $w(n) = \mathbf{o}(n)$, we have $\mathrm{WF}_{\mathcal{A}}(n, Rn, w) \leq 2^{cw(1+\mathbf{o}(1))}$. The other inequality derives from Theorem 1 and Corollary 1.   □

Now, we want to show the same result for the case of NN-ISD. For that purpose it is enough to show that

$$\mathrm{WF}_{\mathrm{NN-ISD}} \geq 2^{\mathbf{o}(w)} \min_p b_a(p),$$

for some $a \in\,]0,1[$, and then proceed as in the proof of Theorem 1 and its Corollary 2. We use the inequality given in the previous section

$$\mathrm{WF}_{\mathrm{NN-ISD}}(n, k, w) \geq \min_{p,\ell} \frac{\binom{n}{w}}{\binom{n-k-\ell}{w-p}\binom{k+\ell}{\frac{7}{8}p}},$$

where ℓ verifies $2^{\ell} = \binom{p}{p/2}\binom{k+\ell-p}{\varepsilon_1}$ with $\varepsilon_1 = \mathbf{O}(p)$. So, when $w = \mathbf{o}(n)$, ε_1 is also $\mathbf{o}(n)$ and

$$2^{\ell} \leq 2^p \binom{k+\ell}{\varepsilon_1}.$$

This is similar to Lemma 2 and we can also deduce $\ell = \mathbf{o}(n)$. So, we can apply the Lemma 3 and obtain

$$\mathrm{WF}_{\mathrm{NN-ISD}} \geq 2^{\mathbf{o}(w)} \min_p b_{\frac{7}{8}}(p),$$

which proves the following corollary.

Corollary 3. *For any code rate R, $0 < R < 1$, if w is a function of n such that $w(n) = \mathbf{o}(n)$, then, when n grows, we have*

$$\mathrm{WF}_{\mathrm{NN-ISD}}(n, Rn, w) = 2^{cw(1+\mathbf{o}(1))} \ \ where \ \ c = \log_2 \frac{1}{1-R}.$$

This resolves the last case of Proposition 2.

4   Comparing with Observations

We confront here our result to estimates of ISD complexity. First in an asymptotic context, then for specific code parameters arising from variants of the McEliece encryption scheme.

4.1   Asymptotic Complexity of ISD Variants

Using ad-hoc optimization techniques, we have computed the asymptotic exponent of all variants of ISD for a code rate $R \in \{0.5, 0.75, 0.875\}$ and various error rates from 0 to the Gilbert-Varshamov bound. We observe in Fig. 3 that the hierarchy is respected throughout the range. This was known up to BJMM-ISD, and expected for NN-ISD. We also observe that the asymptotic exponent $\frac{1}{\tau n} \mathrm{WF}(n, Rn, \tau n)$ obviously tends to $-\log_2(1 - R)$ when $\tau \to 0$.

4.2   Non Asymptotic Complexity of ISD Variants

We examine two case, the QC-MDPC-McEliece scheme [2], and the original McEliece scheme using binary Goppa codes [1].

We compute estimates of the workfactor for various algorithms. Non asymptotic estimates for NN-ISD are not available at this moment, moreover there is a huge polynomial overhead which probably makes the algorithm unpractical at this moment for cryptographic sizes. All our numbers here are given in (log of) number of "vector operations".

In Figs. 4 and 5 we give security of some parameter sets respectively for QC-MDPC-McEliece and Goppa-McEliece. For the same code rate, we give parameters providing the same security with the same code rate when the amount of error is close to the Gilbert-Varshamov bound.

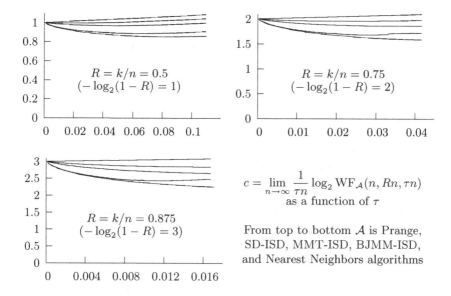

$$c = \lim_{n\to\infty} \frac{1}{\tau n} \log_2 \mathrm{WF}_{\mathcal{A}}(n, Rn, \tau n)$$
as a function of τ

From top to bottom $\mathcal{A}$ is Prange,
SD-ISD, MMT-ISD, BJMM-ISD,
and Nearest Neighbors algorithms

Fig. 3. Asymptotic exponents for variants of ISD and various code rates

(n, k, w)	security bits		
	SD-ISD	MMT-ISD	BJMM-ISD
$(9602, 4801, 84)$	88.7	87.7	85.8
$(19714, 9857, 134)$	138.1	137.1	134.9
$(65536, 32768, 264)$	267.5	266.4	263.3

QC-MDPC codes parameters

(n, k, w)	security bits		
	SD-ISD	MMT-ISD	BJMM-ISD
$(780, 390, 86)$	92.7	90.4	85.5
$(1260, 630, 139)$	148.3	143.8	134.8
$(2520, 1260, 278)$	293.9	283.3	263.2

Same code rates as above, error rate at Gilbert-Varshamov

Fig. 4. Estimates for ISD complexity exponent for QC-MDPC codes

It appears clearly in Fig. 4 that the security of QC-MDPC-McEliece is not reduced by a big amount when using the most elaborate variants of ISD. In fact, because the newest variants are slightly more difficult to implement and require more memory, it is likely that the best attack in practice do not perform better than SD-ISD. This was expected form our result, since for MDPC codes the amount of error is $w = \mathbf{O}(\sqrt{n})$ and is very small compared to the length.

The situation is different for Goppa code, here we have $w = \mathbf{O}(n/\log n)$ and though w is eventually negligible compared to the code length, there is still a huge advantage in using the newest variants for codes of cryptographic size.

(n, k, w)	security bits		
	SD-ISD	MMT-ISD	BJMM-ISD
$(2048, 1608, 40)$	89.5	87.3	81.1
$(4096, 3424, 56)$	144.3	139.5	127.6
$(8192, 6528, 128)$	290.0	280.2	256.2

Goppa codes parameters

(n, k, w)	security bits		
	SD-ISD	MMT-ISD	BJMM-ISD
$(1200, 942, 41)$	92.2	88.5	81.2
$(2400, 2006, 58)$	149.2	141.8	127.6
$(4150, 3307, 132)$	300.1	284.2	255.4

Same code rates as above, error rate at Gilbert-Varshamov

Fig. 5. Estimates for ISD complexity exponent for Goppa codes

5   Conclusion

We have given in this paper a comprehensive way to measure the performance of the various ISD variants by writing the workfactor in the form 2^{cw} were w is the amount errors to be corrected.

The constant c does not vary very much when for the different variants of ISD. Moreover, we have proven that this constant is relatively close to $-\log_2(1-k/n)$ (where n is the code length and k the code dimension) with equality when $w \ll n$.

A   Proof of Proposition 1

Proof (of Proposition 1). We consider the execution of generic_isd (Fig. 2) and use the corresponding notations. If the input (H_0, s_0, w) verify Assumption 1 then so does (H, s, w) inside any particular execution of the main loop.

1. From the assumption, as long as we wish to estimate the cost up to a constant factor, we may assume that there is a unique solution to our problem. In one particular loop, we can only find an error pattern (e'', e') such that its first $n - k - \ell$ bits have weight $w - p$ and its last $k + \ell$ have weight p. This happens with probability at most $P = \frac{\binom{n-k-\ell}{w-p}\binom{k+\ell}{p}}{\binom{n}{w}}$. Thus we expect to execute the main loop, and thus instruction "1:", at least $1/P$ times.

2. To estimate the number of times we have to compute instruction "2:", we need to estimate for any $e' \in \mathbf{F}_2^{k+\ell}$ of weight p the probability that e' leads to a success given that $e'H'^T = s'$.
   If we fix H, the sample space in which we compute the probabilities is $\Omega_H = \{eH^T \mid \text{wt}(e) = w\}$ equipped with a uniform distribution (because of Assumption 1). We consider the two events
   - $\mathcal{S}_H(e') = \{s = (s'', e'H'^T) \in \Omega_H\}$,
   - $\text{Succ}_H(e') = \{eH^T \mid e = (e'', e'), e'' \in \mathbf{F}_2^{n-k-\ell}, \text{wt}(e'') = w - p\}$.

The probability we are interested in is $\mathrm{Pr}_{\Omega_H}(\mathrm{Succ}_H(e') \mid \mathcal{S}_H(e'))$. We have $\mathrm{Pr}_{\Omega_H}(\mathcal{S}_H(e')) \approx 2^{-\ell}$ because we expect the set Ω_H to behave like a set of random vector (true for almost all matrix H). And the set $\mathrm{Succ}_H(e') \subset \Omega_H$ has cardinality $\binom{n-k-\ell}{w-p}$ as it contains for a fixed e', as many elements as we have vectors $e'' \in \mathbf{F}_2^{n-k-\ell}$ of weight $w - p$. Finally

$$\Pr_{\Omega_H}(\mathrm{Succ}_H(e') \mid \mathcal{S}_H(e')) = \frac{\mathrm{Pr}_{\Omega_H}(\mathrm{Succ}_H(e'))}{\mathrm{Pr}_{\Omega_H}(\mathcal{S}_H(e'))} = \frac{\binom{n-k-\ell}{w-p}2^\ell}{\binom{n}{w}}$$

The second part of the statement follows.   □

Proof (of Corollary 1). Using the fact that $\binom{n}{w}$ is proportional to $\frac{2^{nh(w/n)}}{\sqrt{w(1-w/n)}}$, where $h(x) = -x\log_2(x) - (1-x)\log_2(1-x)$ is the binary entropy function, we easily obtain that

$$\log_2 \frac{\binom{(k+\ell)/2}{(1-a)p}\binom{k+\ell}{ap}}{\binom{k+\ell}{p}} = (k+\ell)\left(\frac{h(2(1-a)x)}{2} + h(ax) - h(x)\right)(1+\mathbf{o}(x))$$

where $x = p/(k+\ell)$. An easy study of the above function proves that it is positive for any a, $1 > a \geq 0.5$. Using Proposition 1, if $L \geq \binom{(k+\ell)/2}{(1-a)p}$ then the total contribution of instruction "1:" is at least

$$\frac{\binom{n}{w}L}{\binom{n-k-\ell}{w-p}\binom{k+\ell}{p}} \geq \frac{\binom{n}{w}\binom{(k+\ell)/2}{(1-a)p}}{\binom{n-k-\ell}{w-p}\binom{k+\ell}{p}} \geq \frac{\binom{n}{w}}{\binom{n-k-\ell}{w-p}\binom{k+\ell}{ap}}.$$

Adding to that the contribution of "2:", we obtain the lower bound of the statement.   □

B   Proofs of Main Theorem Section

Proof (of Lemma 1). We have

$$\log(B_a(\ell,p)) \approx \max\left\{\log\left(\frac{\binom{n}{k}}{\binom{n-k-\ell}{w-p}\binom{k+\ell}{ap}}\right), \log\left(\frac{\binom{n}{k}}{\binom{n-k-\ell}{w-p}2^\ell}\right)\right\}.$$

We divide our function in two parts

$$f(\ell,p) = \log\left(\frac{\binom{n}{k}}{\binom{n-k-\ell}{w-p}\binom{k+\ell}{ap}}\right) \quad \text{and} \quad g(\ell,p) = \log\left(\frac{\binom{n}{k}}{\binom{n-k-\ell}{w-p}2^\ell}\right).$$

The function B_a is defined on the domain shown in Fig. 6. Our goal is to show that there is a point $(\hat{\ell},\hat{p}) \in \mathcal{D}$ such that $f(\hat{\ell},\hat{p}) = g(\hat{\ell},\hat{p})$ who minimizes B_a. We will start by studying the interior of $\mathcal{D}$ and we will verify that if B_a achieve its minimum at (ℓ^*,p^*) then there is a point $(\hat{\ell},\hat{p}) \in \mathcal{V}$ which B_a has the same value. Secondly, we will search all possible minimum points in the boundary $\partial \mathcal{D}$ and we will show that again the minimum is attained in a point of $\mathcal{V}$; these two cases will allow us to conclude this theorem.

We suppose $(\ell^*, p^*) \notin \partial \mathcal{D}$ minimizes B_a and it holds that $f(\ell^*, p^*) > g(\ell^*, p^*)$. So, $B_a(\ell, p) = \max\{f(\ell, p), g(\ell, p)\}$ for all (ℓ, p) in a neighborhood U of (ℓ^*, p^*) which does not intercept the boundary. Then,

$$\min_{(\ell, p) \in \mathcal{D}} B_a(\ell, p) = \min_{(\ell, p) \in U} B_a(\ell, p) = \min_{(\ell, p) \in U} f(\ell, p),$$

and in particular $\nabla f(\ell^*, p^*) = (0, 0)$. Since $a \in]0, 1[$, that equality has a unique solution

$$\frac{w - p^*}{n - k - \ell^*} = 0 \text{ or } 1.$$

That means $(\ell, p) \in \partial \mathcal{D}$, so this case is impossible.

In the case where $g(\ell^*, p^*) > f(\ell^*, p^*)$, we deduce similarly $\nabla g = (0, 0)$. And, we obtain

$$\frac{\partial g}{\partial \ell} = -\log\left(1 - \frac{w - p^*}{n - k - \ell^*}\right) - 1 = 0.$$

$$\frac{\partial g}{\partial p} = h'\left(\frac{w - p^*}{n - k - \ell^*}\right) = 0$$

Therefore,

$$\mathscr{L}^* : \quad \frac{w - p^*}{n - k - \ell^*} = \frac{1}{2},$$

this equation defines a line in the plane where $g(\ell, p)$ is constant. We use the function $p_0 : [n - k - 2w, n - k] \to \mathbb{R}$ defined by $p_0(\ell) = w - \frac{n - k - \ell}{2}$ to describe some points in $\mathscr{L}^*$. Now, our objective is to show there is a point belonging to $\mathcal{V}$ in this line $\mathscr{L}^*$. By hypothesis $\ell_0 = n - k - 2w > 0$, so $(\ell_0, p_0(\ell_0)) = (\ell_0, 0) \in \mathscr{L}^* \cap \mathcal{D}$ and

$$g(\ell_0, p_0(\ell_0)) = nh\left(\frac{w}{n}\right) - (n - k - \ell_0) - \ell_0 < nh\left(\frac{w}{n}\right) - (n - k - \ell_0) = f(\ell_0, p_0(\ell_0)).$$

Since $g(\ell^*, p_0(\ell^*)) > f(\ell^*, p_0(\ell^*))$ and the segment of line between $(\ell_0, p_0(\ell_0))$ and $(\ell^*, p_0(\ell^*))$ belongs to $\mathcal{D}$, there is a $\hat{\ell} \in]\ell_0, \ell^*[$ such that $g(\hat{\ell}, p_0(\hat{\ell})) = f(\hat{\ell}, p_0(\hat{\ell}))$. Because $g(\hat{\ell}, p_0(\hat{\ell})) = g(\ell^*, p(\ell^*))$, we conclude that $(\hat{\ell}, p_0(\hat{\ell}))$ is a minimum point for B_a and it belongs to $\mathcal{V}$.

Now, we suppose that the minimum point (ℓ^*, p^*) belongs to the boundary $\partial \mathcal{D}$ and we search all possibles candidates in the boundary. We can divide the boundary into 5 segments of line and we analyze the monotony of f and g respect to ℓ or p. We will obtain that

$$\min_{\partial \mathcal{D}} f(\ell, p) = \min\{f(0, 0), g(0, 0), f(k/a, 0), \max\{f(n - k, w), g(n - k, w)\}\};$$

Since $f(0, 0) = g(0, 0) \leq g(k/a, 0) = f(k/a, 0)$, we focus our analysis on the points $(0, 0)$ and $(n - k, w)$, so it is enough to study the case $(\ell^*, p^*) = (n - k, w)$.

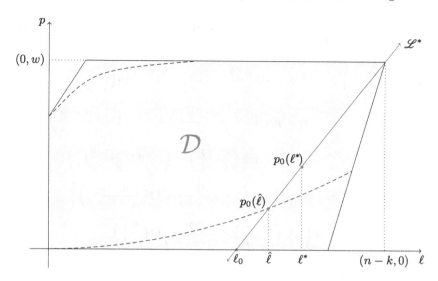

Fig. 6. Definition domain of function B_a

We can analyze f over the line

$$\mathscr{L}_{m_0} : \frac{w-p}{n-k-\ell} = \frac{w}{n-k} = \frac{p}{k+\ell}.$$

We can obtain a derivate function

$$\frac{\partial f}{\partial \ell} = h\left(\frac{w}{n}\right) - \left(-a\frac{w}{n}\log\left(a\frac{w}{n}\right) - \left(1-a\frac{w}{n}\right)\log\left(1-a\frac{w}{n}\right)\right) = h\left(\frac{w}{n}\right) - h\left(a\frac{w}{n}\right) > 0,$$

because $w/n < 1/2$. Therefore, B is increasing respect to ℓ into this line, and B does not achieve its local minimum at $(n-k,w)$; for that reason that minimum is not $B_a(n-k,w)$ in the case $f(n-k,w) > g(n-k,w)$.

In the case of $B_a(\ell^*,p^*) = g(n-k,w) > f(n-k,w)$, we can take any point (ℓ^{**},p^{**}) who belongs to the interior of $\mathcal{D}$ and the line $\mathscr{L}^*$ (which we used before), and we obtain again another point $(\hat{\ell},\hat{p}) \in \mathcal{V}$ as before. □

Proof (of Lemma 2). We take binary logarithm over the third hypothesis and we obtain

$$\frac{\ell}{n} = \frac{p}{n}\left(1 - \log\left(\frac{p}{k+\ell}\right) - \mathbf{O}\left(\frac{p}{k+\ell}\right)\right) + \frac{p}{n}$$

$$\leq \frac{w}{n}\left(2 + \mathbf{O}\left(\frac{w}{k}\right)\right) - \frac{w}{n}\log\left(\frac{w}{k}\right)$$

$$= \frac{w}{n}\left(2 - \log\left(\frac{n}{k}\right) + \frac{n}{k}\mathbf{O}\left(\frac{w}{n}\right)\right) - \frac{w}{n}\log\left(\frac{w}{n}\right)$$

$$= \mathbf{o}(1) - \mathbf{o}(1).$$

So we conclude $\frac{\ell}{n} = \mathbf{o}(1)$. □

Proof (of Lemma 3). It is enough that we analyze the quotient of the respectives terms in these expressions:

$$\log\left(\frac{\binom{n-k-\ell}{w-p}}{\binom{n-k}{w-p}}\right) = (n-k-\ell)h\left(\frac{w-p}{n-k-\ell}\right) - (n-k)h\left(\frac{w-p}{n-k}\right)$$

$$= -(w-p)\left(\log\left(\frac{w-p}{n-k-\ell}\right) + \left(1 + \mathbf{O}\left(\frac{w-p}{n-k-\ell}\right)\right)\right)$$

$$+(w-p)\left(\log\left(\frac{w-p}{n-k}\right) + \left(1 + \mathbf{O}\left(\frac{w-p}{n-k}\right)\right)\right)$$

$$\leq (w-p)\left(\log\left(1 - \frac{\ell}{n-k}\right) + \mathbf{O}\left(\frac{w-p}{n-k-\ell}\right)\right)$$

$$\leq w\left(\log\left(1 - \frac{\ell}{n}\right) + \frac{n}{n-k-\ell}\mathbf{O}\left(\frac{w}{n}\right)\right)$$

$$= w\mathbf{o}(1)$$

In the same way, we obtain

$$\log\left(\frac{\binom{k+\ell}{ap}}{\binom{k}{ap}}\right) \leq ap\left(\log\left(1 + \frac{\ell}{k}\right) + \frac{n}{k+\ell}\mathbf{O}\left(\frac{w}{n}\right)\right) \leq w\mathbf{o}(1).$$

$$\square$$

Proof (of Lemma 4).
  We analyze the derivate of b:

$$b'_a(p) = a\log\left(\frac{ap}{k-ap}\right) - \log\left(\frac{w-p}{n-k-(w-p)}\right).$$

We can see the function b_a is decreasing in a neighborhood of $p = 0$ and increasing in a neighborhood of $p = w$. Moreover, $b''_a(p) > 0$, so $b_a(p)$ is a convex function and the minimization problem has unique solution $\hat{p}$. We analyze the equation $b_a(\hat{p}) = 0$, we obtain

$$\frac{a^a\hat{p}}{w-\hat{p}} = \frac{(k-\hat{p})^a\hat{p}^{1-a}}{n-k-(w-\hat{p})}$$

That implies

$$a^a\frac{\hat{p}}{w} \leq \frac{k^aw^{1-a}}{n-k-w}.$$

We deduce that $\frac{\hat{p}}{w} = \mathbf{O}(\frac{w}{n}^{1-a})$.

$$\square$$

  Now, we have all the asymptotic properties and reductions that we need to prove our principal result. So, we will use the well known Stirling's approximation for binomial coefficient

$$\binom{n}{w} \approx \frac{2^{nh(w/n)}}{\sqrt{w(1-w/n)}},$$

and we will ignore polynomial factors.

Proof (of Theorem 1). The first estimation of c_a, when $w = \mathbf{o}(n)$, gives us

$$c_a(n,k,w) \leq \frac{1}{w} \log \left(B_a(0,0) \right)$$

$$= \frac{1}{w} \left(\log \binom{n}{w} - \log \binom{n-k}{w} \right)$$

$$= \frac{n}{w} h\left(\frac{w}{n}\right) - \frac{n-k}{w} h\left(\frac{w}{n-k}\right)$$

$$= \left(1 - \log \left(\frac{w}{n}\right) + \mathbf{O}\left(\frac{w}{n}\right) \right) - \left(1 - \log \left(\frac{w}{n-k}\right) + \mathbf{O}\left(\frac{w}{n-k}\right) \right)$$

$$= \log \left(\frac{n}{n-k} + \mathbf{O}\left(\frac{w}{n}\right) \right).$$

So, our objective will be show the another inequality. The Lemmas 1, 2 and 3 lets us simplify the equation to that inequality

$$c_a(n,k,w) \geq \mathbf{o}(w) + \min_p \log(b_a(p)).$$

Finally, we analyze the binary logarithm of b_a evaluated in the optimal argument $\hat{p}$:

$$\log(b_a(\hat{p})) = \underbrace{nh\left(\frac{w}{n}\right)}_{(1)} - \underbrace{(n-k)h\left(\frac{w-\hat{p}}{n-k}\right)}_{(2)} - \underbrace{kh\left(\frac{a\hat{p}}{k}\right)}_{(3)}.$$

So, we study these three parts

$$(1): nh\left(\frac{w}{n}\right) = w\left(1 - \log\left(\frac{w}{n}\right) + \mathbf{O}\left(\frac{w}{n}\right) \right)$$

$$(2): (n-k)h\left(\frac{w-\hat{p}}{n-k}\right) = (w-\hat{p})\left(1 - \log\left(\frac{w-\hat{p}}{n-k}\right) + \mathbf{O}\left(\frac{w-\hat{p}}{n-k}\right) \right)$$

$$(3): kh\left(\frac{a\hat{p}}{k}\right) = a\hat{p}\left(1 - \log\left(\frac{a\hat{p}}{k}\right) + \mathbf{O}\left(\frac{a\hat{p}}{k}\right) \right)$$

We group these terms in two sums: the sum of logarithms and the sum of negligible addends:

$$(I) = -w\log\left(\frac{w}{n}\right) + (w-\hat{p})\log\left(\frac{w-\hat{p}}{n-k}\right) + ap\log\left(\frac{a\hat{p}}{k}\right)$$

$$(II) = -w\left(1 + \mathbf{O}\left(\frac{w}{n}\right)\right) + (w-\hat{p})\left(1 + \mathbf{O}\left(\frac{w-\hat{p}}{n-k}\right)\right) + ap\left(1 + \mathbf{O}\left(\frac{a\hat{p}}{k}\right)\right)$$

We continue with the easy part

$$(II) = -w\mathbf{O}\left(\frac{w}{n}\right) + (a-1)\hat{p} + (w-\hat{p})\mathbf{O}\left(\frac{w-\hat{p}}{n-k}\right) + a\hat{p}\mathbf{O}\left(\frac{\hat{p}}{k}\right)$$

$$= -w\mathbf{o}(1) + (a-1)\mathbf{o}(w) + (w-\hat{p})\mathbf{o}(1) + a\mathbf{o}(w)$$

$$= \mathbf{o}(w).$$

Finally,

$$
\begin{aligned}
(I) &= w\left(\log\left(\frac{w-\hat{p}}{n-k}\right) - \log\left(\frac{w}{n}\right)\right) + \hat{p}\left(a\log\left(\frac{ap}{k}\right) - \log\left(\frac{w-\hat{p}}{n-k}\right)\right) \\
&= w\log\left(\frac{w-\hat{p}}{w}\Big/\frac{n-k}{n}\right) + \hat{p}\log\left(a^a\,\frac{\hat{p}^a}{w-\hat{p}}\,\frac{n-k}{k^a}\right) \\
&= w\log\left(\frac{1-\hat{p}/w}{1-k/n}\right) + a\hat{p}\log\left(\frac{a\hat{p}}{w}\right) + \hat{p}\log\left(\frac{w^a}{(w-\hat{p})^a}\right) + \hat{p}\log\left(\frac{n-k}{k^a(w-\hat{p})^{1-a}}\right) \\
&= w\log\left(\frac{1-\hat{p}/w}{1-k/n}\right) + w\left(\mathbf{o}(1) + a\frac{\hat{p}}{w}\log\left(\frac{w}{w-\hat{p}}\right) + \frac{\hat{p}}{w}\log\left(\frac{(n-k)^{1-a}}{(w-\hat{p})^{1-a}}\right)\right) \\
&= w\log\left(\frac{1-\hat{p}/w}{1-k/n}\right) + w\left(\mathbf{o}(1) + (1-a)\frac{\hat{p}}{w}\log\left(\frac{n-k}{w-\hat{p}}\right)\right) \\
&= w\log\left(\frac{1-\hat{p}/w}{1-k/n}\right) + w\left(\mathbf{o}(1) - (1-a)\frac{\hat{p}}{w}\left(\mathbf{O}(1) + \log\left(\frac{n}{w}\right)\right)\right) \\
&= w\log\left(\frac{1-\hat{p}/w}{1-k/n}\right) + w\left(\mathbf{o}(1) + \frac{\hat{p}}{w}\log\left(\frac{w^{1-a}}{n}\right)\right)
\end{aligned}
$$

So, the Lemma 4 implies

$$
(I) = w\log\left(\frac{1-\hat{p}/w}{1-k/n}\right) + w\Big(\mathbf{o}(1) + \mathbf{o}(1)\Big).
$$

Finally, we conclude

$$
c_a(n,k,w) \geq (I) + (II) = w\left(\log\left(\frac{1}{1-R}\right) + \mathbf{o}(1)\right). \qquad \square
$$

References

1. McEliece, R.: A public-key cryptosystem based on algebraic coding theory. In: DSN Progress Report, pp. 114–116. Jet Propulsion Laboratory, California Institute of Technology, Pasadena, CA, January 1978
2. Misoczki, R., Tillich, J.P., Sendrier, N., Barreto, P.S.L.M.: MDPC-McEliece: newMcEliece variants from moderate density parity-check codes. In: IEEE Conference, ISIT 2013, Instanbul, Turkey, pp. 2069–2073, July 2013
3. May, A., Ozerov, I.: On computing nearest neighbors with applications to decoding of binary linear codes. In: Oswald, E., Fischlin, M. (eds.) EUROCRYPT 2015. LNCS, vol. 9056, pp. 203–228. Springer, Heidelberg (2015)
4. Prange, E., Ozerov, I.: The use of information sets in decoding cyclic codes. IRE Trans. **IT–8**, S5–S9 (1962)
5. Berlekamp, E., McEliece, R., van Tilborg, H.: On the inherent intractability of certain coding problems. IEEE Trans. Inform. Theory **24**(3), 384–386 (1978)
6. Alekhnovich, M.: More on average case vs approximation complexity. In: FOCS 2003, pp. 298–307. IEEE (2003)
7. Lee, P.J., Brickell, E.F.: An observation on the security of McEliece's public-key cryptosystem. In: Günther, C.G. (ed.) EUROCRYPT 1988. LNCS, vol. 330, pp. 275–280. Springer, Heidelberg (1988)

8. Stern, J.: A method for finding codewords of small weight. In: Cohen, G., Wolfmann, J. (eds.) Coding Theory and Applications. LNCS, vol. 388, pp. 106–113. Springer, Heidelberg (1989)

9. Dumer, I.: On minimum distance decoding of linear codes. In: Proceedings of 5th Joint Soviet-Swedish International Workshop on Information Theory, Moscow, pp. 50–52 (1991)

10. Canteaut, A., Chabaud, F.: A new algorithm for finding minimum-weight words in a linear code: application to McEliece's cryptosystem and to narrow-sense BCH codes of length 511. IEEE Trans. Inf. Theory $44(1)$, 367–378 (1998)

11. Finiasz, M., Sendrier, N.: Security bounds for the design of code-based cryptosystems. In: Matsui, M. (ed.) ASIACRYPT 2009. LNCS, vol. 5912, pp. 88–105. Springer, Heidelberg (2009)

12. Lange, T., Peters, C., Bernstein, D.J.: Smaller decoding exponents: ball-collision decoding. In: Rogaway, P. (ed.) CRYPTO 2011. LNCS, vol. 6841, pp. 743–760. Springer, Heidelberg (2011)

13. May, A., Meurer, A., Thomae, E.: Decoding random linear codes in $\tilde{\mathcal{O}}(2^{0.054n})$. In: Lee, D.H., Wang, X. (eds.) ASIACRYPT 2011. LNCS, vol. 7073, pp. 107–124. Springer, Heidelberg (2011)

14. Becker, A., Joux, A., May, A., Meurer, A.: Decoding random binary linear codes in $2^{n/20}$: how $1 + 1 = 0$ improves information set decoding. In: Pointcheval, D., Johansson, T. (eds.) EUROCRYPT 2012. LNCS, vol. 7237, pp. 520–536. Springer, Heidelberg (2012)

15. Alekhnovich, M.: More on average case vs approximation complexity. Comput. Complex. $20(4)$, 755–786 (2011)

On the Differential Security of the HFEv-Signature Primitive

Ryann Cartor[1], Ryan Gipson[1], Daniel Smith-Tone[1,2]([✉]), and Jeremy Vates[1]

[1] Department of Mathematics, University of Louisville, Louisville, KY, USA
{ryann.cartor,ryan.gipson,jeremy.vates}@louisville.edu
[2] National Institute of Standards and Technology, Gaithersburg, MD, USA
daniel.smith@nist.gov

Abstract. Multivariate Public Key Cryptography (MPKC) is one of the most attractive post-quantum options for digital signatures in a wide array of applications. The history of multivariate signature schemes is tumultuous, however, and solid security arguments are required to inspire faith in the schemes and to verify their security against yet undiscovered attacks. The effectiveness of "differential attacks" on various field-based systems has prompted the investigation of the resistance of schemes against differential adversaries. Due to its prominence in the area and the recent optimization of its parameters, we prove the security of $HFEv^-$ against differential adversaries. We investigate the newly suggested parameters and conclude that the proposed scheme is secure against all known attacks and against any differential adversary.

Keywords: Multivariate cryptography · HFEv- · Discrete differential · MinRank · Q-rank

1 Introduction and Outline

In the mid 1990s, Peter Shor discovered a way to efficiently implement quantum period finding algorithms on structures of exponential size and showed how the modern world as we know it will change forever once the behemoth engineering challenge of constructing a large scale quantum computing device is overcome. His polynomial time quantum Fourier transforms for smooth integers can be employed to factor integers, to compute discrete logarithms and is powerful enough to efficiently solve hidden subgroup problems for well behaved (usually Abelian) groups. Given the ubiquity of these problems in deployed technologies, our e-society is confronted with the possibility that its public key infrastructure is terminally ill.

It is not known how far this computational cancer may spread, how pervasive exponential quantum speed-ups will prove to be nor how fundamentally wide the gap between feasibility in the classical and quantum world are. Thus we face the task in a rapidly maturing twenty-first century, with ever expanding interconnectivity, of securing open channel communication between unknown

© Springer International Publishing Switzerland 2016
T. Takagi (Ed.): PQCrypto 2016, LNCS 9606, pp. 162–181, 2016.
DOI: 10.1007/978-3-319-29360-8_11

future devices, against machines with unknown capabilities, with an unknown date of inception.

Charged with this challenge is a growing international community of experts in quantum-resistant cryptography. The world-wide effort has spawned international standardization efforts including the European Union Horizon 2020 Project, "Post-Quantum Cryptography for Long-Term Security" PQCRYPTO ICT-645622 [1], ETSI's Quantum Safe Cryptography Specification Group [2], and NIST's Post-Quantum Cryptography Workgroup [3]. The dedication of these resources is evidence that the field of post-quantum cryptography is evolving into a state in which we can identify practical technologies with confidence that they will remain secure in a quantum computing world.

One of a few reasonable candidates for post-quantum security is multivariate cryptography. We already rely heavily on the difficulty of inverting nonlinear systems of equations in symmetric cryptography, and we quite reasonably suspect that security will remain in the quantum paradigm. Multivariate Public Key Cryptography (MPKC) has the added challenge of resisting quantum attack in the asymmetric setting.

While it is difficult to be assured of a cryptosystem's post-quantum security in light of the continual evolution of the relatively young field of quantum algorithms, it is reasonable to start by developing schemes which resist classical attack and for which there is no known significant weakness in the quantum realm. Furthermore, the establishment of security metrics provides insight that educates us about the possibilities for attacks and the correct strategies for the development of cryptosystems.

In this vein, some classification metrics are introduced in [4–6] which can be utilized to rule out certain classes of attacks. While not reduction theoretic proof, reducing the task of breaking the scheme to a known (or often suspected) hard problem, these metrics can be used to prove that certain classes of attacks fail or to illustrate specific computational challenges which an adversary must face to effect an attack.

Many attacks on multivariate public key cryptosystems can be viewed as differential attacks, in that they utilize some symmetric relation or some invariant property of the public polynomials. These attacks have proved effective in application to several cryptosystems. For instance, the attack on SFLASH, see [7], is an attack utilizing differential symmetry, the attack of Kipnis and Shamir [8] on the oil-and-vinegar scheme is actually an attack exploiting a differential invariant, the attack on the ABC matrix encryption scheme of [9] utilizes a subspace differential invariant; even Patarin's initial attack on C^* [10] can be viewed as an exploitation of a trivial differential symmetry, see [5].

As is demonstrated in [4,6,11], many general polynomial schemes can have nontrivial linear differential symmetries. Specifically, in [6], systems of linear equations are presented which can have solution spaces large enough to guarantee the existence of nontrivial linear differential symmetries, while in both [4,11] explicit constructions of maps with nontrivial symmetries are provided. The existence of such symmetries in abundance is the basis of attacks removing the minus modifier as in [7], and depending on the structure of the maps inducing the symmetry, may even provide a direct key recovery attack. Furthermore, the attack of [9] on the ABC simple matrix scheme teaches us that differential invariant techniques are a current concern as well. These facts along with the ubiquity of differential attacks in the literature are evidence that the program developed in [4–6] to verify security against differential adversaries is a necessary component of any theory of security for practical and desirable multivariate cryptosystems.

This challenge leads us to an investigation of the $HFEv$ and $HFEv^-$ cryptosystems, see [12], and a characterization of their differential properties. Results similar to those of [4–6] will allow us to make conclusions about the differential security of $HFEv$, and provide a platform for deriving such results for $HFEv^-$.

Specifically, we reduce the task of verifying trivial differential symmetric structure for a polynomial f to the task of verifying that the solution space of a large system of linear equations related to f has a special form. We elucidate the structure of these equations in the case of the central map of $HFEv$ and provide an algorithm for generating keys which provably have trivial differential symmetric structure. In conjunction with our later results on differential invariants, the proof of concept algorithm verifies that information theoretic security against differential adversaries, as defined in [6], is possible with an instantaneous addition to key generation while maintaining sufficient entropy in the key space to avoid "guess-then-IP" attacks. We then extend these methods to the case of $HFEv^-$, deriving the same conclusion.

Expanding on the methods of [6], we prove the following.

Theorem 1. *Let k be a degree n extension of the finite field $\mathbb{F}_q$. Let f be an $HFEv$ central maps. With high probability, f has no nontrivial differential invariant structure.*

With a minimal augmentation of this method we extend this result to the case of $HFEv^-$.

Theorem 2. *Let f be an $HFEv$ central map and let π be a linear projection. With high probability, $\pi \circ f$ has no nontrivial differential invariant structure.*

Thus, with proper parameter selection, $HFEv^-$ is provably secure against differential adversaries. Together with the existant literature on resistance to algebraic and rank attacks, this security argument provides significant theoretical support for the security of aggressive $HFEv^-$ parameters, such as those presented in [13].

The paper is organized as follows. First, we recall big field constructions in multivariate public key cryptography. Next we review the HFE scheme from [14] and the $HFEv^-$ scheme from [12]. In the following section, we provide criteria for the nonexistence of a differential symmetric relation on the private key of both $HFEv$ and $HFEv^-$ and discuss an efficient addition to key generation that allows provably secure keys to be generated automatically. We next review the notion of a differential invariant and a method of classifying differential invariants. We continue, analyzing the differential invariant structure of $HFEv$

and $HFEv^-$, deriving bounds on the probability of differential invariants in the general case. Next, we review the Q-rank and degree of regularity of $HFEv^-$, and discuss resistance to attacks exploiting equivalent keys. Finally, we conclude, discussing the impact of these results on the $HFEv^-$ pedigree.

2 Big Field Signature Schemes

At Eurocrypt'88, Matsumoto and Imai introduced the first massively multivariate cryptosystem which we now call C^*, in [15]. This contribution was based on a fundamentally new idea for developing a trapdoor one-way function. Specifically, they used finite extensions of Galois fields to obtain two representations of the same function: one, a vector-valued function over the base field; the other, an univariate function over the extension field.

One benefit of using this "big field" structure, is that Frobenius operations in extensions of conveniently sized Galois fields can be modeled as permutations of elements in the small field while computations in the small field can be cleverly coded to utilize current architectures optimally. Thus, one can compute a variety of exponential maps and products with great efficiency and obfuscate a simple structure by perturbing the vector representation.

Typically, a big field scheme is built using what is sometimes called the butterfly construction. Given a finite field $\mathbb{F}_q$, a degree n extension $\mathbb{K}$, and an $\mathbb{F}_q$-vector space isomorphism $\phi : \mathbb{F}_q^n \to \mathbb{K}$, one can find an $\mathbb{F}_q$-vector representation of the function $f : \mathbb{K} \to \mathbb{K}$. To hide the choice of basis for the input and output of f, we may compose two affine transformations $T, U : \mathbb{F}_q^n \to \mathbb{F}_q^n$. The resulting composition $P = T \circ \phi^{-q} \circ f \circ \phi \circ U$ is then the public key. The construction is summarized in the figure below:

$$
\begin{array}{ccccccc}
& & \mathbb{K} & \xrightarrow{\ f\ } & \mathbb{K} & & \\
& & \phi \big\uparrow & & \big\downarrow \phi^{-1} & & \\
\mathbb{F}_q^n & \xrightarrow{\ U\ } & \mathbb{F}_q^n & \xrightarrow{\ F\ } & \mathbb{F}_q^n & \xrightarrow{\ T\ } & \mathbb{F}_q^n
\end{array}
$$

2.1 *HFE*

The Hidden Field Equations (HFE) scheme was first presented by Patarin in [14] as a method of avoiding his linearization equations attack which broke the C^* scheme of Matsumoto and Imai, see [10,15]. The basic idea of the system is to use the butterfly construction to hide the structure of a low degree polynomial that can be inverted efficiently over $\mathbb{K}$ via the Berlekamp algorithm [16], for example.

More specifically, we select an effectively invertible "quadratic" map $f : \mathbb{K} \to \mathbb{K}$, quadratic in the sense that every monomial of f is a product of a constant and two Frobenius multiples of x. Explicitly any such "core" map f has the form:

$$
f(x) = \sum_{\substack{i \le j \\ q^i + q^j \le D}} \alpha_{i,j} x^{q^i + q^j} + \sum_{\substack{i \\ q^i \le D}} \beta_i x^{q^i} + \gamma.
$$

The bound D on the degree of the polynomial is required to be quite low for efficient inversion.

One generates a signature by setting $y = h$, a hash digest, and computing, successively, $v = T^{-1}y$, $u = f^{-1}(v)$ and $x = U^{-1}u$. The vector x acts as the signature.

For verification, one simply evaluates the public polynomials, P, at x. If $P(x)$ which is equal to $T \circ f \circ U(x)$ is equal to y, the signature is authenticated. Otherwise, the signature is rejected.

2.2 *HFEv*⁻

Taking the HFE construction one step further, we may apply the vinegar modifier, adding extra variables $\tilde{x}_1, \ldots \tilde{x}_v$ to be assigned random values upon inversion. The effect of adding vinegar variables is that new quadratic terms, formed from both products of vinegar variables and HFE variables and products among vinegar variables, increase the rank of the public key. The central map of the $HFEv$ scheme has the form:

$$f(\mathbf{x}) = \sum_{\substack{i \leq j \\ q^i + q^j \leq D}} \alpha_{i,j} x^{q^i + q^j} + \sum_{\substack{i \\ q^i \leq D}} \beta_i(\tilde{x}_1, \ldots, \tilde{x}_v) x^{q^i} + \gamma(\tilde{x}_1, \ldots, \tilde{x}_v),$$

where $\alpha_{i,j} \in \mathbb{K}$, $\beta_i : \mathbb{F}_q^v \to \mathbb{K}$ is linear, and $\gamma : \mathbb{F}_q^v \to \mathbb{K}$ is quadratic.

In contrast to HFE, f is a vector-valued function mapping $\mathbb{F}_q^{n+v}$ to $\mathbb{F}_q^n$. The work of [6,17,18] show that representations of such functions over $\mathbb{K}$ are quite valuable. Thus it is beneficial to employ an augmentation of f, adding $n - v$ additional vinegar variables, and say $\hat{y} = \{\tilde{x}_1, \ldots, \tilde{x}_v, \ldots, \tilde{x}_n\}$, where $\tilde{x}_{v+1} = \tilde{x}_{v+2} = \ldots = \tilde{x}_n = 0$. Thus, our core map becomes

$$f(\mathbf{x}) = \hat{f}\left(\begin{array}{c} \hat{x} \\ \hat{y} \end{array}\right).$$

which algebraically identifies f as a bivariate function over $\mathbb{K}$. We may now write f in the following form:

$$f(x, y) = \sum_{\substack{0 \leq i \leq j < n \\ q^i + q^j \leq D}} \alpha_{ij} x^{q^i + q^j} + \sum_{\substack{0 \leq i,j < n \\ q^i \leq D}} \beta_{ij} x^{q^i} y^{q^j} + \sum_{0 \leq i \leq j < n} \gamma_{ij} y^{q^i + q^j}. \quad (1)$$

Here we see an obvious distinction among the types of monomials. We will label the monomials with α coefficients the "HFE monomials," those with β coefficients the "mixing monomials" and the monomials with γ coefficients the "vinegar monomials."

The $HFEv^-$ scheme uses the $HFEv$ primitive f above and augments the public key with the minus modifier. The minus modifier removes r of the public equations. This alteration is designed to destroy some of the information of the big field operations latent in the public key.

3   Differential Symmetry

The discrete differential of a field map $f : \mathbb{K} \to \mathbb{K}$ is given by:

$$Df(a, x) = f(a + x) - f(a) - f(x) + f(0).$$

It is simply a normalized difference operator with variable interval. In [7], the SFLASH signature scheme was broken by exploiting a symmetric relation of the differential of the public key. This relation was inherited from the core map of the scheme.

Definition 1. A *general linear differential symmetry* is a relation of the form

$$Df(Mx, a) + Df(x, Ma) = \Lambda_M Df(a, x),$$

where $M, \Lambda_M : \mathbb{K} \to \mathbb{K}$ are $\mathbb{F}_q$-linear maps.

A differential symmetry exists when linear maps may be applied to the discrete differential inputs in such a way that the effect can be factored out of the differential. Furthermore, we say that the symmetry is *linear* when the relation is linear in the unknown coefficients of the linear maps. It can be shown that any such linear symmetric relation implies the existence of a symmetry of the above form, hence the term "general."

While attacks similar to that of [7,19] exploited some multiplicative relation on central maps of schemes with some algebraic structure over the base field, it was shown in [4] that general linear differential symmetries based on more complex relations exist, in general. Therefore, when analyzing the potential threat of a differential adversary, as defined in [6], it becomes necessary to classify the possible linear differential symmetries. If we succeed in characterizing parameters which provably eliminate nontrivial differential symmetric relations, we prove security against the entire class of differential symmetric attacks, even those utilizing relations not yet discovered.

To this end, we evaluate the security of $HFEv$ against such adversaries. We explicitly consider parameter restrictions which necessarily preclude the existence of any nontrivial differential symmetry.

3.1   Linear Symmetry for HFEv

In our analysis, we will begin by considering the differential of our core map. From the perspective of our adversary, the discrete differential would be

$$D\hat{f}\left(\begin{bmatrix} \hat{a} \\ \hat{b} \end{bmatrix}, \begin{bmatrix} \hat{x} \\ \hat{y} \end{bmatrix}\right) = Df(a, b, x, y).$$

By the bilinearity of $D\hat{f}$ we see that Df is multi-affine; Df is affine in each of its inputs when the remaining inputs are fixed. Evaluating this differential we obtain

$$Df(a,b,x,y) = \sum_{\substack{0 \le i \le j < n \\ q^i + q^j \le D}} \alpha_{i,j}(x^{q^i}a^{q^j} + x^{q^j}a^{q^i})$$

$$+ \sum_{\substack{0 \le i,j < n \\ q^i \le D}} \beta_{i,j}(x^{q^i}b^{q^j} + a^{q^i}y^{q^j}) \qquad (2)$$

$$+ \sum_{0 \le i \le j < n} \gamma_{i,j}(y^{q^i}b^{q^j} + y^{q^j}b^{q^i}),$$

noting that Df is a $\mathbb{K}$-bilinear form in $[a\ b]^T$ and $[x\ y]^T$. For ease of computation, we will choose the following representation for $\mathbb{K}$:

$$x \mapsto [x\ x^q\ x^{q^2}\ \ldots\ x^{q^{n-1}}]^T.$$

Similarly, we may map our oil-vinegar vector as

$$[x\ y] \mapsto [x\ x^q\ x^{q^2}\ \ldots\ x^{q^{n-1}}\ y\ y^q\ y^{q^2}\ \ldots\ y^{q^{n-1}}]^T,$$

and Df is thus represented by the $2n \times 2n$ matrix where the (i,j)th and (j,i)th entries in the upper left $n \times n$ block are the coefficients $\alpha_{i,j}$, and the (i,j)th entries in the upper right block and the (j,i)th entries in the lower left block are the coefficients $\beta_{i,j}$, while the (i,j)th and (j,i)th entries in the lower right block are the coefficients $\gamma_{i,j}$.

Note, that any $\mathbb{F}_q$-linear map $M : \mathbb{K} \to \mathbb{K}$ can be represented by $Mx = \sum_{i=0}^{n-1} m_i x$. Thus, as demonstrated in [6], under our representation,

$$M = \begin{pmatrix} m_0 & m_1 & \cdots & m_{n-1} \\ m_{n-1}^q & m_0^q & \cdots & m_{n-2}^q \\ \vdots & \vdots & \ddots & \vdots \\ m_1^{q^{n-1}} & m_2^{q^{n-1}} & \cdots & m_0^{q^{n-1}} \end{pmatrix}.$$

However, when viewing an $\mathbb{F}_q$-linear map over our vector $\begin{bmatrix} \hat{x} \\ \hat{y} \end{bmatrix}$, we may consider the $2n \times 2n$ matrix

$$\overline{M} = \begin{pmatrix} m_{00,0} & m_{00,1} & \cdots & m_{00,n-1} & m_{01,0} & m_{01,1} & \cdots & m_{01,n-1} \\ m_{00,n-1}^q & m_{00,0}^q & \cdots & m_{00,n-2}^q & m_{01,n-1}^q & m_{01,0}^q & \cdots & m_{01,n-2}^q \\ \vdots & \vdots & \ddots & \vdots & \vdots & \vdots & \ddots & \vdots \\ m_{00,1}^{q^{n-1}} & m_{00,2}^{q^{n-1}} & \cdots & m_{00,0}^{q^{n-1}} & m_{01,1}^{q^{n-1}} & m_{01,2}^{q^{n-1}} & \cdots & m_{01,0}^{q^{n-1}} \\ m_{10,0} & m_{10,1} & \cdots & m_{10,n-1} & m_{11,0} & m_{11,1} & \cdots & m_{11,n-1} \\ m_{10,n-1}^q & m_{10,0}^q & \cdots & m_{10,n-2}^q & m_{11,n-1}^q & m_{11,0}^q & \cdots & m_{11,n-2}^q \\ \vdots & \vdots & \ddots & \vdots & \vdots & \vdots & \ddots & \vdots \\ m_{10,1}^{q^{n-1}} & m_{10,2}^{q^{n-1}} & \cdots & m_{10,0}^{q^{n-1}} & m_{11,1}^{q^{n-1}} & m_{11,2}^{q^{n-1}} & \cdots & m_{11,0}^{q^{n-1}} \end{pmatrix}.$$

For computational reference, we will label each row and column $modulo(n)$, i.e., each coordinate of the entry (i, j), will be represented by a residue class modulo n.

If we assume that f is vulnerable to a differential attack, then there exists a non-trivial linear mapping $\overline{M}$ such that the differential symmetry in (1) is satisfied. To compute such a symmetry inducing map requires the solution of $4n^2$ highly dependent but random equations in the $8n$ unknown coefficients of $\overline{M}$ and Λ_M over $\mathbb{K}$. Since trivial symmetries (such as multiplication by scalars) are exhibited by every map, we know that there exist nontrivial solutions. Even assuming unit time for $\mathbb{K}$-arithmetic operations, for realistic parameters this process is very inefficient; with the more realistic assumption of costly $\mathbb{K}$-arithmetic operations, this task is unsatisfactory in key generation.

To make the solution of such systems of equations more efficient, we derive the structure of the equations and develop a two step process for verifying trivial differential symmetric structure. The first step involves finding equations which only involve a subset of the variables. The existence of such equations is guaranteed by the degree bound of the HFE monomials. This information is then bootstrapped to eliminate many unknown coefficients of $\overline{M}$ resulting in a very small system of equations which can be solved explicitly.

We remark here that this methodology also suggests a method for estimating the probability of the existence of a differential symmetry for the $HFEv$ primitive. The existence of a nontrivial symmetry corresponds to systems for which the rank of the system of equations is less than $8n$. Under the heuristic that under row reduction these systems of equations behave like random $8n \times 8n$ matrices, we obtain a probability of roughly $1 - q^{-1}$ that the scheme has no nontrivial differential symmetry. We note that this heuristic is almost certainly false since trivial symmetries do exist. This quantity does represent a lower bound, however, and thus may offer support for larger base fields.

We begin by considering the entries of the matrix $\overline{M}^T Df + Df\overline{M}$. The contribution of any monomial $\alpha_{i,j} x^{q^i + q^j}$ to the ith row of $Df\overline{M}$ is given by

$$\left(\alpha_{i,j} m^j_{00,-j} \; \alpha_{i,j} m^j_{00,1-j} \; \cdots \; \alpha_{i,j} m^j_{00,-1-j} \; \alpha_{i,j} m^j_{01,-j} \; \alpha_{i,j} m^j_{01,1-j} \; \cdots \; \alpha_{i,j} m^j_{01,-1-j} \right)$$

while the contribution to the jth row is

$$\left(\alpha_{i,j} m^i_{00,-i} \; \alpha_{i,j} m^i_{00,1-i} \; \cdots \; \alpha_{i,j} m^i_{00,-1-i} \; \alpha_{i,j} m^i_{01,-i} \; \alpha_{i,j} m^i_{01,1-i} \; \cdots \; \alpha_{i,j} m^i_{01,-1-i} \right).$$

By symmetry, the ith and jth columns of $\overline{M}^T Df$ are the same as their respective rows.

It is clear that the rows and columns associated with coefficients of vinegar monomials as well as terms associated with mixing monomials may be represented similarly. However, it should be noted that those terms associated with mixing monomials will be multiplied by linear coefficients $m_{00,\cdot}, m_{01,\cdot}, m_{10,\cdot}$, and $m_{11,\cdot}$, while coefficients associated with vinegar variables are multiplied only by linear coefficients $m_{10,\cdot}$ and $m_{11,\cdot}$.

The above patterns can be extended to characterize the contribution to the ith row and jth row of monomials of the form $\beta_{i,j} x^{q^i} y^{q^j}$ and $\gamma_{i,j} y^{q^i + q^j}$, as well.

We note, however, that γ coefficients interact with entries from the lower block matrices while β coefficients interact with coefficients from all block matrices.

Now that we have characterized the left side of (1), we will consider the entries of $\Lambda_{\overline{M}} Df$. For every monomial of f, say $\alpha_{i',j'} x^{q^i+q^j}$, $\beta_{r,s} x^{q^r} y^{q^s}$, or $\gamma_{u,v} y^{q^u+q^v}$, we have under the mapping of $\Lambda_{\overline{M}}$ terms of the form: $\ell \alpha_{i,j}^{q^\ell} x^{q^{i+\ell}+q^{j+\ell}}$, $\ell \beta_{r,s}^{q^{r+\ell}} x^{q^{s+\ell}} y^{q^j}$, and $\ell \gamma_{u,v}^{q^\ell} y^{q^{u+\ell}+q^{v+\ell}}$. Clearly, this results in every nonzero entry, say (r,s), of our Df matrix being raised to the power of q^ℓ and shifted along a forty-five degree angle to entry $(r+\ell, s+\ell)$. Thus, for each monomial in f there are two possible nonzero entries in the ith row, with possible overlap.

This discrete geometrical interpretation of the action of M and D on the coefficients of f is central to this analysis. A graphical representation of these relations is provided in Fig. 1.

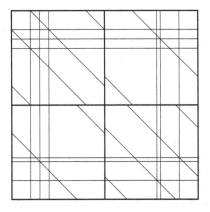

Fig. 1. Graphical representation of the equation $M^T Df + DfM = \Lambda_M Df$ for the $HFEv$ (actually, vC^*) polynomial $f(x) = \alpha_{i,j} x^{q^i+q^j} + \beta_{r,s} x^{q^r} y^{q^s} + \gamma_{u,v} y^{q^u+q^v}$. Horizontal and vertical lines represent nonzero entries in $M^T Df + DfM$ while diagonal lines represent nonzero entries in $\Lambda_M Df$. We may consider this diagram as a genus 4 surface containing straight lines.

As in [6], the possibility of a differential symmetry can be determined by setting the matrix representation of $M^T Df + DfM$ equal to the matrix $\Lambda_M Df$. We will demonstrate an algorithm, given some specific constraints, that will help provide secure keys to be generated automatically.

Due to the structure of our M matrix, we need to work within each $m_{i,j}$ matrix independently. The following algorithm for $m_{0,0}$ extends very naturally to the other 3 matrices. For clarity, all m terms in description below are $m_{0,0}$ terms.

Let $\alpha_{i,j}, \beta_{r,s}, \gamma_{u,v}$ represent the coefficients of our monomials in our core map. Consider the ith row of $M^T Df + DfM$. For all w not occurring as a power of q of our HFE or mixing monomials in f, or difference of powers of q in an exponent of a monomial in f plus i, the (i,w) entry is $\alpha_{i,j} m_{w-j}^{q^j} = 0$ (resp.

$\beta_{i,j} m_{w-j}^{q^j}$). Consider the rth row. For all w not occuring as an exponent of q in a vinegar monomial or as a difference of powers of q in an exponent of a monomial in f plus s, the (r,w)th entry is $\beta_{r,s} m_{k-s}^{q^s} = 0$. Hence, we can use those relations to look for non-zero entries of $m_{0,0}$.

After putting those relations into Algorithm 1, see Fig. 3a, you can generate a set for every i and r, exponents that occur in your core map. Each set provides a list of indices of all possible non-zero m's. For each index not occuring in any such set, the corresponding coefficient m must equal zero due to the fact that there must be a coordinate in the equation $M^T Df + DfM = \Lambda_M Df$ setting a constant multiple of m to zero. Thus, the intersection off all sets generated produces a list of all possible non-zero entries for the sub-matrix $m_{0,0}$.

Once this list is obtained, the variables shown to have value zero are eliminated from the system of equations. After repeating a similar algorithm for each of the remaining three submatrices a significantly diminished system of equations is produced which is then solved explicitly.

After running this algorithm with realistic values satisfying the above constraints and matching the parameter sizes of [13] along with using mild restrictions on the powers of the mixing and vinegar monomials, the only non-zero value obtained is m_0.

We note that it is possible that these restrictions, especially the restriction for these experiments on the number of monomials, place a lower bound on the number of vinegar variables required to achieve such a structure. On the other hand, with numerous small-scale experiments without parameter restrictions and using the full number of monomials we found that structurally the only nonzero value for the matrix $m_{0,0}$ is the m_0 term.

Since we have only a single non-zero term, our $m_{0,0}$ matrix is a diagonal matrix. A similar analysis for each of the remaining submatrices reveals the same structure. Thus we find that the only possible structure for $\overline{M}$ under these constraints satisfying a differential symmetry for $HFEv$ is

$$\overline{M} = \begin{bmatrix} cI & dI \\ \hline dI & cI \end{bmatrix}.$$

Furthermore, we can prove by way of Theorem 2 from [20], that the coefficients $c, d \in \mathbb{F}_q$.

We note that this map induces a trivial differential symmetry. To see this, note that the (nonpartial) differential of any bivariate function is bilinear in its vector inputs. Thus

$$\begin{aligned}
Dg(\overline{M}[a\ b]^T, [x\ y]^T) &= Dg([ca + db\ da + cb]^T, [x\ y]^T) \\
&= Dg([ca + db\ cb + da]^T, [x\ y]^T) \\
&= Dg(c[a\ b]^T, [x\ y]^T) + Dg(d[b\ a]^T, [x\ y]^T) \qquad (3) \\
&= cDg(a, b, x, y) + dDg(b, a, x, y) \\
&= (c + d)Dg(a, b, x, y).
\end{aligned}$$

Consequently, for the parameters provided by Algorithm 1, $HFEv$ provably has no nontrivial differential symmetric structure.

It should be noted that the restrictions provided on the powers of q of the monomials of our f does lower the entropy of our key space and likely raise the number of required vinegar variables to a level which is either unsafe or undesirable. However, there is still plenty of entropy with these restrictions and we obtain provable security against the differential symmetric attack. The restrictions provided are just a base line for this technique and our experiments with small scale examples indicate that even when we insist that every possible monomial satisfying the HFE degree bound is required to have a nonzero coefficient, the generalized algorithm still outputs only the trivial solution. Thus we can achieve provable security with minimal loss of entropy.

3.2 $HFEv^-$

Now, the algorithm extends naturally to $HFEv^-$. Every non-zero entry from the system generated by $HFEv$ is also in that generated by $HFEv^-$, but with a few more, see Fig. 2. We choose a basis in which an example minus projection is a polynomial of degree q^2. For every ith row, we also have for any w not a power of $\alpha + n$ or $\beta + n$ where $n < 2$, the (i, w)th entry is $\alpha_{i,j} m_{w-j}^{q^j} = 0$. For the sth row, for all w not being a power of $\beta + n$ or $r + n$ where $n < 2$, the (s, w)th entry is $\beta_{r,s} m_{w-r}^{q^r} = 0$. A visualization is provided in Fig. 2.

Again, we can use these relations, along with the relations described in the $HFEv$ system, to create a list of sets of all non-zero areas on $m_{0,0}$ using Algorithm 2, see Fig. 3b. Each of these sets contains indices which are possibly non-zero, thus entries not in that set are definitely equal to zero.

By taking the intersection of all the sets, you can find the final locations of non-zero entries for our sub matrix $m_{0,0}$. In doing so, with realistic values from [13], the only non-zero value obtained is m_0. This again gives us security against symmetrical attacks by having M being a block matrix consisting of diagonal matrices with an argument similar to [6].

4   Differential Invariants

Definition 2. Let $f : \mathbb{F}_q^n \to \mathbb{F}_q^m$ be a function. A *differential invariant* of f is a subspace $V \subseteq \mathbb{K}$ with the property that there is a subspace $W \subseteq \mathbb{K}$ such that $dim(W) \leq dim(V)$ and $\forall A \in Span_{\mathbb{F}_q}(Df_i)$, $AV \subseteq W$.

Informally speaking, a function has a differential invariant if the image of a subspace under all differential coordinate forms lies in a fixed subspace of dimension no larger. This definition captures the notion of *simultaneous invariants*, subspaces which are simultaneously invariant subspaces of Df_i for all i, and detects when large subspaces are acted upon linearly.

If we assume the existence of a differential invariant V, we can define a corresponding subspace $V^\perp$ as the set of all elements $x \in \mathbb{K}$ such that the

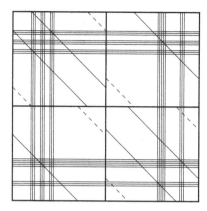

Fig. 2. Graphical representation of the equation $M^T Df + Df M = \Lambda_M Df$ for the $HFEv^-$ with the minus modifier given by the projection $\pi(x) = x^{q^2} + \rho x^q + \tau x$. Horizontal and vertical lines represent nonzero entries in $M^T Df + Df M$ while diagonal lines represent nonzero entries in $\Lambda_M Df$. We note that each triple of lines corresponds to a single monomial in the central map.

dot product $\langle x, Av \rangle = 0 \; \forall v \in V, \forall A \in Span(Df_i)$. We note that this is not the standard definition of an orthogonal complement. $V^\perp$ is not the set of everything orthogonal to V, but rather everything orthogonal to AV, which may or may not be in V. By definition, it is clear that V and $V^\perp$ satisfy the relation

$$dim(V) + dim(V^\perp) \geq n.$$

Assume there is a differential invariant $V \subseteq \mathbb{F}_q^n$, and choose linear maps $M : \mathbb{F}_q^n \to V$ and $M^\perp : \mathbb{F}_q^n \to V^\perp$. For any differential-coordinate-form, we have

$$[Df(M^\perp y, Mx)]_i = (M^\perp y)^T (Df_i(Mx)) \tag{4}$$

Since $M^\perp y$ is in $V^\perp$, and $Df_i Mx \in AV$, we must then have that

$$[Df(M^\perp y, Mx)]_i = (M^\perp a)^T (Df_i(Mx)) = 0 \tag{5}$$

Thus, as derived in [5],

$$\forall y, x \in \mathbb{F}_q^n, Df(M^\perp y, Mx) = 0 \quad \text{or equivalently,} \quad Df(M^\perp \mathbb{F}_q^n, M\mathbb{F}_q^n) = 0 \tag{6}$$

This relation restricts the structure of M and $M^\perp$, and provides a direct means of classifying the differential invariant structure of f.

We follow an analogous strategy to that of [6], adapted to the structure of the central $HFEv^-$ map f. First, we recall a result of [6].

HFEvKeyCheck

Input: An $HFEv$ central map f, a flag flg

Output: Set of indices of coefficients m_i of submatrix m_{00} which are possibly nonzero in a linear map inducing differential symmetry for f.

01. **for** monomial $\alpha_{i,j}x^{q^i+q^j}$ in f
02. $\quad S_i = \{\}$;
03. $\quad S_j = \{\}$;
04. $\quad$ **for** monomial with powers r and s in f
05. $\quad\quad S_i = S_i \cup \{r-j, s-j, i-j+r-s, i-j+s-r\}$;
06. $\quad\quad S_j = S_j \cup \{r-i, s-i, j-i+r-s, j-i+s-r\}$;
07. $\quad$ **end for;**
08. **end for;**
09. **if** flg
10. **then**
11. $\quad$ **return** all S_i;
12. **else**
13. $\quad$ **return** $\bigcap S_i$;
14. **end if;**

(a) Algorithm 1: $HFEv$

HFEv-KeyCheck

Input: An $HFEv^-$ central map $\pi(f)$, the corank of π, r

Output: Set of indices of coefficients m_i of submatrix m_{00} which are possibly nonzero in a linear map inducing differential symmetry for $\pi(f)$.

01. **Call:** HFEvKeyCheck(f,1);
02. **for all** S_i
03. $\quad T_i = \{\}$;
04. $\quad$ **for** j from 0 to $r-1$
05. $\quad\quad T_i = T_i \cup (j + S_i)$;
06. $\quad$ **end for;**
07. **end for;**
08. **return** $\bigcap T_i$;

(b) Algorithm 2: $HFEv^-$

Fig. 3. Algorithms 1 and 2

Proposition 1. *([6]) If A, B are two $m \times n$ matrices, then $rank(A) = rank(B)$ if and only if there exist nonsingular matrices C, D, such that $A = CBD$.*

Without loss of generality we assume that $rank(M^\perp) \leq rank(M)$. If the ranks are equal, then we may apply the proposition and write $M^\perp = SMT$, with S and T nonsingular. If $rank(M^\perp) < rank(M)$, compose M with a singular matrix X so that $rank(XM) = rank(M^\perp)$, and then apply the above result so that $M^\perp = S(XM)T$. Then we can express $M^\perp = S'MT$, where S' is singular. Restating our differential result (6) in this manner, we have that if $M^\perp = SMT$, and $M : \mathbb{F}_q^{n+v} \to V$, then

$$\forall x, y \in \mathbb{F}_q^n, Df(SMTy, MTx) = 0. \tag{7}$$

4.1   Minimal Generators over Intermediate Subfield

For lack of a good reference, we prove the following statement about the structure of the coordinate ring of a subspace of an extension field over an intermediate extension.

Lemma 1. *Let $\mathbb{L}/\mathbb{K}/\mathbb{F}_q$ be a tower of finite extensions with $|\mathbb{L} : \mathbb{K}| = m$ and $|\mathbb{K} : \mathbb{F}_q| = n$. Let V be an $\mathbb{F}_q$-subspace of $\mathbb{L}$. Then $I(V)$ has m multivariate generators over $\mathbb{K}$ of the form*

$$\mathcal{M}_V^{(k)}(x_0, \ldots, x_{m-1}) = \sum_{\substack{0 \le i < n \\ 0 \le j < m}} a_{ijk} x_j^{q^i}.$$

Proof. Choose a basis $\{\overline{e_0} = \overline{1}, \overline{e_1}, \ldots, \overline{e_{m-1}}\}$ for $\mathbb{L}$ over $\mathbb{K}$. Since V is an $\mathbb{F}_q$-subspace of $\mathbb{L}$, the minimal polynomial of V over $\mathbb{L}$, $\mathcal{M}_V(\overline{X}) = \sum_{i=0}^{mn-1} \overline{\alpha_i} \overline{X}^{q^i}$, is $\mathbb{F}_q$-linear. Note that the operations of addition and left multiplication by elements in $\mathbb{L}$ are $\mathbb{K}$-linear, whereas the Frobenius maps are merely $\mathbb{F}$-linear.

Now, since $\mathcal{M}_V(\overline{X})$ is linear it is additive, hence

$$\mathcal{M}_V(\overline{X}) = \mathcal{M}_V \left(\begin{bmatrix} x_0 \\ \vdots \\ x_{m-1} \end{bmatrix} \right) = \sum_{i=0}^{m-1} \mathcal{M}_V(x_i \overline{e_i}).$$

In each summand of $\mathcal{M}_V(x_j \overline{e_j})$, we have

$$(x_j \overline{e_j})^{q^i} = x_j^{q^i} \overline{e_j}^{q^i} = x_j^{q^i} \sum_{i=0}^{m-1} r_i \overline{e_i}$$

for some $r_0, \ldots, r_{m-1} \in \mathbb{K}$. As a vector over $\mathbb{K}$ this quantity is

$$\begin{bmatrix} r_0 x_j^{q^i} \\ \vdots \\ r_{m-1} x_j^{q^i} \end{bmatrix}.$$

Thus $\mathcal{M}_V(x_j \overline{e_j})$ is an m-dimensional vector of $\mathbb{K}$-linear combinations of x_j, $x_j^q, \ldots, x_j^{q^{n-1}}$. Thus $\mathcal{M}_V(\overline{X})$ is of the form

$$\mathcal{M}_V(\overline{X}) = \begin{bmatrix} \mathcal{M}_V^{(0)}(x_0, \ldots, x_{m-1}) \\ \vdots \\ \mathcal{M}_V^{(m-1)}(0, \ldots, x_{m-1}) \end{bmatrix} = \begin{bmatrix} \sum_{\substack{0 \le i \le n \\ 0 \le j \le m}} a_{ij0} x_j^{q^i} \\ \vdots \\ \sum_{\substack{0 \le i \le n \\ 0 \le j \le m}} a_{ij(m-1)} x_j^{q^i} \end{bmatrix},$$

as required.

We note that the minimal polynomials studied in [6] correspond to the special case of the above lemma in which $m = 1$. Given our characterization from Sect. 2.2 of the central map of $HFEv^-$ as a bivariate polynomial over $\mathbb{K}$, we are primarily interested in the $m = 2$ case of Lemma 1.

4.2   Invariant Analysis of $HFEv$

As in [6], we consider $Df(SMTa, MTx)$, where T is nonsingular, S is a possibly singular map which sends V into $V^{\perp}$ and $M : k \to k$ is a projection onto V. Without loss of generality we'll assume that M projects onto V. Then MT is another projection onto V. SMT is a projection onto $V^{\perp}$. An important distinction is that for this case, the a and x above are actually two dimensional vectors over k. Thus $dim(V) + dim(V^{\perp}) \geq n$.

Proof (of Theorem 1). Let us denote by $[\hat{x}\ \hat{y}]^T$ the quantity $MT[x\ y]^T$.
   Suppose we have

$$f(x, y) = \sum_{\substack{0 \leq i \leq j < n \\ q^i + q^j \leq D}} \alpha_{ij} x^{q^i + q^j} + \sum_{\substack{0 \leq i, j < n \\ q^i \leq D}} \beta_{ij} x^{q^i} y^{q^j} + \sum_{0 \leq i \leq j < n} \gamma_{ij} y^{q^i + q^j}.$$

Applying the differential (w.r.t. the vector $[x\ y]^T$) as described in Sect. 3.1, we obtain:

$$\begin{aligned}
Df(a, b, x, y) = &\sum_{\substack{0 \leq i \leq j < n \\ q^i + q^j \leq D}} \alpha_{ij} \left(a^{q^i} x^{q^j} + a^{q^j} x^{q^i} \right) \\
&+ \sum_{\substack{0 \leq i, j < n \\ q^i \leq D}} \beta_{ij} \left(a^{q^i} y^{q^j} + x^{q^i} b^{q^j} \right) \\
&+ \sum_{0 \leq i \leq j < n} \gamma_{ij} \left(b^{q^i} y^{q^j} + b^{q^j} y^{q^i} \right).
\end{aligned} \tag{8}$$

Substituting $SMT[a\ b]^T$ and $MT[x\ y]^T$, we derive

$$Df(S[\hat{a}\ \hat{b}]^T, \hat{x}, \hat{y}) = Df(S_{11}\hat{a} + S_{12}\hat{b}, S_{21}\hat{a} + S_{22}\hat{b}, \hat{x}, \hat{y}).$$

For notational convenience let $\mathring{a} = S_{11}\hat{a} + S_{12}\hat{b}$ and $\mathring{b} = S_{21}\hat{a} + S_{22}\hat{b}$. Plugging in these values in the previous equation we get

$$\begin{aligned}
Df(\mathring{a}, \mathring{b}, \hat{x}, \hat{y}) = &\sum_{\substack{0 \leq i \leq j < n \\ q^i + q^j \leq D}} \alpha_{ij} \left((\mathring{a})^{q^i} \hat{x}^{q^j} + (\mathring{a})^{q^j} \hat{x}^{q^i} \right) \\
&+ \sum_{\substack{0 \leq i, j < n \\ q^i \leq D}} \beta_{ij} \left((\mathring{a})^{q^i} \hat{y}^{q^j} + \hat{x}^{q^i} (\mathring{b})^{q^j} \right) \\
&+ \sum_{0 \leq i \leq j < n} \gamma_{ij} \left((\mathring{b})^{q^i} \hat{y}^{q^j} + (\mathring{b})^{q^j} \hat{y}^{q^i} \right).
\end{aligned} \tag{9}$$

In contrast to the situation with HFE, these monomials are not necessarily independent. By Lemma 1, the generators of $I(V)$ have the form

$$\sum_{0 \leq i < n} r_{ij} x^{q^i} + \sum_{0 \leq i < n} s_{ij} y^{q^i} \quad \text{for } j \in \{1, 2\},$$

where $r_{ij}, s_{ij} \in \mathbb{K}$. Clearly, these expressions evaluate to zero on $(\hat{x}, \hat{y})$. Evaluating (9) modulo $I(V)$ (only on the variables $\hat{x}$ and $\hat{y}$), we obtain:

$$
\begin{aligned}
Df(\hat{a}, \hat{b}, \hat{x}, \hat{y}) = & \sum_{\substack{0 \le i < n \\ 0 \le j < d_x}} \left[\alpha'_{ij}(\hat{a})^{q^i} + \beta'_{ij}(\hat{b})^{q^i} \right] \hat{x}^{q^j} \\
& + \sum_{\substack{0 \le i < n \\ 0 \le j < d_y}} \left[\gamma'_{ij}(\hat{a})^{q^i} + \delta'_{ij}(\hat{b})^{q^i} \right] \hat{y}^{q^j},
\end{aligned}
\tag{10}
$$

where d_x and d_y are the largest powers of $\hat{x}$ (resp. $\hat{y}$) occuring. After the reduction modulo $I(V)$, the remaining monomials $\hat{x}, \ldots, \hat{x}^{q^{d_x}}$ and $\hat{y}, \ldots, \hat{y}^{q^{d_y}}$ are independent. Thus, for $Df(\hat{a}, \hat{b}, \hat{x}, \hat{y}) = 0$, each polynomial expression multiplied by a single $\hat{x}^{q^j}$ or $\hat{y}^{q^j}$ must be identically zero, that is to say that for all $0 \le j \le d_x$

$$
\sum_{0 \le i < n} \left[\alpha'_{ij}(\hat{a})^{q^i} + \beta'_{ij}(\hat{b})^{q^i} \right] = 0
\tag{11}
$$

and for all $0 \le j \le d_y$

$$
\sum_{0 \le i < n} \left[\gamma'_{ij}(\hat{a})^{q^i} + \delta'_{ij}(\hat{b})^{q^i} \right] = 0.
\tag{12}
$$

The left hand sides of (11) and (12) are $\mathbb{F}$-linear functions in $S[\hat{a}\ \hat{b}]^T$. Thus we can express each such equality over $\mathbb{F}$ as

$$
LS \left[\hat{a}_0 \ \cdots \ \hat{a}_{n-1}\ \hat{b}_0 \ \cdots \ \hat{b}_{n-1} \right]^T = 0,
$$

where L is an $n \times 2n$ matrix with entries in $\mathbb{F}$. We note specifically that the coefficients of L depend on V and the choices of coefficients in the central map f. For randomly chosen coefficients retaining the $HFEv$ structure, we expect an L derived from an equation of the form (11) or (12) to have high rank with very high probability, more than $1 - q^{-n}$. Thus the dimension of the intersections of the nullspaces of each L is zero with probability at least $1 - 2q^{-n}$.

Clearly, the condition for these equations to be satisfied is that S sends V to the intersection of the nullspaces of each such L. Thus S is with high probability the zero map on V and so $V^{\perp} = \{0\}$. This generates a contradiction, however, since $2n \le dim(V) + \dim(V^{\perp}) < 2n$. Thus, with probability greater than $1 - 2q^{-n}$, f has no nontrivial differential invariant structure.

4.3 $HFEv^-$

The situation for $HFEv^-$ is quite similar, but the probabilities are slightly different. Specifically one must note that since the condition of being a differential invariant is a condition on the span of the public differential forms, under projection this condition is weaker and easier to satisfy. For specificity, we consider the removal of a single public equation, though, critically, a very similar though notationally messy analysis is easy to derive in the general case.

We may model the removal of a single equation as a projection of the form $\pi(x) = x^q + x$ applied after the central map.

Proof (of Theorem 2). Consider

$$\pi(f(x,y)) = \sum_{\substack{0 \le i \le j < n \\ q^i + q^j \le D}} \alpha_{ij} x^{q^i + q^j} + \sum_{\substack{0 \le i,j < n \\ q^i \le D}} \beta_{ij} x^{q^i} y^{q^j} + \sum_{\substack{0 \le i \le j < n}} \gamma_{ij} y^{q^i + q^j}$$
$$+ \sum_{\substack{0 \le i \le j < n \\ q^i + q^j \le D}} \alpha_{ij}^q x^{q^{i+1} + q^{j+1}} + \sum_{\substack{0 \le i,j < n \\ q^i \le D}} \beta_{ij}^q x^{q^{i+1}} y^{q^{j+1}} + \sum_{\substack{0 \le i \le j < n}} \gamma_{ij}^q y^{q^{i+1} + q^{j+1}}.$$

(13)

Taking the differential, we obtain

$$D(\pi \circ f)(\hat{a}, \hat{b}, \hat{x}, \hat{y}) = \sum_{\substack{0 \le i \le j < n \\ q^i + q^j \le D}} \alpha_{ij} \left((\hat{a})^{q^i} \hat{x}^{q^j} + (\hat{a})^{q^j} \hat{x}^{q^i} \right)$$
$$+ \sum_{\substack{0 \le i,j < n \\ q^i \le D}} \beta_{ij} \left((\hat{a})^{q^i} \hat{y}^{q^j} + \hat{x}^{q^i} (\hat{b})^{q^j} \right)$$
$$+ \sum_{\substack{0 \le i \le j < n}} \gamma_{ij} \left((\hat{b})^{q^i} \hat{y}^{q^j} + (\hat{b})^{q^j} \hat{y}^{q^i} \right)$$
$$+ \sum_{\substack{0 \le i \le j < n \\ q^i + q^j \le D}} \alpha_{ij}^q \left((\hat{a})^{q^{i+1}} \hat{x}^{q^{j+1}} + (\hat{a})^{q^{j+1}} \hat{x}^{q^{i+1}} \right)$$
$$+ \sum_{\substack{0 \le i,j < n \\ q^i \le D}} \beta_{ij}^q \left((\hat{a})^{q^{i+1}} \hat{y}^{q^{j+1}} + \hat{x}^{q^{i+1}} (\hat{b})^{q^{j+1}} \right)$$
$$+ \sum_{\substack{0 \le i \le j < n}} \gamma_{ij}^q \left((\hat{b})^{q^{i+1}} \hat{y}^{q^{j+1}} + (\hat{b})^{q^{j+1}} \hat{y}^{q^{i+1}} \right).$$

(14)

Again, we may evaluate modulo $I(V)$ and collect the terms for the distinct powers of $\hat{x}$ and $\hat{y}$. By the independence of these monomials we obtain the relations

$$\sum_{0 \le i < n} \left[\alpha_{ij}''(\hat{a})^{q^i} + \beta_{ij}'(\hat{b})^{q^i} \right] = 0$$
$$\sum_{0 \le i < n} \left[\gamma_{ij}''(\hat{a})^{q^i} + \delta_{ij}'(\hat{b})^{q^i} \right] = 0.$$

(15)

At this point, the analysis proceeds exactly as in the case of $HFEv$. We once again arrive at the conclusion that with high probability S is the zero map on V, contradicting the existence of a differential invariant. We note here that this analysis works for any projection, though the exact values of the α_{ij}'' and γ_{ij}'' depend on the specific projection and the structure of f.

5   Degree of Regularity, Q-Rank and Parameters

Further considerations for the security of $HFEv^-$ are the degree of regularity, a quantity closely connected to the complexity of algebraic attacks, and the Q-rank of the public key. A careful analysis of each of these quantities reveals that they support the security of $HFEv^-$ against an algebraic attack such as [21] and against the Kipnis-Shamir methodology and its improvements, see [17,18].

In [22], it is shown that an upper bound for the Q-rank of an $HFEv^-$ system is given by the sum of the Q-rank of the HFE component, the number of removed equations, and the Q-rank of the vinegar component. For Gui-96(96, 5, 6, 6), here $q = 2$, $n = 96$, $D = 5$, $v = 6$ and $r = 6$, this quantity is roughly 15. Furthermore, in [13], experimental evidence in the form of analysis of toy variants is provided indicating that this estimate is tight. Thus the complexity of a Kipnis-Shamir style attack is roughly $O(n^3 q^{15n})$.

Also in [22], a formula for an upper bound on the degree of regularity for $HFEv^-$ systems is derived. Given the parameters of Gui-96(96,5,6,6), the degree of regularity is expected to be 9. Further, experiments are provided in [13] supporting the tightness of this approximation formula for toy schemes with n as large as 38. With this degree of regularity the expected complexity of inverting the system via Gröbner basis techniques is given by

$$\binom{96 - 6 + 9}{9}^{2.3766} \approx 2^{93}.$$

We note that an error in the approximation of the degree of regularity can easily change this estimate by a factor of a few thousand. Still, it seems clear that each of these avenues of attack is unviable.

Still another attack vector is to put the entropy of the key space to the test with techniques such as those mentioned in [23] for deriving equivalence classes of keys. With our most restrictive instance of the key verification algorithm in Sect. 3.2, we have a key space consisting of roughly q^{13n} central maps, roughly q^{6n} of which can be seen as equivalent keys as in [23]. Thus provable security against the differential adversary can be achieved with a key space of size far beyond the reach of the "guess-then-IP" strategy.

6   Conclusion

$HFEv^-$ is rapidly approaching twenty years of age and stands as one of the oldest post-quantum signature schemes remaining secure. With the new parameters suggested in [13], $HFEv^-$ has metamorphosed from the very slow form of QUARTZ into a perfectly reasonable option for practical and secure quantum-resistant signatures.

Our analysis contributes to the confidence and optimism which $HFEv^-$ inspires. By elucidating the differential structure of the central map of $HFEv^-$, we have verified that a class of attacks which has proven very powerful against multivariate schemes in the past cannot be employed against $HFEv^-$. In conjunction with the careful analysis of the degree of regularity and Q-rank of the scheme already present in the literature, we have succeeded in showing that $HFEv^-$ is secure against every type of attack known. If the future holds a successful attack against $HFEv^-$ it must be by way of a fundamentally new advance.

References

1. Lange, T., et al.: Post-quantum cryptography for long term security. Horizon 2020, ICT-645622 (2015) http://cordis.europa.eu/project/rcn/194347_en.html
2. Campagna, M., Chen, L., et al.: Quantum safe cryptography and security. ETSI White Paper No. 8 (2015). http://www.etsi.org/images/files/ETSIWhitePapers/QuantumSafeWhitepaper.pdf
3. Moody, D., Chen, L., Liu, Y.K.: Nist pqc workgroup. Computer Security Resource Center (2015). http://csrc.nist.gov/groups/ST/crypto-research-projects/#PQC
4. Smith-Tone, D.: On the differential security of multivariate public key cryptosystems. In: Yang, B.-Y. (ed.) PQCrypto 2011. LNCS, vol. 7071, pp. 130–142. Springer, Heidelberg (2011)
5. Perlner, R., Smith-Tone, D.: A classification of differential invariants for multivariate post-quantum cryptosystems. In: Gaborit, P. (ed.) PQCrypto 2013. LNCS, vol. 7932, pp. 165–173. Springer, Heidelberg (2013)
6. Daniels, T., Smith-Tone, D.: Differential properties of the HFE cryptosystem. In: Mosca, M. (ed.) PQCrypto 2014. LNCS, vol. 8772, pp. 59–75. Springer, Heidelberg (2014)
7. Dubois, V., Fouque, P.-A., Shamir, A., Stern, J.: Practical cryptanalysis of SFLASH. In: Menezes, A. (ed.) CRYPTO 2007. LNCS, vol. 4622, pp. 1–12. Springer, Heidelberg (2007)
8. Shamir, A., Kipnis, A.: Cryptanalysis of the oil & vinegar signature scheme. In: Krawczyk, H. (ed.) CRYPTO '98. LNCS, pp. 257–266. Springer, Heidelberg (1998)
9. Moody, D., Perlner, R., Smith-Tone, D.: An asymptotically optimal structural attack on the ABC multivariate encryption scheme. In: Mosca, M. (ed.) PQCrypto 2014. LNCS, vol. 8772, pp. 180–196. Springer, Heidelberg (2014)
10. Patarin, J.: Cryptanalysis of the Matsumoto and Imai public key scheme of Eurocrypt '88. In: Coppersmith, D. (ed.) CRYPTO 1995. LNCS, vol. 963, pp. 248–261. Springer, Heidelberg (1995)
11. Perlner, R., Smith-Tone, D.: Security analysis and key modification for ZHFE. In: Post-Quantum Cryptography - 7th International Conference, PQCrypto 2016, 24–26 February 2016, Fukuoka, Japan (2016)
12. Patarin, J., Courtois, N.T., Goubin, L.: QUARTZ, 128-bit long digital signatures. In: Naccache, D. (ed.) CT-RSA 2001. LNCS, vol. 2020, pp. 282–297. Springer, Heidelberg (2001)
13. Petzoldt, A., Chen, M., Yang, B., Tao, C., Ding, J.: Design principles for HFEv-based multivariate signature schemes. In: Iwata, T., Cheon, J.H. (eds.) ASIACRYPT 2015. LNCS, vol. 9452, pp. 311–334. Springer, Heidelberg (2015)
14. Patarin, J.: Hidden fields equations (HFE) and isomorphisms of polynomials (IP): two new families of asymmetric algorithms. In: Maurer, U.M. (ed.) EUROCRYPT 1996. LNCS, vol. 1070, pp. 33–48. Springer, Heidelberg (1996)

15. Matsumoto, T., Imai, H.: Public quadratic polynominal-tuples for efficient signature-verification and message-encryption. In: EUROCRYPT, pp. 419–453 (1988)
16. Berlekamp, E.R.: Factoring polynomials over large finite fields. Math. Comput. **24**, 713–735 (1970)
17. Kipnis, A., Shamir, A.: Cryptanalysis of the HFE public key cryptosystem by relinearization. In: Wiener, M. (ed.) CRYPTO 1999. LNCS, vol. 1666, p. 19. Springer, Heidelberg (1999)
18. Bettale, L., Faugère, J., Perret, L.: Cryptanalysis of HFE, multi-HFE and variants for odd and even characteristic. Des. Codes Crypt. **69**, 1–52 (2013)
19. Fouque, P.-A., Macario-Rat, G., Perret, L., Stern, J.: Total break of the ℓ-IC signature scheme. In: Cramer, R. (ed.) PKC 2008. LNCS, vol. 4939, pp. 1–17. Springer, Heidelberg (2008)
20. Smith-Tone, D.: Properties of the discrete differential with cryptographic applications. In: Sendrier, N. (ed.) PQCrypto 2010. LNCS, vol. 6061, pp. 1–12. Springer, Heidelberg (2010)
21. Faugère, J.-C., Joux, A.: Algebraic cryptanalysis of hidden field equation (HFE) cryptosystems using gröbner bases. In: Boneh, D. (ed.) CRYPTO 2003. LNCS, vol. 2729, pp. 44–60. Springer, Heidelberg (2003)
22. Ding, J., Yang, B.-Y.: Degree of regularity for HFEv and HFEv-. In: Gaborit, P. (ed.) PQCrypto 2013. LNCS, vol. 7932, pp. 52–66. Springer, Heidelberg (2013)
23. Wolf, C., Preneel, B.: Equivalent keys in multivariate quadratic public key systems. J. Math. Crypt. **4**, 375–415 (2011)
24. Gaborit, P. (ed.): PQCrypto 2013. Security and Cryptology, vol. 7932. Springer, Heidelberg (2013)
25. Mosca, M. (ed.): PQCrypto 2014. LNCS, vol. 8772. Springer, Heidelberg (2014)

Extension Field Cancellation: A New Central Trapdoor for Multivariate Quadratic Systems

Alan Szepieniec[1,2]([✉]), Jintai Ding[3], and Bart Preneel[1,2]

[1] Department of Electrical Engineering, ESAT/COSIC, KU Leuven, Leuven, Belgium
alan.szepieniec@esat.kuleuven.be
[2] iMinds, Ghent, Belgium
[3] University of Cincinnati, Cincinnati, OH, USA

Abstract. This paper introduces a new central trapdoor for multivariate quadratic (MQ) public-key cryptosystems that allows for encryption, in contrast to time-tested MQ primitives such as Unbalanced Oil and Vinegar or Hidden Field Equations which only allow for signatures. Our construction is a mixed-field scheme that exploits the commutativity of the extension field to dramatically reduce the complexity of the extension field polynomial implicitly present in the public key. However, this reduction can only be performed by the user who knows concise descriptions of two simple polynomials, which constitute the private key. After applying this transformation, the plaintext can be recovered by solving a linear system. We use the minus and projection modifiers to inoculate our scheme against known attacks. A straightforward C++ implementation confirms the efficient operation of the public key algorithms.

Keywords: MQ · Multivariate · Quadratic · Public-key · Post-quantum · Encryption · Mixed-field · Trapdoor

1 Introduction

Since the inception of public-key cryptography, cryptographers have made a huge effort to find new and better computational problems that feature the elusive *trapdoor* — a small piece of information that can turn an otherwise hard to invert function into one that can easily be inverted. This on-going search effort has lead to a tremendous diversification of the computational problems that underpin public-key cryptography. This diversification is a good thing: by keeping all the eggs in separate baskets, a breakthrough in one area is unlikely to spill over to other areas, thus limiting the catastrophic potential of scientific advances.

Of particular interest to this paper is the class of problems known as multivariate quadratic (MQ) systems of equations. Not only do cryptosystems based on this primitive offer performance advantages over well-established ones such as RSA or systems based on elliptic curves, MQ cryptography is also conjectured to be post-quantum — that is to say, it holds promise of resisting attacks on

© Springer International Publishing Switzerland 2016
T. Takagi (Ed.): PQCrypto 2016, LNCS 9606, pp. 182–196, 2016.
DOI: 10.1007/978-3-319-29360-8_12

quantum computers. From this point of view, MQ cryptography is certainly a promising line of research.

The key challenge in the design of MQ cryptosystems is to find a suitable central mapping $\mathcal{F} : \mathbb{F}_q^n \to \mathbb{F}_q^m$ which should be easily invertible in addition to being expressible in terms of multivariate quadratic polynomials. The trapdoor information cannot be recovered efficiently from the public key as it is hidden by two affine transformations. Many central mappings have been proposed, most of which fall in two main categories [32]: single field schemes, such as UOV [17], Rainbow [7] and the triangular variants [31], where the central polynomial system is chosen to have a particular structure that enables efficient inversion; and mixed field schemes, such as C* [19], HFE [22] and Multi-HFE [3], where arithmetic in the base field is mixed with arithmetic in an extension field. However, despite the abundance of proposals, MQ cryptography has an awful track record as most of these proposals have been broken [2,14,18,28,29,32].

Consequently, much research in the area of MQ cryptography has been devoted to patchwork — finding small modifications to existing systems that render specific attacks infeasible. A few examples among many that fall into this category are the minus modifier ("−") [25], which inoculates HFE-type systems against Gröbner basis attacks and linearization attacks; vinegar variables ("v") [17], which combines elements from different trapdoors and like "minus" is capable of making a Gröbner basis attack prohibitively expensive; and projection ("p") [9] which appears to successfully thwart the Dubois *et al.* differential attack [10,11] on SFLASH.

However, the search for modifications to fix broken systems has an equally bad track record. Many of the MQ systems that were supposedly inoculated against some attack by the introduction of a modification, were broken by minor variants of that same attack. For example, both the multivariate generalization and the odd field characteristic variant of HFE were introduced and designed specifically to thwart the algebraic attack on HFE [14]; however, neither variant has managed to withstand cryptanalysis [2]. Another example is given by the fate of SFLASH, one of the three recommended signature schemes of the NESSIE project [1]. The addition of the minus modifier to the basic C* construction did not save the scheme from a new type of differential attack [10,11]. The rapid spawn of attacks that break the inoculated systems seems to suggest the need for a more prudent design strategy: searching for fundamentally different basic principles for MQ trapdoors, rather than tinkering on the edges of existing ones.

Related work. Encryption schemes have been the bane of multivariate quadratic cryptography. No MQ encryption scheme has withstood the test of time, while several MQ *signature* schemes have. However, some very recent results and proposals in this area pose new and interesting challenges for cryptanalysts.

Porras *et al.* proposed a new central trapdoor which they call ZHFE [24]. Up until this point, the extension field polynomial in HFE-based cryptosystem required the number of nonzero coefficients to be small and its degree to be relatively low, so as to allow efficient root calculation. The idea of Porras *et al.* exchanges this single low-degree polynomial for a pair of high-degree polynomials that make up the central map. Additionally, these polynomials are chosen such that there exists a third polynomial, $\Psi(\mathcal{X})$, which is a function of the first two and yet has low degree. In order to invert a given image, it suffices to factorize this third polynomial. As the degree of the polynomials increases, so does the degree of regularity of the system. This increase in the degree of regularity, in turn, renders a direct algebraic attack infeasible, even though the very same attack broke the regular HFE cryptosystem.

Tao *et al.* proposed a multivariate quadratic encryption scheme called Simple Matrix Encryption, or simply ABC Encryption [27]. Their construction is based on a fundamentally new idea: embedding polynomial matrix arithmetic inside the central trapdoor function. The trapdoor can be inverted with high probability because the matrix, albeit evaluated in a single point, can be reconstructed from the output. With high probability this matrix can be inverted, giving rise to a system of linear equations which describe the input.

Our contributions. We introduce a new central trapdoor for multivariate quadratic encryption schemes. Our proposal is a mixed-field scheme — similar to the C* and HFE string of proposals because we use an embedding function to pretend as though a vector of variables in the base field were actually a single variable in the extension field. However, our proposal is notably different from its predecessors, where the restriction on the degree of this embedded polynomial was key both to their efficiency and to their demise; our proposal allows for a high-degree embedded polynomial and undoes this complexity by exploiting the commutative property of the extension field. Our proposal allows for encryption, in stark contrast to most other members of the HFE family.

Like the ABC Encryption Scheme, decryption of a ciphertext consists of essentially solving linear systems. This linear system is parameterized by the particular ciphertext or message: every possible ciphertext or message implicitly defines a unique linear system. Knowledge of the private key allows the user to obtain the linear system efficiently, while the adversary who attacks the system without this crucial information has no advantage to solve the quadratic system.

Like ZHFE, the central map consists of two high-degree extension field polynomials that satisfy a special relation which is obviously hidden from the adversary. The decryption algorithm exploits this relation to turn the otherwise hard inversion problem into an easy one.

Another important similarity between our map and both ABC and ZHFE is that all three are expanding maps, *i.e.*, $\mathbb{F}_q^n \rightarrow \mathbb{F}_q^m$ where $m = 2n$. This commonality is no accident, because in order allow unique decryption, the map must be injective. However, if $m \approx n$, the differential of this nearly-bijective map is readily differentiable from that of a random one — not a desirable property for multivariate quadratic maps to have.

Despite these similarities, the main advantage of our scheme is that its construction is notably *different* from ABC and ZHFE. Consequently, as-yet undiscovered weaknesses or even attacks that affect ABC or ZHFE may leave our scheme intact. Furthermore, this diversification opens the door for a combination of strategies whose end result reaps the benefits of both worlds. Certainly the case of HFEv proves that such a combination may indeed increase both security and performance.

In line with a common theme throughout MQ cryptography, we are unable to prove the security of our scheme or even to reduce it to a plausible computational assumption. An exhaustive list of all known attacks on MQ systems and why they fail against our system is beyond the scope of this paper. Nevertheless, we identify several pertinent attacks that may be launched against a naïve implementation of our scheme, and we propose strategies to thwart them. Patarin's linearization attack [21] is foiled by the minus modifier and repeated applications of the same modifier make the extended MinRank attack [4,18] as well as the direct algebraic attack [14] prohibitively inefficient. The scheme seems naturally resistant to Dubois et al.'s differential attack [10,11], but we nevertheless recommend to use the projection modifier, which is the proper countermeasure against this attack.

Outline. We introduce notation and recall basic properties of MQ systems as well as of extension field embeddings in Sect. 2. Next, Sect. 3 defines the trapdoor proposed in this paper as well as several necessary modifiers. We recommend parameters for 80 bits of security in the first part of Sect. 4 and afterwards discuss the efficiency of our scheme, both from a theoretical point of view and by referencing timing results from a software implementation. Section 5 concludes the text.

2   Preliminaries

2.1   Notation and Definitions

We use small case letters (s) to denote scalars in the base field; extension field elements are denoted by calligraphic capital letters ($\mathcal{C}$); small case bold letters ($\mathbf{v}$) denote column vectors; and regular capital letters are used for matrices (M).

Let $\mathbb{F}_q$ denote the finite field with q elements, which we call the *base field*. With any combination of a finite field $\mathbb{F}_q$ with a polynomial $f(x) \in \mathbb{F}_q[x]$ one can associate a finite ring $\mathbb{E} = \mathbb{F}_q[x]/\langle f(x)\rangle$ of residue classes after division by $f(x)$. If f is irreducible over $\mathbb{F}_q$ and has degree n, then $\mathbb{E} = \mathbb{F}_{q^n}$ is a finite field we call the *extension field*. There exists a natural homomorphism $\varphi : (\mathbb{F}_q)^n \to \mathbb{F}_{q^n}$ that maps a vector $\mathbf{v} = (v_1, \ldots, v_n)^\mathsf{T} \in \mathbb{F}_q^n$ onto an element $\mathcal{V} \in \mathbb{F}_{q^n}$ of the extension field. We can apply this embedding function to the vector of indeterminates $\mathbf{x}$ in order to get the extension field indeterminate $\mathcal{X} = \varphi(\mathbf{x})$.

2.2   Multivariate Quadratic Systems

The public key of an MQ cryptosystem is a system of quadratic polynomials mapping n input variables to m output variables: $\mathcal{P} : \mathbb{F}_q^n \to \mathbb{F}_q^m$; the public operation consists of evaluating this system of polynomials in a point. The secret key consists of a pair of invertible affine mappings on the input and output variables, S and T, and an alternate quadratic system of polynomials, $\mathcal{F} : \mathbb{F}_q^n \to \mathbb{F}_q^m$, such that $\mathcal{P} = T \circ \mathcal{F} \circ S$. The affine transformations are trivially inverted; the central system $\mathcal{F}$ is constructed in such a way that it is also easy to invert. However, the attacker cannot efficiently recover $\mathcal{F}$ from $\mathcal{P}$ and calculate the inverse as $\mathcal{F}$ is hidden by the affine transformations. A schematic overview is given in Fig. 1.

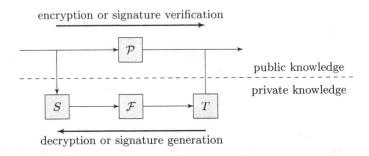

Fig. 1. Schematic representation of multivariate quadratic cryptosystems.

Given a central trapdoor $\mathcal{F}$ it is easy to construct a multivariate quadratic cryptosystem by composing it with two affine transformations. This process is out of the scope of the present paper. Rather, we restrict our attention to the construction of the central trapdoors.

3   Central Map

3.1   The Basic Construction

Let $A \in \mathbb{F}_q^{n \times n}$ be a random matrix over the base field. Then $A\mathbf{x} \in (\mathbb{F}_q[\mathbf{x}])^n$ represents a vector where each element is a linear polynomial in $\mathbf{x}$. And then $\alpha(\mathbf{x}) = \varphi(A\mathbf{x})$ is an extension field element. The square matrix that represents multiplication by $\alpha(\mathbf{x})$ is denoted by $\alpha_m(\mathbf{x}) \in \mathbb{F}_q^{n \times n}$. We use $\alpha(\mathcal{X})$ to stress the fact that α may also be considered as a univariate polynomial in $\mathcal{X}$ over the extension field, regardless of its representation, although the degree of this polynomial is larger than one.

Similarly, let $\beta(\mathbf{x}) = \varphi(B\mathbf{x})$ for a random $n \times n$ matrix $B \in \mathbb{F}_q^{n \times n}$. With these polynomials α and β, we define the central trapdoor as follows:

$$\mathcal{F} : \mathbb{F}_q^n \to \mathbb{F}_q^{2n} : \mathbf{x} \mapsto \begin{pmatrix} \alpha_m(\mathbf{x})\mathbf{x} \\ \beta_m(\mathbf{x})\mathbf{x} \end{pmatrix} . \tag{1}$$

To see how we are able to invert $\mathcal{F}(\mathbf{x}) = \begin{pmatrix} \mathbf{d}_1 \\ \mathbf{d}_2 \end{pmatrix}$, consider first the equality $\alpha(\mathbf{x})\beta(\mathbf{x}) = \beta(\mathbf{x})\alpha(\mathbf{x})$ which holds due to the commutativity of the extension field. We can proceed to construct a system of linear equations in $\mathbf{x}$:

$$\beta_m(\mathbf{x})\mathbf{d}_1 - \alpha_m(\mathbf{x})\mathbf{d}_2 = 0 . \tag{2}$$

While Gaussian elimination is in this case guaranteed to find a solution, this solution need not be unique. Nevertheless, this set of solutions is expected to be small, in accordance with the number of solutions to random linear systems. Moreover, this set can be pruned by iteratively plugging the potential solution into the function $\mathcal{F}$ and verifying that the correct output image $(\mathbf{d}_1; \mathbf{d}_2)$ is produced.

3.2 Modifiers

The trapdoor as described above is insecure. In particular, it is broken by the bilinear attack, the MinRank attack, as well as an algebraic attack using fast Gröbner basis algorithms. We apply the "minus" to inoculate basic EFC against these attacks. While not strictly necessary, "projection" may guard against new differential attacks at very little cost whereas "Frobenius tail" drastically drops the cost of decryption.

Minus. Although Patarin's linearization attack [21] was originally conceived to attack C*, it also applies to unprotected EFC. Indeed, Eq. 2 describes a bilinear polynomial in the plaintext and ciphertext, whose coefficients can be calculated using linear algebra after obtaining enough plaintext-ciphertext pairs. Once these coefficients are known, obtaining a plaintext that matches a given ciphertext is easy. However, dropping just one polynomial from the public key is enough to foil this attack. In this case, the attacker must guess the missing information for every plaintext-ciphertext pair, making them useless for exact linear algebra.

This "minus" modifier, which consists of removing one or more polynomials from the public key [23], is more than just a countermeasure against Patarin's attack. A pair of important results by Ding *et al.* [6,8] indicates that this modifier is much better thought of as a fundamental building block of multivariate quadratic cryptosystems rather than a mere patch. Indeed, not only does the first application of this modifier block Patarin's linearization attack; every repeated application increments by one the rank of the quadratic form associated with the extension field polynomial, rendering the MinRank attack due to Kipnis and Shamir [18] as well as its subsequent improvement by Courtois [4] that much more infeasible. Furthermore, this rank increase in turn increases the degree of regularity of the system, resulting in a similarly infeasible algebraic attack.

The use of this modifier does come at the cost of a performance penalty. In particular, the decryption algorithm must first guess the values of the missing polynomials before undoing the output transformation T. Under this guess, it can proceed to the linear system in Eq. 2 and compute the potential matching plaintext $\mathbf{x}$. If indeed $\mathcal{F}(\mathbf{x}) = (\mathbf{d}_1; \mathbf{d}_2)$, then the correct plaintext was found. If not, then the guess was wrong and the algorithm must start all over again with a new one.

Fortunately, as long as the number of dropped polynomials a is small enough, the correct plaintext will still be found with overwhelming probability. In order for the decryption algorithm to produce the wrong plaintext $\mathbf{x}$ upon decrypting the ciphertext $\mathbf{y}$, there must exist at least two guesses $\mathbf{g}_1 \in \mathbb{F}_q^a$ and $\mathbf{g}_2 \in \mathbb{F}_q^a$ such that both $(\mathbf{y}; \mathbf{g}_1)$ and $(\mathbf{y}; \mathbf{g}_2)$ are in the range of $\mathcal{P}$. If $\mathcal{P}$ is to be modeled as a random function $\mathbb{F}_q^n \to \mathbb{F}_q^{2n-a}$, then its range is a uniform subset of $\mathbb{F}_q^{2n-a}$ of size q^n, and then the probability of this event is approximately $q^n \times q^{-2n+a} = q^{-n+a}$. Consequently, as long as $a \ll n$, the probability of decryption error remains astronomically small.

Figure 2 offers empirical validation of this argument. It shows the probability of decryption error for various even values for a as a function of n. Only when a and n are on the same order of magnitude, is this probability noticeable; when n rises to practical values, this probability does indeed drop to zero.

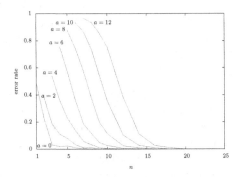

Fig. 2. Observed decryption error rate.

In similar fashion to C^{*-} and HFE^-, this modifier will be denoted by the superscript "$-$", *i.e.*, EFC^-. The number of dropped polynomials will be denoted by a.

Projection. The differential symmetry attacks by Dubois *et al.* [10,11] on SFLASH, a C^* variant, show that the minus operator is not enough to secure it. Dubois *et al.* identify a symmetry in the differential of the C^* map $\mathcal{F}$:

$$D\mathcal{F}(L\mathbf{x}, \mathbf{y}) + D\mathcal{F}(\mathbf{x}, L\mathbf{y}) = \Lambda\mathcal{F}(\mathbf{x}, \mathbf{y})$$

for some matrices L and Λ. The presence of this symmetry proved fatal.

Fortunately, Ding *et al.* [9] show experimentally that a small tweak by the name of "projection" completely foils this line of attack. In particular, pSFLASH projects the input vector $\mathbf{x}$ onto a lower-dimensional space before passing it through the central map. Smith-Tone [26] has since offered a theoretical basis for the efficacy of this modifier. At the core of Smith-Tone's argument is the following theorem:

Theorem 1 (Smith-Tone, [26]). *A polynomial $f : \mathbb{F}_{q^n} \to \mathbb{F}_{q^n}$ with a bilinear differential has the multiplicative symmetry if and only if it has one quadratic monomial summand.*

While the components of EFC do have bilinear differentials, they do not consist of a single quadratic monomial but of a sum of them. For example, the first component is described by $\alpha(\mathcal{X})\mathcal{X} = \sum_{i=0}^{n-1} A_i \mathcal{X}^{q^i+1}$ where the coefficients A_i are with overwhelming probability not all but one equal to zero. Therefore, by Smith-Tone's theorem, the differential multiplicative symmetry is absent with overwhelming probability.

Nevertheless, in anticipation of more general attacks using a similar differential invariant, we follow a perspective offered at the conclusion Smith-Tone's paper: *projection does not destroy the differential symmetry, but pushes it down to a subfield.* Since this modifier is cheap in terms of performance and cannot degrade security, we choose to err on the side of safety and ensure that no such subfield can exist. In particular, we guarantee that the matrices A and B have rank $n - 1$, and that n is a prime number. Moreover, the kernels of A and B do not intersect except at the origin. This modifier will be denoted by the subscript p, *e.g.* EFC_p.

Frobenius Tail in Characteristic Two (or Three). The trapdoor as described so far can be implemented over any base field and unless the minus operator is applied, the rank of the quadratic forms associated with the extension field is two. However, if we restrict to characteristic two, we can naturally increase this rank by adding an extra "tail" term to both expressions. In turn, we must drop fewer equations to ensure the same level of security, and this results in a significant speedup of the decryption algorithm. We will use the subscript t^2 to denote the use of this technique, *e.g.* EFC_{t^2}.

This trick exploits the following property of fields of characteristic two. Let $f(\mathcal{X})$ be a linear function, then $f(\mathcal{X})^3$ is a quadratic function and multiplication by $f(\mathcal{X})$ gives $f(\mathcal{X})^4$ which is once again a linear function.

Let α and β be defined as earlier. Then this enhancement adds the quadratic terms $\alpha(\mathcal{X})^3$ and $\beta(\mathcal{X})^3$ as follows:

$$\mathcal{F} : \mathbb{F}_{2^n} \to \mathbb{F}_{2^n}^2 : \mathcal{X} \mapsto \begin{pmatrix} \alpha(\mathcal{X})\mathcal{X} + \beta(\mathcal{X})^3 \\ \beta(\mathcal{X})\mathcal{X} + \alpha(\mathcal{X})^3 \end{pmatrix}. \tag{3}$$

In order to decrypt $\mathcal{F}(\mathcal{X}) = (\mathcal{D}_1; \mathcal{D}_2)$, the user solves the linear system

$$\alpha(\mathcal{X})\mathcal{D}_2 - \beta(\mathcal{X})\mathcal{D}_1 = \alpha(\mathcal{X})^4 - \beta(\mathcal{X})^4. \tag{4}$$

Afterwards, the set of solutions is pruned based on $\mathcal{F}(\mathcal{X}) = (\mathcal{D}_1; \mathcal{D}_2)$.

A similar trick is possible in fields of characteristic three. For linear functions $f(\mathcal{X})$ the term $f(\mathcal{X})^2$ is quadratic and multiplication by $f(\mathcal{X})$ gives $f(\mathcal{X})^3$ which is once again a linear function. Although this particular Frobenius tail does destroy the common factor in the two polynomials, it merely increases the rank of the quadratic form to three. The use of this trick will be denoted by the subscript t^3.

4 Efficiency

4.1 Recommended Parameters

We predict that the most efficient attack on our system is the algebraic attack using efficient Gröbner basis algorithms such as Faugére's F_4 or F_5 [12,13]. Taking this attack into account, we propose parameters to ensure at least 80 bits of security.

We follow the argument due to Ding et $al.$ [5,8], who develop an upper bound for the degree of regularity of HFE$^-$ systems. In this line of reasoning, the degree of regularity D_{reg} is intricately linked to the rank r of the quadratic form associated with the extension field polynomial. Moreover, a applications of the minus modifier effectively increases this rank by a. Especially for small base fields, the degree of regularity is expected to lie near its upper bound:

$$D_{\text{reg}} \leq \frac{(q-1)(r+a)}{2} + 2 \ . \tag{5}$$

This argument applies to a single quadratic form. However, the central map of EFC consists of two quadratic forms. Nevertheless, we argue that the effect of minus is replicated across both quadratic forms. The polynomials are dropped $after$ the output transformation T is applied, meaning that the effect of the missing information passes through T^{-1} and is not isolated to one quadratic form but spread across both. Although this reasoning underscores the following parameter recommendations, we note it is not perfectly rigorous and warrants further study.

Considering the two components of our central map separately, we see that their rank is $r = 2$. If the Frobenius tail modifiers are applied, this is increased to $r = 4$ and $r = 3$ for characteristics 2 and 3, respectively. For a security level of 80 bits, we recommend to ensure this adjusted rank is at least 12 for $\mathbb{F}_2$ and 8 for $\mathbb{F}_3$.

$$a = \begin{cases} 10 & q = 2, \ n = 83, \ \text{EFC}_p^- \\ 8 & q = 2, \ n = 83, \ \text{EFC}_{pt2}^- \ . \\ 6 & q = 3, \ n = 59, \ \text{EFC}_p^- \end{cases} \tag{6}$$

Then we can estimate the degrees of regularity for these base fields:

$$D_{\text{reg}} \leq \frac{(q-1)(r+a)}{2} + 2 = \begin{cases} 8 & q = 2 \\ 10 & q = 3 \end{cases} . \tag{7}$$

The running time of efficient Gröbner basis algorithms is dominated by Gaussian elimination in the matrix of coefficients associated with the monomials of degree D_{reg}. We can use this bottleneck to estimate the algorithm's total complexity. In particular, the number of monomials of this degree is given by $T = \binom{n}{D_{\text{reg}}} \approx 2^{35}$ both for $n = 83$, $q = 2$ as well as $n = 59$, $q = 3$. Moreover, the number of nonzero monomials is on the order of $\tau = \binom{n}{2} \geq 2^{10}$. Assuming a Wiedemann-type algorithm [30] for sparse Gaussian elimination, this amounts to $\tau T^2 \geq 2^{80}$ in both cases.

Figure 3 offers some experimental evidence in support of this argument. It plots the running time of MAGMA's F_4 algorithm to recover the plaintext from the ciphertext and the public key. The graph on the left starts out with $q = 2$, $n = 35$ and $a = 1$; from there on out, the parameter a increases. The graph on the right lets n vary from 15 to 38 with $q = 2$, and keeps a constant at 10 for the basic trapdoor EFC_p^- (blue circles) and at 8 for the Frobenius tail equivalent EFC_{pt2}^- (red crosses).

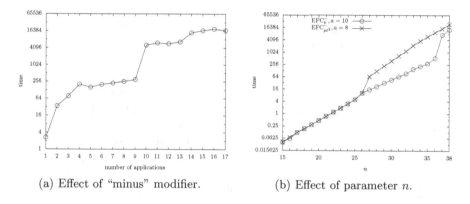

(a) Effect of "minus" modifier.   (b) Effect of parameter n.

Fig. 3. Running time of algebraic attack for various parameters (Color figure online).

The graphs indicate two things. First, the minus modifier enhances security with (nearly) every application, occasionally lifting the system into the next degree of regularity. Second, the Frobenius tail modifier enhances security, even compensating for the rank drop associated with going from $a = 10$ to $a = 8$.

4.2   Complexity

The basic trapdoor, as well as all the modified variants, feature only quadratic terms. Therefore, the transformations T and S should be linear and not affine, and consequently also the public key will consist of only quadratic terms.

The public key consists of $2n - a$ polynomials of degree 2 in n variables. Thus the number of coefficients from $\mathbb{F}_q$ in the public key is $(2n - a) \times \frac{n(n-1)}{2} = n^3 - (a+1)n^2 + an = O(n^3)$ because $a \ll n$. However, we note that there is a considerable amount of redundancy in the public key which we expect can be exploited to produce smaller keys.

The private key consists of two linear transformations S and T, along with a degree-n irreducible polynomial $\psi(z)$, and matrices A and B. This amounts to $n^2 + (2n)^2 + 2(n^2) + n = 7n^2 + n = O(n^2)$ coefficients in $\mathbb{F}_q$.

The most computationally intensive part of the key generation algorithm is the symbolic matrix-vector multiplication — once in $\varphi(A\mathbf{x})\mathbf{x}$ and once in $\varphi(B\mathbf{x})\mathbf{x}$. Both procedures require n^2 polynomial-multiplications, each of which consists of n multiplications in $\mathbb{F}_q$. Since the other steps in the key generation algorithm are less complex, the asymptotic time complexity of this entire algorithm is $O(n^3)$. For the Frobenius tail modifier, this complexity is worse because the additional extension field products $\varphi(A\mathbf{x})(QA\mathbf{x})$ and $\varphi(B\mathbf{x})(QB\mathbf{x})$ (where Q is the matrix associated with the Frobenius map $x \mapsto x^2$) have dense right-side multiplicands. Consequently, the cost of polynomial multiplication rises to n^2 multiplications and the total time complexity of the key generation to $O(n^4)$.

Encryption consists of evaluating $2n - a$ quadratic polynomials in n variables. This comes down to two time steps with unlimited parallelism. Without parallelism, however, each of the $(2n - a) \times (n(n - 1) + 2n)$ base field operations must be executed sequentially and the time complexity is therefore $O(n^3)$.

Decryption consists of the following steps for q^a different guesses, which may be executed in parallel if the resources are available: (1) inversion of T, which requires $(2n)^2$ operations; (2) computation of $\varphi(\mathbf{d}_1)$ and $\varphi(\mathbf{d}_2)$, which requires n vectorized additions for a total of n^2 operations; (3) two matrix multiplications of n^3 operations each, followed by a matrix subtraction; (4) a Gaussian elimination of some $2n^3/3$ operations; (5) inversion of S requiring some n^2 operations; and finally (6) pruning, which has an almost constant expected running time. Thus, decryption has an expected running time of $O(q^a n^3)$. While this expression does involve an exponential factor, the exponent is rather small — on the order of $a \approx \log n$, so that decryption is still practically speaking a polynomial-time algorithm.

Figure 4 emphasizes this exponential behavior by logarithmically plotting the decryption time as a function of a. Even a moderate increase in the number of dropped parameters can make decryption impractically slow.

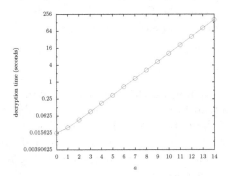

Fig. 4. Decryption time as a function of a for $n = 83$ and $q = 2$.

4.3   Speed

Table 1 shows some timing results obtained from a straightforward C++ implementation on a 64-bit 3.3 GHz Intel CPU. Despite the scheme's obvious capacity

Table 1. Implementation results — timings of key generation, encryption and decryption algorithms along with public key, secret key and ciphertext size.

Construction	Sec. key	Pub. key	Ctxt	Key gen	Enc	Dec
$\mathrm{EFC}_p^-, q = 2, n = 83, a = 10$	48.3 KB	509 KB	20 B	2.45 s	0.004 s	9.074 s
$\mathrm{EFC}_{pt2}^-, q = 2, n = 83, a = 8$	48.3 KB	523 KB	20 B	3.982 s	0.004 s	2.481 s
$\mathrm{EFC}_p^-, q = 3, n = 59, a = 6$	48.8 KB	375 KB	28 B	2.938 s	0.004 s	12.359 s

for parallelism, it is not exploited beyond bit packing and vectorized addition (byte-wise xor) for $\mathbb{F}_2$. The only other optimization that was used was the compiler's optimization flag. For $q = 3$, the sizes are computed by representing elements of $\mathbb{F}_3$ by two bits.

5   Conclusion

Extension Field Cancellation (EFC) is a new construction for central trapdoors in MQ cryptosystems which exploits the commutativity of the extension field in order to cancel the complexity of the extension field polynomials. After cancellation, the plaintext can be obtained by solving a linear system. We anticipate several known attacks and use the projection and minus modifiers to inoculate EFC against these attacks.

We estimate parameters associated with 80 bits of security from the running time of an algebraic attack and offer some experimental validation of its complexity. Our implementation confirms the correctness of our schemes as well as their practical efficiency. Encryption can be done in only a few milliseconds, on par with other post-quantum cryptosystems such as NTRU [16] and McEliece [20]. However, due to the missing information from the minus modifier, decryption takes several seconds.

This minus modifier is an obvious candidate for improvement. While it is necessary for security, any significant number of dropped polynomials constitutes an onerous cost on the decryption function because its running time is exponential in this number. In fact, the minus modifier is ideally suited for MQ *signature* schemes, but ill-suited for MQ *encryption* schemes. The reason is that for signatures, any assignment to the missing variables will do; in contrast, the decryption algorithm must iterate over all possible assignments in order to find the correct plaintext. Any alternative modifier that has the same effect on security but obviates the need for exhaustive search can drastically accelerate decryption.

Another question is to determine to which extent the public keys can be shrunk. While it is difficult to shrink the secret keys without throwing away entropy, the public keys contain a large amount of redundancy. Even a relatively moderate reduction in the public key size can make the cryptosystem a feasible option for applications where the public key size is critical and currently too large.

Acknowledgments. The authors would like to thank the anonymous reviewers for their helpful comments. This work was supported in part by the Research Council KU Leuven: C16/15/058. In addition, this work was supported by the Flemish Government, FWO WET G.0213.11N and by the European Commission through the ICT programme under contract FP7-ICT-2011-284833 PUFFIN, FP7-ICT-2013-10-SEP-210076296 PRACTICE, through the Horizon 2020research and innovation programme under grant agreement No H2020-ICT-2014-644371 WITDOM and H2020-ICT-2014-645622 PQCRYPTO; as well as by grant USDC (NIST) 60NAN15D059 from the Nation Institute of Standards of Technology. Alan Szepieniec is funded by a research grant of the Institute for the Promotion of Innovation through Science and Technology in Flanders (IWT-Vlaanderen).

References

1. NESSIE: New European Schemes for Signatures, Integrity, Encryption 05 November 2014 (2003). https://www.cosic.esat.kuleuven.be/nessie/
2. Bettale, L., Faugère, J., Perret, L.: Cryptanalysis of HFE, multi-HFE and variants for odd and even characteristic. Des. Codes Crypt. **69**(1), 1–52 (2013). http://dx.doi.org/10.1007/s10623-012-9617-2
3. Billet, O., Patarin, J., Seurin, Y.: Analysis of intermediate field systems. IACR Cryptology ePrint Archive 2009, p. 542 (2009). http://eprint.iacr.org/2009/542
4. Courtois, N.T.: The security of Hidden Field Equations (HFE). In: Naccache, D. (ed.) CT-RSA 2001. LNCS, vol. 2020, pp. 266–281. Springer, Heidelberg (2001). http://dx.doi.org/10.1007/3-540-45353-9_20
5. Ding, J., Hodges, T.J.: Inverting HFE systems is quasi-polynomial for all fields. In: Rogaway, P. (ed.) CRYPTO 2011. LNCS, vol. 6841, pp. 724–742. Springer, Heidelberg (2011). http://dx.doi.org/10.1007/978-3-642-22792-9_41
6. Ding, J., Kleinjung, T.: Degree of regularity for HFE. In: IACR Cryptology ePrint Archive 2011, p. 570 (2011). http://eprint.iacr.org/2011/570
7. Ding, J., Schmidt, D.: Rainbow, a new multivariable polynomial signature scheme. In: Ioannidis, J., Keromytis, A.D., Yung, M. (eds.) ACNS 2005. LNCS, vol. 3531, pp. 164–175. Springer, Heidelberg (2005). http://dx.doi.org/10.1007/11496137_12
8. Ding, J., Yang, B.-Y.: Degree of regularity for HFEv and HFEv. In: Gaborit, P. (ed.) PQCrypto 2013. LNCS, vol. 7932, pp. 52–66. Springer, Heidelberg (2013). http://dx.doi.org/10.1007/978-3-642-38616-9_4
9. Ding, J., Yang, B., Cheng, C., Chen, C.O., Dubois, V.: Breaking the symmetry: a way to resist the new differential attack. IACR Cryptology ePrint Archive 2007, p. 366 (2007). http://eprint.iacr.org/2007/366
10. Dubois, V., Fouque, P.-A., Shamir, A., Stern, J.: Practical cryptanalysis of SFLASH. In: Menezes, A. (ed.) CRYPTO 2007. LNCS, vol. 4622, pp. 1–12. Springer, Heidelberg (2007). http://dx.doi.org/10.1007/978-3-540-74143-5_1
11. Dubois, V., Fouque, P.-A., Stern, J.: Cryptanalysis of SFLASH with slightly modified parameters. In: Naor, M. (ed.) EUROCRYPT 2007. LNCS, vol. 4515, pp. 264–275. Springer, Heidelberg (2007). http://dx.doi.org/10.1007/978-3-540-72540-4_15
12. Faugere, J.C.: A new efficient algorithm for computing gröbner bases (f 4). J. Pure Appl. Algebra **139**(1), 61–88 (1999)
13. Faugère, J.C.: A new efficient algorithm for computing gröbner bases without reduction to zero (f5). In: Proceedings of the 2002 International Symposium on Symbolic and Algebraic Computation, ISSAC 2002, pp. 75–83. ACM, New York (2002). http://doi.acm.org/10.1145/780506.780516

14. Faugère, J.-C., Joux, A.: Algebraic cryptanalysis of Hidden Field Equation (HFE) cryptosystems using Gröbner bases. In: Boneh, D. (ed.) CRYPTO 2003. LNCS, vol. 2729, pp. 44–60. Springer, Heidelberg (2003). http://dx.doi.org/10.1007/978-3-540-45146-4_3

15. Gaborit, P. (ed.): PQCrypto 2013. LNCS, vol. 7932. Springer, Heidelberg (2013). http://dx.doi.org/10.1007/978-3-642-38616-9

16. Hoffstein, J., Pipher, J., Silverman, J.H.: NTRU: a ring-based public key cryptosystem. In: Buhler, J.P. (ed.) ANTS 1998. LNCS, vol. 1423, pp. 267–288. Springer, Heidelberg (1998). http://dx.doi.org/10.1007/BFb0054868

17. Kipnis, A., Patarin, J., Goubin, L.: Unbalanced oil and vinegar signature schemes. In: Stern, J. (ed.) EUROCRYPT 1999. LNCS, vol. 1592. Springer, Heidelberg (1999). http://dx.doi.org/10.1007/3-540-48910-X_15

18. Kipnis, A., Shamir, A.: Cryptanalysis of the HFE public key cryptosystem by relinearization. In: Wiener, M. (ed.) CRYPTO 1999. LNCS, vol. 1666, pp. 19–30. Springer, Heidelberg (1999). http://dx.doi.org/10.1007/3-540-48405-1_2

19. Matsumoto, T., Imai, H.: Public quadratic polynomial-tuples for efficient signature-verification and message-encryption. In: Günther, C.G. (ed.) EUROCRYPT 1988. LNCS, vol. 330, pp. 419–453. Springer, Heidelberg (1988). http://dx.doi.org/10.1007/3-540-45961-8_39

20. McEliece, R.J.: A public-key cryptosystem based on algebraic coding theory. DSN Prog. Rep. 42(44), 114–116 (1978)

21. Patarin, J.: Cryptanalysis of the Matsumoto and Imai public key scheme of Eurocrypt 1988. In: Coppersmith, D. (ed.) CRYPTO 1995. LNCS, vol. 963, pp. 248–261. Springer, Heidelberg (1995). http://dx.doi.org/10.1007/3-540-44750-4_20

22. Patarin, J.: Hidden fields equations (HFE) and isomorphisms of polynomials (IP): two new families of asymmetric algorithms. In: Maurer, U.M. (ed.) EUROCRYPT 1996. LNCS, vol. 1070, pp. 33–48. Springer, Heidelberg (1996). http://dx.doi.org/10.1007/3-540-68339-9_4

23. Patarin, J., Goubin, L., Courtois, N.T.: C_-+^* and HM: variations around two schemes of T. Matsumoto and H. Imai. In: Ohta, K., Pei, D. (eds.) ASIACRYPT 1998. LNCS, vol. 1514, pp. 35–50. Springer, Heidelberg (1998). http://dx.doi.org/10.1007/3-540-49649-1_4

24. Porras, J., Baena, J., Ding, J.: ZHFE, a new multivariate public key encryption scheme. In: Mosca, M. (ed.) PQCrypto 2014. LNCS, vol. 8772, pp. 229–245. Springer, Heidelberg (2014). http://dx.doi.org/10.1007/978-3-319-11659-4_14

25. Shamir, A.: Efficient signature schemes based on birational permutations. In: Stinson, D.R. (ed.) CRYPTO 1993. LNCS, vol. 773, pp. 1–12. Springer, Heidelberg (1994). http://dx.doi.org/10.1007/3-540-48329-2_1

26. Smith-Tone, D.: Properties of the discrete differential with cryptographic applications. In: Sendrier, N. (ed.) PQCrypto 2010. LNCS, vol. 6061, pp. 1–12. Springer, Heidelberg (2010). http://dx.doi.org/10.1007/978-3-642-12929-2_1

27. Tao, C., Diene, A., Tang, S., Ding, J.: Simple matrix scheme for encryption. In: Gaborit, P. (ed.) PQCrypto 2013. LNCS, vol. 7932, pp. 231–242. Springer, Heidelberg (2013). http://dx.doi.org/10.1007/978-3-642-38616-9_16

28. Thomae, E.: About the security of multivariate quadratic public key schemes. Ph.D. thesis, Ruhr-Universität Bochum (2013)

29. Thomae, E., Wolf, C.: Cryptanalysis of enhanced TTS, STS and all its variants, or: why cross-terms are important. In: Mitrokotsa, A., Vaudenay, S. (eds.) AFRICACRYPT 2012. LNCS, vol. 7374, pp. 188–202. Springer, Heidelberg (2012). http://dx.doi.org/10.1007/978-3-642-31410-0_12

30. Wiedemann, D.H.: Solving sparse linear equations over finite fields. IEEE Trans. Inf. Theor. **32**(1), 54–62 (1986)
31. Wolf, C., Braeken, A., Preneel, B.: On the security of stepwise triangular systems. Des. Codes Crypt. **40**(3), 285–302 (2006). http://dx.doi.org/10.1007/s10623-006-0015-5
32. Wolf, C., Preneel, B.: Taxonomy of public key schemes based on the problem of multivariate quadratic equations. In: IACR Cryptology ePrint Archive 2005, p. 77 (2005). http://eprint.iacr.org/2005/077

Security Analysis and Key Modification for ZHFE

Ray Perlner[1] and Daniel Smith-Tone[1,2(✉)]

[1] National Institute of Standards and Technology, Gaithersburg, MD, USA
ray.perlner@nist.gov
[2] Department of Mathematics, University of Louisville, Louisville, KY, USA
daniel.smith@nist.gov

Abstract. *ZHFE*, designed by Porras et al., is one of the few promising candidates for a multivariate public-key encryption algorithm. In this article we extend and expound upon the existing security analysis on this scheme. We prove security against differential adversaries, complementing a more accurate and robust discussion of resistance to rank and algebraic attacks. We further suggest a modification, *ZHFE⁻*, a multivariate encryption scheme which retains the security and performance properties of *ZHFE* while optimizing key size in this theoretical framework.

Keywords: Multivariate cryptography · *HFE* · *ZHFE* · Discrete differential · MinRank · Q-rank

1 Introduction

Since the late 1990s, a large international community has emerged to face the challenge of developing cryptographic constructions which resist attacks from quantum computers. The birth of this new discipline is due primarily to the discovery by Peter Shor in the mid 90s, see [1], of algorithms for factoring and computing discrete logarithms in polynomial time on a quantum computing device. The term post-quantum cryptography was coined to refer to this developing field and to emphasize the fact that information security in a quantum computing world is a fundamentally new science.

Today, we face mounting evidence that quantum computing is not a physical impossibility but merely a colossal engineering challenge. With the specter of the death of classical asymmetric cryptography looming on the horizon, it is more important than ever that we develop systems for authentication, confidentiality and key exchange which are secure in the quantum paradigm. We thus are forced to turn to problems of greater difficulty than the classical number theoretic constructs.

Systems of polynomial equations have been studied for thousands of years and have fueled the development of several branches of mathematics from classical to modern times. Multivariate Public Key Cryptography(MPKC) has emerged

© Springer International Publishing Switzerland 2016
T. Takagi (Ed.): PQCrypto 2016, LNCS 9606, pp. 197–212, 2016.
DOI: 10.1007/978-3-319-29360-8_13

from the serious investigation of computational algebraic geometry that reached maturity in the latter half of the last century. Today, we see MPKC as one of a few serious candidates for security in the post-quantum world.

A fundamental problem on which the security of any multivariate cryptosystem rests is the problem of solving systems of quadratic equations over finite fields. This problem is known to be NP-hard, and copious empirical evidence indicates that the problem is hard even in the average case. There is no known significant reduction of the complexity of this problem in the quantum model of computing, and, indeed, if this problem is discovered to be solvable in the quantum model, we can solve all NP problems and the task of securing information might be hopeless in principle. We thus reasonably suspect that MPKC will survive the transition into the quantum world.

Though multivariate cryptosystems almost always suffer from rather large key sizes, the key sizes are rarely so large that they are impractical and these systems can often be quite attractive in certain other aspects of performance. Some systems are very fast, having speeds orders of magnitude faster than RSA, [2–4]. Some schemes combine speed with power efficiency and small signature sizes, [5,6]. Perhaps most importantly, it is generally simple to parameterize multivariate systems in such a way that vastly different properties are derived foiling various attack methodologies.

One great difficulty historically for MPKC is encryption. Though there are several viable options for digital signatures, see [5–8], there is a general absence of long-lived encryption systems. In the last couple of years, a couple of new encryption techniques have been proposed, see [9–11]. These systems are based on the simple idea, proposed by Ding, that the structure of a system of equations can retain injectivity without an extremely restrictive structure if the codomain is of much larger dimension than the domain.

In [12], however, a new and unexpected attack was presented on the ABC simple matrix encryption scheme of [9]. This attack is notable in that the complexity is far less asymptotically than predicted by the analysis in [9], though it does not break the scheme outright. This begs the question of the tightness of the security analyses in [10,11] and the extent to which we can trust in the security of such young schemes in a field which has no significant success history in encryption.

Furthermore, one might ask whether there is some middleground on the ratio of the dimension of the codomain to that of the domain for these multivariate encryption schemes. Even if one concurs that relaxing the relationship between the dimensions of the domain and codomain enhance the security of injective maps, it remains unclear that the disparity should be so large as in the proposed schemes in which there are at least twice as many equations as variables.

In this article we extend and expound upon the security analysis in [11], incorporating some of the theoretical models of assurance presented in [13–15]. We prove security against differential adversaries complementing the discussion of resistance to algebraic attacks provided in [11]. We further elucidate the rank structure of $ZHFE$ and specifically note some necessary, but trivial, key restrictions for security which were apparently overlooked in [11]. We further suggest a modification, $ZHFE^-$, a multivariate encryption scheme which retains the security and performance properties of $ZHFE$ while optimizing key size in this theoretical framework.

The paper is organized as follows. The next section introduces the notion of big field schemes and presents the prototypical such cryptosystem, HFE. In the following section, we define the Q-rank of a multivariate system of equations and discuss the central nature of this concept in the field. The subsequent section presents the $ZHFE$ encryption scheme and calculates some of its inherent parameters. Next we present a thorough security analysis of $ZHFE$, complementing and expanding the analysis provided in [11] and offering security assurance against a differential adversary as well as discussing parameters securing $ZHFE$ against rank and algebraic attacks. Subsequently, we present and analyze $ZHFE^-$, a new multivariate encryption scheme based on $ZHFE$ and the minus modifier. Finally, we note parameter choices for $ZHFE^-$ and discuss the role that the new methodology for multivariate encryption fills in the literature.

2   HFE

Several multivariate cryptosystems belong to a family collectively known as "big field" schemes. Such schemes are constructed using two ideas. The first is an equivalence between functions on a degree n extension k of a finite field $\mathbb{F}_q$ and functions on an n-dimensional $\mathbb{F}_q$-vector space. The second is an isomorphism of polynomials which allows one to hide structure in a function.

To see the equivalence, notice that a vector space isomorphism between k and an n-dimensional vector space over $\mathbb{F}_q$ extends to a vector space isomorphism between the space of univariate functions from k to itself and the space of multivariate n-dimensional vector-valued polynomial functions from $\mathbb{F}_q^n$ to itself. (Specifically, given an isomorphism $\phi : \mathbb{F}_q^n \rightarrow k$ and a function $f : k \rightarrow k$, the function $\phi^{-1} \circ f \circ \phi$ is such a function from $\mathbb{F}_q^n$ to itself; furthermore, this identification is a 1-1 correspondence.)

The second idea, the isomorphism of polynomials, is defined in the following manner.

Definition 1. *Two vector valued multivariate polynomials f and g are said to be* isomorpic *if there exist two affine maps T, U such that $g = T \circ f \circ U$.*

Together these ideas allow us to build an isomorphic copy of a structured univariate map with domain k while hiding the structure. The construction is sometimes called the butterfly construction because of the shape of its defining commutative diagram. Specifically, $P = T \circ \phi^{-1} \circ f \circ \phi \circ U$ produces a perturbed vector-valued version of the structured univariate polynomial f.

The Hidden Field Equations (HFE) scheme was first presented by Patarin in [16] as a method of avoiding his linearization equations attack which broke the C^* scheme of Matsumoto and Imai, see [17] and [18]. The basic idea of the system is to use the butterfly construction to hide the structure of a low degree polynomial that can be inverted efficiently over k via the Berlekamp algorithm [19], for example.

More specifically, we select an effectively invertible "quadratic" map $f : k \rightarrow k$, quadratic in the sense that every monomial of f is a product of a constant and two Frobenius multiples of x. Explicitly any such "core" map f has the form:

$$f(x) = \sum_{\substack{i \leq j \\ q^i + q^j \leq D}} \alpha_{i,j} x^{q^i + q^j} + \sum_{\substack{i \\ q^i \leq D}} \beta_i x^{q^i} + \gamma.$$

The bound D on the degree of the polynomial is required to be quite low for efficient inversion.

The HFE scheme was designed to be used as an encryption or a signature scheme. To generate a signature (or to decrypt), one computes, successively, $v = T^{-1}y$, $u = f^{-1}(v)$ and $x = U^{-1}u$. The vector x is the signature (or the plaintext). For verification (or encryption), one simply evaluates the public polynomials, P, at x. If $P(x)$ which is equal to $T \circ f \circ U(x)$ is equal to y, the signature is authenticated (or the ciphertext is y).

3   Q-Rank

The defining characteristic of HFE, the degree bound, which is necessary for the effective inversion of the central map, ensures that the scheme has low rank as a quadratic form over k, as described below. This property assures that the central map of HFE is vulnerable to Kipnis-Shamir modeling, see [20,21].

Recall that any quadratic map $f : k \rightarrow k$ can be written

$$f(x) = \sum_{0 \leq i,j < n} \alpha_{ij} x^{q^i + q^j}.$$

We can equivalently express f as a vector function over the 1-dimensional k-algebra $\psi : k \rightarrow k^n$ where

$$\alpha \overset{\psi}{\mapsto} \left[\alpha \; \alpha^q \dots \alpha^{q^{n-1}} \right]^T,$$

in the form $f(X) = X^T[\alpha_{ij}]X$ where $X = [x \; x^q \; \dots \; x^{q^{n-1}}]^T$.

Any quadratic form over k can be expressed as a symmetric matrix, and over characteristic $p \neq 2$ a change of basis can be performed which transforms this matrix into an equivalent diagonal form. The rank of this matrix is the rank of the quadratic form. We call this rank the Q-rank of f, that is the rank of f as a quadratic function.

We note here that Q-rank is invariant under polynomial isomorphism, thus the Q-rank of a central map of a cryptosystem is the same as the Q-rank of the public key, unless, of course, the minus or projection modifiers are utilized. We also note that the Q-rank is explicitly exploited in the attacks of [20,21] and plays a central role in the derivation of degree of regularity bounds for several prominent cryptosystems, see [22–24]. Further, there seems to be a complicated relationship between the Q-rank of a field map and the presence of differential symmetric or invariant relations, see, for example [15]. Consequently, Q-rank seems to be emerging as a central concept in multivariate cryptography and in computational algebra.

4   *ZHFE*

ZHFE was introduced in [11]. The idea is to construct an encryption scheme with a high Q-rank central map preventing attacks such as [21] exploiting this weakness. The scheme is notable among "big field" schemes which typically require some low Q-rank map for efficient inversion. Low Q-rank is in fact required for inversion in this setting as well, however, the system attempts to hide the low Q-rank structure in the public key.

The construction concatenates two high degree quadratic maps (with special structure) to form the central map. Specifically, the two general form quadratic maps f_0 and f_1 are derived by constructing a low degree (maximum degree D) cubic map

$$\Psi(x) = x\left[L_{00}f_0(x) + L_{01}f_1\right] + x^q\left[L_{10}f_0 + L_{11}f_1\right], \tag{1}$$

where L_{ij} is a linear map and the square brackets indicate multiplication over k.

To solve for f_0 and f_1 it suffices to set coefficients for the linear maps and for Ψ to recover a system of linear equations in the unknown coefficients of f_0 and f_1. In the homogeneous case, there are collectively $n^2 + n$ coefficients of f_0 and f_1 in k. Due to its low degree and the requirement that it satisfy (1), Ψ is constrained to be of the form

$$\Psi(x) = \sum_{i=0}^{1} \sum_{\substack{i \leq j \leq k \\ q^i + q^j + q^k \leq D}} \alpha_{i,j,k} x^{q^i + q^j + q^k} + \sum_{i=0}^{1} \sum_{\substack{i \leq j \\ q^i + q^j \leq D}} \beta_{i,j} x^{q^i + q^j} + \sum_{i=0}^{1} \gamma_i x^{q^i}. \tag{2}$$

A cubic of the form (2) has n^2 coefficients over k, and thus for *any fixed choice* of Ψ and L_{ij} there are n^2 constraints on a linear system of dimension $n^2 + n$. Thus with probability roughly $1 - q^{-n}$, there is an n-dimensional space of coefficients for the maps f_0 and f_1.

Once, constructed, the central map $(y_0, y_1) = (f_0(x), f_1(x))$ can be inverted by using Berlekamp's algorithm to solve the low degree polynomial equation:

$$\Psi(x) - x\left[L_{00}y_0 + L_{01}y_1\right] - x^q\left[L_{10}y_0 + L_{11}y_1\right] = 0.$$

5   Analysis of *ZHFE*

A few avenues of attack have evolved along with the development of multivariate cryptosystems relying on a hidden large algebra structure. These attacks can be characterized as differential, see [12,25], as minrank, see [20,21], or as algebraic, see [26]. We analyze the security of *ZHFE* against each of these attack models.

5.1   Algebraic

Algebraic attacks attempt to decrypt a given ciphertext y by solving the system of equations $P(x) = y$ directly. The term "algebraic" refers to the fact that these are generic algorithms for solving arbitrary systems of polynomial equations.

While these attacks are not structural, in the sense of being defined based on the structure of the system of equations, the algorithms employed can naturally take advantage of certain properties of the systems. In practice, the complexity of algorithms for solving these systems of equations is closely connected to the degree of regularity of the system.

The degree of regularity of a system of equations is the degree at which the first nontrivial degree fall occurs. Specifically, consider a generating set of an ideal $I = \langle g_1, \ldots, g_m \rangle \in \mathbb{F}_q[x_1, \ldots, x_n]$. We may generate elements of I by selecting polynomials $p_i \in \mathbb{F}_q[x_1, \ldots, x_n]$ and computing

$$\sum_{i=1}^{m} p_i g_i.$$

A degree fall occurs when the degree of this sum is less than the maximum degree of $p_i g_i$. Clearly some degree falls are due to trivial syzygies such as $-g_j g_i + g_i g_j = 0$ and $(g_i^{q-1} - 1)g_i = 0$. The smallest degree, $max_i p_i g_i$ such that the above sum has a nontrivial degree fall is the degree of regularity.

A great deal of literature is devoted to finding bounds for the degree of regularity of quadratic systems, see [22–24,27]. In practice one can find a lower bound for the degree of regularity by studying toy examples of schemes and seeing how the degree of regularity changes as the parameters change.

Such an analysis for $ZHFE$ is quite straight forward. As mentioned in [11] the degree of regularity for toy $ZHFE$ systems matches exactly the degree of regularity for random systems of equations of the same size, at least for relatively small instances. Considering the connection between Q-rank and the degree of regularity as derived in [22–24,27], we conclude that a thorough Q-rank analysis of $ZHFE$ will verify the security of the scheme against algebraic attacks. We perform this analysis in Sect. 5.4.

5.2   Differential Symmetric

As shown in [25], symmetric relations involving the discrete differential of a central map can induce a symmetry in the public key of a multivariate cryptosystem. In certain circumstances, these relations can reveal properties of the extension field structure, and weaken the public key. Indeed one can easily turn the attack on SFLASH of [25], which converts an instance of C^{*-} into a compatible instance of C^*, into a direct key-recovery attack utilizing the derived representation of elements of the extension field.

As shown in [13] the maps inducing a linear differential symmetry for C^* schemes are precisely those corresponding to multiplication by an element of the extension field. Thus one may rightfully expect that nontrivial symmetric relations on the differential of a central map are uncommon. It is shown, however, in [13] and [15] that nontrivial symmetries can and often do exist even for cases as general as HFE.

As a specific example of the phenomenon of differential symmetries for general polynomials, consider the map $f(x) = x^{q^3+q^2} + x^{q^2+1}$ over a degree 6 extension of the characteristic 2 field $\mathbb{F}_q$. One can easily verify that the general linear symmetry structure, defined as

$$Df(La, x) + Df(a, Lx) = \Lambda_L Df(a, x),$$

is satisfied by the selection

$$Lx = \alpha x^{q^4} + \alpha x^q + \beta x \text{ and } \Lambda_L x = 0,$$

where $\alpha^{q^3} = \alpha$ and $\beta^q = \beta$. Thus there is a 4-dimensional $\mathbb{F}_q$-subspace of linear maps L satisfying the above differential symmetric relation for some choice of Λ_L, while the space of all $\mathbb{F}_q$-linear maps from the extension to itself is only of dimension 36. Consequently, a hypothetical cryptosystem based on this map would be vulnerable to an attack removing the minus modifier, similar to [25], among other weaknesses. Quite specifically, the distillation procedure described in [25] is effective in this instance. We note that this scenario is by no means limited to toy examples such as this one or even instances with Q-rank one; thus, the verification of the absence of differential symmetries is an important task for any multivariate cryptosystem, particularly those including the minus modifier.

In analyzing the differential symmetric properties of $ZHFE$, we may directly analyze the public key or we may study the differential of the Ψ map. We consider both interlinked cases explicitly.

The public key P consists of $2n$ polynomials. The defining characteristic of these polynomials is that $P = T(f_0 || f_1)U$. Thus P does not behave like a random system. There exists a low degree cubic map Ψ such that

$$\begin{aligned}
\Psi(Ux) =&(Ux)(L_{00}(T^{-1})_1 P(x) + L_{01}(T^{-1})_2 P(x)) \\
&+ (Ux)^q(L_{10}(T^{-1})_1 P(x) + L_{11}(T^{-1})_2 P(x)).
\end{aligned} \tag{3}$$

We note that $(T^{-1})_i P(x) = f_i(Ux)$. We may now implicitly differentiate this equation obtaining

$$\begin{aligned}
D\Psi(Ua, Ux) =&(Ua)(L_{00}f_0(Ux) + L_{01}f_1(Ux)) \\
&+ (Ua)^q(L_{10}f_0(Ux) + L_{11}f_1(Ux)) \\
&+ (Ux)(L_{00}Df_0(Ua, Ux) + L_{01}Df_1(Ua, Ux)) \\
&+ (Ux)^q(L_{10}Df_0(Ua, Ux) + L_{11}Df_1(Ua, Ux)).
\end{aligned} \tag{4}$$

The above is a biquadratic relation in a and x, and as such doesn't immediately reveal a computational way to recover information about the hidden structure of P. To convert this relation into a form in which we can apply linear algebra techniques we require a second differential. For more information on a more general theory of discrete differential equations, see [28].

Since the differential is symmetric, we get the same answer whether we differentiate with respect to a or to x.

$$
\begin{aligned}
D^2\Psi(Ua, Ub, Ux) =&(Ua)(L_{00}Df_0(Ub, Ux) + L_{01}Df_1(Ub, Ux)) \\
&+ (Ua)^q(L_{10}Df_0(Ub, Ux) + L_{11}Df_1(Ub, Ux)) \\
&+ (Ub)(L_{00}Df_0(Ua, Ux) + L_{01}Df_1(Ua, Ux)) \\
&+ (Ub)^q(L_{10}Df_0(Ua, Ux) + L_{11}Df_1(Ua, Ux)) \\
&+ (Ux)(L_{00}Df_0(Ua, Ub) + L_{01}Df_1(Ua, Ub)) \\
&+ (Ux)^q(L_{10}Df_0(Ua, Ub) + L_{11}Df_1(Ua, Ub)).
\end{aligned}
\tag{5}
$$

Now, due to the fact that Ψ is cubic with a small degree bound, $D^2\Psi$ is a cubic form of low rank. In fact, the existence of linear maps U and $L_{ij}(T^{-1})_j$ such that Eqs. (3) and (5) hold while $D^2\Psi$ has low cubic rank is the defining characteristic of $ZHFE$.

In spite of the existence of this structure, it is unclear how to proceed. One might consider a cubic version of the rank attack from [29], however, the selection of the maps $L_{ij}(T^{-1})_j$ corresponds to solving a minrank problem on a 3-tensor, $D^2\Psi$. Though there is a possibility that the instances of the 3-tensor rank problem arising from this differential equation may lie in a class which are easy to solve, the general 3-tensor rank problem is known to be NP-hard and there does not seem to be any evidence that these instances are any more structured than arbitrary instances of the same rank.

5.3 Differential Invariant

As exemplified in [12] and [30], invariant relations on the differential of a public key can be exploited in key recovery. Although we may analyze the differential invariant structure of the public key of $ZHFE$ directly, there is not in general any nontrivial invariant due to the fact that the structure of $ZHFE$ is hidden in the cubic Ψ map. A couple of generalizations of differential invariants of quadratic functions are derived for higher q-degree functions in [28]. The most relaxed generalization for cubics is given in the following definition.

Definition 2. *A differential invariant of a cubic function f is a pair of subspaces $V_1, V_2 \subseteq k$ for which there exists a subspace W with $dim(W) \leq mindim(V_i)$ such that for all $A \in spanD^2f_i$, we have $D^2f(a, b, x) = 0$ for all $a \in V_1$, $b \in V_2$ and $x \in W^\perp$.*

In the quadratic case, a differential invariant could be seen as a subspace of k on which Df simultaneously acts in every coordinate the same way, that is, always sending that subspace to the same space of linear forms of no larger dimension. In the cubic case we can realize a differential invariant as a subspace V_1 of k and a subspace (defined by V_2) of induced bilinear forms from D^2f each element of which maps V_1 to the same space of linear forms, W, of no larger dimension. The minimum condition on the dimension of W is due to the symmetry of $D^2 f$; we could equivalently consider the subspace V_2 of k and the subspace of bilinear forms from $D^2 f$ induced from V_1.

It is straightforward to show that the Ψ map of $ZHFE$ has no differential invariant structure. Following the technique of [15], without loss of generality, due to the symmetry, we let $\hat{a} \in V_1$, $\hat{b}, \hat{x} \in V_2$, and let S be a surjective linear map from V_2 to W. The existence of a differential invariant implies the equation

$$0 = D^2\Psi(\hat{a}, \hat{b}, S\hat{x})$$
$$= \sum_{\substack{0 \le i,j,l < n \\ q^i + q^j + q^l \le D}} \alpha_{ijl}\hat{a}^{q^i}\hat{b}^{q^j}(S\hat{x})^{q^l}. \tag{6}$$

Since by symmetry D is much smaller than $dim(V_1)$ or $dim(V_2)$, (6) is already reduced modulo the minimal polynomial $\mathcal{M}_{V_1}(a)$ of V_1 as an element in $k[a]$ and modulo the minimal polynomial $\mathcal{M}_{V_2}(b)$ of V_2 as an element in $k[b]$. Thus the collection $\{\hat{a}, \hat{a}^q, \dots, \hat{a}^{q^{d_1}}, \hat{b}, \dots, \hat{b}^{q^{d_2}}\}$ is independent in $k[a,b]/\langle\mathcal{M}_{V_1}(a), \mathcal{M}_{V_2}(b)\rangle$. Therefore, we obtain the equations

$$\sum_{\substack{0 \le i,j < n \\ q^i + q^j + q^l \le D}}^{0 \le l < n} \alpha_{ijl}(S\hat{x})^{q^l} = 0.$$

We then obtain the analogous result of [15]; statistically, S must be the zero map on V_2, contradicting the nontriviallity of the differential invariant. Furthermore, we also obtain the result that if any power of q is unique there is no nontrivial differential invariant.

5.4 Q-Rank

A further attack vector for $ZHFE$ is to perform a minrank attack using the Kipnis-Shamir methodology of [20] and the improved version in [21]. The attack searches for a low rank k-linear combination of the differentials of the public key. The general minrank problem is known to be NP-complete, see [31] but in practice the complexity depends on the lowest rank map in the space.

It was shown in [21] that the smallest such rank is equal to the smallest Q-rank of the image of the public key under any full rank $\mathbb{F}_q$-linear map. Notice that for (1) to hold we must have that the $x^{q^i+q^j}$ term in $L_{00}f_0 + L_{01}f_1$ to have coefficient 0 for $q^i + q^j + 1 > D$ and $i, j \neq 1$. This restriction induces a relation on the quadratic representations of $L_{00}f_0$ and $L_{01}f_1$. Specifically, if

$$L_{00}f_0(x) + L_{01}f_1(x) = \begin{bmatrix} x \\ x^q \\ \vdots \\ x^{q^{n-1}} \end{bmatrix}^T \begin{bmatrix} \alpha_{00} & \frac{\alpha_{01}}{2} & \cdots & \frac{\alpha_{0(n-1)}}{2} \\ \frac{\alpha_{01}}{2} & \alpha_{11} & \cdots & \frac{\alpha_{1(n-1)}}{2} \\ \vdots & \vdots & \ddots & \vdots \\ \frac{\alpha_{0(n-1)}}{2} & \frac{\alpha_{1(n-1)}}{2} & \cdots & \alpha_{(n-1)(n-1)} \end{bmatrix} \begin{bmatrix} x \\ x^q \\ \vdots \\ x^{q^{n-1}} \end{bmatrix},$$

then $\alpha_{ij} = 0$ for $q^i + q^j > D$ and $i, j \neq 1$. Thus $L_{00} f_0 + L_{01} f_1$ has the form

$$
\begin{bmatrix}
\alpha_{00} & \frac{\alpha_{01}}{2} & \frac{\alpha_{02}}{2} & \cdots & \frac{\alpha_{0D}}{2} & 0 & \cdots & 0 \\
\frac{\alpha_{01}}{2} & \alpha_{11} & \frac{\alpha_{12}}{2} & \cdots & \frac{\alpha_{1D}}{2} & \frac{\alpha_{1(D+1)}}{2} & \cdots & \frac{\alpha_{1(n-1)}}{2} \\
\alpha_{02} & \frac{\alpha_{12}}{2} & \alpha_{22} & \cdots & \frac{\alpha_{2D}}{2} & 0 & \cdots & 0 \\
\vdots & \vdots & \vdots & \ddots & \vdots & \vdots & \ddots & \vdots \\
\frac{\alpha_{0,D}}{2} & \frac{\alpha_{1D}}{2} & \frac{\alpha_{2D}}{2} & \cdots & \alpha_{DD} & 0 & \cdots & 0 \\
0 & \frac{\alpha_{1(D+1)}}{2} & 0 & \cdots & 0 & 0 & \cdots & 0 \\
\vdots & \vdots & \vdots & \ddots & \vdots & \vdots & \ddots & \vdots \\
0 & \frac{\alpha_{1(n-1)}}{2} & 0 & \cdots & 0 & 0 & \cdots & 0
\end{bmatrix},
$$

and has rank no more than $\lceil log_q(D) \rceil + 2$. Hence, if L_{ij} are nonsingular, the $Q - rank$ of $f_0 \| f_1$ is bounded by $\lceil log_q(D) \rceil + 2$.

In spite of the alarming relation derived above, Q-rank does not appear to be a weakness for ZHFE when one selects L_{ij} to have reasonable corank. One can check that for small r, insisting that L_{ij} have corank r increases the possible Q-rank of $f_0 \| f_1$ by $2r$. Also, having L_{ij} with even moderately large corank doesn't produce a non-negligible probability of decryption ambiguity due to the zero expectation of the dimension of the intersection of the kernels of L_{ij}. Furthermore, recall that we have at least n degrees of freedom over k in selecting f_0 and f_1 for *any* choice of L_{ij}. Thus the Kipnis-Shamir attack, which is exponential in the Q-rank of the scheme, is trivially thwarted with simple parameter restrictions, though we note that the lack of such restriction on the rank of L_{ij} in [11] is apparently an oversight.

5.5 Equivalent Keys

In [32], the question of the number of equivalent keys for multivariate cryptosystems is explored. This question is quite relevant for $ZHFE$, as well, since there can clearly be multiple private keys allowing one to decrypt a public key. The danger in this vein would be if there is insufficient entropy in public keys due to massive redundancy in private keys.

To analyze the number of equivalent keys, we first determine the number of possible pairs f_0, f_1 satisfying (1) for a fixed Ψ and L_{ij}. As mentioned in Sect. 4, a map of the form Ψ has n^2 coefficients over k, and due to the degree bound only s of these can be nonzero. Thus with L_{ij} fixed, we have $n^2 + n$ unknown coefficients for f_0 and f_1 over k, and so we have $n^2 + n - (n^2 - s) = n + s$ degrees of freedom in choosing the pair f_0, f_1 for a fixed private key.

Next we consider the same relation with f_0, f_1 fixed. For specificity, let $f_i(x) = \sum_{0 \leq v \leq w < n} \alpha_{ivw} x^{q^v + q^w}$. Given the existence of L_{ij} and Ψ, we have the relation

$$
\Psi(x) = \sum_{t=0}^{1} \sum_{i=0}^{n-1} \sum_{0 \leq v \leq w < n} l_{0ti} \alpha_{tvw}^{q^i} x^{q^{v+i} + q^{w+i} + 1}
$$

$$
+ \sum_{t=0}^{1} \sum_{i=0}^{n-1} \sum_{0 \leq v \leq w < n} l_{1ti} \alpha_{tvw}^{q^i} x^{q^{v+i} + q^{w+i} + q}, \tag{7}
$$

where l_{ijl} are the unknown coefficients of the linearized polynomial form of L_{ij}. There are implicitly $n^2 - s$ linear relations on the $4n$ unknown coefficients of L_{ij}, as well as the rank restrictions on these maps; thus, for $n > 4$ we expect an unique solution, and thus an unique Ψ as well.

Given a public key, there is a fixed relationship $P = T(f_0 \| f_1)U$. We note that different choices of T can be accommodated by different choices of L_{ij} by (3). In contrast, statistically there is only one selection of U which maintains the structure of the key. Thus $M(f_0 \| f_1)$, $L_{ij}(M^{-1})_i$, Ψ form distinct equivalent private keys for all invertible M. One can see this result as indicating that the security of $ZHFE$ is more closely related to the IP1S problem than the IP problem.

We therefore have roughly q^{4n^2} equivalent private keys for any given public key. Since there are $q^{5n^2 + sn}$ possible choices of private keys, there are on the order of $q^{n^2 + sn}$ nonequivalent public keys. Consequently, there is sufficient entropy in public keys.

6 $ZHFE$ Key Modification, $ZHFE^-$

6.1 Design

As mentioned in the previous section, there are many degrees of freedom in selecting f_0 and f_1, even when Ψ and L_{ij} for $(i, j) \in \{0, 1\}^2$ are fixed. These facts naturally lead to the question of whether it is possible to develop a "minus" modification of $ZHFE$ preserving the essential injectivity of the original scheme.

Analogous to the analysis in the last section, we compute the degrees of freedom in selecting f_0 and f_1 when the L_{ij} for $(i, j) \in \{0, 1\}^2$ are fixed and when the degree bound for Ψ is fixed. Because we are decreasing the dimension of f_0 or f_1 or both, we compute over $\mathbb{F}_q$.

Recall from Sect. 5 that there are n^2 possible nonzero coefficients of a cubic polynomial of the form of Ψ over k, and that with only the degree bound restriction, $n^2 - s$ of these must be zero. Expressing this fact over $\mathbb{F}_q$, we see that there are $n^3 - sn$ linear constraints. Considering the maps $L_{i,j}$ to be of corank c, we require an additional $2cn - 2n$ relations to be satisfied, for a total of $n^3 - sn + 2cn - 2n$ linear constraints. Allow the total combined output dimension of f_0 and f_1 over $\mathbb{F}_q$ to be $n+t$. Since there are $\binom{n}{2} + n = \binom{n+1}{2}$ homogeneous quadratic monomials in each coordinate, there are $(n + t)\binom{n+1}{2}$ coefficients in our linear system.

$$(n + t)\binom{n + 1}{2} \geq n^3 - sn + 2cn - 2n$$

$$(n + 1)t \geq n^2 - n - 2s + 4c - 4.$$

For realistic values of s, it is possible to get t as low as $n - 2$, and $n - 1$ is always possible. Thus we consider removing two public equations. For symmetry and simplicity, we choose to remove one coordinate from each of f_0 and f_1, making them both maps from $\mathbb{F}_q^n$ to $\mathbb{F}_q^{n-1}$.

Remark 1. *This technique makes $ZHFE^-$ much more similar to small field schemes. The central map is no longer defined as a pair of maps over the extension field.*

Generation of the central map proceeds exactly as in $ZHFE$, with the exception that the linear maps L_{ij} are now representable as $n \times (n-1)$ matrices with entries in $\mathbb{F}_q$. As with $ZHFE$ we identify the image of L_{ij} with k to obtain relation (1).

Inversion of the central map proceeds exactly as with $ZHFE$. Now since both f_0 and f_1 map into a smaller space, there is a possibility of decryption failure beyond that of $ZHFE$. Under the heuristic that f_0 and f_1 are random quadratic maps from $\mathbb{F}_q^n$ to $\mathbb{F}_q^{n-1}$, one computes the probability that $f_0(y)\|f_1(y) = f_0(x)\|f_1(y)$ for a fixed x to be q^{2-2n}. While f_0 and f_1 are not random, we expect this quantity to be correct, and therefore the probability of decryption failure is increased by q^{2-2n}. Assuming parameters similar to $ZFHE$, this probability is roughly 2^{-300}, which is well within reason.

6.2   Analysis

The differential analysis from the previous section carries over nearly verbatim to the case of $ZHFE^-$. In particular, the 3-tensor structure of the differential remains essentially the same, though over a slightly diminished space. We therefore conclude that $ZHFE^-$ is as secure as $ZHFE$ against a differential symmetric or invariant attack.

Further, the degree of regularity of a subset of a system of relations is bounded below, as noted in [22], by the degree of regularity of the entire system. Thus, in comparison with any full rank $ZHFE$ scheme of the same Q-rank, the degree of regularity is at least as high, and so once again the resistance to algebraic attacks and attacks in the Kipnis-Shamir model is reduced to Q-rank analysis.

Unlike the differential security criteria, Q-rank is not monotone with respect to the composition of projections, a fact which can be seen by observing that $g(x) \in k[x]$, where k is an even degree n extension of $\mathbb{F}_q$, defined by $g(x) = x^{2q^{n/2}} + x^2$ clearly has Q-rank 2, whereas the composition with the projection $\pi(x) = x^{q^{n/2}} - x$ produces

$$\pi(g(x)) = (x^{2q^{n/2}} + x^2)^{q^{n/2}} - (x^{2q^{n/2}} + x^2)$$
$$= x^{2q^n} + x^{2q^{n/2}} - x^{2q^{n/2}} - x^2 = 0.$$

This strange result is due to the fact that $g(x)$ maps into a subfield L of k of degree $n/2$ over $\mathbb{F}_q$, and π is the minimal polynomial of L. To verify that this phenomenon does not preclude the use of the minus modifier, we find a bound on the reduction of Q-rank for $ZFHE^-$.

First, we note that all options for removing two equations are equivalent with respect to Q-rank. Therefore our specification that the dimension of each f_i for $i \in \{0,1\}$ is reduced by one suffices for Q-rank analysis. In this case, the minus modifier projects f_i onto a hyperplane. There is a basis in which this codimension one projection is given by $\pi(x) = x^q - x$. Since Q-rank is invariant under isomorphism, we may take $\tilde{f}_i$ isomorphic to f_i with respect to this basis.

Relative to this basis we may view the operation of projection on the associated matrices to be raising each element to the power q, shifting one unit down and to the right, and subtracting the original, thusly:

$$
\pi \begin{bmatrix} \alpha_{11} & \alpha_{12} & \cdots & \alpha_{1,n} \\ \vdots & \vdots & \ddots & \vdots \\ \alpha_{n,1} & \alpha_{n,2} & \cdots & \alpha_{n,n} \end{bmatrix} = \begin{bmatrix} \alpha_{n,n}^q - \alpha_{11} & \alpha_{n,1}^q - \alpha_{12} & \cdots & \alpha_{n,n-1}^q - \alpha_{1,n} \\ \vdots & \vdots & \ddots & \vdots \\ \alpha_{n-1,n}^q - \alpha_{n,1} & \alpha_{n-1,1}^q - \alpha_{n,2} & \cdots & \alpha_{n-1,n-1}^q - \alpha_{n,n} \end{bmatrix}.
$$

We are assured that this operation does not reduce the rank by more than one and thus the Q-rank of the public key is reduced by at most two. Since we can control the Q-rank via selection of L_{ij}, we conclude that $ZHFE^-$ is secure against the Kipnis-Shamir minrank attack.

6.3 Suggested Parameters

In this section we propose practical parameters for a realistic implementation of $ZHFE^-$. Since the most costly operations, encryption and decryption, utilize algorithms identical to those of $ZHFE$, and due to the tightness between the security analyses of the two schemes, we recommend parameters similar to those of the original scheme.

In an earlier version of this manuscript, we suggested as a parameter set $(q, n, D, r, c) = (7, 55, 105, 2, 6)$, where q is the size of the base field, n is the degree of the extension k over $\mathbb{F}_q$, D is the degree bound for Ψ (in this case $105 = 2*7^2 + 7$), r is the number of equations removed, and c is the corank of the parameters L_{ij}, having non-intersecting kernels. In discussions with the authors of [33], it became apparent that we overlooked the added restrictions from insisting on corank 6 matrices L_{ij}. Furthermore, we may have been overcautious about the risk of the Q-rank property of $ZHFE$. Any linear system derived from the Q-rank property is inherently overdefined, and so we dare to be more aggressive. Based in part on their analysis, we propose new parameters for our scheme:

$$108 - ZHFE^- : \quad (q, n, D, r, c) = (7, 55, 393, 2, 3).$$

The experiments of the authors of [33] support the viability of these parameters while retaining the significant advance in key generation efficiency even in the minus case.

These parameters correspond to a public key Q-rank of approximately 6, and a degree of regularity of 9 (est.). Given the overdefined nature of the Q-rank attacks and the above analysis verifying resistance to all other known attacks, we conclude that these parameters achieve a security level greater than 80 bits. The performance and security data are essentially the same as the original scheme with L_{ij} of the same moderate corank, 3.

The main differences between $ZHFE^-$ and its progenitor with the same parameters is key size and encryption time. Since a plaintext is in $\mathbb{F}_7^{55}$, its length is 165 bits. The ciphertext lies in $\mathbb{F}_7^{2*55-2}$ and is thus 324 bits in length. Thus the public key size is determined by the storage requirements of 108 equations in 55 variables over $\mathbb{F}_7$. This quantity is roughly $63.1K$. In comparison, the public key size of $110 - ZHFE(7, 55, 105, 6)$ is $64.3K$, which is about 2% larger. Finally, since $ZHFE^-$ has about 2% fewer public equations than $ZHFE$, encryption is about 2% faster.

7   Conclusion

For many years, multivariate cryptography has had effective tools for building secure and efficient post-quantum signature schemes, but has had much less success for encryption. New schemes such as $ZHFE$ and ABC are promising candidates to fill that gap. Nonetheless, being trapdoor constructions, these schemes can only be trusted after a detailed security analysis.

This work provides much of the security analysis needed to establish trust in the $ZHFE$ construction. In addition to the existing analysis of the difficulty of applying direct algebraic attack to $ZHFE$, we analyze the scheme's security against differential attacks, specify parameters precluding rank attacks, and verify resistance to IP-based equivalent-key attacks. This analysis serves to elucidate the structure of the $ZHFE$ public key, but does not break the cryptosystem, reinforcing the likelihood that the scheme is indeed secure.

The elucidation of the structure of $ZHFE$ also allows us to propose the modified scheme $ZHFE^-$. $ZHFE^-$ modifies the core map of $ZHFE$ and thereby reduces its key size, while still remaining secure with respect to the attacks analyzed above. While the reduction in key size is relatively small, it opens up the possibility of using Ding's idea of constructing an injective multivariate encryption map whose codomain is much larger than its domain, without requring the dimension of the codomain to exceed that of the domain by a factor of two or more, as do all existing schemes that use this approach.

References

1. Shor, P.W.: Polynomial-time algorithms for prime factorization and discrete logarithms on a quantum computer. SIAM J. Sci. Stat. Comp. **26**, 1484 (1997)
2. Yang, B.-Y., Lee, F.Y.-S., Cheng, C.-M., Chen, A.I.-T., Kuo, E.L.-H., Ding, J., Chen, T.-R., Chen, M.-S.: SSE Implementation of Multivariate PKCs on Modern x86 CPUs. In: Clavier, C., Gaj, K. (eds.) CHES 2009. LNCS, vol. 5747, pp. 33–48. Springer, Heidelberg (2009)
3. Chen, A.I.-T., Chen, C.-H.O., Chen, M.-S., Cheng, C.-M., Yang, B.-Y.: Practical-Sized instances of multivariate PKCs: rainbow, TTS, and ℓIC-derivatives. In: Buchmann, J., Ding, J. (eds.) PQCrypto 2008. LNCS, vol. 5299, pp. 95–108. Springer, Heidelberg (2008)
4. Cheng, C.-M., Chen, J.-M., Yang, B.-Y., Chen, B.-R.: Implementing minimized multivariate PKC on low-resource embedded systems. In: Clark, J.A., Paige, R.F., Polack, F.A.C., Brooke, P.J. (eds.) SPC 2006. LNCS, vol. 3934, pp. 73–88. Springer, Heidelberg (2006)

5. Ding, J., Schmidt, D.: Rainbow, a new multivariable polynomial signature scheme. In: Ioannidis, J., Keromytis, A.D., Yung, M. (eds.) ACNS 2005. LNCS, vol. 3531, pp. 164–175. Springer, Heidelberg (2005)
6. Chen, M.S., Yang, B.Y., Smith-Tone, D.: Pflash - secure asymmetric signatures on smart cards. Lightweight Cryptography Workshop 2015 (2015). http://csrc.nist.gov/groups/ST/lwc-workshop2015/papers/session3-smith-tone-paper.pdf
7. Kipnis, A., Patarin, J., Goubin, L.: Unbalanced oil and vinegar signature schemes. In: Stern, J. (ed.) EUROCRYPT 1999. LNCS, vol. 1592, p. 206. Springer, Heidelberg (1999)
8. Patarin, J., Courtois, N.T., Goubin, L.: QUARTZ, 128-Bit long digital signatures. In: Naccache, D. (ed.) CT-RSA 2001. LNCS, vol. 2020, p. 282. Springer, Heidelberg (2001)
9. Tao, C., Diene, A., Tang, S., Ding, J.: Simple matrix scheme for encryption. In: [35], pp. 231–242
10. Ding, J., Petzoldt, A., Wang, L.: The cubic simple matrix encryption scheme. In: [34], pp. 76–87
11. Porras, J., Baena, J., Ding, J.: Zhfe, a new multivariate public key encryption scheme. In: [34], pp. 229–245
12. Moody, D., Perlner, R.A., Smith-Tone, D.: An asymptotically optimal structural attack on the ABC multivariate encryption scheme. In: [34], pp. 180–196
13. Smith-Tone, D.: On the differential security of multivariate public key cryptosystems. In: Yang, B.-Y. (ed.) PQCrypto 2011. LNCS, vol. 7071, pp. 130–142. Springer, Heidelberg (2011)
14. Perlner, R.A., Smith-Tone, D.: A classification of differential invariants for multivariate post-quantum cryptosystems. In: [35], pp. 165–173
15. Daniels, T., Smith-Tone, D.: Differential properties of the HFE cryptosystem. In: [34], pp. 59–75
16. Patarin, J.: Hidden Fields Equations (HFE) and Isomorphisms of Polynomials (IP): two new families of asymmetric Algorithms. In: Maurer, U.M. (ed.) EUROCRYPT 1996. LNCS, vol. 1070, pp. 33–48. Springer, Heidelberg (1996)
17. Patarin, J.: Cryptanalysis of the matsumoto and imai public key scheme of eurocrypt '88. In: Coppersmith, D. (ed.) CRYPTO 1995. LNCS, vol. 963, pp. 248–261. Springer, Heidelberg (1995)
18. Matsumoto, T., Imai, H.: Public quadratic polynominal-tuples for efficient signature-verification and message-encryption. In: EUROCRYPT, pp. 419–453 (1988)
19. Berlekamp, E.R.: Factoring polynomials over large finite fields. Math. Comput. **24**, 713–735 (1970)
20. Kipnis, A., Shamir, A.: Cryptanalysis of the HFE public key cryptosystem by relinearization. In: Wiener, M. (ed.) CRYPTO 1999. LNCS, vol. 1666, p. 19. Springer, Heidelberg (1999)
21. Bettale, L., Faugère, J., Perret, L.: Cryptanalysis of hfe, multi-hfe and variants for odd and even characteristic. Des. Codes Crypt. **69**, 1–52 (2013)
22. Gama, N., Dubois, V.: The degree of regularity of HFE systems. In: Abe, M. (ed.) ASIACRYPT 2010. LNCS, vol. 6477, pp. 557–576. Springer, Heidelberg (2010)
23. Hodges, T.J., Ding, J.: Inverting HFE systems is quasi-polynomial for all fields. In: Rogaway, P. (ed.) CRYPTO 2011. LNCS, vol. 6841, pp. 724–742. Springer, Heidelberg (2011)
24. Ding, J., Yang, B.Y.: Degree of regularity for hfev and hfev-. In: [35], pp. 52–66

25. Fouque, P.-A., Shamir, A., Stern, J., Dubois, V.: Practical cryptanalysis of SFLASH. In: Menezes, A. (ed.) CRYPTO 2007. LNCS, vol. 4622, pp. 1–12. Springer, Heidelberg (2007)

26. Faugère, J.-C., Joux, A.: Algebraic cryptanalysis of hidden field equation (HFE) cryptosystems using gröbner bases. In: Boneh, D. (ed.) CRYPTO 2003. LNCS, vol. 2729, pp. 44–60. Springer, Heidelberg (2003)

27. Ding, J., Kleinjung, T.: Degree of regularity for HFE-. IACR Cryptology ePrint Archive 2011, 570 (2011)

28. Smith-Tone, D.: Discrete geometric foundations for multivariate public key cryptography. (In Submission)

29. Goubin, L., Courtois, N.T.: Cryptanalysis of the TTM cryptosystem. In: Okamoto, T. (ed.) ASIACRYPT 2000. LNCS, vol. 1976, p. 44. Springer, Heidelberg (2000)

30. Gligoroski, D., Perret, L., Samardjiska, S., Faugère, J.-C., Thomae, E.: A Polynomial-Time Key-Recovery attack on MQQ cryptosystems. In: Katz, J. (ed.) PKC 2015. LNCS, vol. 9020, pp. 150–174. Springer, Heidelberg (2015)

31. Buss, J.F., Frandsen, G.S., Shallit, J.O.: The computational complexity of some problems of linear algebra. J. Comput. Syst. Sci. **58**, 572–596 (1999)

32. Wolf, C., Preneel, B.: Equivalent keys in multivariate quadratic public key systems. J. Math. Crypt. **4**, 375–415 (2011)

33. Baena, J., Cabarcas, D., Escudero, D., Porras-Barrera, J., Verbel, J.: Efficient zhfe key generation. In: Post-Quantum Cryptography - 7th International Conference, PQCrypto 2016, Fukuoka, Japan, February 24–26, 2016, Proceedings (2016)

34. Mosca, M. (ed.): Post-Quantum Cryptography. LNCS, vol. 8772. Springer, Switzerland (2014)

35. Gaborit, P. (ed.): Post-Quantum Cryptography. LNCS, vol. 7932. Springer, Heidelberg (2013)

Efficient ZHFE Key Generation

John B. Baena[1], Daniel Cabarcas[1], Daniel E. Escudero[1],
Jaiberth Porras-Barrera[2], and Javier A. Verbel[1(✉)]

[1] Universidad Nacional de Colombia, Sede Medellín, Medellín, Colombia
{jbbaena,dcabarc,deescuderoo,javerbelh}@unal.edu.co
[2] Facultad de Ingeniería, Tecnológico de Antioquia, Medellín, Colombia
jporras6@tdea.edu.co

Abstract. In this paper we present a new algorithm to construct the keys of the multivariate public key encryption scheme ZHFE. Constructing ZHFE's trapdoor involves finding a low degree polynomial of q-Hamming-weight-three, as an aid to invert a pair of q-Hamming-weight-two polynomials of high degree and high rank. This is done by solving a large sparse linear system of equations. We unveil the combinatorial structure of the system in order to reveal the hidden structure of the matrix associated with it. When the system's variables and equations are organized accordingly, an almost block diagonal shape emerges. We then exploit this shape to solve the system much faster than when ZHFE was first proposed. The paper presents the theoretical details explaining the structure of the matrix. We also present experimental data that confirms the notable improvement of the key generation complexity, which makes ZHFE more suitable for practical implementations.

Keywords: Multivariate public key cryptography · Encryption schemes · ZHFE · Block diagonal matrix

1   Introduction

The eventual construction of large quantum computers has triggered the creation and development of research in Post-Quantum Cryptography (PQC) [1]. PQC is the branch of cryptography that is dedicated to the study of cryptosystems that have the potential to resist quantum computer attacks. If such computers were built, Shor's algorithm could be used to factorize integers and solve the Discrete Logarithm Problem (DLP) in polynomial time [14]. This scenario would annihilate most of our current security protocols, causing a worldwide catastrophe.

Multivariate Public Key Cryptography (MPKC) [4] is an appealing Post-Quantum alternative. The public key in an MPKC is usually a set of multivariate quadratic polynomials over a finite field. A direct attack is to solve a system of multivariate quadratic equations. Solving a random such system is an $\mathcal{NP}$-hard problem [8], and at the moment there is no known quantum algorithm that can solve this problem efficiently. On the other hand, the computations on MPKC's are usually very efficient.

© Springer International Publishing Switzerland 2016
T. Takagi (Ed.): PQCrypto 2016, LNCS 9606, pp. 213–232, 2016.
DOI: 10.1007/978-3-319-29360-8_14

Although efficient and secure MPK signature schemes do exist (cf. [5]), no MPK encryption scheme has prevailed. One of the most researched alternative for PKC encryption is the HFE cryptosystem, proposed in 1996 by Patarin [10]. The idea behind HFE is to hide a core low degree polynomial over a large field by means of two invertible affine transformations over a small field. The composition of these maps, via a vector space isomorphism, yields the public key polynomials. The restriction on the core polynomial degree is necessary to make decryption possible. However, this restriction introduces a weakness in HFE exploited by Faugère and Joux [7] to break HFE over the binary field through a direct algebraic attack. The case of odd characteristic remained open until Faugère et al. [2] improved the Kipnis-Shamir attack [9] and broke some related HFE schemes.

Porras et al. [13] recently proposed an alternative to avoid both the direct algebraic attack [6] and the Kipnis-Shamir attack [2]. They proposed a reduction method to construct and invert pairs of q-Hamming-weight-two polynomials of high degree and high rank. Using these polynomials they introduced a new family of multivariate trapdoor functions. The trapdoor information includes a low degree polynomial Ψ of q-Hamming weight three, used to invert the multivariate trapdoor function consisting of two polynomials F and $\tilde{F}$ of q-Hamming weight two. The polynomial Ψ is a linear combination of Frobenius powers of F and $\tilde{F}$ lifted to q-Hamming weight three by multiplying by X and X^q. Ψ can be found by solving a large sparse linear system of equations resulting from vanishing the high degree terms.

Based on the new trapdoor function, they proposed an HFE-type encryption scheme named ZHFE [12]. They presented theoretical and practical evidence that supports their claim that ZHFE resists the main attacks against this kind of schemes, namely, the direct algebraic attack [6] and the Kipnis-Shamir attack [2]. They also showed that encryption and decryption speed are comparable with their counterparts in the HFE challenge 1 [10]. The main drawback of ZHFE is that the vanishing equation system is very large. Solving it directly requires a lot of time and memory. This situation represents an obstacle to consider ZHFE for practical security protocols.

Our Contribution

In this paper we propose a new method for generating the ZHFE private key efficiently. The main idea of this method is to conveniently sort the variables and equations of the vanishing equation system coming from the reduction method introduced in [12,13], in order to unveil its hidden structure. With this suitable order, the matrix associated with this system presents a shape close to a block diagonal matrix, as shown in Fig. 1.

The math required to expose the matrices' hidden structure is important in its own right. We carefully explain the combinatorial structure of Frobenius powers of q-Hamming-weight-two univariate polynomials. We explain how they match and mismatch when raised to q-Hamming weight three through multiplication by q-Hamming-weight-one monomials.

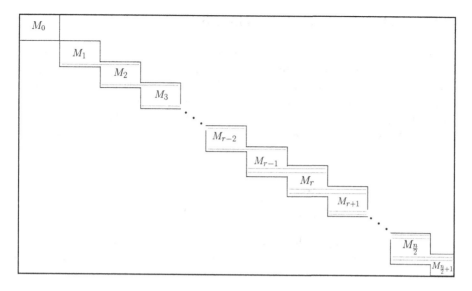

Fig. 1. Hidden structure of the matrix associated with the system $\mathcal{S}$.

Understanding the vanishing equation system leads in the first place to a direct and fast algorithm to construct its matrix. Moreover, we propose an algorithm to solve the vanishing equation system very efficiently. More precisely, the algorithm finds an element in the null space of an almost block diagonal matrix over a finite field. We improved the asymptotic complexity from $\mathcal{O}(n^{3\omega})$ in a naive approach to $\mathcal{O}(n^{2\omega+1})$, where n is the number of variables of the public ZHFE polynomials and $2 \leq \omega \leq 3$ is a constant that depends on the specific Gaussian elimination algorithm used. Moreover, for practical parameters, our experiments show that the proposed key generation algorithm is much faster than the one proposed in [12,13]. We reduced key generation time from a couple of days to only a few minutes.

Another important contribution of this paper is that the new method for solving the vanishing equation system does not require as much memory as the method used in [12,13]. This is because we do not need to work with the complete matrix of Theorem 2, but instead we now work with each block separately. Moreover, once a block is used, it can be deleted, thus in total we are significantly reducing the memory usage.

All these improvements turn ZHFE into an interesting alternative as a Post-Quantum public key encryption scheme.

The paper is organized as follows. In Sect. 2, we review the main features of the ZHFE encryption scheme. In Sect. 3, we present the new method for solving the vanishing equation system, and in Sect. 4, we discuss the complexity of the new method and present experimental data that confirms the efficiency of the new algorithm. In Sect. 5 we discuss some remarks about security, and we finalize giving some conclusions in Sect. 6.

2   The ZHFE Encryption Scheme

The authors in [13] introduced a special reduction method to construct new candidates for multivariate trapdoor functions using q-Hamming-weight-two polynomials of high degree and high rank. The idea of their construction is as follows. Let n be a positive integer, $\mathbb{F}$ a finite field of size q, and $g(y) \in \mathbb{F}[y]$ a degree n irreducible polynomial. Consider the field extension $\mathbb{K} = \mathbb{F}[y]/(g(y))$ and the vector space isomorphism $\varphi \colon \mathbb{K} \to \mathbb{F}^n$ defined by $\varphi\left(u_1 + u_2 y + \ldots + u_n y^{n-1}\right) = (u_1, u_2, \ldots, u_n)$. Take two HFE polynomials over $\mathbb{K}$ of the form

$$F(X) = \sum a_{ij} X^{q^i + q^j} + \sum b_i X^{q^i} + c, \text{ and}$$

$$\tilde{F}(X) = \sum \tilde{a}_{ij} X^{q^i + q^j} + \sum \tilde{b}_i X^{q^i} + \tilde{c}.$$

Denote by $F_0, F_1, \cdots, F_{n-1}$ the Frobenius powers of F, and by $\tilde{F}_0, \tilde{F}_1, \cdots, \tilde{F}_{n-1}$ the Frobenius powers of $\tilde{F}$. Let Ψ_0 and Ψ_1 be the q-Hamming-weight-three polynomials defined by

$$\Psi_0 = X\left(\alpha_1 F_0 + \cdots + \alpha_n F_{n-1} + \beta_1 \tilde{F}_0 + \cdots + \beta_n \tilde{F}_{n-1}\right), \text{ and}$$

$$\Psi_1 = X^q\left(\alpha_{n+1} F_0 + \cdots + \alpha_{2n} F_{n-1} + \beta_{n+1} \tilde{F}_0 + \cdots + \beta_{2n} \tilde{F}_{n-1}\right).$$

Fix a positive integer D such that every univariate polynomial equation over $\mathbb{K}$ of degree less than D is solved efficiently using Berlekamp's algorithm. Choose the scalars $\alpha_i, \beta_i \in \mathbb{K}$ uniformly at random. Then, determine coefficients $a_{ij}, b_i, c, \tilde{a}_{ij}, \tilde{b}_i, \tilde{c} \in \mathbb{K}$, such that the q-Hamming-weight-three polynomial $\Psi = \Psi_0 + \Psi_1$ has degree less than D. This leads to a sparse linear equation system over the small field $\mathbb{F}$ with more variables than equations and thus with nontrivial solutions. This vanishing equation system has about n^3 variables, so finding its solution via the Gaussian elimination process has complexity $\mathcal{O}(n^{3\omega})$, where $2 \leq \omega \leq 3$ is a constant that depends on the specific Gaussian elimination algorithm used.

The multivariate trapdoor function is built in a similar way as the HFE public key is constructed. Choose $G = (F, \tilde{F})$ as the core map, and then select two invertible affine transformations $S : \mathbb{F}^n \to \mathbb{F}^n$ and $T : \mathbb{F}^{2n} \to \mathbb{F}^{2n}$. The multivariate trapdoor function is the map $P : \mathbb{F}^n \to \mathbb{F}^{2n}$ given by

$$P(x_1, \cdots, x_n) = \left(T \circ (\varphi \times \varphi) \circ G \circ \varphi^{-1} \circ S\right)(x_1, \cdots, x_n).$$

Porras et al. used this multivariate trapdoor function to introduce a new encryption scheme named ZHFE [12]. The ZHFE public key includes the field $\mathbb{F}$ and its structure, and the trapdoor function $P(x_1, \cdots, x_n)$. The private key includes the low degree polynomial Ψ, the two invertible affine transformations S and T, and the scalars $\alpha_1, \cdots, \alpha_{2n}, \beta_1, \cdots, \beta_{2n}$. The inversion of the core map G is accomplished by means of the low degree polynomial Ψ, the scalars $\alpha_1, \cdots, \alpha_{2n}, \beta_1, \cdots, \beta_{2n}$, and Berlekamp's algorithm.

3   New Method

In this section we describe a new method to build the function Ψ necessary to create the private key in ZHFE. First, we enumerate adequately the coefficients of the polynomial F and $\tilde{F}$ in order to show the hidden structure of the matrix associated with the vanishing equation system. Next, we propose a method to solve efficiently the structured vanishing equation system.

3.1   Structure of the Matrix

The vanishing equation system arises from equating to zero the coefficients of terms in $\Psi = \Psi_0 + \Psi_1$ of degree greater than or equal to D. We carefully explain the combinatorial structure of the Frobenius powers of F and $\tilde{F}$. We explain how they match and mismatch when raised to q-Hamming-weight-three through multiplication by q-Hamming-weight-one monomials.

We will consider the case when n is even. The case when n is odd is similar and even easier. Our analysis focuses on the q-Hamming-weight-three terms of Ψ, because q-Hamming-weight-two terms lead to and independent and much simpler system. For $k \in \{0, \ldots, \frac{n}{2}\}$ let $\mathcal{A}_k$ be the subset of $\mathbb{Z}_n \times \mathbb{Z}_n$

$$
\mathcal{A}_k := \begin{cases} \{(i, (k+i) \mod n)\mid 0 \le i < n\} & \text{if } 0 \le k < \frac{n}{2}, \\ [5pt] \{(i, k+i)\mid 0 \le i < \frac{n}{2}\} & \text{if } k = \frac{n}{2}. \end{cases}
$$

Let $\mathcal{A}$ be the union of the $\mathcal{A}'_i$s. Each element (i, j) from $\mathcal{A}$ represents the q-Hamming-weight-two term $X^{q^i + q^j}$ of an HFE polynomial. Note that each possible q-Hamming-weight-two term $X^{q^i + q^j}$ appears on a single $\mathcal{A}_i$. Moreover, if $(i, j) \in \mathcal{A}$ then $(j, i) \notin \mathcal{A}$.

Consider two HFE polynomials F and $\tilde{F}$. We denote by Z_h the coefficient of $X^{q^i + q^j}$ in F or $\tilde{F}$, where $h \in \mathbb{Z}^+$ depends on (i, j) and on which polynomial the term $Z_h X^{q^i + q^j}$ belongs to. We aim to sort these terms according to the partition $\{\mathcal{A}_k\}_{k=0}^{\frac{n}{2}}$ of $\mathcal{A}$. For $(i, j) \in \mathcal{A}_k$, the coefficient of $X^{q^i + q^j}$ in F will be indexed by $2nk + i$ so that they range from $2nk$ to $2nk + n - 1$, and we will index the coefficient of $X^{q^i + q^j}$ in $\tilde{F}$ by $2nk + n + i$ so that they range from $2nk + n$ to $2nk + 2n - 1$.

Similarly, we index the coefficients of the q-Hamming-weight-one monomials by setting $Z_{n(n+1)+i}$ and $Z_{n(n+1)+n+i}$ to be the coefficients of X^{q^i} in F and $\tilde{F}$, respectively. With the terms indexed in this fashion, F and $\tilde{F}$ are as follows

$$
F(X) = \sum_{k=0}^{\frac{n}{2}} \left(\sum_{(i,j) \in \mathcal{A}_k} Z_{2nk+i} X^{q^i + q^j} \right) + \sum_{i=1}^{n-1} Z_{n(n+1)+i} X^{q^i} + C,
$$

$$
\tilde{F}(X) = \sum_{k=0}^{\frac{n}{2}} \left(\sum_{(i,j) \in \mathcal{A}_k} Z_{2nk+n+i} X^{q^i + q^j} \right) + \sum_{i=1}^{n-1} Z_{n(n+1)+n+i} X^{q^i} + \tilde{C}.
$$

For $0 \le k \le \frac{n}{2}$, we define **the k–th part of F** as

$$_k F(X) := \sum_{(i,j) \in \mathcal{A}_k} Z_{2nk+i} X^{q^i+q^j}.$$

For $(i,j) \in \mathcal{A}_k$, the Frobenius powers of $X^{q^i+q^j}$ mod $\left(X^{q^n} - X\right)$ fall within a set indexed by $\mathcal{A}_k$, moreover, the k–th part of F^{q^ℓ} is equal to the k–th part of F, raised to the power q^ℓ. In order to prove this, we introduce the following definition.

Definition 1. For $(i,j) \in \mathcal{A}_k$, and $\ell \in \mathbb{Z}_n$ we define

$$i \ominus \ell := \begin{cases} i - \ell \bmod n \ if \ k \ne \frac{n}{2} \\ i - \ell \bmod \frac{n}{2} \ if \ k = \frac{n}{2}. \end{cases}$$

Proposition 1. For $0 \le \ell \le n-1$, $_k\left[F(X)^{q^\ell}\right] = [_k F(X)]^{q^\ell}$.

Proof.

$$[_k F(X)]^q = \left(\sum_{(i,j) \in \mathcal{A}_k} Z_{2nk+i} X^{q^i+q^j} \right)^q \mod (X^{q^n} - X)$$

$$= \left(\sum_{(i,j) \in \mathcal{A}_k} Z^q_{2nk+i} X^{q^{i+1}+q^{j+1}} \right) \mod (X^{q^n} - X)$$

$$= \sum_{(i,j) \in \mathcal{A}_k} Z^q_{2nk+(i\ominus 1)} X^{q^i+q^j}.$$

So, by iterating this ℓ times, we obtain

$$_k\left[F(X)^{q^\ell}\right] = \sum_{(i,j) \in \mathcal{A}_k} Z^{q^\ell}_{2nk+(i\ominus \ell)} X^{q^i+q^j} = [_k F(X)]^{q^\ell}.$$

Using the notation for the ℓ–th Frobenius power of F as F_ℓ, we have $_k[F_\ell] = [_k F]_\ell$. Since the $\mathcal{A}_k$'s are mutually disjoint, if $2 < q$ and $(i,j) \in \mathcal{A}_k$, the only term in F_ℓ that has the monomial $X^{q^i+q^j}$ is $Z^{q^\ell}_{2nk+(i\ominus \ell)} X^{q^i+q^j}$. We thus get the following result.

Corollary 1. If $(i,j) \in \mathcal{A}_k$ and $s \in \{0,1\}$, then the coefficient of $X^{q^s+q^i+q^j}$ in Ψ_s is

$$\sum_{\ell=0}^{n-1} \alpha_{ns+\ell+1} Z^{q^\ell}_{2nk+(i\ominus \ell)} + \sum_{\ell=0}^{n-1} \beta_{ns+\ell+1} Z^{q^\ell}_{2nk+n+(i\ominus \ell)}.$$

This corollary determines the coefficients of the q-Hamming-weight-three monomials in Ψ_0 and Ψ_1. Since $\Psi = \Psi_0 + \Psi_1$, in order to determine the coefficients of the q-Hamming-weight-three monomials of Ψ, we only need to find the q-Hamming-weight-three monomials that Ψ_0 and Ψ_1 share. The following lemma gives the conditions under which this holds

Lemma 1. *Assume $2 < q$, $(i, j) \in \mathcal{A}_k$ and $(s, t) \in \mathcal{A}$.*

1. *For $0 \le k < \frac{n}{2}$, $q^0 + q^i + q^j = q^1 + q^s + q^t$ if and only if*
   (a) $i = 1$, $s = 0$ and $j = t$, or
   (b) $j = 1$, $t = 0$ and $i = s$.
2. *For $k = \frac{n}{2}$, $q^0 + q^i + q^j = q^1 + q^s + q^t$ if and only if $i = 1, s = j = \frac{n}{2} + 1$ and $t = 0$.*

Proof. Throughout this proof we will use the uniqueness of the q-ary expansion of integers. Suppose $q^0 + q^i + q^j = q^1 + q^s + q^t$. If $i = j$, then $q^0 + 2q^i = q^1 + q^s + q^t$, but this is absurd since $q > 2$ and q^1 does not appear in the q-ary expansion of $q^0 + 2q^i$. Now, if $i \ne j$, the uniqueness of the q-ary expansion of $q^0 + q^i + q^j$ shows us that one of the following cases must hold:

1. $i = 1, s = 0$ and $j = t$
2. $j = 1, t = 0$ and $i = s$
3. $i = 1, t = 0$ and $j = s$
4. $j = 1, s = 0$ and $i = t$.

Suppose $0 \le k < \frac{n}{2}$. We now show that cases 3 and 4 are not possible. Suppose $i = 1, t = 0$ and $j = s$, then $(s, 0) \in \mathcal{A}$ and therefore $s > \frac{n}{2}$, but $j = s$, then $(1, j) \in \mathcal{A}_k$ with $0 \le k < \frac{n}{2}$ and $j > \frac{n}{2}$, but this is a contradiction since in this case $\frac{n}{2} > k = j - 1 > \frac{n}{2} - 1$, so case 3 is not possible. Now, if case 4 holds, i.e., if $j = 1, s = 0$ and $i = t$, proceeding as before we see that $(0, t) \in \mathcal{A}$ and so $t \le \frac{n}{2}$, but then $(i, 1) \in \mathcal{A}_k$ with $0 \le k \le \frac{n}{2}$ and $i = t \le \frac{n}{2}$, which is absurd since $(1, i) \in \mathcal{A}_k$ (note this also shows that case 4 is not possible when $k = \frac{n}{2}$). It is straightforward to see that cases 1 and 2 are actually achievable.

Now suppose $k = \frac{n}{2}$. We claim that only case 3 is possible. Indeed, case 4 is not possible as we pointed out in the previous paragraph. Suppose case 1 holds, then $i = 1, s = 0$ and $j = t$ and therefore $(1, j) \in \mathcal{A}_{\frac{n}{2}}$, then $j = \frac{n}{2} + 1 = t$ so $(0, \frac{n}{2} + 1) \in \mathcal{A}$, which is absurd since $(\frac{n}{2} + 1, 0) \in \mathcal{A}_{\frac{n}{2}-1} \subseteq \mathcal{A}$. If case 2 holds, i.e., $j = 1, t = 0$ and $i = s$, we would then have $(i, 1) \in \mathcal{A}_{\frac{n}{2}}$, but this is absurd since there is no element of this form in $\mathcal{A}_{\frac{n}{2}}$. Finally, the only possibility left is case 3, which is only achievable by taking $i = 1, s = j = \frac{n}{2} + 1$ and $t = 0$. $\qed$

We can now precisely describe the coefficients of the q-Hamming-weight-three monomials in Ψ.

Proposition 2. *If $2 < q$ and $(i, j) \in \mathcal{A}_k$, then the coefficient of $X^{q^0 + q^i + q^j}$ in Ψ is one of the following:*

$$(i) \quad \sum_{p=0}^{1} \left[\sum_{\ell=0}^{n-1} \left(\alpha_{pn+\ell+1} Z_{2n(k+p)+((i-p)\ominus\ell)}^{q^\ell} + \beta_{pn+\ell+1} Z_{2n(k+p)+n+((i-p)\ominus\ell)}^{q^\ell} \right) \right]$$

$$(ii) \quad \sum_{p=0}^{1} \left[\sum_{\ell=0}^{n-1} \left(\alpha_{pn+\ell+1} Z_{2n(k-p)+((\frac{n}{2}p+1)\ominus\ell)}^{q^\ell} + \beta_{pn+\ell+1} Z_{2n(k-p)+n+((\frac{n}{2}p+1)\ominus\ell)}^{q^\ell} \right) \right]$$

$$(iii) \quad \sum_{p=0}^{1} \left[\sum_{\ell=0}^{n-1} \left(\alpha_{pn+\ell+1} Z_{2n(k-p)+(i\ominus\ell)}^{q^\ell} + \beta_{pn+\ell+1} Z_{2n(k-p)+n+(i\ominus\ell)}^{q^\ell} \right) \right]$$

$$(iv) \quad \sum_{\ell=0}^{n-1} \alpha_{\ell+1} Z_{2nk+(i\ominus\ell)}^{q^\ell} + \sum_{\ell=0}^{n-1} \beta_{\ell+1} Z_{2nk+n+(i\ominus\ell)}^{q^\ell}$$

Moreover, (i) holds if $i = 1$ and $k \neq \frac{n}{2}$, (ii) holds if $i = 1$ and $k = \frac{n}{2}$, (iii) holds if $j = 1$ and (iv) holds otherwise.

Proof. Let $(i,j) \in \mathcal{A}_k$. Suppose at first that $i = 1$ and $k \neq \frac{n}{2}$. Note that in this case $(0,j) \in \mathcal{A}_{k+1}$. By Corollary 1, the coefficient of $X^{q^0+q^1+q^j}$ in Ψ_0 is

$$\sum_{\ell=0}^{n-1} \alpha_{\ell+1} Z_{2nk+(1\ominus\ell)}^{q^\ell} + \sum_{\ell=0}^{n-1} \beta_{\ell+1} Z_{2nk+n+(1\ominus\ell)}^{q^\ell}.$$

By Lemma 1, the only monomial in Ψ_1 equal to $X^{q^0+q^1+q^j}$ is $X^{q^1+q^0+q^j}$, whose coefficient by Corollary 1 is

$$\sum_{\ell=0}^{n-1} \alpha_{n+\ell+1} Z_{2n(k+1)+(0\ominus\ell)}^{q^\ell} + \sum_{\ell=0}^{n-1} \beta_{n+\ell+1} Z_{2n(k+1)+n+(0\ominus\ell)}^{q^\ell}.$$

Since $\Psi = \Psi_0 + \Psi_1$, the coefficient of $X^{q^0+q^1+q^j}$ in Ψ is

$$\sum_{\ell=0}^{n-1} \alpha_{\ell+1} Z_{2nk+(1\ominus\ell)}^{q^\ell} + \sum_{\ell=0}^{n-1} \beta_{\ell+1} Z_{2nk+n+(1\ominus\ell)}^{q^\ell}$$

$$+ \sum_{\ell=0}^{n-1} \alpha_{n+\ell+1} Z_{2n(k+1)+(0\ominus\ell)}^{q^\ell} + \sum_{\ell=0}^{n-1} \beta_{n+\ell+1} Z_{2n(k+1)+n+(0\ominus\ell)}^{q^\ell},$$

i.e.,

$$\sum_{p=0}^{1} \left[\sum_{\ell=0}^{n-1} \left(\alpha_{pn+\ell+1} Z_{2n(k+p)+((1-p)\ominus\ell)}^{q^\ell} + \beta_{pn+\ell+1} Z_{2n(k+p)+n+((1-p)\ominus\ell)}^{q^\ell} \right) \right].$$

Now suppose $i = 1$ and $k = \frac{n}{2}$, i.e. $i = 1$ and $(i,j) \in \mathcal{A}_k$. Clearly $j = \frac{n}{2} + 1$. By Corollary 1, the coefficient of $X^{q^0+q^1+q^{\frac{n}{2}+1}}$ in Ψ_0 is

$$\sum_{\ell=0}^{n-1} \alpha_{\ell+1} Z_{2nk+(1\ominus\ell)}^{q^\ell} + \sum_{\ell=0}^{n-1} \beta_{\ell+1} Z_{2nk+n+(1\ominus\ell)}^{q^\ell}.$$

By Lemma 1, the only monomial in Ψ_1 equal to $X^{q^0+q^1+q^{\frac{n}{2}+1}}$ is $X^{q^1+q^{\frac{n}{2}+1}+q^0}$, and by Corollary 1, its coefficient is

$$\sum_{\ell=0}^{n-1} \alpha_{n+\ell+1} Z_{2n(k-1)+((\frac{n}{2}+1)\ominus\ell)}^{q^\ell} + \sum_{\ell=0}^{n-1} \beta_{n+\ell+1} Z_{2n(k-1)+n+((\frac{n}{2}+1)\ominus\ell)}^{q^\ell}.$$

Then, the coefficient of $X^{q^1+q^{\frac{n}{2}+1}+q^0}$ in Ψ is

$$\sum_{\ell=0}^{n-1} \alpha_{\ell+1} Z_{2nk+(1\ominus\ell)}^{q^\ell} + \sum_{\ell=0}^{n-1} \beta_{\ell+1} Z_{2nk+n+(1\ominus\ell)}^{q^\ell}$$

$$+ \sum_{\ell=0}^{n-1} \alpha_{n+\ell+1} Z_{2n(k-1)+((\frac{n}{2}+1)\ominus\ell)}^{q^\ell} + \sum_{\ell=0}^{n-1} \beta_{n+\ell+1} Z_{2n(k-1)+n+((\frac{n}{2}+1)\ominus\ell)}^{q^\ell},$$

i.e.,

$$\sum_{p=0}^{1} \left[\sum_{\ell=0}^{n-1} \left(\alpha_{pn+\ell+1} Z_{2n(k-p)+((\frac{n}{2}p+1)\ominus\ell)}^{q^\ell} + \beta_{pn+\ell+1} Z_{2n(k-p)+n+((\frac{n}{2}p+1)\ominus\ell)}^{q^\ell} \right) \right].$$

The other cases are obtained in a similar fashion.

Recall that the polynomial Ψ is constructed so that its degree is smaller than an adequate parameter D. Therefore, we get a system $\mathcal{S}$ of vanishing equations, where the variables are the coefficients of the polynomials F and $\tilde{F}$, and each equation corresponds to the coefficient of every term in Ψ of degree higher than D equated to zero. From now on, we refer to the variables of the form $Z_{2nk+pn+(i\ominus\ell)}^{q^\ell}$, with $p \in \{0,1\}$, as the variables associated with the group $\mathcal{A}_k$; and to the coefficient of $X^{q^s+q^i+q^j}$ in Ψ equated to zero as the (s,i,j) equation. The matrix associated with this system has a very distinct structure as stated in the following theorem.

Theorem 1. *Let n, q, and D be positive integers such that $2 < q$, $1 < r = \lceil \log_q D \rceil < \frac{n}{2}$, and $q + 2q^{r-1} < D \le q^r$. Then, we can reorganize adequately the rows of the matrix associated with $\mathcal{S}$ so that it has the form shown in Fig. 1, and for $0 \le k \le \frac{n}{2}$, the size of the submatrix M_k is $a \times b$, with*

$$a = \begin{cases} 2(n-r+k) & \text{if} \quad k < r \\ 2n & \text{if} \quad r \le i < \frac{n}{2} \\ n & \text{if} \quad k = \frac{n}{2} \end{cases} \quad \text{and} \quad b = \begin{cases} 2n^2 & \text{if} \quad k \ne \frac{n}{2} \\ n^2 & \text{if} \quad k = \frac{n}{2} \end{cases}.$$

Proof. Note first that the condition $q + 2q^{r-1} < D \le q^r$ guarantees that for each $(i,j) \in \mathcal{A}$, $D \le q + q^i + q^j$ if and only if $D \le q^0 + q^i + q^j$, and they are both true only if $i \ge r$ or $j \ge r$. So given $0 \le k \le \frac{n}{2}$, the number of (s,i,j) equations such that $D \le q^s + q^i + q^j$, where $s \in \{0,1\}$ and $(i,j) \in \mathcal{A}_k$, is equal to twice the number of elements $(i,j) \in \mathcal{A}_k$ such that $i \ge r$ or $j \ge r$, i.e.

$$\begin{cases} 2(n-r+k) & \text{if} \quad k < r \\ 2n & \text{if} \quad r \le k < \frac{n}{2} \\ 2\frac{n}{2} & \text{if} \quad k = \frac{n}{2}. \end{cases}$$

For $0 < k \leq \frac{n}{2}$, we have $(0, k) \in \mathcal{A}_k$ and $(1, k) \in \mathcal{A}_{k-1}$, so by Proposition 2 the $(0, 1, k)$ equation only contains variables associated with the groups $\mathcal{A}_{k-1}$ and $\mathcal{A}_k$. On the other hand, for $0 \leq k < \frac{n}{2} - 1$ and $(i, 0) \in \mathcal{A}_k$, $(i, 1) \in \mathcal{A}_{k+1}$ and by the Proposition 2 the $(0, i, 1)$ equation only contains variables associated with $\mathcal{A}_k$ and $\mathcal{A}_{k+1}$. Furthermore, note that $(\frac{n}{2} + 1, 0) \in \mathcal{A}_{\frac{n}{2}-1}$ and $(1, \frac{n}{2} + 1) \in \mathcal{A}_{\frac{n}{2}}$, so the $(0, 1, \frac{n}{2} + 1)$ equation contain only variables associated with $\mathcal{A}_{\frac{n}{2}-1}$ and $\mathcal{A}_{\frac{n}{2}-1}$.

According to Lemma 1 and Corollary 1, if $(i, j) \in \mathcal{A}_k$ and $i, j \notin \{0, 1\}$, then the $(0, i, j)$, $(1, i, j)$ equations only contain variables associated with $\mathcal{A}_k$. Then, for each k the elements of the form $(0, j)$, $(1, j + 1)$, $(i, 0)$ and $(i + 1, 0)$ are the only ones that have elements associated with a group different to $\mathcal{A}_k$. So, given $0 < k < \frac{n}{2}$, the number of equations in $\mathcal{S}$ that contain variables associated with $\mathcal{A}_k$ and $\mathcal{A}_{k+1}$ is equal to the number of elements $(i, j) \in \mathcal{A}_k$ such that $i = 1$ and $j \geq r$; or $j = 0$ and $i \geq r$. Similarly, the number of equations in $\mathcal{S}$ that contain variables associated with $\mathcal{A}_k$ and $\mathcal{A}_{k-1}$ is equal to the number of elements $(i, j) \in \mathcal{A}_k$ such that $i = 0$ and $j \geq r$; or $j = 1$ and $i \geq r$. Finally, the number of equations in $\mathcal{S}$ that only contain variables associated with $\mathcal{A}_k$ is equal to the number of elements $(i, j) \in \mathcal{A}_k$, such that $i, j \notin \{0, 1\}$.

Clearly, for each $(i, i) \in \mathcal{A}_0$ with $i \geq r$, the $(0, i, i)$ and $(1, i, i)$ equations appear in the system $\mathcal{S}$ and only have variables associated with $\mathcal{A}_0$. So, for any equation of the system $\mathcal{S}$ there are two possibilities, either it does not contain variables associated with $\mathcal{A}_0$ or it only contains variables associated with $\mathcal{A}_0$.

Suppose $1 < k \leq r - 2$. Even though by Proposition 2 the $(1, 0, k)$ equation contains variables associated with $\mathcal{A}_{k-1}$ and $\mathcal{A}_k$, that equation does not appear in the system because $k \leq r$. Analogously, we conclude that the $(0, 1, k+1)$ equation does not appear in the system. On the other hand, $(n - k, 0), (n - k + 1, 1) \in \mathcal{A}_k$, and since $1 < k \leq r - 2$ and $r < \frac{n}{2}$, then $r < n - k < n - 1$ and so the $(1, n - k, 0)$ equation appears in the system; and by Proposition 2 it has variables associated with $\mathcal{A}_k$ and $\mathcal{A}_{k+1}$. Also, since $r < n - k + 1 \leq n - 1$, the $(0, n - k + 1, 1)$ equation appears in the system and contains variables associated with $\mathcal{A}_{k-1}$ and $\mathcal{A}_k$. Consequently, for $1 < k \leq r - 2$ the system $\mathcal{S}$ only has one equation that contains variables associated with $\mathcal{A}_k$ and $\mathcal{A}_{k-1}$, and $\mathcal{S}$ only has one equation that contains variables associated with $\mathcal{A}_k$ and $\mathcal{A}_{k+1}$. For every other equation in $\mathcal{S}$, either it only contains variables associated with $\mathcal{A}_k$ or it does not contain variables associated with $\mathcal{A}_k$ at all.

Now, if $k = r - 1$, then $(0, r - 1), (1, r) \in \mathcal{A}_{r-1}$. The $(1, 0, r - 1)$ equation has variables associated with $\mathcal{A}_{r-1}$ and $\mathcal{A}_{r-2}$, but it does not appear in the system. Clearly, the $(0, 1, r)$ equation is the only one in $\mathcal{S}$ that contains variables associated with $\mathcal{A}_{r-1}$ and $\mathcal{A}_r$. If in particular $2 < r < \frac{n}{2}$, then $r < \frac{n}{2} + 1 < n - (r - 1) < n - 1$. Thus, $r < n - (r - 1) + 1 \leq n - 1$ and finally we have that

$$(n - (r - 1), 0) = (0 + (n - (r - 1)), (r - 1) + (n - (r - 1)) \bmod n), \text{ and}$$
$$(n - (r - 1) + 1, 1) = (0 + (n - (r - 1)) + 1, (r - 1) + (n - (r - 1) + 1) \bmod n).$$

Therefore, $(n - (r - 1), 0), (n - (r - 1) + 1, 1) \in \mathcal{A}_{r-1}$ and, by Proposition 2, the $(1, n - (r - 1), 0)$ equation appears in the system and contains variables associated with $\mathcal{A}_r$ and $\mathcal{A}_{r-1}$. Likewise, the $(0, n - (r - 1) + 1, 1)$ equation appears in the system and has variables associated with $\mathcal{A}_{r-1}$ and $\mathcal{A}_{r-2}$. Notice that, if $r = 2$, then $\mathcal{A}_{r-1} = \mathcal{A}_1$, and $(0,1)$ is the unique element of the form $(i, 1)$ in $\mathcal{A}_1$. Consequently, and since $0, 1 < r$, no equation contains variables associated with $\mathcal{A}_{r-1}$ and $\mathcal{A}_{r-2}$ in the system; in contrast, if $r > 2$, there is only one equation in $\mathcal{S}$ that contains variables associated with $\mathcal{A}_{r-1}$ and $\mathcal{A}_{r-2}$, namely, the $(0, n - (r - 1) + 1, 1)$ equation.

If $r \le k < \frac{n}{2}$, then $\frac{n}{2} \le n - k < n - k + 1 \le n - 1$. By similar reasons as above, the $(1, 0, k)$ and $(0, n - k + 1, 1)$ equations are the only ones in $\mathcal{S}$ that have variables associated with $\mathcal{A}_k$ and $\mathcal{A}_{k-1}$. Furthermore, the $(0, 1, k + 1)$ and $(1, n - k, 0)$ equations are the only ones in $\mathcal{S}$ that have variables associated with $\mathcal{A}_k$ and $\mathcal{A}_{k-1}$. All equations of the form (s, i, j) with $(i, j) \in \mathcal{A}_k$ are in $\mathcal{S}$, and they only contain variables associated with $\mathcal{A}_k$.

For $k = \frac{n}{2}$, the $(1, 0, \frac{n}{2})$ and $(0, 1, \frac{n}{2} + 1)$ equations are the only ones that contain variables associated with $\mathcal{A}_{\frac{n}{2}-1}$ and $\mathcal{A}_{\frac{n}{2}}$. Moreover, the (s, i, j) equations with $s \in \{0, 1\}$ and $(i, j) \in \mathcal{A}_{\frac{n}{2}}$ are the only ones in $\mathcal{S}$ that contain variables associated with $\mathcal{A}_{\frac{n}{2}}$.

Therefore, we can reorganize the rows of the matrix associated with the vanishing equation system $\mathcal{S}$ so that it has the desired structure.

Remark 1. The conditions $1 < r < \frac{n}{2}$ and $q + 2q^{r-1} < D \le q^r$ in Theorem 1 are merely technical. If we omit these conditions, the matrix is still quite structured but it is a bit harder to describe. Moreover, these conditions do not restrict much the values D can take. For example, if we choose the parameters suggested in [12] for a practical implementation of ZHFE, $q = 7$ and $n = 56$, then r could be in the interval $[1, 28]$ and the possible values for D are as shown in Table 1.

Table 1. Possible values of D for $q = 7$ and $n = 56$.

r	Without the restriction	With the restriction
2	$7 < D \le 49$	$21 < D \le 49$
3	$49 < D \le 343$	$105 < D \le 343$
4	$343 < D \le 2401$	$693 < D \le 2401$

3.2   The Matrix over the Small Field

Recall that we aim at determining the coefficients Z_k such that the polynomial Ψ has degree less than D. Initially, each coefficient Z_k is seen as a variable. In that way, every term of the form $\alpha_{ns+\ell+1} Z_k^{q^\ell}$ in Ψ can be seen as an $\mathbb{F}$-linear transformation from $\mathbb{K}$ to $\mathbb{K}$. Since the big field $\mathbb{K}$ is a vector space over the small field $\mathbb{F}$, any $\mathbb{F}$-linear transformation $\mathbb{K} \to \mathbb{K}$ can be seen as an $\mathbb{F}$-linear transformation $\mathbb{F}^n \to \mathbb{F}^n$. Let $A_{ns+\ell}$ be the matrix over $\mathbb{F}$ that represents the $\mathbb{F}$-linear transformation $Z \mapsto \alpha_{ns+\ell+1} Z^{q^\ell}$ with respect to the canonical basis.

Let (i, j) be an element in $\mathcal{A}_k$ for some $k \neq \frac{n}{2}$. We know that the coefficient of $X^{q^s + q^i + q^j}$ in Ψ_s is

$$\sum_{\ell=0}^{n-1} \alpha_{ns+\ell+1} Z_{2nk+(i\ominus\ell)}^{q^\ell} + \sum_{\ell=0}^{n-1} \beta_{ns+\ell+1} Z_{2nk+n+(i\ominus\ell)}^{q^\ell}. \tag{1}$$

We can see the expression in (1) as an $\mathbb{F}$-linear transformation $T_{s,i}^k : \mathbb{K}^{2n} \to \mathbb{K}$, such that its $(ns+i)$-th variable is $Z_{2nk+ns+i}$, where $s \in \{0, 1\}$ and $i = 0, \ldots n-1$. In that way, the matrix that represents $T_{s,i}^k$ is $[A|B]$ with

$$A = \left[A_{ns+i} \middle| A_{ns+i-1} \middle| \cdots \middle| A_{ns} \middle| A_{ns+n-1} \middle| \cdots \middle| A_{ns+(i+1)} \right],$$
$$B = \left[B_{ns+i} \middle| B_{ns+i-1} \middle| \cdots \middle| B_{ns} \middle| B_{ns+n-1} \middle| \cdots \middle| B_{ns+(i+1)} \right],$$

where $A_{ns+\ell}$ and $B_{ns+\ell}$ are the matrices that represent the $\mathbb{F}$-linear transformations $\alpha_{ns+\ell+1} Z^{q^\ell}$ and $\beta_{ns+\ell+1} Z^{q^\ell}$, respectively. Furthermore, the matrix that represents the $\mathbb{F}$-linear transformation T_k from $\mathbb{K}^{2n}$ to $\mathbb{K}^{2n}$, defined by

$$T_k = (T_{0,0}^k, \cdots, T_{0,n-1}^k, T_{1,0}^k, \cdots T_{1,n-1}^k),$$

is as shown in Fig. 2.

A_0	A_{n-1}	A_{n-2}	$\cdots$	A_1	B_0	B_{n-1}	B_{n-2}	$\cdots$	B_1
A_1	A_0	A_{n-1}	$\cdots$	A_2	B_1	B_0	B_{n-1}	$\cdots$	B_2
A_2	A_1	A_0	$\cdots$	A_3	B_2	B_1	B_0	$\cdots$	B_3
$\vdots$	$\vdots$	$\vdots$	$\ddots$	$\vdots$	$\vdots$	$\vdots$	$\vdots$	$\ddots$	$\vdots$
A_{n-2}	A_{n-3}	A_{n-4}	$\cdots$	A_{n-1}	B_{n-2}	B_{n-3}	B_{n-4}	$\cdots$	B_{n-1}
A_{n-1}	A_{n-2}	A_{n-3}	$\cdots$	A_0	B_{n-1}	B_{n-2}	B_{n-3}	$\cdots$	B_0
A_n	A_{2n-1}	A_{2n-2}	$\cdots$	A_{n+1}	B_n	B_{2n-1}	B_{2n-2}	$\cdots$	B_{n+1}
A_{n+1}	A_n	A_{2n-1}	$\cdots$	A_{n+2}	B_{n+1}	B_n	B_{2n-1}	$\cdots$	B_{n+2}
A_{n+2}	A_{n+1}	A_n	$\cdots$	A_{n+3}	B_{n+2}	B_{n+1}	B_n	$\cdots$	B_{n+3}
$\vdots$	$\vdots$	$\vdots$	$\ddots$	$\vdots$	$\vdots$	$\vdots$	$\vdots$	$\ddots$	$\vdots$
A_{2n-2}	A_{2n-3}	A_{2n-4}	$\cdots$	A_{2n-1}	B_{2n-2}	B_{2n-3}	B_{2n-4}	$\cdots$	B_{2n-1}
A_{2n-1}	A_{2n-2}	A_{2n-3}	$\cdots$	A_n	B_{2n-1}	B_{2n-2}	B_{2n-3}	$\cdots$	B_n

Fig. 2. Matrix representation of $T_k : \mathbb{K}^{2n} \to \mathbb{K}^{2n}$.

Similarly, for $(i, j) \in \mathcal{A}_{\frac{n}{2}}$, we can define the $\mathbb{F}$-linear transformation $T_{s,i}^{\frac{n}{2}}$ from $\mathbb{K}^n$ to $\mathbb{K}$, so that the matrix that represents $T_{s,i}^{\frac{n}{2}}$ is $[A|B]$ with

$$A = \left[A_{ns+i} + A_{ns+\frac{n}{2}+i} \middle| \cdots \middle| A_{ns} + A_{ns+\frac{n}{2}} \middle| A_{ns+n-1} + A_{ns+\frac{n}{2}-1} \middle| \cdots \middle| A_{ns+(i+1)} + A_{ns+\frac{n}{2}+(i+1)} \right],$$
$$B = \left[B_{ns+i} + B_{ns+\frac{n}{2}+i} \middle| \cdots \middle| B_{ns} + B_{ns+\frac{n}{2}} \middle| B_{ns+n-1} + B_{ns+\frac{n}{2}-1} \middle| \cdots \middle| B_{ns+(i+1)} + B_{ns+\frac{n}{2}+(i+1)} \right].$$

The matrix that represents the $\mathbb{F}$-linear transformation

$$T_{\frac{n}{2}} = (T_{0,1}^{\frac{n}{2}}, \ldots, T_{0,\frac{n}{2}-1}^{\frac{n}{2}}, T_{1,0}^{\frac{n}{2}}, \ldots, T_{1,\frac{n}{2}-1}^{\frac{n}{2}})$$

is presented in Fig. 3.

A_0 $+A_{\frac{n}{2}}$	$A_{\frac{n}{2}-1}$ $+A_{\frac{n}{2}-1}$	$\cdots$		A_1 $+A_{\frac{n}{2}+1}$	B_0 $+B_{\frac{n}{2}}$	$B_{\frac{n}{2}-1}$ $+B_{\frac{n}{2}-1}$	$\cdots$		B_1 $+B_{\frac{n}{2}+1}$
A_1 $+A_{\frac{n}{2}+1}$	A_0 $+A_{\frac{n}{2}}$	$\cdots$		A_2 $+A_{\frac{n}{2}+2}$	B_1 $+B_{\frac{n}{2}+1}$	B_0 $+B_{\frac{n}{2}}$	$\cdots$		B_2 $+B_{\frac{n}{2}+2}$
$\vdots$	$\vdots$	$\ddots$		$\vdots$	$\vdots$	$\vdots$	$\ddots$		$\vdots$
$A_{\frac{n}{2}-1}$ $+A_{n-1}$	$A_{\frac{n}{2}-2}$ $+A_{n-2}$	$\cdots$		A_0 $+A_{\frac{n}{2}}$	$B_{\frac{n}{2}-1}$ $+B_{n-1}$	$B_{\frac{n}{2}-2}$ $+B_{n-2}$	$\cdots$		B_0 $+B_{\frac{n}{2}}$
A_n $+A_{n+\frac{n}{2}}$	$A_{n+\frac{n}{2}-1}$ $+A_{n+\frac{n}{2}-1}$	$\cdots$		A_{n+1} $+A_{n+\frac{n}{2}+1}$	B_n $+B_{n+\frac{n}{2}}$	$B_{n+\frac{n}{2}-1}$ $+B_{n+\frac{n}{2}-1}$	$\cdots$		B_{n+1} $+B_{n+\frac{n}{2}+1}$
A_{n+1} $+A_{n+\frac{n}{2}+1}$	A_n $+A_{n+\frac{n}{2}}$	$\cdots$		A_{n+2} $+A_{n+\frac{n}{2}+2}$	B_{n+1} $+B_{n+\frac{n}{2}+1}$	B_n $+B_{n+\frac{n}{2}}$	$\cdots$		B_{n+2} $+B_{n+\frac{n}{2}+2}$
$\vdots$	$\vdots$	$\ddots$		$\vdots$	$\vdots$	$\vdots$	$\ddots$		$\vdots$
$A_{n+\frac{n}{2}-1}$ $+A_{2n-1}$	$A_{n+\frac{n}{2}-2}$ $+A_{2n-2}$	$\cdots$		A_n $+A_{n+\frac{n}{2}}$	$B_{n+\frac{n}{2}-1}$ $+B_{2n-1}$	$B_{n+\frac{n}{2}-2}$ $+B_{2n-2}$	$\cdots$		B_n $+B_{n+\frac{n}{2}}$

Fig. 3. Matrix representation of $T_{\frac{n}{2}} : \mathbb{K}^n \to \mathbb{K}^n$.

Recall that the homogeneous system $\mathcal{S}$ contains all (s, i, j) equations such that $q^s + q^i + q^j \geq D$, where $s \in \{0, 1\}$ and $(i, j) \in \mathcal{A}$. Theorem 1 explains the hidden structure of the matrix associated with $\mathcal{S}$. We now consider $\mathcal{S}$ with the order given in Theorem 1, so that the i-th equation in $\mathcal{S}$ can be seen as $L_i(Z_0, \ldots, Z_N) = \mathbf{0}$, where L_i is an $\mathbb{F}$-linear transformation from $\mathbb{K}^N$ to $\mathbb{K}$ and N is two times the number of variables of the polynomial F. In that way, $\mathcal{S}$ can be seen as $L(Z_1, \ldots, Z_N) = \mathbf{0}$, where $L = (L_1, \ldots, L_t)$ and t is the number of equations in the system $\mathcal{S}$.

Theorem 2. *Let $n, q,$ and D be positive integers such that $q > 2$, $1 < r = \lceil \log_q D \rceil < \frac{n}{2}$ and $q + 2q^{r-1} < D \leq q^{r-1}$. Then, the matrix $\tilde{M}$ that represents the $\mathbb{F}$-linear transformation L is formed by $\frac{n}{2} + 1$ submatrices $\tilde{M}_0, \ldots, \tilde{M}_{\frac{n}{2}}$ arranged in the same way as in the matrix in Fig. 1. For $0 \leq i \leq \frac{n}{2}$, the size of the submatrix $\tilde{M}_i$ is $a \times b$, where*

$$a = \begin{cases} 2n(n-r-i) & \text{if } i < r \\ 2n^2 & \text{if } r \le i < \frac{n}{2} \,, \\ n^2 & \text{if } i = \frac{n}{2} \end{cases} \qquad b = \begin{cases} 2n^2 & \text{if } i \ne r \\ n^2 & \text{if } i = \frac{n}{2}. \end{cases}$$

Remark 2. The blocks $\tilde{M}_i$ and $\tilde{M}_{i+1}$ overlap in a block of pn rows if and only if the blocks M_i and M_{i+1} overlap in p rows.

Remark 3. The submatrices $\tilde{M}_0, \ldots, \tilde{M}_{\frac{n}{2}}$ are small modifications of the matrix in Fig. 2. More precisely, for $r \le k < \frac{n}{2}$, $\tilde{M}_k$ can be obtained simply by permuting the rows of the matrix in Fig. 2, placing in the upper part the rows that come from equations in $\mathcal{S}$ with variables associated with both $\mathcal{A}_k$ and $\mathcal{A}_{k-1}$. Also, for $0 \le k \le r-1$, $\tilde{M}_k$ can be obtained by removing the blocks of rows that represent expressions with $(i,j) \in \mathcal{A}_k$, $i < r$ and $j < r$, and adequately permuting rows as above.

Note that Theorem 2, together with the description of the submatrices above, provide a direct and fast algorithm to construct the matrix $\tilde{M}$. Given α_i's and β_i's we construct $A_{ns+\ell}$ and $B_{ns+\ell}$ as the matrices that represent the $\mathbb{F}$-linear transformations $Z \mapsto \alpha_{ns+\ell+1} Z^{q^\ell}$ and $Z \mapsto \beta_{ns+\ell+1} Z^{q^\ell}$, respectively. Then, we assemble the matrices in Figs. 2 and 3 for all k's, and sort their rows according to Remark 3. Finally, we put them together as described in Theorem 2. However, as we will see in the next subsection, we never really have to construct the whole matrix $\tilde{M}$. Since we just aim at finding a non-trivial element in its null space, we can exploit its structure to do so more efficiently.

3.3   An Algorithm to Solve the System

In this section, we will first describe an algorithm for finding random elements in the null space of the matrix $\tilde{M}$. The algorithm is based on the hidden structure of the matrix unveiled in Theorem 2. Then, we will discuss the probability that this algorithm terminates.

As seen in Sect. 3.2, the matrix $\tilde{M}$ is almost block diagonal, with blocks $\tilde{M}_1, \ldots, \tilde{M}_{\frac{n}{2}}$ overlapping in a few rows. In order to illustrate the method, suppose we have only two blocks $\tilde{M}_1, \tilde{M}_2$. We first split each block in two blocks U_i and L_i so that the matrix has the form

$$\tilde{M} = \begin{bmatrix} U_1 & 0 \\ L_1 & U_2 \\ 0 & L_2 \end{bmatrix}.$$

Next we find an element $\mathbf{y}_2$ in the null space of L_2. Then, we compute $\mathbf{r} = U_2 \mathbf{y}_2$. Then we find an element $\mathbf{y}_1$ such that $\begin{bmatrix} U_1 \\ L_1 \end{bmatrix} \mathbf{y}_1 = \begin{bmatrix} 0 \\ -\mathbf{r} \end{bmatrix}$. It is easy to see that

$\tilde{M} \begin{bmatrix} \mathbf{y}_1 \\ \mathbf{y}_2 \end{bmatrix} = 0$. This process can be iterated through the whole matrix regardless of the number of blocks.

To formally describe the algorithm, we introduce the following notation. For $r \leq i \leq \frac{n}{2}$, let L_i be the matrix that results from removing the first $2n$ rows from $\tilde{M}_i$, and let L_i be the matrix that results from removing the first n rows from $\tilde{M}_i$, for $2 \leq i < r$. For each $2 \leq i \leq \frac{n}{2}$, U_i is the matrix such that $\tilde{M}_i = \begin{bmatrix} U_i \\ L_i \end{bmatrix}$ (for $i = 1$, we define $U_1 = \tilde{M}_1$). The expression $\mathbf{y} \xleftarrow{\$} W$ denotes that $\mathbf{y}$ is an element chosen uniformly at random from the set W. Algorithm 1 describes an algorithm to find a solution of the equation $\tilde{M}\mathbf{y} = 0$.

Algorithm 1. Finds an element in the null space of $\tilde{M}$

Input: $\tilde{M}_0, \tilde{M}_1, \ldots, \tilde{M}_{\frac{n}{2}}$, blocks of $\tilde{M}$ as described in Theorem 2

1: $W := \left\{ \mathbf{z} \mid L_{\frac{n}{2}}\mathbf{z} = \mathbf{0} \right\}$
2: **for** $i = \frac{n}{2}, \ldots, 1$ **do**
3:      $\mathbf{y}_i \xleftarrow{\$} W$
4:      $\mathbf{r}_i := U_i \mathbf{y}_i$
5:      $W := \left\{ \mathbf{z} \mid L_i\mathbf{z} = \begin{bmatrix} \mathbf{0} \\ -\mathbf{r}_i \end{bmatrix} \right\}$
6:      **if** $W = \emptyset$ **then**
7:          **stop algorithm**
8: $W := \left\{ \mathbf{z} \mid \tilde{M}_0\mathbf{z} = \mathbf{0} \right\}$
9: $\mathbf{y}_0 \xleftarrow{\$} W$
10: **return** $\mathbf{y} = [\mathbf{y}_0, \mathbf{y}_1, \ldots, \mathbf{y}_{\frac{n}{2}}]^T$

It is easy to see that if this algorithm terminates, the output $\mathbf{y}$ is an element in the null space of $\tilde{M}$. Moreover, the converse is also true.

Proposition 3. *If $\boldsymbol{x}$ is a vector in the null space of the matrix $\tilde{M}$, then $\boldsymbol{x}$ can be the output of Algorithm 1.*

Proof. Let $\mathbf{x}$ be an element in the null space of $\tilde{M}$, say $\mathbf{x} = [x_1, x_2, \ldots, x_t]^T$, with $t = n^2(n+1)$. For $0 < i \leq \frac{n}{2}$, we define $\mathbf{x}_i = [x_{t_{i-1}+1}, x_{t_{i-1}+2}, \ldots, x_{t_i}]^T$, where $t_i := 2in^2$, for $0 < i < \frac{n}{2}$, $t_0 := 0$ and $t_{\frac{n}{2}} := t$. Since $\mathbf{x}$ is an element in the null space of $\tilde{M}$ and $\tilde{M}_i = \begin{bmatrix} U_i \\ L_i \end{bmatrix}$, then

$$L_{\frac{n}{2}}\mathbf{x}_{\frac{n}{2}} = \mathbf{0}.$$

Let us define the vector $\mathbf{r}_{\frac{n}{2}}$ as

$$\mathbf{r}_{\frac{n}{2}} = U_{\frac{n}{2}}\mathbf{x}_{\frac{n}{2}}.$$

Since $\mathbf{x}$ is a element in the null space of $\tilde{M}$, we must have that

$$L_{\frac{n}{2}-1}\mathbf{x}_{\frac{n}{2}-1} = \begin{bmatrix} \mathbf{0} \\ -\mathbf{r}_{\frac{n}{2}} \end{bmatrix}.$$

So, $\mathbf{x}_{\frac{n}{2}-1}$ belongs to the solution set of the equation

$$L_{\frac{n}{2}-1}\mathbf{z} = \begin{bmatrix} \mathbf{0} \\ -\mathbf{r}_{\frac{n}{2}}. \end{bmatrix}$$

In general, for $0 \leq i < \frac{n}{2}$, $\mathbf{x}_{i-1}$ belongs to the solution set of the equation

$$L_i\mathbf{z} = \begin{bmatrix} \mathbf{0} \\ -\mathbf{r}_{i+1}, \end{bmatrix}$$

where $\mathbf{r}_i = U_i\mathbf{x}_i$.

This proposition shows that every element of the null space of $\tilde{M}$ can be output by Algorithm 1. Moreover, the element in the null space is still chosen with uniform distribution. This is because Algorithm 1 obtains each element $\mathbf{x}$ by finding its projections $\mathbf{x}_i$, and this is performed uniformly.

Algorithm 1 does not always terminate. In case it fails, we would have to run it again. However, we claim that the probability of failure is very small. Note that the termination of the Algorithm 1 depends on W not being empty for each $i = \frac{n}{2}, \ldots, 1$. So, a sufficient condition to guarantee that the Algorithm 1 terminates is that each matrix L_i be of full rank. Therefore, for a uniformly random instance of ZHFE, the probability that the Algorithm 1 terminates is greater than the probability that for each i the rank of L_i is equal to its number of rows. In order to give an estimate for this probability, we ran extensive experiments for different values of n and computed the rank of L_i for $i = r, \ldots, \frac{n}{2}$ (see Table 2). For every single instance and for each $i = r, \ldots, \frac{n}{2}$, the matrix L_i was full rank.

Table 2. Computation of the rank of the L_i's with $q = 7$ and $D = 106$. For every generated instance, the matrices are full rank.

n	Number of instances
8	80000000
16	4000000
32	100000
56	5000

4   Complexity of the New Method

The new method introduced in this paper to solve the vanishing equation system finds an element in the null space of an almost-block diagonal matrix with $\frac{n}{2} + 1$ blocks, as depicted in Fig. 1. The size of each block is at most $2n^2 \times 2n^2$, so reducing each block to its echelon form has complexity $\mathcal{O}\left((n^2)^{\omega}\right)$, where the parameter $2 \leq \omega \leq 3$ is a constant that depends on the specific Gaussian elimination algorithm used (e.g., $\omega = 3$ for a classical Gaussian elimination algorithm and $\omega < 2.376$ for an asymptotically improved algorithm). Therefore, the complexity of the new method is $\mathcal{O}\left(n\left(n^2\right)^\omega\right) = \mathcal{O}\left(n^{2\omega+1}\right)$. This improves the naive approach used in [12], which costs $\mathcal{O}\left(\left(n^3\right)^\omega\right) = \mathcal{O}\left(n^{3\omega}\right)$, if a dense Gaussian elimination algorithm is used. Since the matrix of the vanishing equation system is sparse, even the old method could take advantage of its sparsity. Although the complexity of sparse algorithms is harder to compare with, our experiments confirm a significant improvement against sparse methods too.

We performed experiments in order to compare the new method with the one used in [12] for solving the vanishing equation system. We built different ZHFE private keys using both methods. In Table 3 we present these results for different sets of parameters. All the experiments were performed using Magma v2.21-1 [3] on a server with a processor Intel(R) Xeon(R) CPU E5-2609 0 @ 2.40GHz, running Linux CentOS release 6.6. It is important to notice that the experiments for the old method where performed on Magma using the *Nullspace* command. Magma's *Nullspace* implementation exploits the matrix sparsity using the Markowitz Pivot Strategy. Hence, in practice, we are comparing our new method with an sparse matrix solving algorithm.

Table 3. Private key generation: comparison between the new and old methods.

Method			New method		Old method		
q	D	n	CPU time [s]	Memory [MB]	n	CPU time [s]	Memory [MB]
7	106	8	0.07	≤32	8	0.43	≤32
7	106	16	1.46	≤32	16	25.41	131
7	106	32	67.29	64	32	2285.44	3452
7	106	56	1111.26	235	55[a]	216076.27	53619
17	106	8	0.08	≤32	8	0.45	≤32
17	106	16	2.02	68	16	26.63	160
17	106	32	122.86	93	32	2095.94	3785
17	595	56	2712.63	353	55[a]	226384.28	59658

[a]Experiments run on a different machine: Magma V2.20-2 on a Sun X4440 server, with four Quad-Core AMD OpteronTM Processor 8356 CPUs running at 2.3 GHz.

Note the significant reduction in the time needed to construct the keys for ZHFE. It is also evident that, for the new method, the memory needed to build the ZHFE keys is considerably less than the memory needed in [12].

5 Remarks About Security

Although a more rigorous study of the security of ZHFE is out of the scope of this paper, this aspect is not affected by the proposed key generation improvement. The matrix $\tilde{M}$ is simply a rearrangement of the sparse matrix used in the original approach to construct the ZHFE private key. Moreover, Proposition 3 guarantees that the new algorithm would not miss any solution of the system and as remarked in Sect. 3, the solution is chosen under the same uniform distribution. This matrix $\tilde{M}$ has about n^2 free variables, so the size of its null space is about q^{n^2}. This number is huge for practical values of the parameters. Thus, in principle, the unveiled structure of the matrix $\tilde{M}$ does not represent an obvious threat to the security of ZHFE. Nevertheless, this aspect should be considered more deeply and will be part of future research.

The security of ZHFE was studied in detail in [12], and we base the pertinence of this paper on those arguments. Nevertheless, it recently came to our attention new works exposing a rank weakness on the original ZHFE [11,15]. Perlner and Smith-Tone prove that if we write $\Psi(X) = X(L_{11}F + L_{12}\tilde{F}) + X^q(L_{21}F + L_{22}\tilde{F})$, and the L_{ij} maps have full rank, then the rank of ZHFE is no larger than $\lceil \log_q D \rceil + 2$ [11]. They also argue that if we select the L_{ij} maps to have reasonable corank c, then the Q-rank does not appear to be a weakness for ZHFE. They further propose a "minus" modification of ZHFE, called ZHFE$^-$, which adds a projection to the original ZHFE, by removing r polynomials from the public key. They recommend the following parameters for this new proposal:

$$\text{ZHFE}^- : \qquad (q, n, D, r, c) = (7, 55, 105, 2, 6).$$

They claim that with these parameters the public key Q-rank is about 12, and the degree of regularity is estimated to be 9, which implies a security level of at least 80 bits.

We performed extensive experiments to see how our new key generation method behaves for the parameters proposed in [11]. We found that for the parameters $(q, n, D, r, c) = (7, 55, 105, 2, 6)$, both the new and old methods produce only the trivial solution $\Psi(X) = 0$, even though the kernel is not trivial. We also found that for those parameters, c must be chosen in $\{1, 2\}$ for a nontrivial $\Psi(X)$ to exist. Using a different value for q, we realised that for $(q, n, D, r) = (3, 55, 105, 2)$, the corank c must be chosen in $\{1, 2, 3\}$ for a nontrivial $\Psi(X)$ to exist. We also found that if we want to obtain a nontrivial $\Psi(X)$ for $(q, n, D, r) = (3, 55, 170, 2)$, the corank c must be chosen in $\{1, 2, 3, 4\}$. Again, in all these cases both the new and old methods work fine. In order to construct a ZHFE key using L_{ij} maps with corank $c = 6$, the parameter D must be increased. We discovered for instance that the new and old methods work for $(q, n, D, r, c) = (3, 56, 1462, 2, 6)$. Table 4 shows the results of the experiments run for some choices of the parameters.

According to our extensive experiments, we can say that our new algorithm works flawlessly, when we use L_{ij} maps with positive corank, including the case $c = 6$. Moreover, we can say that for any fixed set of parameters, the original method finds a nontrivial $\Psi(X)$ if and only if the new algorithm finds a nontrivial $\Psi(X)$.

Table 4. Computation of ZHFE keys for $(q, D, c) = (3, 1462, 6)$, $(q, D, c) = (3, 490, 5)$ and $(q, D, c) = (3, 170, 4)$. For every generated instance, the algorithm terminated successfully

n	Number of instances
16	400000
32	5000
56	400

6   Conclusions

We have proposed a novel way to solve the vanishing equation system necessary to construct keys in ZHFE. By exposing its almost-block diagonal structure, we unleashed a series of improvements in ZHFE key generation. We can now construct the matrix associated with the system faster, and store it more efficiently. Moreover, we can find solutions to the system asymptotically faster. These improvements turn ZHFE from an only theoretical proposal, into a viable Post-Quantum public key encryption scheme.

In order to achieve these, we had to understand the combinatorial structure of Frobenius powers of q-Hamming-weight-two univariate polynomials. We expect this understanding will serve as a tool to explore a bigger family of encryption schemes, i.e., generalizations of ZHFE in which the polynomial Ψ is obtained multiplying by more than two powers of the form X^{q^i}.

We also found that, in terms of success, our new algorithm works just as good as the original method, when considering L_{ij} maps with positive corank, as proposed in [11].

We foresee further improvements in ZHFE derived from this work. Since the vanishing equation system has several free variables, we can fix some variables for all instances of the trapdoor function. Knowing the structure of the matrix allows us to do so in a way that further speeds up key generation, and reduces secret key size.

We must not discard the theoretical results of this paper as a useful tool to get a better understanding of the security of ZHFE.

Acknowledgements. This work was partially supported by "Fondo Nacional de Financiamiento para la Ciencia, la Tecnología y la Innovación Francisco José de Caldas", Colciencias (Colombia), Project No. 111865842333 and Contract No. 049-2015. We would like to thank Jintai Ding, Ludivic Perret, and Felipe Cabarcas for useful discussions. We would also like to thank the reviewers of PQCrypto 2016 for their constructive reviews and suggestions. And last but not least, we thank the Facultad de Ciencias of the Universidad Nacional de Colombia sede Medellín for granting us access to the Enlace server, where we ran most of the experiments of this paper.

References

1. Bernstein, D.J., Buchmann, J., Dahmen, E.: Post-quantum Cryptography, 1st edn. Springer, Heidelberg (2009)
2. Bettale, L., Faugère, J.C., Perret, L.: Cryptanalysis of HFE, multi-HFE and variants for odd and even characteristic. Des. Codes Crypt. **69**(1), 1–52 (2013)
3. Bosma, W., Cannon, J., Playoust, C.: The Magma algebra system. I. The user language. J. Symbolic Comput. **24**(3–4), 235–265 (1997). http://dx.doi.org/10.1006/jsco.1996.0125, computational algebra and number theory (London, 1993)
4. Ding, J., Gower, J.E., Schmidt, D.S.: Multivariate Public Key Cryptosystems. AISC, vol. 25. Springer, New York (2006)
5. Ding, J., Schmidt, D.: Rainbow, a new multivariable polynomial signature scheme. In: Ioannidis, J., Keromytis, A.D., Yung, M. (eds.) ACNS 2005. LNCS, vol. 3531, pp. 164–175. Springer, Heidelberg (2005)
6. Faugère, J.C.: A new efficient algorithm for computing Gröbner bases (F_4). J. Pure Appl. Algebra **139**(1–3), 61–88 (1999). Effective methods in algebraic geometry (Saint-Malo, 1998)
7. Faugère, J.-C., Joux, A.: Algebraic cryptanalysis of hidden field equation (HFE) cryptosystems using Gröbner bases. In: Boneh, D. (ed.) CRYPTO 2003. LNCS, vol. 2729, pp. 44–60. Springer, Heidelberg (2003)
8. Garey, M.R., Johnson, D.S.: Computers and Intractability: A Guide to the Theory of NP-Completeness. W. H. Freeman & Co., New York (1990)
9. Kipnis, A., Shamir, A.: Cryptanalysis of the HFE public key cryptosystem by relinearization. In: Wiener, M. (ed.) CRYPTO 1999. LNCS, vol. 1666, pp. 19–30. Springer, Heidelberg (1999)
10. Patarin, J.: Hidden fields equations (HFE) and isomorphisms of polynomials (IP): two new families of asymmetric algorithms. In: Maurer, U.M. (ed.) EUROCRYPT 1996. LNCS, vol. 1070, pp. 33–48. Springer, Heidelberg (1996)
11. Perlner, R.A., Smith-Tone, D.: Security analysis and key modification for ZHFE. In: Proceedings of the 7th International Conference Post-Quantum Cryptography, PQCrypto 2016, 24–26 February 2016, Fukuoka, Japan (2016, to appear)
12. Porras, J., Baena, J., Ding, J.: ZHFE, a new multivariate public key encryption scheme. In: Mosca, M. (ed.) PQCrypto 2014. LNCS, vol. 8772, pp. 229–245. Springer, Heidelberg (2014)
13. Porras, J., Baena, J., Ding, J.: New candidates for multivariate trapdoor functions. Rev. Colomb. Matemáticas **49**, 57–76 (2015)
14. Shor, P.W.: Polynomial-time algorithms for prime factorization and discrete logarithms on a quantum computer. SIAM Rev. **41**(2), 303–332 (1999). (Electronic)
15. Zhang, W., Tan, C.H.: Personal communication (2015)

Additively Homomorphic Ring-LWE Masking

Oscar Reparaz[⊠], Ruan de Clercq, Sujoy Sinha Roy, Frederik Vercauteren, and Ingrid Verbauwhede

COSIC/KU Leuven and iMinds, Kasteelpark Arenberg 10, 3001 Leuven, Belgium
{oscar.reparaz,ruan.declercq,sujoy.sinharoy,frederik.vercauteren,
ingrid.verbauwhede}@esat.kuleuven.be

Abstract. In this paper, we present a new masking scheme for ring-LWE decryption. Our scheme exploits the additively-homomorphic property of the existing ring-LWE encryption schemes and computes an additive-mask as an encryption of a random message. Our solution differs in several aspects from the recent masked ring-LWE implementation by Reparaz et al. presented at CHES 2015; most notably we do not require a masked decoder but work with a conventional, unmasked decoder. As such, we can secure a ring-LWE implementation using additive masking with minimal changes. Our masking scheme is also very generic in the sense that it can be applied to other additively-homomorphic encryption schemes.

1 Introduction

Most public-key cryptography deployed today will not withstand attacks by a quantum computer. Shor's algorithm [Sho99] can break RSA, discrete logarithms and elliptic-curve cryptography in polynomial time using a quantum computer. The National Security Agency (NSA) has recently announced that quantum computing is a threat to the existing public key infrastructure, and has recommended a transition to quantum resistant public key algorithms [nsa15]. In recent years significant progress was made to improve public-key cryptosystems based on computational problems that will remain secure even in the presence of powerful quantum computers. Regev's *learning with errors* (LWE) problem [Reg05] and its ring variant, known as the *ring*-LWE problem have become very popular in designing public key encryption, key exchange, digital signature and homomorphic encryption schemes. Several recent publications such as [PG14, PDG14, RVM+14, GOPS13, RVV14, dCRVV15, APS13, LSR+15, BSJ15, POG15] show that ring-LWE based encryption and digital signature schemes are faster and relatively easier to implement compared to elliptic curve cryptography (ECC) algorithms.

Though secure against quantum computing, ring-LWE based cryptography offers no inherent protection against side-channel attacks [Koc96]. It is well-known that a vanilla, unprotected implementation of a cryptographic algorithm running on an embedded device can be broken if the adversary can observe a side-channel, such as the instantaneous power consumption, the EM radiation

© Springer International Publishing Switzerland 2016
T. Takagi (Ed.): PQCrypto 2016, LNCS 9606, pp. 233–244, 2016.
DOI: 10.1007/978-3-319-29360-8_15

or some timing information. A particularly effective method to extract secrets, such as cryptographic keys or passwords, from embedded devices is Differential Power Analysis (DPA) [KJJ99].

Masking [CJRR99, GP99] is a provable sound countermeasure against DPA. First-order masking works by probabilistically splitting every intermediate into two shares such that each share is statistically independent from the intermediate. This property ought to preserve through the entire computation. A masking scheme defines how the computation on masked data should be performed. Masking, of course, comes at a cost. Masked implementations incur area, time and energy overheads. In public-key cryptosystems, the decryption operation is normally the prime target for DPA protections, as it is the component that manipulates long-term secrets.

Post-quantum cryptosystems are not yet as mature as RSA, Diffie-Hellman or ECC. There is ongoing research to determine the exact security offered by a concrete parameter choice, to determine which padding schemes should be used, to design fast and memory-efficient implementations that can compete with classical public-key cryptography and to write protected implementations against side-channel analysis.

A first step in a masked ring-LWE implementation is the work [RRVV15], hereafter referred to as the CHES 2015 approach. This approach takes an unmasked ring-LWE processor and adds masking with a bespoke, customized masked decoder. The overhead is roughly 2.6 times more cycles and the impact in area is very small.

Our contribution. In this paper we propose a new masking scheme to protect the secret key during decryption operations in ring-LWE cryptosystems. Our masking scheme is based on the additively homomorphic nature of the existing ring-LWE encryption. A mask is computed by encrypting a random message and then the mask is added to the ciphertext. This operation randomizes the ciphertext and mitigates the side-channel leakage problem.

Our solution has the advantage compared to the CHES 2015 approach that we do not require additional hardware (nor software) to compute the final decoding operation. The masking scheme is applicable to both hardware and software implementations. A caveat of our approach is that we need to place additional assumptions on the underlying arithmetic hardware compared to the CHES 2015 approach.

2   Background

For a complete view of the system, we describe the entire ring-LWE cryptosystem. In this paper we focus on the DPA security of the ring-LWE decryption operation.

Notation. We denote by $R = \mathbb{F}_q[x]/(f(x)), +, *$ a modular polynomial ring over base field $\mathbb{F}_q$. When we want to access a specific coefficient of a polynomial s we write $s[i]$. The operation $\oplus$ is the xor operation on bits or strings of bits.

Review of ring-LWE based encryption scheme. In the literature there are several encryption schemes based on the ring-LWE problem, for example [LPR10,FV12,BLLN13] etc. The major algorithms in these encryption schemes are: key-generation, encryption and decryption. These algorithms perform message-encoding, discrete Gaussian sampling, polynomial addition/subtraction/multiplication, and decoding as the primitive operations.

In this paper, we use the scheme proposed by Lyubashevsky, Peikert, and Regev (LPR) [LPR10]. Though our masking scheme is generic and works with the other ring-LWE encryption schemes, we choose the LPR scheme for the analysis mainly due to the availability of several efficient implementations [PG14, RVM+14,GOPS13,dCRVV15,LSR+15,POG15] and due to the existence of a DPA resistant masked implementation [RRVV15].

The three main operations in the LPR encryption scheme are described below. The parameters are (n, q, σ) where n is the dimension of polynomial ring, q is the modulus and σ is the standard deviation of the discrete Gaussian distribution.

- *Key generation.* Two polynomials r and s are generated by sampling the coefficients from the discrete Gaussian distribution. Next a new polynomial $p = r - g * s$ is computed where g is a globally known base polynomial. The key generation outputs s as the secret key and p as the public key.
- *Encryption.* The n-bit input plaintext is encoded as a ring element $\bar{m} \in R$ by multiplying the bits by $q/2$. The encryption operation generates three error polynomials e_1, e_2 and e_3 using the discrete Gaussian sampler. These error polynomials are used as noise. The ciphertext is a pair of polynomials (c_1, c_2) where $c_1 = g * e_1 + e_2$ and $c_2 = p * e_1 + e_3 + \bar{m}$.
- *Decryption.* In the decryption phase s is used to compute the intermediate message $\tilde{m} = c_1 * s + c_2$. This intermediate plaintext contains noise. Next, a decoding is performed to recover the original plaintext bits: $m_{\text{recovered}} = decode(\tilde{m})$. The simplest decoder just compares each coefficient of $\tilde{m}$ with $q/2$: if the distance is small (i.e. $< q/4$) it returns 1 otherwise it returns 0.

Among all the computations, polynomial multiplication is the costliest. Most of the reported implementations use the Number Theoretic Transform (NTT) to accelerate the polynomial multiplications. In the implementation in [RVM+14] the ciphertext is kept in the NTT domain to reduce the number of NTTs and inverse NTTs (INTTs). When c_1, c_2 and s are in the NTT domain, the plaintext bits are computed as $m_{\text{recovered}} = decode(\text{INTT}(c_1 \cdot s + c_2))$. Here $\cdot$ is the coefficient-wise multiplication operator.

Review of CHES2015 approach. The paper [RRVV15] proposes to mask the ring-LWE decryption by additively splitting the secret s into two shares s', s'' such that $s = s' + s''$. The masked decryption proceeds as follows: it first computes one branch

$$a' = \text{INTT}(c_1 \cdot s' + c_2), \qquad (1)$$

then proceeds with the computation of the second branch:

$$a'' = \text{INTT}(c_1 \cdot s'') \qquad (2)$$

and finally outputs the pair of the mask bit and the masked message bit $(m', m'') = $ masked-decoder(a', a'').

The random splitting of s into two shares s' and s'' works as a countermeasure against DPA during the coefficient-wise multiplications. The main difficulty is the masked-decoder block. This block performs the threshold th computation in the masked domain, yielding Boolean masked results m' and m''. Inside the decoder block, the two input shares a' and a'' are compared with a lookup table to check if a set of rules is satisfied or not. When the rules are not satisfied, the shares are refreshed by adding and subtracting a small refreshment-value Δ with the two shares, and then checking the rules again. The masked decoder implementation in [RRVV15] performs the refreshing operation 16 times in order to achieve constant time decoding with high success probability.

3   Additively Homomorphic Ring-LWE Masking

Core idea. The central idea is that the LPR encryption scheme presented in Sect. 2 is additively homomorphic. This means that for any two ciphertexts (c_1, c_2) and (c_1', c_2') corresponding to the respective encryptions of m and m' under the same public key, $(c_1 + c_1', c_2 + c_2')$ will be an encryption of $(m \oplus m')$. Hence we can write the following equation:

$$\text{decryption}(c_1, c_2) \oplus \text{decryption}(c_1', c_2') = \text{decryption}(c_1 + c_1', c_2 + c_2') \qquad (3)$$

This additive homomorphism can be exploited to randomize the computation of the decryption operation. The randomization technique is explained below.

The proposed randomized decryption. To perform the decryption of (c_1, c_2) in a randomized way, the implementation follows the following steps:

1. Internally generate a random message m' unknown to the adversary
2. Encrypt m' to (c_1', c_2')
3. Perform decryption$(c_1 + c_1', c_2 + c_2')$ to recover $m \oplus m'$.

The masked recovered message is the tuple $(m', m \oplus m')$.

This approach has the nice property of not requiring a masked decoder. One can use an unprotected decoder function. The obvious disadvantage is that extra circuitry or code is required to perform the encryption. Another disadvantage is the increased decryption failure rate. When two ciphertexts are added, the amount of noise increases. The added noise increases the decryption failure rate as we will see in Sect. 4.3.

4   Discussion

4.1   Analysis

First-order DPA. Our countermeasure can be thought of as ciphertext blinding. Note that there is no attacker-known, nor attacker-controlled inputs that are mixed with the secret key s. Thus, straightforward first-order DPA attack does not immediately apply. Nevertheless, more refined first-order DPA attacks do apply.

First-order attacks. Note that the key is not masked. Thus, we do not claim theoretic first-order security. Our randomization makes it harder for the attacker to model the power consumption (and thus harder to DPA). In Appendix A we describe a strategy to detect whether $s[i] = 0$ or $s[i] \neq 0$, which leads to an entropy loss. This seems not to significantly affect security for the following reason. First, remember that s is handled in the NTT domain, so that the probability of the event $s[i] = 0$ is $1/q$. If there are w coefficients for which $s[i] = 0$, the dimension is effectively reduced by w. Since $q > n$, we expect w to be very small and thus not to lose much in the dimension of the system. The same effect can occur at a smaller scale, exploiting intermediates from within the multiplication. In this situation, the consequences are more serious. Therefore, the underlying hardware must ensure that intermediates from inside the multiplication are noisy enough to be hard to exploit in this way.

4.2 Comparison with Previous Work

In this section we compare our solution with the CHES 2015 approach.

Offline precomputations. Our solution allows to precompute the encryption of m' into (c_1', c_2'). This follows since m' is independent from the message m to be decrypted. In contrast, the CHES 2015 approach does not allow to precompute any of the values from Eq. 1 nor Eq. 2. This potential precomputation minimizes the impact of the countermeasure on the running time, as detailed in the next section.

Simplicity. The implementation complexity of our solution is remarkably low, both in software or hardware. In comparison, the CHES 2015 approach would need a careful implementation of the masked decoder block. This block is delicate to implement. In particular, the practitioner should pay careful attention to leaking distances if implemented in software, since during the masked decoding both shares are handled in contiguous temporal locations. In hardware comparable observations apply during the implementation of the masked tables.

In contrast, our approach is very easy to implement. The implementation handles both shares of all intermediates far from each other, minimizing the possibility of unintended interferences between shares (and thus first-order leaks).

Is the masked decoder needed? In this paragraph we would like to point out an important difference between the CHES 2015 approach and the one presented in Sect. 3. Namely, in this paper we do not require a masked decoder, while the CHES 2015 solution does. One can wonder if the masked decoder of the CHES 2015 approach is really needed: after all, Eq. 3 may seem to imply that the decoding function is linear. However, this is clearly not the case.

The difference is that, in our additively-homomorphic masking scheme the inputs to the decoder are coefficients resulting from the *proper* decryption with respect to the secret key s, and hence the input coefficients are distributed around 0 or $q/2$. Whereas in the CHES 2015 approach, the shared coefficients a' and a''

in (Eqs. 1 and 2) are not *individually* proper decryptions of a valid message; and hence are uniformly distributed in $(\mathbb{F}_q, \mathbb{F}_q)$. This is why the CHES 2015 requires a custom decoder, whereas our masking scheme does not.

4.3 Error Rates

The LPR encryption scheme is probabilistic in nature, i.e. the decryption of a valid ciphertext may produce an incorrect plaintext with a small probability. A decryption failure occurs when the noise in the coefficient-to-be-decoded exceeds the threshold value of the decoder. In our additive masking scheme the addition of two ciphertexts also adds the noises present in the two ciphertexts: the error coefficients in the new ciphertext could be at most one bit larger than the error coefficients in the two ciphertexts. This larger noise increases the decryption failure rate. To know the exact decryption failure rate we performed experiments for the parameter set $(n, q, \sigma) = (256, 7681, 4.51)$ [GFS+12] corresponding to a medium-level security. The parameter set was used in [PG14, RVM+14, dCRVV15, LSR+15, POG15] to implement encryption schemes. When the masking is turned off, the decryption failure rate is 3.6×10^{-5} per bit. The failure rate increases to 3.3×10^{-3} per bit when the masking turned on.

The increase in the decryption failure rate can be compensated at the cost of a minor deterioration in the security by using the techniques as follows.

– The modulus q can be increased by one bit. This increment in the size of q (from 13 bits to 14 bits) does not slow down our software implementation since the underlying processor architecture is 32 bit, and hence the processing times for both 13 and 14 bit coefficients are the same.
– As suggested by one of the anonymous reviewers, decreasing the standard deviation σ of the discrete Gaussian distribution may be more effective than increasing the size of q as the final noise is in the order of σ^2.

5 Implementation Results

The presented masking scheme is suitable for implementation both in hardware and software. We wrote a reference version of the proposed countermeasure in C99. The implementation follows the same lines as de Clercq et al. [dCRVV15].

Overheads. The overhead of our solution with respect to an unprotected decryption is one random message generation, one extra encryption and one coefficient addition. This incurs a negligible code size increase if the encryption operation is available. In terms of speed, the costliest process is the encryption. It is 2.8 times slower than the decryption. However, this computation can be performed in advance before even knowing the ciphertext to be decrypted.

6 Experimental Results

In this section we describe the key-recovery DPA attacks on an ARM Cortex-M4 processor that we performed to assess the security of our solution.

Experimental setup. We compiled the reference implementation with `arm-none-eabi-gcc` version 4.8.4 20140526 without any special optimization flags (note that we do not aim at maximum speed or code efficiency). We flashed an STM32F407VGT6 microcontroller featuring an ARM Cortex-M4 core running at 168 MHz (full speed) and an RNG that "delivers 32-bit random numbers generated by an integrated analog circuit"[1]. We collected contactless power measurements by placing a Langer LF-R 400 magnetic field probe in the vicinity of the chip power supply circuitry as indicated in Fig. 6. Traces are synchronized by a GPIO pin.

Methodology. We follow a standard methodology to assess the security of our countermeasure. We first attack our implementation when the source of randomness is switched off—that is, the whole computation is deterministic. This is equivalent to switching off the countermeasure. Therefore, attacks are expected to work against this mode of operation. Nevertheless, successful attacks in this scenario serve to confirm that the experimental setup is indeed sound. In the second part of our analysis we switch on the randomness to observe security gained exclusively by the countermeasure.

We assume that when the adversary places hypotheses on certain key coefficients, he knows all other key coefficients. This allows the adversary to easily predict intermediates deep into the computation. This adversarial model may seem quite strong; however, due to the mathematical structure of the scheme it is possible to predict deep intermediates with low effort.

An overview EM trace is depicted in Fig. 1. The trace spans the entire protected computation as described in Sect. 3. Features of this EM trace are more visually recognisable in the cross-correlation picture of Fig. 2. We can recognize

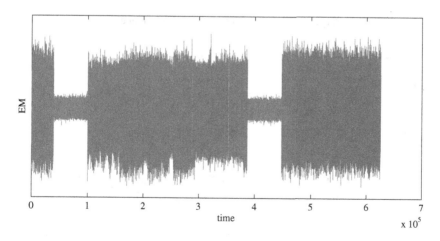

Fig. 1. An exemplary EM trace covering the whole protected decryption. Data series with large number of samples are difficult to plot; patterns are more visible with other plotting techniques cf. Fig. 2.

---

[1] http://www.st.com/web/en/resource/technical/document/datasheet/ DM00037051.pdf.

the two most time-consuming blocks: the encryption of m' and the subsequent computation of decryption$(c_1 + c'_1, c_2 + c'_2)$.

Masks off. We modeled the power consumption of a 32-bit register holding the result of a MUL instruction as the Hamming distance between two consecutive values, and applied standard CPA [BCO04]. When the randomization is switched off the CPA attack is successful. In this scenario the adversary learns the "random"

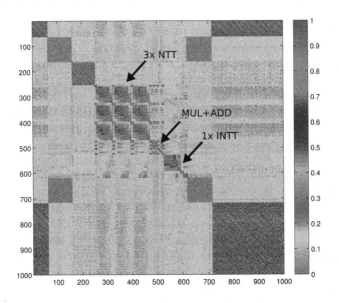

Fig. 2. Cross-correlation of a single trace.

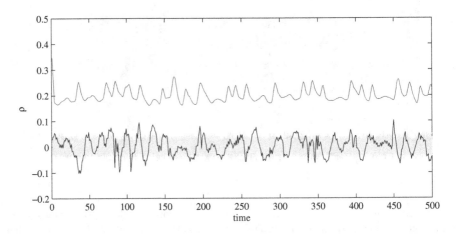

Fig. 3. Top: EM trace in the region where the modular multiplication is performed. The time axis spans around 10 instructions, including MUL.W. Bottom: CPA results. Correct key coefficient hypothesis in black; incorrect hypotheses in grey. Masks off.

values, he can predict any intermediate, and thus the attack is expected to work. Nevertheless, this confirms that the setup is sound.

Figure 3 shows the result of correlating 5000 traces against predictions of an intermediate that appears towards the end of the INTT computation. Note that there are plenty of time samples that allow key-recovery; this is because this intermediate is handled at many other times during the execution of the decryption block.

The evolution of the Pearson's correlation coefficient as the number of traces increases is plotted in Fig. 4. We can see that starting from 1000 measurements the attack is successful.

Masks on. We repeated the same procedure when the randomness is switched on. This is equivalent to activating the countermeasure. At the time of this writing,

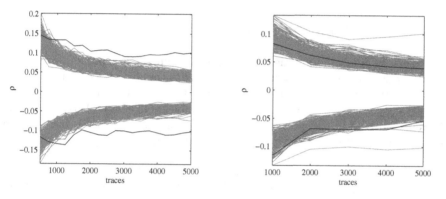

Fig. 4. Evolution of CPA results masks off.   **Fig. 5.** Evolution of CPA results masks on.

Fig. 6. Setup photography showing the orientation of the H-field pick-up probe.

we had available 5000 traces. as Fig. 5 shows. The countermeasure makes harder the DPA attack: the correlation for the correct key hypothesis does not stand out among other key hypothesis. We acknowledge that it is suspiciously high. A more detailed study is planned for the extended version of this paper.

7   Conclusion

In this paper we proposed a new masking scheme for protecting ring-LWE decryption against differential power analysis based attacks. The proposed masking technique is more generic than the state of the art and can be applied to all ring-LWE encryption schemes that are additively homomorphic. Moreover we showed that the masking scheme is easy to implement and does not require any masked decoder circuit or software.

A   An Attack on the Multiplication

An adversary could mount the following attack with a zero-value power model to recover only whether $s[i] = 0$ or not. Note that the distribution of $(c_1 + c_1') \cdot s$ when $s = 0$ and $c_1 + c_1'$ is uniform random is different from the distribution of $(c_1 + c_1') \cdot s$ when $s \neq 0$. This effect resembles [GT02], with the important difference that here the attacker has no control over $(c_1 + c_1')$ and that the outcome of the attack is recovering only whether $s[i] = 0$ or not.

1. locate time samples where $(c_1 + c_1')[i] \cdot s[i]$ is handled $i \in \{0, \ldots, 255\}$.
2. cluster $(c_1 + c_1')[i] \cdot s[i]$ into two groups according to mean power consumption (or variance).
3. tag the two groups as $s[i] = 0$ or $s[i] \neq 0$.

References

[APS13] Aysu, A., Patterson, C., Schaumont, P.: Low-cost and area-efficient FPGA implementations of lattice-based cryptography. In: 2013 IEEE International Symposium on Hardware-Oriented Security and Trust (HOST), pp. 81–86 (2013)

[BCO04] Brier, E., Clavier, C., Olivier, F.: Correlation power analysis with a leakage model. In: Joye, M., Quisquater, J.-J. (eds.) CHES 2004. LNCS, vol. 3156, pp. 16–29. Springer, Heidelberg (2004)

[BLLN13] Bos, J.W., Lauter, K., Loftus, J., Naehrig, M.: Improved security for a ring-based fully homomorphic encryption scheme, Cryptology ePrint Archive, Report 2013/075 (2013). http://eprint.iacr.org/

[BSJ15] Boorghany, A., Sarmadi, S.B., Jalili, R.: On constrained implementation of lattice-based cryptographic primitives and schemes on smart cards. ACM Trans. Embed. Comput. Syst. **14**(3), 42 (2015)

[CJRR99] Chari, S., Jutla, C.S., Rao, J.R., Rohatgi, P.: Towards sound approaches to counteract power-analysis attacks. In: Wiener, M. (ed.) CRYPTO 1999. LNCS, vol. 1666, pp. 398–412. Springer, Heidelberg (1999) [dCRVV15] de Clercq, R., Roy, S.S., Vercauteren, F., Verbauwhede, I.: Efficient software implementation of ring-lwe encryption. In: Nebel, W., Atienza, D. (ed.) Proceedings of the 2015 Design, Automation & Test in Europe Conference & Exhibition, Grenoble, France, 9–13 March 2015, pp. 339–344. ACM (2015)

[FV12] Fan, J., Vercauteren, F.: Somewhat practical fully homomorphic encryption, Cryptology ePrint Archive, Report 2012/144 (2012). http://www.eprint.iacr.org/

[GFS+12] Göttert, N., Feller, T., Schneider, M., Buchmann, J., Huss, S.: On the design of hardware building blocks for modern lattice-based encryption schemes. In: Prouff, E., Schaumont, P. (eds.) CHES 2012. LNCS, vol. 7428, pp. 512–529. Springer, Heidelberg (2012)

[GOPS13] Güneysu, T., Oder, T., Pöppelmann, T., Schwabe, P.: Software speed records for lattice-based signatures. In: Gaborit, P. (ed.) PQCrypto 2013. LNCS, vol. 7932, pp. 67–82. Springer, Heidelberg (2013)

[GP99] Goubin, L., Patarin, J.: DES and differential power analysis. In: Koç, Ç.K., Paar, C. (eds.) CHES 1999. LNCS, vol. 1717, pp. 158–172. Springer, Heidelberg (1999)

[GT02] Golic, J.D., Tymen, T.: Multiplicative masking and power analysis of AES, cryptographic hardware and embedded systems - CHES 2002. In: Kaliski Jr, Burton S., Koç, Çetin Kaya, Paar, Christof (eds.) CHES 2002. LNCS, vol. 2523, pp. 198–212. Springer, Heidelberg (2002)

[KJJ99] Kocher, P.C., Jaffe, J., Jun, B.: Differential Power Analysis. In: Wiener, M. (ed.) CRYPTO 1999. LNCS, vol. 1666, pp. 388–397. Springer, Heidelberg (1999)

[Koc96] Kocher, P.C.: Timing attacks on implementations of Diffie-Hellman, RSA, DSS, and other systems. In: Koblitz, N. (ed.) CRYPTO 1996. LNCS, vol. 1109, pp. 104–113. Springer, Heidelberg (1996)

[LPR10] Lyubashevsky, V., Peikert, C., Regev, O.: On ideal lattices and learning with errors over rings. In: Gilbert, H. (ed.) EUROCRYPT 2010. LNCS, vol. 6110, pp. 1–23. Springer, Heidelberg (2010)

[LSR+15] Liu, Z., Seo, H., Roy, S.S. Großschädl, J., Kim, H., Verbauwhede, I.: Efficient ring-lwe encryption on 8-bit avr processors, Cryptology ePrint Archive, Report 2015/410 (2015). http://eprint.iacr.org/

[nsa15] Cryptography today, Last Modified on 19, Aug 2015. https://www.nsa.gov/ia/programs/suiteb_cryptography/index.shtml

[PDG14] Pöppelmann, T., Ducas, L., Güneysu, T.: Enhanced lattice-based signatures on reconfigurable hardware. In: Batina, L., Robshaw, M. (eds.) CHES 2014. LNCS, vol. 8731, pp. 353–370. Springer, Heidelberg (2014)

[PG14] Pöppelmann, T., Güneysu, T.: Towards practical lattice-based public-key encryption on reconfigurable hardware. In: Lange, T., Lauter, K., Lisoněk, P. (eds.) SAC 2013. LNCS, vol. 8282, pp. 68–86. Springer, Heidelberg (2014)

[POG15] Pöppelmann, T., Oder, T., Güneys, T.: High-performance ideal lattice-based cryptography on 8-bit atxmega microcontrollers, Cryptology ePrint Archive, Report 2015/382 (2015). http://eprint.iacr.org/

[Reg05] Regev, O.: On lattices, learning with errors, random linear codes, and cryptography. In: Proceedings of the Thirty-seventh Annual ACM Symposium on Theory of Computing, New York, NY, USA, STOC 2005, pp. 84–93. ACM (2005)

[RRVV15] Reparaz, O., Roy, S.S., Vercauteren, F., Verbauwhede, I.: A masked ring-LWE implementation. In: Güneysu, T., Handschuh, H. (eds.) CHES 2015. LNCS, vol. 9293, pp. 683–702. Springer, Heidelberg (2015)

[RVM+14] Roy, S.S., Vercauteren, F., Mentens, N., Chen, D.D., Verbauwhede, I.: Compact ring-LWE cryptoprocessor. In: Batina, L., Robshaw, M. (eds.) CHES 2014. LNCS, vol. 8731, pp. 371–391. Springer, Heidelberg (2014)

[RVV14] Roy, S.S., Vercauteren, F., Verbauwhede, I.: High precision discrete gaussian sampling on FPGAs. In: Lange, T., Lauter, K., Lisoněk, P. (eds.) SAC 2013. LNCS, vol. 8282, pp. 383–401. Springer, Heidelberg (2014)

[Sho99] Shor, P.W.: Polynomial-time algorithms for prime factorization and discrete logarithms on a quantum computer. SIAM Review. **41**, 303–332 (1999)

A Homomorphic LWE Based E-voting Scheme

Ilaria Chillotti[1]([✉]), Nicolas Gama[1,2], Mariya Georgieva[3],
and Malika Izabachène[4]

[1] Laboratoire de Mathématiques de Versailles, UVSQ, CNRS,
Université Paris-Saclay, 78035 Versailles, France
ilaria.chillotti@uvsq.fr
[2] Inpher, Lausanne, Switzerland
[3] Gemalto, 6 rue de la Verrerie, 92190 Meudon, France
mariya.georgieva@gemalto.com
[4] CEA LIST, Point Courrier 172, 91191 Gif-sur-Yvette Cedex, France
malika.izabachene@cea.fr

Abstract. In this paper we present a new post-quantum electronic-voting protocol. Our construction is based on LWE fully homomorphic encryption and the protocol is inspired by existing e-voting schemes, in particular Helios. The strengths of our scheme are its simplicity and transparency, since it relies on public homomorphic operations. Furthermore, the use of lattice-based primitives greatly simplifies the proofs of correctness, privacy and verifiability, as no zero-knowledge proof are needed to prove the validity of individual ballots or the correctness of the final election result. The security of our scheme is based on classical SIS/LWE assumptions, which are asymptotically as hard as worst-case lattice problems and relies on the random oracle heuristic. We also propose a new procedure to distribute the decryption task, where each trustee provides an independent proof of correct decryption in the form of a *publicly verifiable ciphertext trapdoor*. In particular, our protocol requires only two trustees, unlike classical proposals using threshold decryption via Shamir's secret sharing.

Keywords: E-vote · Post quantum · Fully homomorphic encryption · Lattice based protocol · LWE

1 Introduction

Electronic-voting aims at providing several elaborated properties. Basically, an e-voting protocol should ensure privacy and verifiability. The first one prevents anyone from retrieving the vote of a particular user, and the second one allows each voter to verify that his vote appears in the bulletin board (individual verifiability) and ensures that the final count of votes corresponds to the votes of legitimate voters (universal verifiability). Also, the scheme is correct when the outcome of the election counts the votes of the honestly generated votes. Among other desirable properties for e-voting schemes, there are strong forms

© Springer International Publishing Switzerland 2016
T. Takagi (Ed.): PQCrypto 2016, LNCS 9606, pp. 245–265, 2016.
DOI: 10.1007/978-3-319-29360-8_16

of privacy such as receipt-freeness, coercion-resistance and ballot independence. Defining security properties for electronic based systems has long been debated and the design of secure e-voting protocols achieving all these properties happens to be more intricate than for traditional paper-based systems. Several proposal appeared over the last years and could be categorized in different ways, depending on how the privacy is guaranteed or the tally function is implemented. However, until now, the security of all provably secure protocols still rely on classical assumptions. This means that these proposed schemes could all be compromised if efficient quantum computers arise. Therefore, designing a quantum resistant e-voting scheme is very challenging, and it is a promising approach to comfort people in using e-voting protocols. This paper is a first step towards this goal.

In this paper we present a new e-voting protocol build on post quantum cryptographic primitives: unforgeable lattice-based signatures, LWE-based homomorphic encryption and trapdoors for lattices. The scheme is inspired by existing e-voting protocols, in particular Helios [2], which has already been used for medium-scale elections (and its variant Belenios). However, our scheme differs in two principal ways. The underlying primitive is different: Helios [1] is a remote e-voting protocol based on the additive property of ElGamal (which is broken by Shor's quantum algorithm). Since additive homomorphism lacks some expressiveness, each voter must ensure that the plaintext encrypted in their ballot has a specific shape, suitable for homomorphic additions. For example, if the voter gives one ciphertext per candidate, he must prove that all these ciphertexts encrypt 0, except the one corresponding to the chosen candidate, which encrypts 1. Proving such semantic properties on the plaintext without revealing its content was usually achieved using zero-knowledge proofs. In our protocol, the fully homomorphic encryption based on Ducas and Micciancio [13] bootstrapping allows to efficiently transform full-domain ciphertexts into such ciphertexts with specific semantic. This effectively removes the need of a ZK proof.

Helios uses another zero-knowledge proof in the final phase of the voting protocol, when the trustees decrypt the final result of the votes and must prove that this result is correct without revealing their own secret. In our protocol, this proof is replaced by *publicly verifiable ciphertext trapdoors*, which are produced using techniques borrowed from trapdoor-based lattice signatures, GPV [15], or [21], based on Ajtai's SIS problem.

Interestingly, combining these publicly verifiable ciphertext trapdoors with the inherent randomness of LWE-samples simplifies a lot the proof of a variant of the strongest game-based ballot privacy recently introduced by [5, Definition 7], since all the proposed oracles (except one) essentially follow the protocol, and the simulator, which is usually the most complex part of the game, is simply the identity function.

Our protocol also satisfies correctness and verifiability in the sense of [17]. In order to deter the bulletin board from stuffing itself, we add an additional authority in charge of providing each user with a private and public credential which allows him to sign his vote. This solution was already used in the variant of Helios proposed in [10]. And to compute his vote, the user encrypts his vote expressed as a sequence of 0/1, and signs the ciphertext along its public credential and sends it to the bulletin board. Cortier and Smyth [11, 24] shows that homomorphic based e-voting protocols and in particular Helios could be vulnerable to replay attacks that allow a user to cast a vote related to a previously cast ballot. This type of attacks could possibly incur a bias on the vote of other users and break privacy. Although this attack has a small impact in practice, the model for privacy should capture such attacks. Until now, this attack is prevented by removing ballots which contains a ciphertext that does already appear in a previously cast ballot. This operation is called cipherext weeding. This strategy would not work with fully homomorphic schemes, as bootstrapping operations would allow an attacker to re-randomize duplicated ballots beyond anything one can detect.

In this paper, we use the one-wayness of the bootstrapping to create some "plaintext-awareness" auxiliary information. This auxiliary information is not needed to prove the verifiability of the scheme. This information could be viewed as another encryption of the same ballot, hence it does not leak information on the plaintext vote. The only purpose of this auxiliary information is to guarantee that the ballot has not been copied or crafted from other ballots in the bulletin board as publicly viewed by other users. Thus, the voter sends this info with his ballot, which remains encrypted in the bulletin board until the end of the voting phase. At this point, for the sake of transparency, it could be safely revealed to everyone. In practice, we model this temporarily private channel by giving a public key to the bulletin board, and letting him reveal the private key at the end of the voting phase.

Finally, in order to guarantee privacy even when some of the authorities keys are corrupted, we show that our encryption scheme can be distributed among t trustees. Instead of using a threshold decryption based on Shamir's secret sharing, we rely on a simple concatenated LWE scheme. Each of the trustees carries its own decryption part, and any attempt to cheat is publicly detected. On one hand, we lose the optional ability to reconstruct the result if some trustees attempt a denial of service (which can be prevented anyway by taking the appropriate legal measures). On the other hand, once the public key has been set, we detect any attempt to cheat even if all the trustees collude. And as a bonus, our protocol can be instantiated with only two trustees which operate independently. In comparison, at least three trustees are needed for Shamir's interpolation, and if they all collude, they could produce a valid proof for a false result.

Open Problems: Our definition of an e-voting scheme differs from previous ones in that the bulletin board is carried with an additional secret to decide whether a ballot should be cast or not, but this secret key could be publicly disclosed after the voting phase. We define correctness and verifiability as in [17] and propose an adaptation of the recent definition of privacy [5] to our setting. Due to the constraint on the validation of a ballot before it is cast, the definition of the strong consistency property [5, Definition 8] does not adapt properly to our setting, and thus, we leave the definition of proper extensions to strong correctness and strong consistency and privacy models against a malicious bulletin board and/or corrupted registration authority for a future work.

Finally, our proof of privacy relies on an arguably strong assumption, where a properly randomized bootstrapping function is modeled as a random oracle. We require this assumption in order to successfully simulate the Tally in the privacy game, and to a lesser extent, when we use Micciancio and Peikert's trapdoors to sample small solutions for SIS without revealing information on the trapdoor or on the keys. Proving the same result in the standard model is still an open problem.

2   Preliminaries

In the following, we specify the definition and the properties we consider for our e-voting protocol.

2.1   Definition of Single Pass E-voting Schemes

In a single pass e-voting scheme, each user publishes only one message to cast his vote in the bulletin board. A voting scheme is specified by a family of result functions denoted as $\rho : (\mathcal{I} \times \mathbb{V})^* \to \mathcal{R}$ where $\mathbb{V}$ is the set of all possible vote, $\mathcal{I}$ is the set of voter's identifiers, $\mathcal{R}$ specifies the space of possible result. A voting scheme is also associated to a re-vote policy. In our case, we will assume that the last vote is taken into account. The entities are:

- A_1: the authority that handles the registration of users and updates the public list of legitimate voters.
- BB, the bulletin board; The bulletin board checks the well-formedness of received ballots before they are cast. In our model, we assume that BB uses a secret key to perform a part of this task but the secret could be revealed after the voting phase.
- $\mathcal{T}$: a set of trustee(s) in charge of setting up their own decryption keys, and computing the final tally function.

Let λ denote the security parameter. We denote as ℓ the number of candidates, L an upper bound on the number of voters and t the number of trustees. We denote as $\mathcal{L}_\mathcal{U}$ a public list of users set at empty at the beginning. To simplify, we assume an authenticated private channel between the trustees. For our description, we will be given $\mathcal{S} = (\mathsf{KeyGenS}, \mathsf{Sign}, \mathsf{VerifyS})$ an existentially unforgeable scheme and $\mathcal{E} = (\mathsf{KeyGenE_{BB}}, \mathsf{Enc_{BB}}, \mathsf{Dec_{BB}})$ a non-malleable encryption scheme both assumed quantum resistant. The algorithms associated to a single pass e-voting scheme could be defined as follows:

- $(\mathsf{sk} = (\mathsf{sk}_1, \ldots, \mathsf{sk}_t), \mathsf{params}) \leftarrow \mathsf{Setup}(1^\lambda, t, \ell, L)$: Each trustee chooses its secret key sk_i and publishes a public information pk_i and proves that it knows the corresponding secret w.r.t the published public key.

The bulletin board runs $(\mathsf{pk}_{\mathsf{BB}}, \mathsf{sk}_{\mathsf{BB}}) \leftarrow \mathsf{KeyGenE}_{\mathsf{BB}}(1^\lambda)$, it publishes $\mathsf{pk}_{\mathsf{BB}}$ and keeps $\mathsf{sk}_{\mathsf{BB}}$ private. This step implicitly defines the public pk of the e-voting scheme that includes $\mathsf{pk}_{\mathsf{BB}}$. The parameters params includes the public key pk, the numbers t, ℓ, L, the list $\mathcal{L}_\mathcal{U}$ and the set of valid votes $\mathbb{V}$. All these parameters are taken as input to all the following algorithms.

- $(\mathsf{usk}, \mathsf{upk}) \leftarrow \mathsf{Register}(1^\lambda, \mathsf{id})$: on input a security parameter and a user identity, it provides the secret part of the user credential usk and its public part upk. It updates the public list $\mathcal{L}_\mathcal{U}$ with upk.
- $b \leftarrow \mathsf{Vote}(\mathsf{pk}, \mathsf{usk}, \mathsf{upk}, v)$: It takes as input a secret credential and public credential that possibly inclides id and a vote $v \in \mathbb{V}$. It outputs a ballot b which consists in a content message that includes upk, an encryption c of v, an auxiliary information aux encrypted using the key $\mathsf{pk}_{\mathsf{BB}}$ and a version number num plus a signature of this content message under the secret usk.
- $\mathsf{ProcessBB}(\mathsf{BB}, b, \mathsf{sk}_{\mathsf{BB}})$ As long as the bulletin board is open, when the bulletin board manager receives a ballot b: its parses it as $(\mathsf{aux}, \mathsf{upk}, c, \mathsf{num}, \sigma)$, verifies that $\mathsf{upk} \in \mathcal{L}_\mathcal{U}$ and uses upk to verify the signature of the ballot. Then he decrypts aux using $\mathsf{sk}_{\mathsf{BB}}$. And it performs a validity check on b and upk and finally verifies the revote policy with the version number. If b passes all these checks, it is added in BB, otherwise BB remains unchanged.
- $(\Pi_1, \ldots, \Pi_t) \leftarrow \mathsf{Tally}(\mathsf{BB}, \mathsf{sk}_1, \ldots, \mathsf{sk}_t)$: Once the voting phase is closed and the public bulletin board is published together with $\mathsf{sk}_{\mathsf{BB}}$, each trustee $T \in \mathcal{T}$ takes as input the public bulletin board BB, and its own secret key to produce a partial proof Π_i, which is publicly disclosed.
- $\mathsf{VerifyTally}(\mathsf{BB}, (\Pi_1, \ldots, \Pi_t))$: (public) takes as input t partial proofs associated to a given bulletin board BB and verifies that each individual proof Π_i is correct, and uses all of them to decrypt. It outputs a final result r and $\bot$ in case of failure.

Correctness. In this paper, we only address correctness in the case where the bulletin board is supposed to be honest. In particular, it is not allowed to stuff itself or suppress valid ballots cast by honest users. Correctness for an e-voting scheme states that, if users follow the protocol, then the tally leads to the result of the election on the submitted votes. Considering an honest execution as follows: Assume $(\mathsf{sk}, \mathsf{params} = (\mathsf{pk}, \ldots)) \leftarrow \mathsf{Setup}(1^\lambda, t, \ell, L)$ and $p = \#\mathcal{V} = \#\mathcal{I}$, where $\mathcal{V}$ is the set of valid votes whose users' identifiers lie in $\mathcal{I} = \{\mathsf{id}_1, \ldots, \mathsf{id}_p\}$. Denote as BB_i the set of the first i valid ballots cast corresponding to valid votes in $\mathcal{V}$. Then $\mathsf{ProcessBB}(\mathsf{BB}_{i-1}, b_i, \mathsf{sk}_{\mathsf{BB}})$ adds $b_i \leftarrow \mathsf{Vote}(\mathsf{pk}, \mathsf{usk}, \mathsf{upk}, v_i)$ in BB_{i-1} for all $i \leq p$ and some $\mathsf{id} \in \mathcal{I}$ s.t. $(\mathsf{usk}, \mathsf{upk}) \leftarrow \mathsf{Register}(1^\lambda, \mathsf{id})$. Also $(\Pi_1, \ldots, \Pi_t) \leftarrow \mathsf{Tally}(\mathsf{BB}_p, \mathsf{sk})$ where $\mathsf{VerifyTally}(\mathsf{BB}_p, (\Pi_1, \ldots, \Pi_t)) = r$ and $r = \rho(v_1, \ldots, v_p)$.

2.2 Security Model

Privacy. Several models for privacy have been introduced over the last years. In this paper, we will use a simulation-based definition inspired from the definition recently proposed in [5]. The challenger maintains two bulletin boards BB_0 and BB_1. It randomly chooses $\beta \in \{0, 1\}$ and the adversary will be given access to

BB_β. The adversary can corrupt a subset of the trustees and the adversary can vote for candidate of his choice and cast ballots. The tally is computed on the real board in both worlds. At the end, it should not be able to tell the difference. The procedures and oracles given as access to the adversary in the definitional game are defined as follows:

- $\mathsf{Init}(1^\lambda, t, \ell, L)$: This procedure is run at the beginning interactively by the challenger and the adversary. The lists $\mathcal{L}_\mathcal{U}$ (published), $\mathcal{L}'_\mathcal{U}$ (kept by the challenger) of registered users and $\mathcal{L}_{\mathcal{CU}}$ of corrupted users are initialized at empty. The adversary might corrupt a subset ($< t$) of trustees when running the Setup algorithm and deviate from the algorithm specification. At the end, the non-corrupted secret keys are derived as well as the BB's secret key $\mathsf{sk}_{\mathsf{BB}}$ and the public parameters $(t, \ell, L, \mathcal{L}_\mathcal{U}, \mathbb{V}, \mathsf{pk})$ are published.
- $\mathsf{ORegister}(\mathsf{id})$: it checks whether an entry $(\mathsf{id}, *)$ appears in $\mathcal{L}'_\mathcal{U}$. If yes, it aborts, otherwise it runs the algorithm $\mathsf{Register}(1^\lambda, \mathsf{id})$. It updates $\mathcal{L}_\mathcal{U}$ and $\mathcal{L}'_\mathcal{U}$ with upk_id and $(\mathsf{id}, \mathsf{upk}_\mathsf{id})$ respectively. It outputs upk_id.
- $\mathsf{OCorruptU}(\mathsf{id})$: it checks whether $(\mathsf{id}, *)$ appears in $\mathcal{L}_{\mathcal{CU}}$. If yes, it returns the corresponding usk_id. Otherwise it checks whether id has been registered using $\mathcal{L}'_\mathcal{U}$. If not, it calls $\mathsf{ORegister}$ on input id. It outputs $(\mathsf{upk}_\mathsf{id}, \mathsf{usk}_\mathsf{id})$ and updates $\mathcal{L}_{\mathcal{CU}}$ with $(\mathsf{id}, \mathsf{upk}_\mathsf{id}, \mathsf{usk}_\mathsf{id})$.
- $\mathsf{OVote}(\mathsf{id}, v_0, v_1)$: if some entry $(\mathsf{id}, \mathsf{upk}_\mathsf{id}, \mathsf{usk}_\mathsf{id})$ does not exist in $\mathcal{L}'_\mathcal{U}$ or $v_0, v_1 \notin \mathbb{V}$, it halts. Else, it updates $\mathsf{BB}_i \leftarrow \mathsf{BB}_i \cup \{\mathsf{Vote}(\mathsf{pk}, \mathsf{upk}_\mathsf{id}, \mathsf{usk}_\mathsf{id}, v_i)\}$ for $i = 0, 1$. Here the adversary has access to the public view of BB and thus to the associated ballot b.
- $\mathsf{OCast}(\mathsf{id}, b)$: if $\mathsf{upk}_\mathsf{id} \notin \mathcal{L}_\mathcal{U}$, it halts. Otherwise it parses b and checks its validity w.r.t upk_id and the auxiliary information inside the submitted ballot using $\mathsf{sk}_{\mathsf{BB}}$. If b passes the checks, it adds b to BB_i for $i = 0, 1$.
- $\mathsf{OTally}()$: This procedure is run only once when the voting phase is closed. It runs $(\Pi_1, \dots, \Pi_t) \leftarrow \mathsf{Tally}(\mathsf{BB}_0, \mathsf{sk}_1, \dots, \mathsf{sk}_t)$ s.t. $r = \mathsf{VerifyTally}(\mathsf{BB}_0, (\Pi_1, \dots, \Pi_t))$. For $\beta = 0$, it returns $(\Pi_1, \dots, \Pi_t)$. For $\beta = 1$, it returns $(\Pi'_1, \dots, \Pi'_t) \leftarrow \mathsf{SimTally}(\Pi_1, \dots, \Pi_t, \mathsf{info})$ s.t. $r' = \mathsf{VerifyTally}(\mathsf{BB}_1, (\Pi'_1, \dots, \Pi'_t))$, where info includes auxiliary information known by the simulator $\mathsf{SimTally}$, and thus not the trustee's private keys. If $r \neq r'$, it halts.

And we define the experiment $\mathsf{Exp}^{\mathsf{bpriv}, \beta}_{\mathcal{A}, \mathsf{Vote}}(\lambda)$ in Fig. 1.

Definition 2.1. We say that a voting protocol Vote has the *ballot privacy* property if there exists an efficient simulator $\mathsf{SimTally}$ such that, for any PPT[1] adversary $\mathcal{A}$, it holds that $\left| \Pr\left[\mathsf{Exp}^{\mathsf{bpriv}, \beta}_{\mathcal{A}, \mathsf{Vote}}(\lambda) = \beta\right] - \frac{1}{2} \right|$ is negligible in λ.

Verifiability. We say that a voting protocol Vote is verifiable if it ensures that the tally verification algorithm does not accept two different results for the same view of the public bulletin board. This condition has to be verified even if in the

---

[1] Probabilistic Polynomial Timing.

Experiment $\mathsf{Exp}^{\mathsf{bpriv},\beta}_{\mathcal{A},\mathsf{Vote}}(\lambda)$

$(\mathbf{pk},\mathbf{sk}) \leftarrow \mathsf{Setup}(1^\lambda, t, \ell, L)$

$\beta' \leftarrow \mathcal{A}^{\mathsf{ORegister},\mathsf{OCorruptU},\mathsf{OVote},\mathsf{OCast},\mathsf{OTally}}(\mathsf{BB}_\beta)$

Experiment $\mathsf{Exp}^{\mathsf{ver}}_{\mathcal{A},\mathsf{Vote}}(\lambda)$

$(\mathsf{params}, \mathsf{sk}_{\mathsf{BB}}, \mathsf{BB}, (\Pi_1, \ldots, \Pi_t), (\Pi'_1, \ldots, \Pi'_t)) \leftarrow \mathcal{A}^{\mathsf{ORegister},\mathsf{OCorruptU}}$

let $r = \mathsf{VerifyTally}(\mathsf{BB}, (\Pi_1, \ldots, \Pi_t))$

let $r' = \mathsf{VerifyTally}(\mathsf{BB}, (\Pi'_1, \ldots, \Pi'_t))$

if $r \neq \perp$ and $r' \neq \perp$ and $r \neq r'$ return 1, else return 0

Fig. 1. The experiments $\mathsf{Exp}^{\mathsf{bpriv},\beta}_{\mathcal{A},\mathsf{Vote}}(\lambda)$ and $\mathsf{Exp}^{\mathsf{ver}}_{\mathcal{A},\mathsf{Vote}}(\lambda)$

presence of malicious adversary corrupting all users except $\mathcal{A}_1$. The adversary still have access to the $\mathsf{ORegister}, \mathsf{OCorrupt}$ oracles.

We define the experiment $\mathsf{Exp}^{\mathsf{ver}}_{\mathcal{A},\mathsf{Vote}}(\lambda)$ in Fig. 1.

Definition 2.2. We say that a voting protocol Vote is *verifiable* if for any PPT adversary $\mathcal{A}$, it holds that $Succ^{\mathsf{ver}}(\mathcal{A}) = \Pr\left[\mathsf{Exp}^{\mathsf{ver}}_{\mathcal{A},\mathsf{Vote}}(\lambda) = 1\right]$ is negligible in λ.

3 (Cryptographic) Building Blocks

Our scheme is built on the following post-quantum building blocks: Existentially unforgeable Signatures, Non-malleable Encryption, LWE-based Homomorphic Encryption, Trapdoors for lattices.

3.1 Signatures

The signature is used by the voter to sign the ballot. The security of the signature scheme in our protocol should be based on post-quantum assumptions. In our scheme, we rely on the hardness of finding short vectors in a lattice. One example of lattice-based signature was proposed in [12] inspired by Lyubashevsky's scheme [19].

3.2 Scale-Invariant LWE Encryption

Our protocol strongly relies on the Learning With Errors problem, first introduced by Regev in [23], and improved to obtain ring variants [20] and homomorphic encryption [4,7,8,13,16].

To ease the presentation, we use a normal form notation for LWE which captures its inherent scale-invariant property by working directly in the unit torus $\mathbb{T} = \mathbb{R}/\mathbb{Z}$, not only for the right member like in Regev's original description [23], but also for the left member (i.e. no modulus q or other technical rounding). The LWE secret is decomposed as bits. This separates the main hardness parameters (i.e. entropy of secret and error rate) from implementation or optimization technicalities (which takes the form of some unspecified, and not so important discretization group). Furthermore, this representation is easy to obtain from any classical representation, and will allow us to study homomorphic protocols by reasoning directly on the (hidden) plaintext and the continuous noise.

Definition 3.1 (LWE Scale-Invariant Normal Form). Let $\alpha \in \mathbb{R}^+$ be a noise parameter, $(s_1, ..., s_n)$ be a uniformly distributed binary secret in $\mathbb{B}^n$, and $G \subseteq \mathbb{T}^n$ be a sufficiently dense[2] finite discretization group. We note $\mathsf{LWE}(s, \alpha, G)$ the following scale-invariant Learning with errors instance. A random LWE Sample from $\mathsf{LWE}(s, \alpha, G)$ of a message $\mu \in \mathbb{T}$ is mathematically defined as an element $(a, b) \in G \times \mathbb{T}$ where: the left term $a = (a_1, ..., a_n) \in G \subset \mathbb{T}^n$ is (indistinguishable from) a uniform sample of G and the right term b is equal to $\sum_{i=1}^n s_i a_i + \mu + e \in \mathbb{T}$ where e is statistically close from a zero-centered continuous Gaussian sample of $\mathbb{T}$ of parameter α.

Definition 3.2 (Phase). We define the *phase* of a LWE sample $(a, b) \in \mathbb{T}^n \times \mathbb{T}$ as $\varphi_s((a, b)) = b - \sum_{i=1}^n s_i a_i \in \mathbb{T}$.

As a straightforward example, a classical sample $(a, b) \in \mathbb{Z}_q^n$ of integer LWE with binary secret and binary noise, denoted as $\mathsf{binLWE}(n, q, 1.4)$ in [6] or [13] corresponds to the normal form sample $(\frac{a}{q}, \frac{b}{q}) \in \mathbb{T}^{n+1}$. In this case, the left member is uniformly distributed over the discretized group $G = (\frac{1}{q}\mathbb{Z}/\mathbb{Z})^n$, and the error rate α is $\approx 1/q$. If the secret is not binary, classical binary-decomposition methods (see for instance the $\mathsf{BitDecomp}$ and $\mathsf{PowersOfTwo}$ methods from [7, Sect. 3.2]) can quickly put the sample into normal form.

Security. The security of LWE therefore relies on the two other parameters: the number n of bits or entropy in the secret, and the Gaussian error parameter α. Figure 3 in the appendix summarizes the practical secure choices for (n, α), according to standard lattice reduction estimates (see [9]). In particular, for α equal to 2^{-10}, 2^{-30} or 2^{-50}, LWE is 128-bit secure as soon as $n \geq 300$, 800 and 1500 respectively, if no better attack than the lattice embedding exists. Furthermore, for any α and $n = \Omega(\log(1/\alpha))$, LWE asymptotically benefits from the worst-case to average case reduction (see [3,15,22,23] or [14] depending on the shape of G).

The choice of the discretization group G controls the efficiency, but not the security of LWE. Indeed, as a simple reformulation of the Modulus-dimension reduction from [6, Corollaries 3.2 and 3.3, Theorem 4.1] or the Group switching from [14, Lemma 6.3, Corollary 6.4], groups $G \subset \mathbb{T}^n$ can be swapped as long as

---

[2] Technically speaking, the smoothing parameter of the real lattice $G + \mathbb{Z}^n$ must be smaller than $\alpha/\sqrt{2n}$, as implied by [14] or [6].

they are sufficiently dense to not interfere with the result of the phase (i.e. decryption) function from Definition 3.1. Since this function is $1/\sqrt{n}$-lipschitzian from $\mathbb{T}^n \to \mathbb{T}$, and has a precision α, it means that $\#G$ can always be chosen as small as $\log_2(\#G) = \tilde{O}(n \log_2(\alpha))$, which will be assumed in the remaining of the paper.

3.3 LWE Symmetric Encryption

In Definition 3.1, we define LWE samples with continuous messages $\mu \in \mathbb{T}$. The meaning of this message is natural for freshly generated LWE samples, but is less obvious when a sample is obtained as a combination of other samples. In all cases, the message μ and resp. the noise parameter α of a LWE sample c can mathematically (and not computationally) be defined as the center and resp. the Gaussian parameter of the distribution of its phase $\varphi_s(c)$. Here, the probability space consists in re-sampling all Gaussian error terms of all fresh LWE samples, and in resampling all random choices that were made in decomposition or bootstrapping algorithms.

Given a security parameter λ, the noise amplitude $\bar{\alpha}$ is the smallest distance such that $|\mu - \varphi_s(c)| \leq \bar{\alpha}$ with probability $\geq 1 - 2^{-\lambda}$. It typically means $\bar{\alpha} = \alpha \cdot \sqrt{\lambda/\pi}$. For a fixed security parameter, amplitude and parameters are just proportional one to each other. Bootstrapping and decryption operations are in general easier to present in terms of amplitude rather than parameter, because it better depicts the actual noise that we get.

To algorithmically extract the message from a LWE sample c like in usual decryption algorithms, we need an external information on the message: usually, μ belongs to a discrete message space $\mathcal{M}$ of packing radius $\geq \bar{\alpha}$. In this case, the message of c is computed by rounding its phase $\varphi_s(c)$ to the closest point in $\mathcal{M}$. We note this $\mathsf{LWEDecrypt}_{\mathcal{M},s}(c)$. And in this context, we will also write $\mathsf{LWESymEncrypt}_{s,\alpha,G}(\mu)$ the operation which consists in generating a random $\mathsf{LWE}(s, \alpha, G)$ sample of $\mu \in \mathcal{M}$.

3.4 Homomorphism

LWE samples satisfy a straightforward linear homomorphism property, which follows from continuous Gaussian convolution:

Proposition 3.3 (Linear Homomorphism). *Let $c_1, \ldots, c_p$ be p independent LWE samples of messages $\mu_1, \ldots, \mu_p \in \mathbb{T}$ and noise parameters $\alpha_1, \ldots, \alpha_p$, and let $x_1, \ldots, x_p \in \mathbb{Z}$ be p integer coefficients. Then the sample $c = \sum_{i=1}^{p} x_i c_i$ is a valid encryption of the message $\mu = \sum_{i=1}^{p} x_i \mu_i$ with square noise parameter $\alpha^2 \leq \sum_{i=1}^{p} x_i^2 \alpha_i^2$.*

If non-linear operations are needed, one may use the following theorem, which can be viewed as an abstracted (and slightly generalized) version of the Bootstrapping theorem of Ducas and Micciancio [13].

Theorem 3.4 (General Bootstrapping Theorem). *Let* λ *denote a security parameter. Let* $\mathcal{E} = LWE(s, \beta, G)$ *and* $\mathcal{E}' = LWE(s', \alpha, G')$ *be two instances of LWE with respective* n *and* n'*-bit secrets* $s \in \mathbb{B}^n$ *and* $s' \in \mathbb{B}^{n'}$*. We note* $\bar{\alpha}$ *and* $\bar{\beta}$ *their respective noise amplitudes. Let* $\mathcal{M} \subseteq \mathbb{T}$ *be an input message space at distance* d *from* $\{-\frac{1}{4}, \frac{1}{4}\}$*, and* N *be a power of two at least of the order of* $\sqrt{(\lambda n)/(d^2 - \bar{\beta}^2)}$*. If* (n, β) *and* $(n', \alpha/\lambda\sqrt{n(N + n\log(\beta))})$ *are both* λ*-bit secure LWE parameters, then, there exists a bootstrapping key* $BK_{[(s,\bar{\beta}) \to (s',\bar{\alpha})]}$ *and a polynomial bootstrapping algorithm which takes as input the bootstrapping key, a sample from* $\mathcal{E}$ *and two points* $(\mu'_0, \mu'_1) \in \mathbb{T}^2$ *of our choice, and simulates the following algorithm without knowing the secrets:*

$$Bootstrap_{BK}(c, \mu'_1, \mu'_0) =$$

$$\begin{cases} LWESymEncrypt_{s',\alpha,G'}(\mu'_1) & \textbf{\textit{if }} d(\varphi_s(c), \frac{1}{2}) < d(\varphi_s(c), 0) \\ LWESymEncrypt_{s',\alpha,G'}(\mu'_0) & \textbf{\textit{otherwise.}} \end{cases}$$

Historically, the first bootstrapping notions were just designed to suppress the input noise of a ciphertext, and optionally to switch its encryption key. But from a plaintext point of view, bootstrapping was just the identity function. In contrast, the bootstrapping function from Theorem 3.4, and which is implicitly used by [13], evaluates the comparator operator (or mux) between its three arguments.

[13] provides a concrete example of $BK_{[(s,\frac{1}{4}-\varepsilon) \to (s,\frac{1}{16})]}$ bootstrapping key for any 500-bit key s, which has 128-bit security and whose bootstrapping algorithm runs in about 700 sequential ms, and which we intend to reuse. They use this key to fully-homomorphically simulate NAND gates between LWE samples of noise amplitude $\bar{\alpha} = \frac{1}{16}$ and message space $\mathcal{M} = \{0, \frac{1}{4}\}$, just by doing $HomNAND(c_1, c_2) = Bootstrap_{BK}((0, \frac{5}{8})\text{-}c_1\text{-}c_2, \frac{1}{4}, 0)$. However, for the final step of our protocol, we will also need to bootstrap to a much lower noise amplitude, which is not covered in [13], although their construction works with minor adjustments.

Theorem 3.4 implies that the output of the bootstrapping function is indistinguishable from a fresh LWE sample of μ'_0 or μ'_1. In fact, it even seems to behave like a good collision-resistant one-way function, especially if we re-randomize the input sample by adding a random combination of the public key. However, for verifiability purposes, one may also wish to control the randomness to reproduce some computations. To simplify the analysis, we will therefore model bootstrapping as a random oracle:

Assumption 3.5 (Bootstrapping as a Random Oracle). In the conditions of Theorem 3.4, the Bootstrap function is assimilated to a random oracle which returns a fresh LWE sample of μ'_b where $b = 1$ iff. $dist(\varphi_s(c), \frac{1}{2}) < dist(\varphi_s(c), 0)$. In particular, the left term a' is always indistinguishable from uniform over G'.

3.5 Publicly Verifiable Decryption for LWE

In the previous section, the LWE normal form with secret $s \in \mathbb{B}^n$ has been presented in a symmetric key manner. To allow public encryption, one usually publishes a polynomial number $m = \Omega(n \log(1/\alpha))$ of random LWE samples of the message 0 with noise parameter α. This is the public key $\mathsf{pk} \in (G \times \mathbb{T})^m$. The public key can equivalently be written as a $m \times (n+1)$ matrix $\mathsf{pk} = [M|\boldsymbol{y}]$ of $\mathbb{T}$ where $\boldsymbol{y} = M\boldsymbol{s}^t + \mathsf{error}$. Public encryption of a message $\mu \in \mathbb{T}$ can then achieved by summing a random subset (of rows) of the public key, and adding the trivial ciphertext $(0, \mu)$ to the result. We call this operation $\mathsf{LWEPubEncrypt}_{\mathsf{pk}}(\mu)$.

In the protocol we will present, this allows a voter to encrypt his vote. Then the BB can publicly use the bootstrapping theorem to homomorphically evaluate whatever circuits produces the (encrypted) final result. And in the end, some trustee must decrypt this result using the secret key. If decrypting a LWE ciphertext on a discrete message space is easy, proving to everyone that the decryption is correct without revealing anything on the LWE secret key requires some more work.

To do so, we adopt a strategy which is borrowed from Lattice-based signatures like GPV [15]. To allow a public decryption of $\boldsymbol{c} \in G \times \mathbb{T}$, we reveal a small integer combination $(x_1, \ldots, x_m)$ of the public key pk which could have been used to encrypt $\boldsymbol{c}$, as in the following definition:

Definition 3.6 (Publicly Verifiable Ciphertext Trapdoor). Let $\mathsf{LWE}(\boldsymbol{s}, \alpha, G)$ be a LWE instance, and $\mathsf{pk} = [M|\boldsymbol{y}] \in (G \times \mathbb{T})^m$ a public key, and $\mathcal{M}$ a discrete message space of packing radius $\geq d$. Let $\boldsymbol{c} = (\boldsymbol{a}, b)$ be a sample with noise amplitude $\leq \bar{\delta}$ and $\beta = \sqrt{(d^2 - \bar{\delta}^2)/\bar{\alpha}^2}$, we say that $\boldsymbol{x} = (x_1, \ldots, x_m) \in \mathbb{Z}^m$ is a ciphertext trapdoor of $\boldsymbol{c}$ if $\|\boldsymbol{x}\| \leq \beta$ and if $\boldsymbol{x} \cdot M = \boldsymbol{a}$ in G.

Anyone who knows the public key can verify the correctness of the ciphertext trapdoor. Furthermore, since the difference $\boldsymbol{c} - \boldsymbol{x} \cdot \mathsf{pk}$ is a trivial ciphertext $(\boldsymbol{0}, b')$ of phase b' of the same message $\mu \in \mathcal{M}$ with noise amplitude $<d$, this reveals the message in the same time.

Of course, finding a small combination of random group elements which is close to some target is related to the subset sum, or the SIS family of problems, which are hard in average. Luckily, the framework proposed in [21], and which we briefly summarize in the next paragraph, introduces an efficient trapdoor solution.

Definition 3.7 (Master Trapdoor as in Definition 5.2 of [21]). Let $\mathsf{LWE}(\boldsymbol{s}, \alpha, G)$ be a λ-bit secure instance of LWE. A Gadget $\mathsf{Gad} \in G^{m'}$ is some publicly known superincreasing generating family of G, such that any element $a \in G$ can be decomposed as a small (or binary) linear combination of Gad. Let A be a uniformly distributed family in $G^{m-m'}$, and let R be a $m' \times (m-m')$ integer matrix with (small) subGaussian entries. We define the matrix $M = \begin{bmatrix} A \\ A' \end{bmatrix} \in G^m$ where $A' = \mathsf{Gad} - R \cdot A$. We call R a *master trapdoor*, and its corresponding public key is $\mathsf{pk} \in (G \times \mathbb{T})^m$, whose i-th row is $\mathsf{pk}_i = (M_i | M_i \cdot \boldsymbol{s} + e_i)$ for some Gaussian noise e_i of parameter α. The master trapdoor verifies the condition $\mathsf{Gad} = [R| \mathit{Id}_{m-m'}] \cdot M$ and the parameters $m, m', m - m' = O(\log_2(\#G))$.

Theorem 3.8 (Adapted from Theorem 5.1 of [21]). *Let* $c \in G \times \mathbb{T}$ *be a* *LWE*(s, δ, G) *sample on a message space of packing radius* $> 2\bar{\delta}$, R *a master trap-* *door of parameter* γ *and* pk *an associated public key with noise* $< \bar{\delta}/\bar{\gamma}\log(\#G)^{1.5}$. *Given* c *and* R, *one may efficiently compute a ciphertext trapdoor* x *for* c *of* *norm* $O(\beta \log(\#G)^{1.5})$. *This trapdoor can decrypt* c, *as in Definition 3.6. Fur-* *thermore, the distribution of the ciphertext trapdoors of* c *is statistically close to* *some discrete Gaussian distribution on* $\mathbb{Z}^m$, *of parameter* $O(\beta \log(\#G)^{0.5})$, *and* *thus, does not reveal any information about* R.

Like square roots oracles for RSA moduli, ciphertext trapdoors are trivially vulnerable to chosen ciphertext attacks, so they should only be invoked on the output of some good hash function, or some random oracle. It is the case for all provable instantiations of trapdoor-based lattice signatures like GPV [15] or [21], and in this paper, we will use the output of the bootstrapping algorithm, which can also be viewed as a random oracle by Assumption 3.5.

3.6 Concatenated LWE, with Distributed Decryption

To prevent a single authority from decrypting individual ballots, or to guaranty privacy in the long term, even if all but one trustee leak their private key, we need to split the LWE secret key among multiple trustees. We do not propose a threshold decryption like Shamir's secret sharing scheme, but instead, a simple concatenation of LWE systems where all the trustees must do their part of the decryption, and any cheater is publicly detected. This requirement seems suffi-cient for an e-voting scheme, and has the additional benefit of being achievable with only two trustees.

Let LWE(s_i, α, G_i) for $i \in [1, t]$ be λ-bit secure instances of LWE, and pk$_i =$ $[M_i | y_i] \in (G \times \mathbb{T})^m$ be the corresponding public keys with associated master trapdoors R_i. We call concatenated LWE the LWE instance whose private key is $s = (s_1 | \dots | s_t)$, discretization group is $G = G_1 \times \dots \times G_t$, and public key is

$$\mathsf{pk} = \begin{bmatrix} M_1 & 0 & 0 & y_1 \\ 0 & \ddots & 0 & \vdots \\ 0 & 0 & M_t & y_t \end{bmatrix} \tag{1}$$

To decrypt such LWE ciphertext (with publicly verifiable decryption) $c = (a_1 | \dots | a_t, b) \in G \times \mathbb{T}$, each of the t trustee independently use his master trapdoor R_i to provide a ciphertext trapdoor Π_i of $(a_i, 0)$, and like in the previous section, the concatenated ciphertext trapdoor $\Pi = (\Pi_1 | \dots | \Pi_t)$ is a ciphertext-trapdoor for c.

Finally, note that even if all trustees leak their private keys except s_1, R_1 (we take 1 for simplicity), then decrypting c rewrites in decrypting the $LWE(s_1, \alpha', G_1)$ ciphertext (a_1, b') where $b' = b - \sum_{i=2}^{t} a_i \cdot s_i$. This is by definition still λ-bit secure. In other words, even in case of collusions between the trustees, the whole scheme remains secure as long as one trustee is honest.

4 Detailed Description of Our E-voting Protocol

4.1 Setup Phase

The bulletin board manager generates a pair of keys $(\mathsf{pk_{BB}}, \mathsf{sk_{BB}}) = \mathsf{KeyGenE_{BB}}(1^\lambda)$ and publishes $\mathsf{pk_{BB}}$.

The trustees setup the concatenated LWE scheme presented in Sect. 3.6: each trustee generates its own separate LWE secret key $s_i \in \mathbb{B}^n$, its own master trapdoor R_i, and a corresponding public key $\mathsf{pk}_i \in (G \times \mathbb{T})^m$.

Thus, the secret key sk_i of each trustee consists in R_i and s_i. Without revealing any information on s_i, they must provide a proof that the public key pk_i is indeed composed of $\mathsf{LWE}(s_i, \alpha)$ samples of 0, because it is a requirement for the correctness of the decryption with ciphertext trapdoors. To do so, the trustees may for instance use the NIZK proof defined in [18, Sect. 2.2]. Once the existence of s_i is established, the trustees do not necessarily need to prove that they know the secrets s_i or R_i, although, the simple fact that they can output valid ciphertext trapdoors prove it anyways, by standard LWE-to-SIS or decision-to-search reduction arguments.

The main public key pk is the tensor product defined in Eq. (1).

The main secret key $s = (s_1, \ldots, s_t)$ must be secure for low noise rates, like $O(1/L^{1.5})$, which means that the number of secret bits is larger than usual. To perform homomorphic operations efficiently, the trustees define two other secret keys $s^{(f)}$ and $s^{(m)}$ for a noise rate $1/16$ and their corresponding public key $\mathsf{pk}^{(f)}$ and $\mathsf{pk}^{(m)}$ (they may still use a concatenated scheme, although this time, they don't need a master trapdoor for that).

Finally, they provide three bootstrapping keys: $\mathrm{BK}_1 := \mathrm{BK}_{[(s^{(f)}, \frac{1}{4}) \to (s^{(m)}, \frac{1}{4})]}$, $\mathrm{BK}_2 := \mathrm{BK}_{[(s^{(m)}, \frac{1}{4}) \to (s^{(m)}, \frac{1}{16})]}$, and a larger one for low noise amplitude $\mathrm{BK}_3 := \mathrm{BK}_{[(s^{(m)}, \frac{1}{4}) \to (s, \frac{1}{L^{3/2}})]}$. Since a bootstrapping key essentially consists in a public LWE encryption of each individual bit of the private key, each trustee can independently provide their part of the bootstrapping keys. Bootstrapping with BK_1 or BK_2 can be done in less than 700ms using the implementation of [13]. BK_3 uses secrets which are typically twice as large, and since the bootstrapping is essentially quartic in n, one should expect a slowdown by some constant factor ≈ 16.

4.2 Voter Registration

$\mathsf{Register}(1^\lambda, \mathsf{id})$: The authority A_1 runs $(\mathsf{upk_{id}}, \mathsf{usk_{id}}) \leftarrow \mathsf{KeyGenS}(1^\lambda)$. Its adds $\mathsf{upk_{id}}$ in $\mathcal{L}_\mathcal{U}$ and outputs $(\mathsf{upk_{id}}, \mathsf{usk_{id}})$.

4.3 Voting Phase

In our scheme, we suppose that the number of candidates $\ell = 2^k$ is a power of two. If it is not the case, we can always add null candidates. Then, if we choose a random value for the vote, no candidate will be favorite over the others. A valid vote v is thus assimilated to an integer between 0 and $\ell - 1$.

Vote(pk, usk, upk, v): each user computes the binary decomposition $(v_0, \ldots, v_{k-1}) \in \{0,1\}^k$ s.t $v = \sum_{j=0}^{k-1} v_j 2^j$. Let $\hat{v}_j$ denote $\frac{1}{2}v_j \in \mathbb{T}$, he encrypts each bit as $c_j = \mathsf{LWEPubEncrypt}_{\mathsf{pk}(f)}(\hat{v}_j)$ with noise amplitude $< \frac{1}{4}$. It bootstraps the c'_js as follow: $c'_j = \mathsf{Bootstrap}_{BK_1}(c_j, \frac{1}{2}, 0)$. It computes aux $= \mathsf{Enc}_{\mathsf{BB}}(\mathsf{pk}_{\mathsf{BB}}, (c_0, \ldots, c_{k-1})\|\mathsf{upk})$. It returns the final ballot $b = (\mathsf{content}, \sigma)$, where content $= (\mathsf{aux}, \mathsf{upk}, (c'_0, \ldots, c'_{k-1}), \mathsf{num})$ and $\sigma = \mathsf{Sign}(\mathsf{usk}, \mathsf{content})$ and where num is the version number of the ballot for the revote policy[3].

4.4 Processing a Ballot in BB

All the procedures performed by the BB and described in this section are summarized in Fig. 2.

Validity Checks on a Ballot. $\mathsf{ProcessBB}(\mathsf{BB}, b, \mathsf{sk}_{\mathsf{BB}})$: upon reception of a ballot b, it parses it as $(\mathsf{content}, \sigma)$, with content $= (\mathsf{aux}, \mathsf{upk}, (c'_0, \ldots, c'_{k-1}), \mathsf{num})$.

BB verifies that upk $\in \mathcal{L}_{\mathcal{U}}$ and checks whether $\mathsf{VerifyS}(\mathsf{upk}_{\mathsf{id}}, \mathsf{content})$.

It verifies that each $c_j \in G \times \mathbb{T}$. It computes $(c_0, \ldots, c_{k-1})\|\mathsf{upk}' = \mathsf{Dec}_{\mathsf{BB}}(\mathsf{sk}_{\mathsf{BB}}, \mathsf{aux})$. It checks whether $\mathsf{upk}' == \mathsf{upk}$ and whether $c'_j = \mathsf{Bootstrap}_{BK_1}(c_j, \frac{1}{2}, 0)$ for all $j = 0, \ldots, k-1$. Then, it checks the revote policy with the version number num and adds the ballot if all the validity checks passed. Note that a syntaxical check on the c_j's is enough. Note also that unlike classical e-voting protocol, no semantic check or zero-knowledge proof is needed at this step, since all binary message are valid choices.

BB Homomorphic Operation. Then, BB applies a sequence of public homomorphic operations on the encrypted vote $(c'_1, \ldots, c'_k)$. These homomorphic operations do not require the presence of the voter, and can therefore be performed offline by the cloud. To simplify, we will just describe what happens on the cleartext.

1. *Pre-Bootstrapping.* $\mathsf{Bootstrap}_{BK_2}(c'_j, \frac{1}{4}, 0)$ is applied on each c'_j to cancel its uncontrolled input noise and reduce it to $\frac{1}{16}$, and also to reexpress its content on the $\{0, \frac{1}{4}\}$ message space, which is suitable for boolean homomorphic operations.

2. *Homomorphic binary expansion.* In order to compute the sum of the votes (homomorphically), BB transforms the vector $\hat{v} = (\hat{v}_0, \ldots, \hat{v}_{k-1}) \in \{0, \frac{1}{4}\}^k$ into its characteristic vector $\hat{w} = \frac{1}{4}(w_0, \ldots, w_{\ell-1}) = (0, \ldots, 0, \frac{1}{4}, 0, \ldots, 0)$ of length ℓ (number of the possible choices of votes) with a $\frac{1}{4}$ at position v. This transformation is very easy and, for every h of binary decomposition $h = \sum_{i=0}^{k-1} h_i 2^i$, w_h corresponds to this boolean term:

---

[3] The revote policy consists in accepting the last vote sent for upk: BB accepts to overwrite a ballot for upk iff the new version number is strictly larger than the previous one.

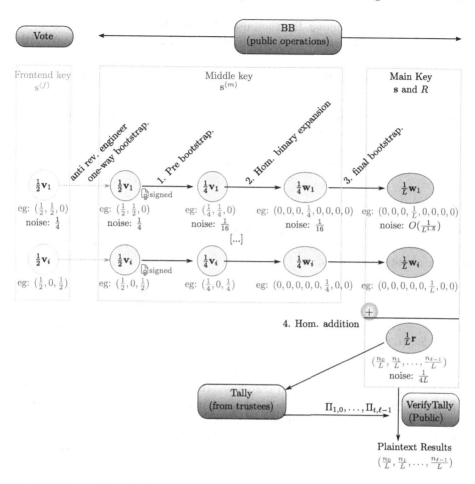

Fig. 2. Schematic of the protocol In red and green an example: red means encrypted, green means decrypted (Color figure online)

$$w_h(v) = \left(\bigwedge_{\substack{i \in [0, k-1] \\ h_i = 0}} \overline{v_i} \right) \wedge \left(\bigwedge_{\substack{i \in [0, k-1] \\ h_i = 1}} v_i \right)$$

The formula seems complicated, but it is just a conjunction of k variables v_i or their negation ($k = \log_2 \ell$ is in general smaller than 5 in typical elections).

These conjunctions can be easily evaluated on ciphertexts using these homomorphic gates, keeping in mind that $\mathsf{Bootstrap}_{BK_2}$ runs in less than 700 ms, as in [13]:

$$\mathsf{HomAND}(c_1, c_2) = \mathsf{Bootstrap}_{BK_2}((\mathbf{0}, -\tfrac{1}{8}) + c_1 + c_2, \tfrac{1}{4}, 0)$$
$$\mathsf{HomANDNot}(c_1, c_2) = \mathsf{Bootstrap}_{BK_2}((\mathbf{0}, \tfrac{1}{8}) + c_1 - c_2, \tfrac{1}{4}, 0)$$

3. *Generalized Bootstrapping.* BB then uses the main bootstrapping key BK_3 to convert these ℓ ciphertexts into a new ciphertext of $(0, \ldots, 0, \frac{1}{L}, 0, \ldots, 0)$ with noise $O(L^{-3/2})$.

This consists in applying $\mathsf{Bootstrap}_{\mathrm{BK}_3}((\mathbf{0}, \frac{1}{8}) + c, \frac{1}{L}, 0)$ to each of the ℓ ciphertexts.

4. *Homomorphic addition.* At the end of the voting phase, BB sums (homomorphically) all ciphertexts, which yields to the final LWE ciphertexts $(C_0, \ldots, C_{\ell-1})$ of $(\frac{n_0}{L}, \ldots, \frac{n_{\ell-1}}{L})$, with noise $O(L^{-1})$. No bootstrapping is needed for this step, it just uses the standard addition on ciphertexts.

4.5   Tallying and Verification

Denote as $(C_0, \ldots, C_{\ell-1})$ the final ciphertext processed by BB. Each LWE sample C_j encodes the message $\frac{n_j}{L}$ with noise amplitude $O(1/L)$, where n_j is the number of votes for candidate j.

$\mathsf{Tally}(\mathsf{BB}, \mathsf{sk} = (\mathsf{sk}_1, \ldots, \mathsf{sk}_t))$: for each C_j, the trustees independently perform the distributed decryption described in Sect. 3.6, and publish a ciphertext trapdoor $\Pi_{i,j} \in \mathbb{Z}^m$ (for $i = 1, \ldots, t$ and $j = 0, \ldots, \ell - 1$) as in Definition 3.6, which is revealed to everyone.

$\mathsf{VerifyTally}(\mathsf{BB}, (\Pi_1, \ldots, \Pi_t))$: given the main public key pk, anyone is able to check the validity of the ciphertext trapdoors. If a trapdoor $\Pi_{i,j}$ is invalid, it publicly proves that the i-th trustee is not honest and in this case $\mathsf{VerifyTally}$ returns $\perp$. If all the trapdoors are valid, anyone can use $(\Pi_{1,j}, \ldots, \Pi_{t,j})$ to decrypt C_j, and thus, recover n_j for all j, which gives the number of votes for the candidate j. This gives the result of the election. And $\mathsf{VerifyTally}$ returns the result $(n_0, \ldots, n_{\ell-1})$.

5   Correctness and Security Analysis

5.1   Correctness and Verifiability

In order to prove verifiability and correctness, we show that our scheme verifies this more general theorem.

Theorem 5.1 (Intermediate theorem for proving Verifiability and Correctness). *Let* pk *be a valid e-voting public key (this includes also* $\mathsf{pk}^{(f)}$, $\mathsf{pk}^{(m)}$, *and the bootstrapping keys* BK_1, BK_2, BK_3 *with the parameters defined in Sect. 4.1, together with their respective NIZK proofs of validity). Let* $\mathcal{S}$ *be an existentially unforgeable scheme and* $\mathcal{E}$ *a non-malleable encryption scheme both quantum resistant. Let* BB *be a sequence of bits that can syntaxically be interpreted as the public view of a bulletin board after the end of the voting phase: i.e. a BB key pair (*$\mathsf{sk}_{\mathsf{BB}}$, $\mathsf{pk}_{\mathsf{BB}}$), *a list* $[b_1, \ldots, b_p]$ *of ballots where each*

$b_i = (\mathsf{aux}, \mathsf{upk}, \boldsymbol{c'}, num, \sigma)$ *passed the verification check from* ProcessBB *and the whole sequence of public homomorphic operations from Sect. 4.4 until the final ciphertexts. Then, the following facts holds with overwhelming probability*

1. *For each* $b_i \in$ BB, *let* $(\mathsf{upk}, \mathsf{usk})$ *be the credential pair associated to this ballot, there exists a unique* $v_i \in \mathbb{V} = [0, \ell - 1]$ *such that* b_i *can be expressed as* $\mathsf{Vote}(\mathsf{pk}, \mathsf{upk}, \mathsf{usk}, v_i)^4$.
2. *If* BB *was produced in less than* 2^λ *elementary operations, then each ballot* b_i *has been generated with the knowledge of its associated* usk.
3. *The final* ℓ *ciphertexts after all the homomorphic operations in* BB *are* $\mathsf{LWE}(\mathsf{sk}, 1/L^{1.5}, G)$ *samples of the plaintext result* $\boldsymbol{r} = \rho(v_1, \ldots, v_p)$.
4. *For all integer matrix* $(\Pi_1, \ldots, \Pi_t) \in \mathbb{Z}^{\ell t m}$, $\mathsf{VerifyTally}(\mathsf{BB}, \Pi_1, \ldots, \Pi_t)$ *is equal to either* $\boldsymbol{r}$ *or* $\perp$.

The theorem holds even if one does not perform the check on the auxiliary information, and thus, providing $(\mathsf{sk_{BB}}, \mathsf{pk_{BB}})$ *is optional.*

Proof (Sketch). Suppose that the hypothesis of the theorem are satisfied.

1. Let $b_i \in$ BB be a ballot. By construction it can be parsed as $b_i = (\mathsf{aux}, \mathsf{upk}, \boldsymbol{c'}, num, \sigma)$, and since b_i passes the tests from ProcessBB, $\mathsf{Dec}(\mathsf{sk_{BB}}, \mathsf{aux}) = (\mathsf{upk}, \boldsymbol{c})$ where $\boldsymbol{c'} = \mathsf{Bootstrap}_{BK_1}(\boldsymbol{c}, \frac{1}{2}, 0)$. Let $\boldsymbol{c''} = \mathsf{Bootstrap}(BK_2, \boldsymbol{c'}, \frac{1}{4}, 0)$ be the result of the pre-bootstrapping of $\boldsymbol{c'}$. Then v_i is the integer whose binary decomposition is $\boldsymbol{m} = 4 \cdot \mathsf{LWEDecrypt}_{\mathsf{sk}(m), 0, \frac{1}{4}((\boldsymbol{c''}))}$. Then by Theorem 3.4 on the bootstrapping, $\boldsymbol{c}$ encodes necessarily $\frac{1}{2}\boldsymbol{m}$ with noise amplitude $\frac{1}{4}$, and thus, b_i can be expressed as $\mathsf{Vote}(\mathsf{pk}, \mathsf{upk}, \mathsf{usk}, v_i)$. Reciprocally, if b_i is expressed as $\mathsf{Vote}(\mathsf{pk}, \mathsf{upk}, \mathsf{usk}, x)$, then we get back the same $v_i = x$ since we are just encrypting, bootstrapping twice and decrypting. This proves unicity.
2. Each ballot b_i contains a signature σ, which cannot be forged in less than 2^λ elementary operations without the private key usk assuming $\mathcal{S}$ is secure.
3. From the plaintext point of view, computing the binary expansion to transform the vote into its characteristic vector and summing these characteristic vectors (over L) yields the correct result. By Theorem 3.4, the same operations are correct on the ciphertexts, which proves that the ciphertexts that are decrypted by the Tally encrypt the correct election result $\boldsymbol{r} = \rho(v_1, \ldots, v_p)$.
4. Let $(\Pi_1, \ldots, \Pi_t) \in \mathbb{Z}^{\ell t m}$ be an integer matrix. If $\mathsf{VerifyTally}(\mathsf{BB}, \Pi_1, \ldots, \Pi_t)$ is not $\perp$, then $\Pi_1, \ldots, \Pi_t$ form ciphertexts trapdoors for the final ciphertexts, which satisfy the conditions of Definition 3.6. Therefore, $\mathsf{VerifyTally}(\mathsf{BB}, \Pi_1, \ldots, \Pi_t)$ is the decryption of the final ciphertexts, which are the election result $\boldsymbol{r} = \rho(v_1, \ldots, v_p)$ by point 3.

Corollary 1 (Correctness). *Assuming that the signature scheme* $\mathcal{S}$ *is existentially unforgeable and* $\mathcal{E}$ *is a non-malleable encryption scheme and that the public homomorphic operations performed by the* BB *are correct, then our protocol is* Correct.

---

[4] the v_i exists and is unique, but b_i might have been generated without its knowledge, or more generally, without calling the Vote procedure.

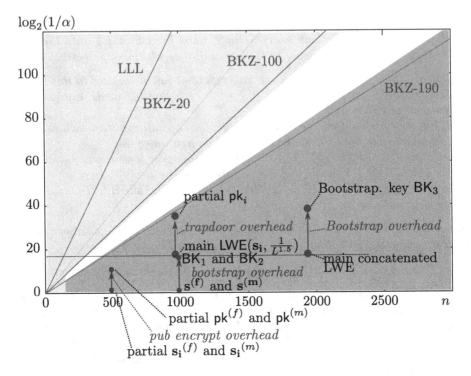

Fig. 3. 128-bit secure LWE parameters, as a function of (n, α)

Proof. The Correctness is a direct consequence of Theorem 5.1, in the particular case where the public view of BB is generated by honest voters which follow the protocol, and $\Pi_1, \ldots, \Pi_t$ are generated by the Tally function.

Corollary 2 (Verifiability). *Assuming that* BB *accepts only valid ballots and that all other operations performed by the* BB *are public, then our protocol is verifiable in the sense of Definition 2.2.*

Proof. The Verifiability is a direct consequence of point 4 of Theorem 5.1. In fact, it states that the sole possible results of VerifyTally can be $r = \rho(v_1, \ldots, v_p)$ or $\perp$. This implies that the result of the game defined in Fig. 1 is equal to 0 with overwhelming probability.

5.2   Privacy

Theorem 5.2. *Assuming Assumption 3.5 holds, our protocol verifies* Privacy *in the sense of Definition 2.1.*

Proof (Sketch). The challenger sets two empty bulletin boards BB_0 and BB_1 picks a random bit β. The adversary may choose at most $k \leq t - 1$ LWE secrets

$s_1, \ldots, s_{k-1} \in \mathbb{B}^n$ and the challenger chooses the remaining $t - k$ secrets randomly and independently (even from the ones chosen by the adversary). As long as one trustee's secret key part is uniformly generated and unknown from the adversary, the three LWE instances generated in the Setup are λ-bit secure. All the oracles ORegister, OCorrupt, OCast, Tally and VerifyTally follow the normal protocol described in Sect. 4. The OVote oracle follows the protocol to vote v_0 on BB_0 and v_1 on BB_1, but it chooses the output of the random oracle[5] $\mathsf{Bootstrap}_{BK_3}$ function on BB_1 so that it uses exactly the same left-hand term for corresponding samples in BB_0 and BB_1. Since the left term of a LWE sample is uniform in G, this is consistent with the expected output distribution of $\mathsf{Bootstrap}_{BK_3}$. Finally, SimTally is simply the identity function, since all LWE samples in BB_0 and BB_1 have the same left term, and the ciphertext trapdoors only depends on it. The only oracle which depends on a secret that is unknown to the adversary is Tally. We already know from Theorem 3.8 that the ciphertext trapdoors of the tally do not leak any information on the master trapdoors, nor on the LWE secret. It remains to show that the result of the election does not bring any new information to the adversary. Obviously, the attacker does not get any information from OVote, since he knows the ballot plaintexts. And finally, our auxiliary information prevents the adversary from using public data in BB_β to craft a valid ballot for OCast. $\qquad\square$

6   Discussion and Conclusion

In this paper, we presented a new post quantum e-voting protocol. Our new scheme is simple and the procedures are transparent. The construction exploits the versality of LWE-based homomorphic encryption to build a scheme reaching all the security properties, without relying on zero knowledge proofs for proving the validity of a vote, nor correct decryption. Instead, we make use of ciphertext trapdoors and rely on a new way to distribute LWE decryption which is not based on Shamir secret sharing to ensure the public verifiability of the decryption of the final result. We also introduce a new approach for preventing replay attacks, by using the one-wayness of the bootstrapping letting the user send some encrypted auxiliary information. We leave as a possible direction for future work the extension of our model to a possibly dishonest bulletin board. Lastly, our scheme is a first instantiation of an LWE-based e-voting protocol and we leave as an open problem the improvement of our scheme that would make lattice-based e-voting scheme close to practice.

Acknowledgments. This work has been supported in part Fonds Unique Interministériel (FUI)through the CRYPTOCOMP project and the EIT Digital project HC@WORKS.

---

[5] This works well in the random oracle model as in Assumption 3.5. Getting it in the standard model remains open.

Appendix

Assuming a medium-scale election with $L \approx 2000$ voters, the main partial keys should allow a $1/L^{1.5} \approx 2^{-17}$ noise parameter. Taking into account the overhead for publicly verifiable ciphertext trapdoors and bootstrapping key, the overall scheme can easily be instantiated with at most 2000-bit secrets.

References

1. Adida, B., de Marneffe, O., Pereira, O., Quisquater, J.-J.: Electing a university president using open-audit voting: analysis of real-world use of Helios. In: Proceedings of the 2009 Conference on Electronic Voting Technology/Workshop on Trustworthy Elections (2009)
2. Adida, B., de Marneffe, O., Pereira, O.: Helios voting system. http://www.heliosvoting.org
3. Ajtai, M.: The shortest vector problem in L_2 is NP-hard for randomized reductions. In: Proceedings of 30th STOC. ACM (1998). ECCC as TR97-047
4. Alperin-Sheriff, J., Peikert, C.: Faster bootstrapping with polynomial error. In: Garay, J.A., Gennaro, R. (eds.) CRYPTO 2014, Part I. LNCS, vol. 8616, pp. 297–314. Springer, Heidelberg (2014)
5. Bernhard, D., Cortier, V., Galindo, D., Pereira, O., Warinschi, B.: A comprehensive analysis of game-based ballot privacy definitions. In: Proceedings of the 36th IEEE Symposium on Security and Privacy (S&P 2015), San Jose, CA, USA, May 2015. IEEE Computer Society Press
6. Brakerski, Z., Langlois, A., Peikert, C., Regev, O., Stehlé, D.: Classical hardness of learning with errors. In: Proceedings of the 45th STOC, pp. 575–584. ACM (2013)
7. Brakerski, Z.: Fully homomorphic encryption without modulus switching from classical GapSVP. In: Safavi-Naini, R., Canetti, R. (eds.) CRYPTO 2012. LNCS, vol. 7417, pp. 868–886. Springer, Heidelberg (2012)
8. Brakerski, Z., Vaikuntanathan, V.: Efficient fully homomorphic encryption from (standard) LWE. In: FOCS, pp. 97–106 (2011)
9. Chen, Y., Nguyen, P.Q.: BKZ 2.0: better lattice security estimates. In: Lee, D.H., Wang, X. (eds.) ASIACRYPT 2011. LNCS, vol. 7073, pp. 1–20. Springer, Heidelberg (2011)
10. Cortier, V., Galindo, D., Glondu, S., Izabachène, M.: Election verifiability for Helios under weaker trust assumptions. In: Kutyłowski, M., Vaidya, J. (eds.) ICAIS 2014, Part II. LNCS, vol. 8713, pp. 327–344. Springer, Heidelberg (2014)
11. Cortier, V., Smyth, B.: Attacking and fixing Helios: an analysis of ballot secrecy. In: CSF, pp. 297–311. IEEE Computer Society (2011)
12. Ducas, L., Durmus, A., Lepoint, T., Lyubashevsky, V.: Lattice Signatures and Bimodal Gaussians. In: Canetti, R., Garay, J.A. (eds.) CRYPTO 2013, Part I. LNCS, vol. 8042, pp. 40–56. Springer, Heidelberg (2013)
13. Ducas, L., Micciancio, D.: FHEW: bootstrapping homomorphic encryption in less than a second. In: Oswald, E., Fischlin, M. (eds.) EUROCRYPT 2015. LNCS, vol. 9056, pp. 617–640. Springer, Heidelberg (2015)
14. Gama, N., Izabachène, M., Nguyen, P.Q., Xie, X.: Structural lattice reduction: generalized worst-case to average-case reductions. IACR Cryptology ePrint Archive 2014, p. 48 (2014)

15. Gentry, C., Peikert, C., Vaikuntanathan, V.: Trapdoors for hard lattices and new cryptographic constructions. In: STOC (2008)
16. Gentry, C., Sahai, A., Waters, B.: Homomorphic encryption from learning with errors: conceptually-simpler, asymptotically-faster, attribute-based. In: Canetti, R., Garay, J.A. (eds.) CRYPTO 2013, Part I. LNCS, vol. 8042, pp. 75–92. Springer, Heidelberg (2013)
17. Juels, A., Catalano, D., Jakobsson, M.: Coercion-resistant electronic elections. In: Chaum, D., Jakobsson, M., Rivest, R.L., Ryan, P.Y.A., Benaloh, J., Kutylowski, M., Adida, B. (eds.) Towards Trustworthy Elections. LNCS, vol. 6000, pp. 37–63. Springer, Heidelberg (2010)
18. Laguillaumie, F., Langlois, A., Libert, B., Stehlé, D.: Lattice-based group signatures with logarithmic signature size. In: Sako, K., Sarkar, P. (eds.) ASIACRYPT 2013. LNCS, vol. 8270, pp. 41–61. Springer, Heidelberg (2013)
19. Lyubashevsky, V.: Lattice signatures without trapdoors. In: Pointcheval, D., Johansson, T. (eds.) EUROCRYPT 2012. LNCS, vol. 7237, pp. 738–755. Springer, Heidelberg (2012)
20. Lyubashevsky, V., Peikert, C., Regev, O.: On ideal lattices and learning with errors over rings. In: Gilbert, H. (ed.) EUROCRYPT 2010. LNCS, vol. 6110, pp. 1–23. Springer, Heidelberg (2010)
21. Micciancio, D., Peikert, C.: Trapdoors for Lattices: Simpler, Tighter, Faster, Smaller. In: Pointcheval, D., Johansson, T. (eds.) EUROCRYPT 2012. LNCS, vol. 7237, pp. 700–718. Springer, Heidelberg (2012)
22. Micciancio, D., Peikert, C.: Hardness of SIS and LWE with small parameters. In: Canetti, R., Garay, J.A. (eds.) CRYPTO 2013, Part I. LNCS, vol. 8042, pp. 21–39. Springer, Heidelberg (2013)
23. Regev, O.: On lattices, learning with errors, random linear codes, and cryptography. In: STOC, pp. 84–93 (2005)
24. Smyth, B.: Replay attacks that violate ballot secrecy in Helios (2012)

Author Index

Printed in the United States
By Bookmasters